Colonizing Leprosy

STUDIES IN SOCIAL MEDICINE

Allan M. Brandt and Larry R. Churchill, editors

Michelle T. Moran

Colonizing Leprosy

IMPERIALISM AND

THE POLITICS OF

PUBLIC HEALTH IN

THE UNITED STATES

The University of North Carolina Press
Chapel Hill

Designed by Heidi Perov
Set in Cycles and The Sans
by Keystone Typesetting, Inc.
Manufactured in the United States of America

The paper in this book meets the guidelines for permanence and durability of the Committee on Production Guidelines for Book Longevity of the Council on Library Resources.

Library of Congress Cataloging-in-Publication Data
Moran, Michelle Therese, 1967–
Colonizing leprosy : imperialism and the politics of public health in the United States / Michelle T. Moran.
p. ; cm. — (Studies in social medicine)
Includes bibliographical references and index.
ISBN 978-0-8078-3145-8 (cloth: alk. paper)
ISBN 978-0-8078-5839-4 (pbk.: alk. paper)
1. Leprosy—United States—History. 2. Colonialism—United States—History. I. Title. II. Series.
[DNLM: 1. Kalaupapa (Hawaii) 2. United States Marine Hospital No. 66 (Carville, La.) 3. Public Health Service Hospital at Carville, La. 4. Leprosy—History—United States. 5. Colonialism—History—United States. 6. Health Policy—United States. 7. History, 19th Century—United States. 8. History, 20th Century—United States. 9. Patient Isolation—History—United States. 10. Prejudice—United States. WC 335 M829ca 2007]
RA644.L3M6779 2007
362.196'99800973—dc22

2007008206

cloth   11 10 09 08 07   5 4 3 2 1
paper   11 10 09 08 07   5 4 3 2 1

To Andrew
  For Everything

CONTENTS

Illustrations

Maps

ACKNOWLEDGMENTS

A wide array of people provided the guidance, expertise, assistance, and support that have made this book possible. To all who are mentioned, and to those who have been inadvertently omitted, know that you have my heartfelt thanks.

The many archivists and repository staff members who helped me locate materials and guided me through various bureaucratic mazes have my sincerest gratitude. Many thanks to Marjorie Ciarlante of the National Archives, Stephen Greenberg and Douglas Atkins of the History of Medicine Division at the National Library of Medicine, Annabelle Steinbach of the former Hansen's Disease Archives and Library at what was once the Gillis W. Long Hansen's Disease Center, Carolyn Ching of the Hawaii Medical Library, Judy Bolton of Louisiana State University Libraries Special Collections, Neal Hatayama of the Hawai'i State Library, Geoffrey A. White of the Hawai'i State Archives, Nancy Morris of the University of Hawai'i-Mānoa Library Special Collections, DeSoto Brown of the Bishop Museum Archives, Sister Genevieve Keusenkothen of the Daughters of Charity of St. Vincent dePaul West Central Province Archives, Jennifer Lloyd of the Louisiana State University Medical Center Library, and the countless helpful librarians at the University of Illinois. Special thanks to Patrick Ragains of the University of Nevada's Getchell Library for his assistance in tracking down government documents and scanning images.

I am particularly grateful to the communities at Kalaupapa and Carville for their hospitality during my too-brief visits. In addition to the tour guides at Kalaupapa, I wish to thank Dr. Alfred Morris and Dr. Mona Bomgaars of the State of Hawaii Department of Health and Mike McCarten, administrator of the Kalaupapa Settlement, for their assistance. At the former Gillis W. Long Hansen's Disease Center, Josie Major and Julia Elwood provided helpful guidance. Many thanks to Nancy and Willie for their spirited assistance, engaging stories, and thoughtful gifts of food.

Archival research cannot be conducted without material support. The

Pew Program in Religion and American History at Yale University, the Graduate College at the University of Illinois at Urbana-Champaign, and the UIUC Women's Studies Program granted me financial assistance for the dissertation phase of this project. A postdoctoral fellowship from the University of Nevada, Reno, provided additional support. Special thanks to Judy Coode, Tim Watson, Jenny Lloyd, and John and Yvonne Moran for opening their homes to me during various research trips, providing not only shelter and sustenance but also emotional support and welcome diversions.

I am happy to be able to thank my mentors and teachers, especially those at the University of Illinois, to whom I owe an enormous intellectual debt. I am profoundly grateful to my graduate adviser, Leslie Reagan, for introducing me to the history of medicine and for providing a continuing source of support for this project and for me. Special thanks go to Antoinette Burton, who arrived at UIUC at just the right moment to shape my thinking on imperialism and encourage me to pursue this work. Mark Leff, Sonya Michel, and Paula Treichler each contributed insights and thoughtful commentary that helped me better contextualize the political, gendered, and cultural dimensions of the project. Evan Melhado and Kristin Hoganson gave close readings to early chapters and offered cogent critiques. For the guidance of Liz Pleck, Kathy Oberdeck, and Lillian Hoddeson, I am deeply appreciative. Thanks is long overdue for the mentorship of David Moore and Nancy Anderson, which began during my undergraduate years and helped convince me that a study of the past might make for an interesting future.

The graduate student community at the University of Illinois Department of History fostered a collegial and stimulating environment in which to study, and I am privileged to have worked with many generous and intellectually engaged people. Thanks to Cathy Adams, Kate Bullard, Jon Coit, Matt Gambino, Jen Edwards, Sace Elder, Rose Holz, Raka Nandi, Lynnea Magnuson, Kathy Mapes, Caroline Waldron Merithew, Jeff Sahadeo, Robert Saxe, Kerry Wynn, and everyone associated with the Graduate Symposium on Women's and Gender History. I am particularly grateful to Dawn Flood, Ruth Fairbanks, Elisa Miller, and Paula Rieder for their continuing support and friendship.

The Berkshire Conference on the History of Women, the American Association for the History of Medicine, and the American Society of Church History provided stimulating forums in which I could share my ideas at various stages of this project. Thanks to Sharla Fett, Brenda Stevenson, Warwick Anderson, and Dolores Liptak for their thoughtful comments, and to audience members for their questions and interest. I am also grateful to members of the History Colloquium at the University of Nevada, Reno. In particular, I wish to recognize the advice and collegiality of Marie Boutte, Scott Casper, Linda Curcio, Greta de Jong, and Bill Rowley.

I owe a real debt to Sian Hunter for her patience and wisdom in shepherding me through the publication process. The readers for the University of North Carolina Press gave my manuscript thoughtful consideration and offered helpful suggestions on how to refine my argument and enliven my prose. Thanks to all the people at UNC Press for their help in the mystical process of transforming a manuscript into a book, especially Ron Maner and Eric Schramm.

Truly, no words are adequate to express my gratitude to Andrew Nolan, who has read every word of every draft and provided the most enthusiastic and unwavering support of this project. His contributions to this work are immeasurable. Be it ever so humble a thank you, this book is dedicated to him.

Introduction

In May 1946, a Paramount newsreel segment entitled "In Sickness and In Health: Husband Seeks to Join Wife in Leper Colony" introduced movie-goers to the story of Hans and Gertrude Hornbostel. According to this "story of devotion," Hans, a U.S. Army major who survived the Bataan death march, wanted permission to accompany his wife as she sought treatment at the federal leprosarium in Carville, Louisiana. Gertrude had contracted leprosy while imprisoned by Japanese forces at Santa Thomas in the Philippines. Audiences were assured that Gertrude's hope for a cure at Carville were "excellent." Once she entered the facility, however, she would not be able to leave until doctors determined that she no longer posed a threat to public health. Regulations prohibited Hans, who did not have leprosy, from entering the facility with his wife. Seeking to sway health officials by taking their story to the public, the Hornbostels made a compelling case that as a happily married couple of thirty-three years, and one that had already experienced the trauma of separation during the war, they deserved to remain together at Carville. "Whom God hath joined let no man put asunder," Gertrude Hornbostel recited in the newsreel. "Yes, and that's why I want to stay with you," her husband replied, putting his arm around her shoulder. The couple kissed as the segment ended.[1]

In 1952, movie audiences viewing the anti-Communist picture *Big Jim McLain* saw another story of leprosy unfold on the big screen. In this film, John Wayne plays the title character, an agent for the House Un-American Activities Committee tracking down members of the Communist Party in Hawai'i. McLain grows concerned when his investigations lead him to the leprosy settlement at Kalaupapa, on the island of Moloka'i. As his plane lands on the peninsula, he admits, "Frankly leprosy scares me—scares most people I guess." He enters a small medical office to interrogate a Nurse Numaka, who confesses that she had been a Communist for eleven years "before I came to my senses." During their discussion, she leaves her desk to enter an adjoining children's ward, where she props up the crib of a cooing infant so that two visiting Hawaiian parents—leprosy patients—can see their baby from the other side of a wall of windows. The nurse explains to McLain that all infants are taken from their mothers immediately upon delivery, to be removed to the mainland after six months. After relating that medical officials do this to protect the children, Nurse Numaka explains why she took a post at Kalaupapa. "I thought, I suppose, that I might atone for the injury I had done humanity by helping these unfortunates."[2]

Both of these clips connected leprosy to enduring stereotypes. Each film segment marked the disease as a foreign contagion, one cultivated in the "incredible filth" of a Japanese prison camp in the Philippines, the other contained within an isolated Hawaiian peninsula. Each labeled individuals with the disease as dangerous contaminants requiring isolation from the general public. Each invoked the stigmatized term "leper" to link the disease to scriptural images of marginalization and ostracism. As John Wayne's character prepares to enter Kalaupapa, for instance, he speaks of the fear that he felt as a child when he listened to his mother reading the Bible, recalling "the chill that ran up and down backs when she said the ancient word—leper." Indeed, the scriptwriter for *Big Jim McLain*, in seeking a metaphor to characterize postwar Communism as deviant, foreign, and contagious, could find no more powerful image than leprosy.

These filmmakers built dramatic tension by showcasing the incongruence between leprosy as an ancient and foreign contagion and its presence in modern America, but they also potentially allowed audiences to find alternative meanings within these stories. Despite the assumptions viewers may have held about leprosy, those watching the Paramount newsreel saw an ordinary American couple faced with a disease that clearly was not consigned to the past or to less developed parts of the world. Those attending a showing of *Big Jim McLain* saw two seemingly healthy parents standing not in a dilapidated stone asylum or a filthy grass hut but in a modern medical facility staffed by a uniformed nurse. Neither Gertrude Hornbostel nor the Kalaupapa patients featured in these films manifested visible symptoms of the disease. They were presented as sympathetic human beings whose disease had the potential to separate them from those whom they loved. They were depicted as potentially active agents who had cause to challenge policies that isolated and marginalized them.

These two cinematic artifacts are also instructive in demonstrating how imperialism shaped leprosy in the modern United States. Gertrude Hornbostel claimed to have contracted leprosy when she was imprisoned in the

Philippines, a U.S. territory until 1946, whereas the fictional Jim McLain encounters leprosy in the U.S. territory of Hawai'i. Both clips reminded audiences that leprosy had a very real presence in the postwar United States, despite its image as a disease separated from the modern nation by time and space. Health officials sought to contain it within the U.S. Marine Hospital at Carville, Louisiana, and the Kalaupapa settlement in Moloka'i, Hawai'i, two facilities that had emerged in the imperial age of the late nineteenth and early twentieth centuries. U.S. encounters with places where leprosy was widespread in this era had raised fears of its contagion and prompted the development of institutions and policies to contain what was increasingly viewed as a foreign threat encroaching on the national body. The United States had acquired the leprosy settlement on Moloka'i when it took possession of the Hawaiian Islands in 1898. Ongoing debates over the potential danger that leprosy posed to the mainland led the U.S. Public Health Service to establish a federal leprosarium in Louisiana in 1921. By reminding audiences of these two sites, these film clips demonstrated how Americans in the post–World War II era continued to confront concerns about the vulnerability of the U.S. mainland to exotic dangers lurking in not-so-far-away places. Though viewers watching the clips might accept the need for institutions to contain those with this disease, however, these images also raised questions about the fairness of policies that prevented Hans from accompanying Gertrude and that kept the loving Kalaupapa couple from raising their own child. The cinematic representations thus implicitly underscored challenges to the notion that isolation served as the best approach to the disease, hinting at a potential for resisting and questioning policies regulating leprosy in these institutions.

How these two institutions for the care and management of leprosy emerged in a country where the disease was not widespread, how the disease came to represent an exotic danger that required strict containment, and how various groups sought to mobilize their own understandings of leprosy to challenge and reconfigure medical regulations and popular stereotypes surrounding this disease is the subject of this book. *Colonizing Leprosy* provides the first history of the disease in the United States to examine the active interplay among imperialism, public health policy, and patient activism in the creation, development, and maintenance of leprosy institutions in Kalaupapa and Carville.[3] By examining leprosy in both Hawai'i and Louisiana, this work shows not only how public health policy emerged as a tool of empire in the colonies, but also how imperial ideologies became embedded within mainland medical practices. The interaction between colony and mainland yielded diverse and often contradictory policies of treatment and containment for leprosy. Doctors and medical administrators in both Hawai'i and Louisiana reconceptualized leprosy as a colonial disease requiring strict isolation, even as they adapted regulations developed at one site to the other, changing the rules to conform to their ideas of how "natives" and "Americans" could and should be treated. Patients, for their part, formed communities, mobilized to protest restrictive regulations, and promoted their own ideas about the nature of their disease, demonstrating how medical policies faced challenges both in the colony and on the mainland. This case study of leprosy helps us begin to appreciate the degree to which imperialism and public health policy became intertwined in debates over the constitution and health of American political and social bodies.

The idea that leprosy represented a foreign threat or a throwback to ancient times is an impression that often still resonates among those unfamiliar with contemporary medical understandings of the disease. Current medical literature identifies leprosy as a mildly communicable and chronic bacterial disease caused by *Mycobacterium leprae*. The disease is also known as Hansen's disease, named for Norwegian physician Gerhard Armauer Hansen, who first identified the rod-shaped bacillus linked to leprosy in 1873.[4] Despite its early identification, health officials today remain uncertain as to how exactly the disease is transmitted. Contrary to popular assumption, the disease is not highly infectious, and health officials theorize that respiratory droplets from infected individuals might spread the *M. leprae* bacillus to individuals who come into extended contact with people who have untreated cases of Hansen's disease. About five years commonly elapses between first exposure to the bacillus and the onset of the disease, though incubation periods can last twenty years or longer. Hansen's disease primarily produces a degeneration of skin tissue, mucus membranes, and peripheral nerves. As the disease progresses, patients may experience skin discoloration, lesions, and ulcerations; hair loss, particularly on the face; muscle paralysis; and bone absorption of fingers and toes. In its most advanced stages, Hansen's disease can cause blindness and organ failure. The disease does not eat away flesh nor cause limbs to fall away, as popular images suggest. Severe injury can occur, however, from the indirect consequences of nerve damage.[5]

These more disfiguring aspects of the disease, coupled with its deep-rooted associations with sinfulness and social exclusion, have infused it with a powerful stigma that has proven more difficult to eradicate than the disease itself. Biblical and medieval writings identified leprosy as a punishment for sin and outlined strict guidelines for separating those with the disease from the healthy. The Old Testament book of Leviticus instructed priests to label those with leprosy "unclean" and cast them from society. During the Middle Ages, religious communities established Lazar houses in Western Europe to contain and care for those with leprosy. Before being sent to such institutions, people with leprosy received the same religious rites as those performed for the dying, reinforcing the idea that someone with the disease was one of the "living dead." Under medieval law, those with leprosy could lose their property and rights of citizenship. They were, however, still allowed to wander and beg in the streets to remind communities of God's punishment for immoral living.[6] The 1179 Lateran Council mandated greater segregation of people with leprosy and linked their disease to matters of sexual licentiousness. Labeling someone as a "leper" became a powerful method of ostracism and persecution.[7] While the disease declined in Europe in the sixteenth century, it lived on as a metaphor for social exclusion.

It was during the age of empire that leprosy reemerged as a tangible threat to Western bodies, while retaining its stigma as a symbol of filth, defilement, and sin. The combination of Christian missionary ventures, scientific medicine, and U.S. imperial activities in the late 1800s helped produce an image of leprosy as a foreign menace that posed a physical danger to Americans. In the latter half of the nineteenth century, Protestant and Catholic missionaries wrote articles that connected religious desires to convert nonbelievers with humanitarian impulses to heal the sick. These religious workers wrote accounts of their sojourns among people with leprosy that evoked biblical interpretations of the disease as punishment for sinful living and that exploited its physical ravages to help generate monetary support for their proselytizing efforts.[8] Even as missionaries in India, China, and the Philippines drew on scriptural imperatives and the language of religious faith to portray those with leprosy as uncivilized savages in need of Western intervention, the increasingly accepted germ theory of disease helped legitimate the idea that people with leprosy posed a threat of contamination.[9] Physicians and public health officials replaced earlier understandings of leprosy as a hereditary condition with a new theory portraying it as a communicable disease caused by the spread of a specific bacterium. This interpretation justified targeting people with leprosy as contagions and requiring isolation to protect public health. Accounts of U.S. imperial expansion in the Caribbean and Pacific, where leprosy was widespread, reinforced notions of the disease as a by-product of ways of life that Americans imagined as primitive. Ambivalence over the acquisition of such territories as Hawai'i, the Philip-

pines, and Guam sometimes manifested itself in public concern that diseased bodies could now gain easy access into the mainland United States.
Religion, scientific medicine, and imperial conquest comfortably supported
this new representation of leprosy, and policymakers dusted off the model
of the medieval Christian lazaretto and reconfigured it as a modern American medical institution.

Leprosy thus provides a useful lens for examining the broad and complex
networks that conjoined the United States and its colonies. In recent years,
scholars have begun to demonstrate how the U.S. acquisition and management of an empire influenced domestic policies and a sense of national
identity. This scholarship has helped to displace older narratives that ignored the impact of imperialism on the daily lives of Americans.[10] Ann
Laura Stoler has urged U.S. historians to continue broadening their understanding of imperialism by paying greater attention to the transnational
connections among imperial projects throughout the globe. She specifically
calls for a focus on the "intimacies of empire" where imperial rule was
implemented, contested, and negotiated.[11] Historians of medicine, with eyes
trained on the body, are particularly well situated to examine these intimate
arenas. In the case of leprosy, scholars can investigate how physicians and
public health officials regularly patrolled racial and imperial boundaries
through their attempts to police the sexual lives of patients, limit child-
bearing, intervene in child rearing, and regulate the creation and maintenance of domestic spaces.[12] *Colonizing Leprosy* analyzes such policies to place
the United States in dialogue with other regimes over the management of
disease within the imperial landscape and to understand the dynamic ex-
changes flowing between colony and mainland.

Modern American understandings of leprosy and the medical policies
that sought to manage, treat, and contain the disease took shape within this
imperial context.[13] In Hawai'i, public health practices sometimes served as
tools of empire, as territorial leprosy programs buttressed claims that U.S.
domination of the islands amounted to a beneficent "civilizing mission."
Territorial officials denigrated indigenous medical practices as inefficient
and even dangerous, because they left Hawaiians vulnerable not only to
sickness but to extinction. Asserting that U.S. imperialism informed medical policies does not suggest, however, that this is simply a narrative of
a dominant nation imposing its will upon a hapless and distant colony.
Rather, this work builds upon historical, anthropological, and postcolonial
studies of imperialism in which colonies have emerged as dynamic sites of
contest, negotiation, and invention that reshaped the worlds of both colo-

nized and colonizer.[14] Without denying the violence and coercion that accompanied U.S. intervention into Hawai'i, I show how U.S. public health officials and politicians in the territory found their power circumscribed by Hawaiian resistance and recalcitrance and their agendas reshaped by their encounters with Hawaiians' alternative visions of medical knowledge and treatment.

At the same time, the maintenance of empire created a complex web of interactions that bound together individuals throughout the mainland and colonies.[15] What Bernard S. Cohn has termed the "investigative modality" used by westerners to study and control colonized bodies abroad was also employed at home.[16] Political and medical officials used medical surveys, inspections, and examinations—as well as medical reports that quantified data and defined research—to create a Hawaiian "leper" during the late 1800s that could be controlled and contained. These very processes also provided models for public health services on the mainland. Medical practitioners and policymakers applied cultural assumptions about leprosy and its sufferers that had been cultivated during the colonization of Hawai'i to treatments and practices used at Carville in the 1900s. By comparing policies in both the colony and the mainland, this work explicitly demonstrates that the transfer of medical knowledge and practice operated in multiple directions and in often unexpected ways.[17] Hawai'i did not always operate as the ideal laboratory, nor were practices of bodily surveillance, incarceration, and invasive examination solely practiced on the racialized and colonized "Other"—these practices were transported back to and sometimes inaugurated on mainland bodies in order to better understand the disease.[18]

Colonizing Leprosy contextualizes the Progressive medical directives that informed early leprosy policies to suggest that there were connections between the management of the U.S. empire and efforts to control rising immigrant populations at home. Much of the previous scholarly work on leprosy has focused on the question of how traditional notions of leprosy as a disease of the sinful and unclean remained intact even as scientific understandings of leprosy challenged such ideas.[19] Previous scholarship described the decision to create a federal leprosarium as an exception to the Progressive era's "enlightened amelioration of stigma" associated with other illnesses and blamed biblical teachings and medieval traditions for motivating politicians to treat people with leprosy more harshly than other disease sufferers.[20] This interpretation overlooks the degree to which U.S. policies governing leprosy were consistent with Progressive public health practices that targeted certain individual groups—based on class, ethnicity, race, and gender—for isolation and censure because of their presumed connection to contagious diseases or mental illness. Stigma and quarantine represented significant components of late-nineteenth- and early-twentieth-century public health measures, often aimed at recent arrivals who were seen as threatening the health of the American civic body.[21] Medical restrictions on immigrant populations during the late 1800s and early 1900s took shape within a broader framework of interventionist public health policies at home and abroad, which strongly influenced congressional debates over the establishment of a national leprosarium. Fears that the presumed primitivism and disease in the newly acquired colonies posed a threat to civilized and healthy bodies also shaped policies within leprosy institutions, as officials sought to impose strict discipline upon patients. Indeed, for the first half of the twentieth century, people who entered the facilities at Carville or Kalaupapa found themselves effectively incarcerated for life.

Yet histories that have highlighted the tragedy of imprisoning people with this disease within isolated institutions have often forfeited an examination of patient agency to emphasize instead the beneficence and bravery of those who came to rescue them. The myth of the powerless "leper" has been promoted most notably in histories of the Reverend Damien de Veuster, the Belgian Catholic priest and missionary who came to Kalaupapa in 1873. Numerous representations of "Father Damien" have cast him as the savior of uncivilized and defenseless Hawaiians who floundered in their state of isolation before his arrival brought order, morality, and succor.[22] The fact that Damien died in 1889 of complications from leprosy has long been used to define the disease as dangerously contagious and to cement his status as a selfless martyr. As anthropologist Pennie Moblo has shown, casting a Western missionary in the role of savior to native Hawaiians who were helpless without foreign protection and assistance ignores the ways in which patients at Kalaupapa managed to establish a functioning community before Damien arrived and continued to engage actively in the process of managing it after his death.[23] This book demonstrates that the multiple histories Moblo has uncovered from Damien's time continued to inform debates over Hawaiian governance and U.S. imperial intervention in the islands throughout the twentieth century.

One key theme that emerges from this comparative study is the manner in which different groups struggled to frame leprosy in ways that made the disease meaningful to them. Charles E. Rosenberg has asserted, "In some ways disease does not exist until we have agreed that it does, by perceiving, naming, and responding to it."[24] While politicians, patients, physicians, and community members may have "agreed" that leprosy existed, they had different understandings of what the disease represented and how it should be treated. Excavating and analyzing the multiple discourses about leprosy allows us to make sense of how different groups constructed leprosy as both biological condition and cultural label from the late nineteenth to the mid-twentieth centuries. No single definition of leprosy existed during this time; rather, multiple discourses competed for dominance, each with its own representation of the disease. Medical discourses portrayed those with leprosy as highly contagious and disfigured, missionaries saw these sufferers as sinful and unclean, and popular accounts depicted those with the disease as foreign threats. Patients in leprosy institutions countered such images with a language describing their condition in what they hoped were neutral terms as a treatable, mildly contagious illness. This emphasis on language is not to deny the materiality of leprosy, or to slight the physical and emotional pain experienced by those whose lives were shaped by a painful and deforming disease. Rather, the attempt to unpack the cultural construction of leprosy serves to recognize the significance of discourse for delimiting, shaping, and giving meaning to the disease. As Paula Treichler has explained, "Language is not a substitute for reality; it is one of the most significant ways we know reality, experience it, and articulate it; indeed, language plays a powerful role in producing experience and in certifying that experience as 'authentic.'"[25] Public health officials and patients could neither contain nor contest leprosy without first labeling it in their terms.

The medical terminology often viewed as the most straightforward and materially grounded method of defining disease is itself the product of social and cultural contests, and a variety of groups debated who had the authority to name and define leprosy throughout this period.[26] As Bruno Latour and Steve Woolgar observed in their study of scientists at work in the laboratory, "Argument between scientists transforms some statements into figments of one's subjective imagination, and others into facts of nature."[27] Many Hawaiians at the Kalaupapa settlement, for example, challenged the process by which public health officials attempted to construct clinically a biomedical reality in which the leprosy bacillus was a dangerous contagion. Even patients on the mainland, most of whom accepted Western medicine as well qualified to gather the critical knowledge necessary to find a cure for their disease, refused to accept as "fact" that leprosy was highly contagious and required strict isolation.

A study of the language of leprosy, far from slighting the lived experience of people with the disease, helps reveal the extent to which leprosy policies were enacted upon and contested by real human beings whose humanity and active engagement have often been overlooked in histories of the disease.²⁸ Historians have often viewed institutionalized patients as particularly passive and isolated, subject to the law of the asylum or sanitarium that labeled them as dangerously abnormal and inassimilable into society.²⁹ Contrary to depictions of leprosy patients as incapacitated objects relegated to institutions that completely divorced them from the outside world, patients in both Kalaupapa and Carville worked to carve largely autonomous spaces for themselves and to forge alliances with groups on the outside.³⁰ They resisted and manipulated public health regulations to gain some measure of control over their lives. For example, patients at Carville in the 1940s began publishing their own newspaper, *The Star*, as a means of educating the public and offering a counter-definition and name for their disease. People incarcerated in Kalaupapa voted in local elections for politicians who promised to address their concerns. Both groups mobilized outside support for their causes when they felt that health officials ignored their demands. Patients in both Hawai'i and Louisiana recognized the ways in which leprosy policies labeled them as deviant bodies deemed unfit to live within mainstream society. The diverse group of residents at the two leprosy institutions sought to overturn restrictive policies and create new identities for themselves by eradicating the negative connotations of leprosy.

Efforts by patients to gain control over the naming and management of their disease provide an early demonstration of a movement to democratize medicine, which has been widely viewed as a distinctively late-twentieth-century phenomenon.³¹ Leprosy patients developed and used an activist network to orchestrate resistance to medical practice and to develop their own interpretation of their disease. While the patient groups at Kalaupapa and Carville, limited in scale and influence, could not match the resources and numbers mobilized by advocates for breast cancer and HIV/AIDS patients, they clearly engaged in collective action in an attempt to improve their conditions and to bring about a broader social change in understandings of their disease.³² Residents of Kalaupapa and Carville mobilized, generated resources, formed alliances with outside groups, countered state and professional efforts to stifle them, manipulated social symbols, and established solidarity to challenge the dominant medical interpretation of their disease and to alter public policies that incarcerated them in institutions. Paying attention to these patient efforts further demonstrates how Western medicine was contested and politicized rather than emerging neatly as a stable body of incontrovertible truths.

Even as patients proposed alternative methods for identifying and describing their disease, however, many patient activists still drew upon a medical discourse to define their disease. Decades before Susan Sontag's efforts to strip diseases of their cultural metaphors, leprosy patient activists worked to replace the term "leprosy" with "Hansen's disease" (HD), which was one major strategy for eliminating the stigma surrounding their illness and encouraging the public to view them not as "lepers" but simply as individuals with a chronic medical condition.[33] This did pose a challenge to the authority of medical professionals, but patients still found themselves constrained by the very medical framework that had labeled them as contaminants. Deborah Lupton has demonstrated how groups who draw on a medical discourse while criticizing the medical establishment's approach to defining and managing a disease find themselves caught in a paradoxical relationship to scientific medicine.[34]

Many patient activists failed to appreciate the degree to which medical understandings of leprosy were colonial understandings. Residents in these institutions hoped that medical knowledge of leprosy would provide a strictly "scientific" and thereby value-free understanding of their disease. Definitions, images, and treatments related to leprosy, however, had taken shape in a colonial setting and still retained the colonialist assumptions and nationalist aspirations of the public health officials and physicians who developed and delivered them. These medical professionals composed a significant part of the colonial regime that had identified Hawaiians as the uncivilized, unclean, and undisciplined "Other."[35] Westerners reconceptualized leprosy and those who contracted it as uniquely "primitive" and dangerous contaminants, a concept which then promoted popular understandings of the disease as highly contagious and found only in societies unschooled in modern notions of proper sanitation and cleanliness. Kelvin Santiago-Valles has explored how this process of inventing and deploying categories of racialized and cultural difference and disparity created "the structural circumstances that turn such diseases into the 'natural' . . . conditions of certain populations by turning such populations into social problems."[36] Many Americans thus justified their intervention in Hawaiian affairs and ultimately their annexation of the islands in large part as the necessary action of a superior and benevolent civilization to assist and supervise those in need of surveillance and guidance. Medical framing of leprosy as a foreign contagion provided a powerful rationale for Western political and social domination of the Hawaiian Islands.

Exploring the connections and contrasts between the leprosy institutions in Hawai'i and Louisiana offers a unique examination of how colonialism affected policies and people both in the crucible of empire and at home. The establishment of leprosy facilities in Hawai'i and Louisiana demonstrated the remarkable success that public health officials had enjoyed in gaining the authority to inspect the bodies of citizens, identify certain individuals as threats to the public health, and confine them within specialized institutions. Doctors and medical administrators did not simply replicate on the mainland what had been developed in the territory, however. Inside the institutions, officials developed different sets of regulations to conform to differing expectations of how varied groups of patients could and should behave. Racialized and gendered assumptions of Hawaiians as promiscuous, unruly, and ignorant in the ways of Western medicine initially led health officials to favor a more open design for Kalaupapa. In Carville, health officials imposed more restrictive policies and mandated that patients follow the dictates of a modern medical institution. The Kalaupapa settlement provided a model for its Louisiana counterpart, but it was patients at Carville who acted as ideal test subjects in medical research. Only after physicians had been successfully treating patients in Carville with experimental sulfone drugs for several years in the 1940s did they transport the treatment to Hawai'i after World War II.

Patients in both Louisiana and Hawai'i attempted to create autonomous spaces within their institutions while allying themselves with outside groups to challenge policies that regulated their sexual lives, limited their ability to have and raise children, restricted their domestic space, and even in some instances eliminated their right to vote. They also attempted to recast their disease, rejecting the labels of primitive, unclean, and immoral embodied in such terms as "leper." Many patients believed that by renaming leprosy as Hansen's disease, they could strip it of its stigma and unify patients through a shared identity. Patients in the two institutions found themselves mobilizing in different ways, however, as Carville activists could stake a claim to U.S. citizenship that many Hawaiians could not or did not want. While patients helped end the policy of enforced incarceration in the 1950s, they had less success in altering the public's view of the disease. In part, this stemmed from the different cultural matrices that had shaped residents at Kalaupapa and Carville, which made the search for a universally understood, value-neutral disease more complicated than patient activists realized. Imperial legacies and medical definitions could bring leprosy to the consciousness of Americans, but they could not make it an "American" disease.

The first part of *Colonizing Leprosy* examines how the intersection of U.S. colonialism, Western religion, and scientific medicine shaped the construction of leprosaria in Louisiana and Hawai'i during the late nineteenth and early twentieth centuries. The first chapter, "Protecting the National Body," examines how U.S. empire building in the late 1800s precipitated congressional debates over the need to protect American health by constructing a federal leprosy institution on the mainland. U.S. imperialist interventions in such places as Hawai'i intersected with missionary practices and the germ theory of disease to forge a new representation of leprosy as a highly contagious foreign menace. As physicians emphasized the primitive nature of "natives" as carriers of disease, tolerance for U.S. citizens with leprosy decreased. In 1889, Congress began a debate lasting almost thirty years over what steps to take to suppress leprosy in the United States. The sensational trips of patient John Early to Washington, D.C., in the early 1900s show how at least one patient with leprosy saw the possibility of federal intervention in a different light. He hoped a federal law would provide improved care for patients, but ironically, when Early mingled with the Washington elite, he helped spur passage of a 1917 law that established a federal leprosarium dedicated more to isolating patients than to treating them. Four years later, Congress agreed upon the Catholic-administered Louisiana Leper Home as the new federal site.

"Creating a Colonial Disease" focuses on nineteenth-century leprosy settlements in Hawai'i to explore how medicine and Christianity acted as tools of colonial subjugation and how Hawaiian resistance revealed the contingent nature of Western colonial authority in the islands. A group led by U.S. businessmen seized control of the Hawaiian Islands in 1893, and the new government they established used health policy to bolster its authority over a defiant Hawaiian community. Western health officials imposed harsh policing measures upon those with leprosy, and they justified this action by arguing that Hawaiians were succumbing to this disease at a dangerously rapid pace. Hawaiians with leprosy, along with their friends and relatives, often refused to comply with the Western-influenced Board of Health. A deadly 1893 standoff between Provisional Government officials and a group of Hawaiians with leprosy in the Kalalau Valley of Kaua'i highlighted the struggle between an emerging colonial government and its reluctant subjects. Westerners asserted their power by rounding up a substantial percentage of the Hawaiian population with leprosy and containing them at the Kalihi Receiving Station in Honolulu and the Kalaupapa Settlement on

Moloka'i. Hawaiian resistance and community building continued within these institutions, however, demonstrating that the imposition of colonial control was never complete.

On the mainland, religious and scientific traditions combined to create an establishment in Louisiana whose architects focused more on containment than medical treatment. "Sacred Duties, Public Spaces" examines the Louisiana Leper Home during its years as a state-run institution. From its beginning in 1894, limited state funding and an isolated setting ensured that the home's primary purpose would be removing people with leprosy from the broader population rather than developing innovative medical treatment. Leprosy's religious connotations, coupled with a tradition of religious health care in Louisiana, allowed the state to enlist the Daughters of Charity of St. Vincent de Paul as administrators of the home in 1896. While the sisters dramatically improved the material condition of the Louisiana home, their presence reinforced public perceptions of leprosy patients as "unclean" and suggested that their care was a religious rather than a medical responsibility. Patients in the home both drew upon and countered the sisters' religious administration to shape their own conception of what a leprosy institution should be. They envisioned a hospital that would provide medical care without religious oversight, allowing patients the freedom to interact physically with each other as well as the outside world.

The second half of the book examines the evolution and interaction of these two institutions and demonstrates how patients worked to undermine the walls that contained them and to alter popular understandings of leprosy. "Institutionalizing American Leprosy" looks at both the Kalaupapa leprosy settlement in Hawai'i and the newly established U.S. National Leprosarium in Louisiana during the first third of the twentieth century. During this period, the influence of imperialism and its relationship to Western medicine proved crucial factors in shaping these medical institutions and their patient communities. U.S. health officials and physicians who hoped to establish state-of-the-art research and treatment facilities for leprosy in the Hawaiian Islands encountered resistance from Hawaiian patients, who organized to protest medical decisions and experimentation prescribed by doctors. When broad plans for making Kalaupapa into an international research site dimmed, public health officials moved the center of their operations to the mainland arena at the National Leprosarium in Carville, which the federal government acquired in 1921. Officials believed that patients there would prove more willing to accept the promises and premises of Western medicine, as well as the systems of surveillance and institutional discipline that accompanied this knowledge. Racial assumptions regarding the behaviors of Hawaiians and Americans were grounded on imperial foundations and resulted in two different institutions in Hawai'i and Louisiana. Despite the intensified regulations that operated to ensure containment, patients at both institutions demonstrated that they were not totally isolated from the outside world and that they could effectively draw on outside allies to support patient interests.

Patients and officials at each institution mobilized in the 1930s and 1940s around questions of U.S. identity and nationality to actively debate policies of incarceration and definitions of leprosy. "Leprosy and Citizenship" explores how patient communities in Louisiana and Hawai'i each attempted to advance their particular visions of appropriate treatment for the disease. Hawaiians worked to build an autonomous community at the isolated Kalaupapa settlement, where they fought with territorial officials who depicted them as "deviant" bodies requiring proper isolation to protect healthy Americans. Territorial health officers took care to show mainland Americans how they coached leprosy patients in Western medical habits, and they presented their containment of leprosy as a demonstration of Hawai'i's fitness as a future U.S. state. In contrast, patients at Carville highlighted their status as Americans to challenge containment and other public health regulations there as unjustified restrictions of their freedom. World War II exacerbated differences between the Kalaupapa and Carville institutions, as Carvillians sought to distance themselves rhetorically from colonial patients. Residents at the Louisiana facility successfully built alliances with veterans' organizations and deployed wartime rhetoric to demand civil liberties and freedom from incarceration. Their assertions of citizenship as a basis for these changes, however, reinforced images that linked leprosy to foreign bodies who posed a threat to American public health. Wartime contingencies may have labeled patients in Hawai'i more indelibly as non-westerners, but their containment also afforded them greater latitude to shape a distinctively Hawaiian community whose members could criticize and challenge American intervention and medical administration.

"Negotiating an End to Segregation" shows how patients in the postwar era successfully overturned restrictive regulations that mandated their isolation yet found it more difficult to eradicate the social stigma surrounding their disease. Linking their efforts to end the policy of segregation to the success of drug therapy, Carville patients successfully used a rhetoric of medical progress to convince public health officials that the policy of strict segregation no longer held any medical validity. Patients could receive treatment at local outpatient clinics and no longer needed to abandon friends and family to go to an isolated institution. Such policies dispersed the patient community, however, and ultimately weakened efforts to sustain an attack on the cultural stigma surrounding their disease. The patient community in Hawai'i, meanwhile, fractured between those supporting an outpatient movement similar to the one in Carville and those seeking to retain an interethnic Hawaiian community of patients within Kalaupapa. As Hawai'i became a state, some Hawaiians with leprosy positioned themselves as part of the national body and thereby distanced themselves from perceptions that linked leprosy with savagery and foreignness. Residents remaining at Kalaupapa, however, sought to retain their interethnic and strongly indigenous Hawaiian identity and thereby challenge Western medical policy that had sought to control and contain them. Even as segregation ended, colonial legacies continued to shape treatments of leprosy and its image as a distinctly foreign disease.

CHAPTER ONE

Protecting the National Body

In June 1914, leprosy patient and Spanish-American War veteran John Ralston Early made national headlines simply by taking a room in a hotel. After escaping a Puget Sound quarantine station and trekking across North America, Early checked into the fashionable Hotel Willard in the District of Columbia under an assumed name. He considered his accommodations carefully, selecting an establishment favored by members of Congress, ambassadors, and even Vice President Thomas Marshall and his wife. After spending a few days mixing with hotel guests, he notified the city health inspector of his condition and location. Early then gathered a small pool of reporters at the Willard to explain the purpose of his actions and reveal his true identity.[1] He said that he had planned the trip to protest the enforced isolation that he and other leprosy patients faced and to demand that the national government provide better care for people in his situation. He explained, "I knew that if I mingled among the well-to-do and the rich and exposed them to contagion that they would arise out of self-protection and further my plan of a national home."[2] He announced to the reporters, "No matter what my trials are here, I will fight for my constitutional right as a citizen of the United States, and I will resist any effort to ship me to some place where I don't want to go."[3] To some extent, Early's stunt had its desired effect. Although he was arrested and quarantined in an isolated facility on the banks of the Anacostia River, his actions reignited a decades-old debate over the need for a federal facility that would care for Americans with leprosy. The wheels of legislation moved slowly, and Congress did not pass a bill to establish a national leprosarium until 1917, but legislators, physicians, and public health professionals often invoked the name of John Early when making their case for federal intervention in the treatment and containment of leprosy.[4]

Physicians and public health officials had been petitioning Congress to establish a national leprosarium since the 1880s, spurred in large part by concerns that U.S. imperial interventions in places where leprosy was endemic might spread the disease within the borders of the mainland. State and local health officials who had been treating scattered cases of leprosy over the years began to press the U.S. government for assistance in handling what they characterized as a foreign and stigmatized disease, while some federal health officials encouraged the national government to oversee the treatment of people with leprosy as a means of expanding their authority in matters of public health. Although efforts by both these groups produced investigations into the prevalence of the disease in the United States and on the practicality of establishing a national facility, public health officials failed to move the House and Senate to take decisive action.

John Early managed to do what health professionals could not: convince members of Congress that they might find themselves exposed to the disease. Early had hoped to challenge state and local policies that required strict isolation for people with leprosy and to demand a federal facility dedicated to better treatment for those who had contracted the disease, but he instead frightened legislators into protecting themselves and their constituents who also feared the disease. No longer certain that leprosy could be kept out of the country through immigration regulations, members of Congress came to view the disease as a hidden internal menace that needed to be identified and contained to protect the health of the national body. They recognized that possessing an empire meant that U.S. citizens such as Early—missionaries, government officials, soldiers, and merchants—who had lived, worked, and fought in overseas territories could pose a contagious threat when they returned to the mainland. Early's invocation of his citizenship also suggested to some lawmakers that the federal government had a responsibility to care for these Americans serving in colonial settings. Congress finally decided to authorize an institution in 1917, though it took another four years before the U.S. government federalized the existing Louisiana Leper Home and created a national leprosarium. Legislators ultimately determined that such a facility was necessary, in part because they hoped to provide a humane site of care for Americans, but primarily because they wanted to contain an internal threat to the nation.

Diagnosing a National Illness

Congressional debates over leprosy during the late nineteenth and early twentieth centuries both responded to and induced changes in the ways physicians, public health officials, and politicians conceptualized the disease and sought to contain it. State and local officials before this period had established their own methods of treating and containing those with leprosy in their communities, but they now began to turn to the federal government for assistance. Where once they had seen occurrences of leprosy as isolated (although repugnant and dangerous) incidents, they now came to view them as linked to broader patterns of national intervention in world affairs, particularly imperialist ventures. Where in the past they had attributed fears of leprosy to concerns over its physical effects and biblical connotations of sinful living, they increasingly incorporated apprehension of foreign contamination into their characterizations of the disease. When members of Congress began to investigate the prevalence of leprosy in the United States in response to concerns from individual constituents, their investigations helped reconfigure the disease as a national problem. Congressional debates brought together leprosy specialists from both state and colonial contexts, paving the way for a national policy that would blend colonial methods of disease control with mainland public health practices.

Leprosy had been a documented presence in the United States for more than 100 years when members of Congress first began to debate its prevalence during the 1880s. Not indigenous to the United States, leprosy was thought to have entered several specific regions of the country from a variety of immigration streams. The first known cases were identified in Louisiana during the mid-eighteenth century, though scholars debate whether French Acadians or the Spanish West Indian slave trade brought the disease. During the nineteenth century, physicians connected leprosy in the Midwest (particularly Minnesota and Wisconsin) with Scandinavian immigrants, in California with Pacific rim and Latin American immigrants, and in New York with a multivaried group of European and Asian immigrants.[5] Although the disease had links with immigrant groups from its earliest appearance in the United States, leprosy did not acquire its reputation as a fearful foreign contaminant requiring national management until the late nineteenth century.

No locality established a mandatory incarceration policy for all people with leprosy, though health officials often placed certain patients who lacked suitable caregivers in specialized facilities. A leprosy hospital established on the outskirts of New Orleans during the late eighteenth century closed in 1804 as a result of charges that none of the five patients it held actually had the disease, but the city's Charity Hospital treated more than one hundred leprosy patients between 1805 and 1894.[6] In an 1888 survey of Minnesota, Wisconsin, and the Dakotas, Norwegian physician Gerhard Armauer Hansen estimated that 160 Scandinavians with leprosy had emigrated to the

United States since the mid-nineteenth century, with only 13 patients surviving at the time of the survey. He wrote to state public health officials to suggest that a proposed rigid policy of segregation would prove unnecessary, as the disease did not appear to be spreading.[7] Health officials in California and New York required that physicians report identified cases of leprosy, but neither state outlined a policy of how to contain or treat such cases. Lack of a coherent policy led to an uneven handling of patients. Immigrants without families tended to end up in urban pest houses, while other leprosy patients were allowed to convalesce within their homes.[8]

During the late nineteenth century, state and local public health officials and physicians began to urge federal officials to establish a national leprosarium to contain those who had contracted the disease. This request for U.S. government intervention marked an abrupt departure in health policies, as responsibility for the health care of citizens had previously rested with individual states and localities. Significantly, the first requests for assistance came not from Minnesota and Louisiana, states where the disease was endemic, but from regions unaccustomed to dealing regularly with leprosy. A Florida physician in 1889 and the Philadelphia Board of Health in 1892 based their claims for government aid on the premise that leprosy posed such a grave threat to public health that it required strict incarceration. Since these communities held few leprosy patients, doctors and health officials argued that constructing specialized institutions for the care of a few contagious individuals would place too great a burden on their communities. These medical professionals argued that the federal government could provide one or two institutions for all leprosy patients in the nation, conveniently relieving local communities of both the financial costs and the social affliction of harboring people with leprosy.[9]

The sense that leprosy posed a unique strain on local communities stemmed in part from its historical stigma, which assumed a new significance during the late nineteenth and early twentieth centuries in part through the efforts of Christian missionaries.[10] These religious workers evoked the disease's religious connotations in writings and church lectures detailing missionary ventures among leprosy patients in a variety of colonial contexts. Both Protestant and Catholic missionaries operated under the conviction that attending to physical needs served a specifically spiritual function, both in saving souls and serving as an example of Christ's teachings.[11] Their writings drew explicit connections between the disease that they encountered and the one that was described in the Bible, connections that emphasized the depiction of those with leprosy as "unclean" and drew authority from Christ's command to the apostles to "Heal the sick, cleanse the lepers."[12] Articles on missionary work dealt with leprosy patients in Africa, Hawai'i, China, and India, and the authors of these accounts suggested that contemporary outbreaks of the disease existed primarily among "uncivilized" populations whose communities proved unwilling or incapable of properly caring for these "poor creatures."[13] These reports by missionaries directed attention to a disease many thought extinct and reinforced leprosy's image as a dangerous contaminant requiring strict segregation. The writings also suggested that westerners had a responsibility to assist those deemed primitive by spreading both the Christian religion and Western notions of health and cleanliness.

The 1889 death in Hawai'i of Belgian Catholic missionary Joseph de Veuster, known as Father Damien, became a particularly powerful symbol of religious sacrifice for leprosy and attracted global attention to the disease. After arriving at the Hawaiian leprosy settlement on the island of Moloka'i in 1873 to improve patient care and provide spiritual guidance, Damien contracted the disease himself. Although few medical or religious personnel had acquired the disease in years of dealing with leprosy patients, Damien's case reinforced the notion that leprosy was a highly contagious and life-threatening illness. Word of his death, sensationalized in newspaper accounts, biographies, and memoirs, heightened public awareness of the disease and called attention to its presence both abroad and in the United States.[14] As one 1890 article on leprosy in Louisiana argued, the story of Damien could be employed to arouse public interest in attending to those with the disease within the United States. The author concluded, "Why should not we too do something in memory of Father Damien? What shall we do for these our own lepers?"[15]

For many physicians and public health officials, the answer to this question was to enlist federal assistance in identifying leprosy's pervasiveness in the United States and in establishing a national policy for containing it. At the 1894 meeting of the Congress of American Surgeons and Physicians (CASP), Dr. James White invoked the case of Damien to assert the contagiousness of leprosy and the need for prompt government action to control it.[16] The Congress devoted half a day of its three-day conference to leprosy, including discussions that outlined its prevalence in such colonial settings as the Hawaiian Islands, Cuba, Jamaica, and Panama. To medical men such as Dr. Joseph D. Bryant, the leprosy patient was by nature foreign and represented a threat not only to American physical well-being, but to an American way of life. He described those with leprosy as "a kind of human maelstrom, that engulfs and swallows everything of use that enters the circle of its influence, and yields nothing . . . that is necessary to American comfort and prosperity."[17] White, Bryant, and other physicians at the meeting asserted that the federal government had a responsibility to use the benefits of scientific progress to sustain civilization and shield the American public from foreign contagions like leprosy. U.S. Surgeon General Walter Wyman brought the afternoon's discussion about U.S. leprosy policy to a close with a specific plan for convincing the U.S. Congress about the necessity for federal intervention. He proposed that the CASP petition members of Congress to appoint a committee of specialists to investigate the prevalence of the disease and to determine how it should be contained, suggesting that such a course of action would produce information that could relieve public anxiety and potentially place the disease under national control.[18] The attention devoted to the disease suggested that the conference attendees saw leprosy policy as a suitable avenue for pursuing one of their primary goals: to promote the importance of the American medical profession in protecting the welfare of the nation. Within two weeks, CASP members presented their petition to Congress.[19]

Surgeon General Wyman saw in leprosy an opportunity to enlarge the scope and power of the slowly expanding Marine Hospital Service (MHS, which later evolved into the U.S. Public Health Service) over the health of Americans. During the 1880s and 1890s, MHS physicians and public health officials translated people's fears over rising numbers of immigrants and an Asiatic cholera scare into increased regulatory control for the service over who or what could enter the United States. Congress passed a law in 1891 mandating individual health inspections for all immigrants entering the country, to be conducted by physicians of the MHS. Passage of a national quarantine law in 1893 required that all foreign vessels receive a health certificate from the U.S. consul before leaving their home ports for the United States, with the MHS providing the personnel to conduct inspections in foreign ports. Before landing cargo or passengers in the United States, the captain of a ship had to present an MHS certificate to the Collector of Customs. This law also authorized the MHS to examine all interstate facilities and regulations. A fledgling hygienic laboratory established in New York to study cholera and yellow fever further enlarged the scope of the service's power. Having facilitated this expanding authority in the areas of quarantine and contagious disease investigation, Wyman helped translate anxieties about foreign contamination into increased government intervention in the public health arena.[20]

By the end of the nineteenth century, MHS involvement in national health issues had become so customary that some members of Congress believed the service already had the authority to mount a nationwide investigation into leprosy. In 1898, Senator Orville Platt of Connecticut wondered why the MHS needed a new law passed before it could launch an investigation of the disease.[21] He learned that while Congress had defined a role for the MHS in investigating contagious disease, the Surgeon General required congressional approval before spending any money on such an effort.[22] Seeking to gain such authorization from the Senate, Wyman drew attention to the contagious nature of leprosy and warned that "when introduced into a country . . . history shows that it invariably spreads."[23] While the Senate approved a small $5,000 sum for the investigation in 1898, the surgeon general had less success in mustering concern in the House, which failed to act on the measure.[24]

Even as members of Congress debated the need to investigate the disease, U.S. acquisition of Pacific territories in 1898 galvanized support for a federal investigation into the prevalence of leprosy in the United States. In 1897, New York dermatologist Prince A. Morrow speculated that a proposal to annex the Hawaiian Islands and their "leprous population" to the United States would expose the American population to the disease. Asserting that existing quarantine measures would be ineffective, as leprosy could not be detected in its earliest stages, Morrow charged that annexation "would create conditions favorable to the dissemination of the seeds of leprosy in this country."[25] American physician Burnside Foster reiterated those concerns once annexation became a reality in 1898, urging federal investigation of the disease to help address the potential influx of people with leprosy. "Many of those who either know or suspect that they have the disease will undoubtedly attempt to escape to this country," Foster warned.[26] Such commentaries prompted House members to consider how contagious diseases running rampant in the "tropics" could put American health at risk.[27] Representative Alexander Dockery of Missouri asserted that a leprosy investigation "is no doubt a proper precaution, which is made necessary by the acquisition of Hawai'i and some other undesirable possessions." A majority of House members agreed and passed the bill in February 1899.[28]

Investigating Leprosy in America

When President William McKinley signed the bill calling for a leprosy survey into law on 2 March 1899, he helped further Surgeon General Wyman's goal of expanding MHS authority and federal control over the nation's health.[29] Conducting a nationwide survey and formulating a national policy for a specific disease represented a new endeavor for the federal service. The process of identifying the scope of leprosy's spread throughout the nation required a central agency with the authority to demand cooperation from qualified medical practitioners in each state and territory, along with the money and bureaucratic support to tabulate responses, assess findings, develop recommendations, and work to implement them. MHS officials sent questionnaires to local health officials requesting information on the numbers of people with leprosy within their districts and how they were treated. Commission members reviewed the 2,530 responses from the 2,819 counties they polled to calculate the prevalence of the disease within various regions, to identify the kinds of policies and institutions established to handle patients with leprosy, and to assess the effectiveness of local measures.[30] The leprosy investigation provided a precedent for future nationwide studies of health-related matters.

Changing conceptions of disease and bacteriology heightened fears regarding the contagious nature of leprosy and empowered physicians to take interventionist measures in the name of protecting public health. Although the germ theory of disease spread unevenly through medical and public circles, it commanded increasing authority during the late 1800s as bacteriologists identified the sources of anthrax, diphtheria, typhoid, cholera, and tuberculosis. As doctors linked diseases to specific contagions, disease prevention increasingly focused on identifying and curing those who were sick rather than on general sanitation measures.[31] For much of the nineteenth century, doctors had conceived of leprosy as a hereditary disease, but Hansen's 1873 identification of *Mycobacterium leprae* as the causative agent of leprosy lent credence to the idea that someone with the disease could transmit it to others. The identification of the leprosy bacillus, however, led neither to the creation of a preventive vaccine nor to a method of treatment, but instead to calls for isolating patients. North Dakota legislators petitioned Congress in 1899 to establish a national institution for leprosy patients, emphasizing the incurable and contagious nature of the disease, its threat to public health, and the inability of local authorities to handle it. According to these local officials, only the federal government had the means to oversee the disease, "which baffles the skill of medical science."[32]

Media reports of Hawaiian leprosy patients and the death of Father Damien, along with the belief that those with the disease forfeited their right to live within the United States, prompted California legislators to make more drastic demands for isolation. In 1901, they called for a leprosy policy that would transport anyone with the disease out of their state and even off the continent. In February 1901, Senator George Perkins presented to Congress a joint resolution of the California legislature that called for the removal of all leprosy patients in the United States to an expanded leprosy hospital on the Hawaiian island of Molokaʻi. The island already supported a leprosy settlement on its Kalaupapa peninsula, and legislators hailed its favorable climate and inaccessibility as ideal attributes for the proper facility to handle people from the mainland who had the disease.[33] Such extreme measures formed part of a broader pattern of racial intolerance and racialized notions of disease that circulated along the Pacific coast. Some California medical professionals pronounced leprosy a disease of Chinese immigrants and used the disease as a means to target the population as a physical and moral threat to white residents.[34] Members of Congress took no action on the California resolution, however, and postponed further consideration of the leprosy issue until the Marine Hospital Service revealed the results of its survey.

The conclusions released by the MHS commission in 1902 reflected the colonialist experiences and practices of the health officials who served on it. The doctors charged with conducting the investigation—Joseph H. White, George Vaughan, and Milton Rosenau—had extensive experience in colonial quarantine and contagious disease research. White and Vaughan investigated yellow fever and diphtheria overseas during the Spanish-American War in 1898 and participated in developing a harsh quarantine measure for San Francisco's Chinatown during a 1900 outbreak of bubonic plague.[35] Rosenau oversaw the military's sanitation policies in Cuba following the 1898 war with Spain.[36] The experiences of these medical officers shaped their ideas regarding the kind of intervention the federal government could make into the lives of those perceived to threaten U.S. interests. Although they conceded that leprosy proved less threatening than sensationalist accounts suggested, the commission's physicians concluded that leprosy posed a significant enough threat to warrant the establishment of a federal leprosarium or two.[37] This proposed policy of identifying those who had a communicable disease and isolating them from the public reflected prevailing public health assumptions; however, creating a national institution to contain all those who had a particular disease represented a significant expansion of federal authority in the realm of public health. The commissioners based their argument for such an expansion on a model constructed from the experiences they had and from the practices they developed in colonial settings.

Rather than recommend the creation of local sanatoria across the continent (comparable to those established for tuberculosis patients) or the placement of leprosy patients within contagious disease wards of general hospitals, the commission suggested the creation of institutions that sounded similar to the one already established on Moloka'i. Reports from MHS officials who had investigated the Hawaiian leprosy settlement celebrated the wide expanse of the peninsula set aside for leprosy patients, the government-provided cottages and rations, the beautiful setting, the fertile grounds suitable for cultivation, and the variety of recreational activities available to patients.[38] As a result, the commission advocated that the national leprosaria should be located in "a salubrious climate . . . where the inmates can have unlimited and unrestrained outdoor exercise and occupation, roaming over well-kept grounds, enjoying pleasant vistas, or engaged in tilling fertile fields." Suggesting that the support of such patients should be a federal responsibility, it further advised that the government provide all basic necessities for patients admitted to such institutions.[39]

Despite its efforts to portray leprosy as a national threat requiring immediate action, the MHS found itself forced to explain why a federal leprosarium would be necessary in the mainland United States, where the disease was much less widespread than in Hawai'i. The MHS investigation had identified only 278 cases of leprosy in the nation, a number that did not suggest a dangerous epidemic. Concluding that this number did not accurately represent the real extent of the disease, commission members attempted to explain what they saw as an unreasonably low figure for leprosy patients. Many cases escaped detection due either to the lack of cooperation from officials who failed to send information or to the mild nature of early cases that could not be identified, the report's authors argued. They also attributed the low number to the reluctance of leprosy patients to admit the true nature of their disease, which was based partly on their awareness of the stigma attached to the illness and the wretched condition of pest houses to which they could be sent. Commission members did concede that the number of patients with leprosy in the United States was relatively low, but they suggested that this low prevalence made local containment and care all the more inefficient and expensive. For the commission, the very presence of leprosy—however small—posed a danger. The report emphasized that only 72 of the 278 identified cases were isolated, indicating that "proper institutions" were needed, "not only for the sake of the sick but as a protection to the well."[40]

Public health officials and physicians struggled to balance these two components of their mission: to care for those afflicted with disease and to protect the health of the general public. That many leprosy patients received indifferent care or worse troubled these officials, who urged strongly that any federal institutions should be designed more as homes than as sites of incarceration. The authors of the report recommended that the facilities "be made as attractive as it is possible to make them, so as not to be looked upon as a species of poorhouse or prison by the victims of the disease." Still, the commission members bluntly asserted that the motivation to make such facilities pleasant stemmed in part from their desire to lure people with the disease to them.[41] They reasoned that if patients did not feel they were being restrained (even though they were), they would come forward and present themselves for treatment. In this way, public health officials could remove them from the community. The MHS commission strongly favored the International Leprosy Conference's determination in 1897 that "every leper is dangerous to his surroundings, the danger varying with the nature and extent of his relations therewith."[42] The more segregated the leprosy patient, the commission reasoned, the better for the public. So while the recommendation that the institution be placed in a pleasant climate—in the open spaces of the arid Southwest, on an island in the Gulf of Mexico, or off the Pacific coast—was couched as a benefit to patients, the isolated nature of the sites proved the dominant determining factor in the final selection of a national leprosarium.[43]

The report reflected the commission members' enduring sense that leprosy remained a disease most closely identified with Asian, Pacific Islander, and Caribbean populations, despite their own evidence to the contrary. Although the survey identified more than half of the patients as having contracted the disease in the United States, the commission reported that many of these people must have "brought the disease with them from foreign lands," with China, the Hawaiian Islands, and the West Indies singled out as the likely sources of contagion. The public health officials specifically drew attention to figures gleaned from an 1898 investigation of Hawai'i, claiming that they explained how the disease could be introduced from the nation's new "transoceanic possessions."[44]

While leprosy had been prevalent throughout Europe during the Middle Ages, by the late nineteenth century it was often categorized as a "tropical disease," a term applied to many contagious diseases that Western physicians encountered in their colonial medical practices. Rather than emerging from accurate understandings of the "natural" origin of such diseases, this new category arose from European desires to bolster their knowledge of unfamiliar diseases in order to protect imperial colonizers. This new conceptualization reshaped the way people came to understand disease in the late nineteenth century.[45] The British conducted a leprosy survey of India during the early 1890s to assess the disease's potential threat to the empire, for example, and their study helped reconceptualize leprosy as a tropical disease. Identifying leprosy in this way explicitly situated it outside of the Western world, while suggesting that scientific medicine could categorize, contain, and manage the disease through proper study.[46] Still, British medical officials did not develop a coherent leprosy policy until the early twentieth century, when they adapted the strict segregationist policy followed in Hawai'i to their own colonies in India and South Africa.[47]

This reconception of leprosy as a tropical disease led to a bifurcated system of classifying both leprosy and the people who had it. Doctors recognized that some people who had contracted the disease came from northern climes and recommended they be treated differently from other people with leprosy. In the MHS report to the Senate, a few doctors pointed out that a significant number of those who contracted the disease outside the United States came from the Scandinavian countries of Norway and Sweden. Dr. H. M. Bracken of the Minnesota Board of Health suggested that the U.S. government establish two separate facilities, one for people from the north and one for those from tropical and semitropical climes. As he explained, "It would not be humane to transport those who by inheritance and birth belong in a tropical climate to a leprosarium in Minnesota, while on the other hand people of Scandinavian or Icelandic origin should not be sent to Louisiana or the Hawaiian Islands."[48] While such a decision may seem to have been motivated by a concern for patients' comfort, it also revealed the ways in which notions of racial and ethnic difference, climate, region, and disease became closely intertwined.[49] To some physicians, European leprosy (and consequently those who contracted it) was inherently different from tropical leprosy and required separate accommodations and treatment.

Just as physicians and public health officials cited Asian and island locales more frequently as threats to American soil, so too did they look to those regions when theorizing about how and why leprosy spread. Their hypotheses often incorporated racialized notions of difference, grounded in assumptions of foreign inferiority and uncivilized behavior. Dr. A. W. Hitt speculated that the ingestion of "rotten fish," a practice that he asserted was common among Filipinos and Indians, provoked leprosy. He connected the rapid spread of the disease in Hawai'i to the "common poi bowl," into which individuals would dip their fingers to partake of communal meals.[50] Dr. D. A. Carmichael contended that shared sleeping mats, clothing, and pipes; "bad hygienic surroundings"; and "kissing, nose rubbing, and cohabitation" provided ways for Hawaiians to transmit the disease.[51]

Failure to shun those with leprosy provided the most visible symbol of Hawaiian savagery, which highlighted the subsequent need for American supervision and intervention in the islands, according to some U.S. physicians. The threat of contagion arose, Carmichael argued, from the Hawaiian "tolerance of the leper—that is, he was treated as a member of the family, and never as an outcast."[52] In the eyes of public health professionals, civilized society showed a healthy fear of leprosy and took appropriate steps to isolate those with the disease from the rest of the community. If other societies failed to properly accommodate those with a contagious disease, they consigned themselves to "uncivilized" status and thereby justified American intervention and acquisition. U.S. public health officials used the commission report to suggest that they would save the colonized from themselves.

Tapping into the intolerance of leprosy that mainland Americans possessed, the commission included in its report photographs of those in advanced stages of leprosy in order to persuade Congress to develop a policy of segregation. The images came from Dr. A. W. Hitt's personal collection of sixteen lantern slides he gathered during his travels to India in 1894. The images did not resemble late-nineteenth-century clinical photographs as much as mid-nineteenth-century medical representations that focused on unusual deformities, suggesting that the physician framed the images more for their shock value than for medical interest. While most clinical photography had begun in the 1890s to focus on the site of pathology, blacking out nondiseased portions of the body and attempting to maintain the anonymity of the patient,[53] Hitt generally framed the entire patient in ways that emphasized both the exoticism and the deformity of those with leprosy. As such, the pictures appeared as a kind of portrait gallery of monstrosities. One of the images in the collection did not even represent a patient with leprosy, but an Indian barber. The caption read, "He uses the same razor to shave lepers, syphilitics, and men who are free from these diseases. The razor is cleaned by wiping it on his dirty loin cloth." The barber and client, pictured crouching on a dirt floor, clad only in loin cloths, established a sense of the alien, the oversexualized, and the unhygienic. Other images depicted leprosy patients with misshapen hands held forward like claws, or with unseeing eyes staring glassily heavenward, or with large tubercles obliterating any recognizable mouth, nose, or cheek.[54] No captions accompanied

Image of lantern slide from Dr. A. W. Hitt depicting an Indian barber and client, presented to the U.S. Senate Committee on Public Health and National Quarantine, 1902.

the pictures of patients; the idea that their physical disfigurement reflected moral and mental incapacitation was presumably self-evident.

Doctors attempted to motivate the government to take action by heightening public fears through written descriptions of leprosy's physical ravages. Hitt sent to Congress an 1897 speech in which he identified and described in grotesque detail two different forms of the disease. The anesthetic variety, said to focus on the nerves, ultimately mutilated the hands, feet, and face; "the nose sinks in, and leaves a ghastly looking patient, whose face can never be forgotten." The advanced stage of the second variety, tubercular leprosy, affected the skin and produced "greasy" and "shining" masses on the face, causing the patient "to look simply frightful."[55] Hitt's descriptions read like a recounting of horrors witnessed at a show of carnival performers labeled "freaks." In recommending segregation of leprosy patients, Dr. R. D. Murray of the MHS suggested that leprosy transformed people into creatures who should be and even wanted to be ostracized. "Lepers shun people instinctively," he asserted, "but remain human for a long time; and lepers

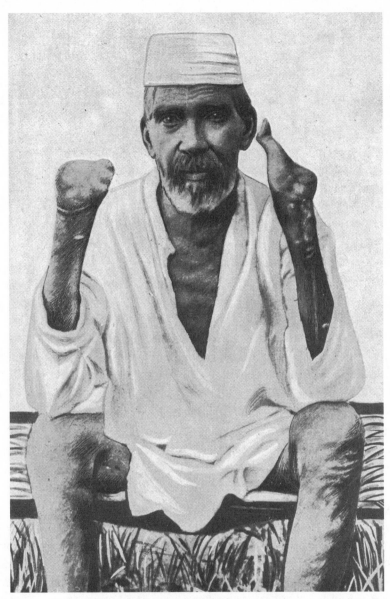

Image of lantern slide from Dr. A. W. Hitt depicting an Indian man with leprosy, presented to the U.S. Senate Committee on Public Health and National Quarantine, 1902. Hitt's description of such pictures emphasized visible physical deformities and reduced people with leprosy to static objects. One could view the man's direct gaze and carriage, however, as a challenge to leprosy's stigma and an assertion of his humanity.

fear lepers." If members of Congress missed Murray's distinction between "lepers" and "people," they could not help but recognize his later bestialization of leprosy patients when he said, "Lepers are like rats and rattlesnakes— where there is one, there is or was another not far off."[56] Like vermin, those with leprosy were to be eliminated from the society at large, where they were viewed as capable only of skulking about, spreading disease. The dehumanizing manner in which Hitt and other physicians described patients seemed to reflect a sense held by those who studied the disease that a person with leprosy ceased to be human during the advanced stages of the sickness. Such beings, these medical professionals argued, needed to be removed from society and placed in strict isolation.

Designing a National Leprosarium

The development of a federal leprosy policy illustrates how U.S. imperialism had far-reaching consequences for the administration of U.S. public health. After the publication of the 1902 report, Congress adopted a two-pronged approach to American leprosy policy that revealed a determination to maintain separate approaches for the mainland and U.S. territories. Hawai'i had been a U.S. possession since 1898, but many members of Congress and U.S. medical officials sought to keep many of its inhabitants— particularly the sick—rigidly segregated from those on the mainland. In December 1904, the House of Representatives considered two separate bills regarding leprosy: one to investigate the leprosy problem in Hawai'i, and the other to provide a federal leprosarium for the segregation of patients with leprosy in the mainland United States.[57] Despite legislators' insistence on treating Hawaiian leprosy independently from the disease on the mainland, much of what health officials recommended for a national leprosy policy emerged from a Hawaiian context. While legislators and physicians worked to prevent importation of "diseased" territorial residents into the mainland, they viewed Hawai'i as providing a positive model for understanding and managing leprosy.

Even as U.S. public health officials worked to make distinctions between colonial and mainland leprosy policy, they held up Hawai'i as an example of how segregation could contain the spread of the disease. Health officials had intensified a system of surveillance to police the inhabitants of the islands after westerners deposed Queen Lili'uokalani in 1893. Building on segregation policies developed under the Hawaiian monarchs, Western public health officials after 1893 segregated a dramatically higher number of people with leprosy, established methods of medical record keeping, and enacted more stringent regulations governing the activities of those diagnosed with leprosy.[58] In recommending the Senate version of the bill that would fund leprosy care within Hawai'i, Surgeon General Wyman spoke approvingly of a territorial Board of Health report that detailed the cooperation between health officials and district deputy sheriffs in rounding up "suspects," described the process of examination at an investigation station in Honolulu, and discussed how those diagnosed with the disease were sent to a segregated settlement on Moloka'i.[59] Wyman supported the strict segregation policy established in the islands and welcomed the opportunity for increased federal support of Hawaiian efforts to contain the disease. Such a policy presented mainland politicians and health officials with a strong precedent for how to manage leprosy at home.

Federal discussions of leprosy also spurred debate over Hawai'i as an ideal site for medical research, drawing further distinctions between the primary purposes of colonial and mainland institutions. Whereas the 1904 bill providing for the creation of a federal leprosarium on the mainland delineated its primary function as containment, the bill providing funds for leprosy in Hawai'i focused instead on the creation of an "experiment station." This legislation, ostensibly created to provide federal money for "the care and treatment" of leprosy patients in Hawai'i, detailed the benefits of allowing doctors to learn from the sizable number of patients in an isolated setting "where every clinical feature of the disease can be seen and studied to advantage."[60] The bill emphasized the value of a facility where U.S. physicians and medical researchers could study, analyze, and test Hawaiian patients to acquire knowledge for the benefit of Americans at home.

The fact that the MHS targeted the Moloka'i leprosy settlement as a site for scientific investigation in 1904 underlines medicine's participation in the colonization of the Hawaiian Islands. Medical officials saw Moloka'i as a site to be exploited for research and experimentation that would yield information applicable to the mainland and beyond. Such methods form part of what Bernard S. Cohn refers to as the "investigative modality," a process by which a colonial society could be identified, categorized, and controlled.[61] Debate in Congress emphasized this colonialist element. When one House member stated that he assumed the bill would create a hospital for the care of Hawaiian leprosy patients, the sponsor of the bill corrected him by explaining that it would create a "laboratory" for studying leprosy, where patients would be admitted for the purpose of allowing U.S. doctors to investigate the disease.[62] The measure raised little objection in Congress and passed in March 1905.[63]

The separate bill calling for the establishment of a U.S. leprosarium within the continental United States did not fare as well, suggesting that members of Congress still had difficulty conceptualizing leprosy as an "American" problem. Surgeon General Wyman attempted to counter this ambivalence by stimulating social revulsion toward the disease and drawing attention to its presence on the mainland.[64] He referred to Dr. Hitt's lantern slides included in the 1902 MHS report to remind members of Congress that the "effects of the disease are loathsome beyond description," causing anyone who contracted it to become "an object shunned by his fellow men and even by his relatives." Wyman's proposed measures further depicted those with leprosy as offensive by emphasizing that the bill provided pay and a half for all health officials employed at the leprosarium as fair compensation for jobs that medical officials portrayed as hazardous. Specifically, he called attention to the daily physical contact medical practitioners would have with leprosy patients, "whose lesions and mutilations are not only unsightly, but often disgusting to the last degree."[65] While alluding to the danger of contagion, the language most often used to describe the disease dwelled on its repugnant physical effects, suggesting that the mental anguish suffered from looking at the deformities wrought by leprosy was at least equal to the physical threat of infection.

Wyman also took the opportunity to reiterate points made in the 1902 report regarding the efficacy of establishing a federal institution, and he attempted to ease concerns that such a leprosarium would pose a financial burden to the nation. He pointed to the uneven state-level administration of the disease and described the creation of a national leprosarium as part of a broader policy that would standardize leprosy medical administration and care.[66] While insisting that the creation of individual institutions throughout the country would be onerous for state governments, he contended that the federal government already had at its disposal public land suitable for a leprosarium, as well as qualified professionals in the Public Health and Marine Hospital Service who would be responsible for administering the institution. A national site, staffed with federal employees, would accept all leprosy patients who voluntarily offered themselves for admission, or who (more likely) were committed there by a state or territorial board of health.[67]

Only patients from within the continental United States would be welcome at this institution, despite the fact that many residents of Hawai'i, the Philippines, and Puerto Rico had the disease. Congress and federal medical officials saw these new territories as American possessions, but did not consider their inhabitants "Americans."[68] The bill providing for a federal leprosarium explicitly stated "that no leper shall be brought from any territorial possession without the continental boundaries of the United States." The sponsor of the legislation attempted to assuage any fear that establishing such an institution would allow territorial residents entry into the mainland when he firmly stated that "there is no possibility of one of them [Hawaiian leprosy patients] coming under the terms of this bill."[69]

Debates over the suitability of creating a federal leprosarium demonstrated how the leprosy patient, no matter what his or her country of origin, came to embody the diseased "Other," a person unwelcome in any mainland locality. While most members of Congress agreed that leprosy in the United States posed a problem, none of them wanted to allow the government to build a leprosarium in their home state. Others protested the establishment of such a site anywhere within the continental borders. One congressman explained, "I have no objection to the establishment of a leprosarium in the insular possessions, but I do object to forcing on Arizona or New Mexico a leprosarium as more likely to lead to the spread of leprosy in those territories than to stamp out what little there is in the balance of the United States." Revisiting the 1901 proposal of California legislators, Representative John Stephens of Texas suggested in the 1905 debates that all leprosy patients could be rounded up on the mainland and sent to the Moloka'i settlement in Hawai'i. Even mainland U.S. citizens who contracted the disease, according to this way of thinking, forfeited their rights of citizenship by threatening the national body and left themselves vulnerable to expulsion to a colony. While Representative William Hepburn of Iowa chided Stephens for recommending that "Americans" be "expatriated" and banished "thousands of miles across the sea," other representatives rejoined that members should not advise placing in another state or territory what they would not accept in their own.[70]

The very definition of territory underwent close scrutiny, as members of Congress differentiated lands within the continental borders of the United States from the newly acquired island possessions in the Pacific. The contrast highlights the ways in which Americans saw their continental expansion in a separate light from their acquisition of an overseas empire.[71] The territories of Arizona and New Mexico were expected to become U.S. states, but politicians differed over the future of such new acquisitions as Hawai'i, viewing them more as valuable properties to be exploited than as future partners in the union. Delegates from the continental territories in particular sought to distinguish themselves from the new possessions, reminding members of Congress of their role in "taming the West" and their need to attract the population necessary to attain statehood. Delegate John Wilson of Arizona territory waxed eloquent about the early settlers who fought off "the wild Indian," "conquered the desert," and established "peaceful communities," only to be threatened with "the leper" from "abroad." Delegate Bernard Rodey from the territory of New Mexico asserted that placing a federal leprosarium within the arid Southwest would make it more difficult for Arizona and New Mexico to lure settlers. Invoking popular perceptions of the "leper" as outcast, Rodey asked, "How would you gentlemen in the States like to have the tinkling bell sounding and the white shroud of the leper stalking through your back yard in the morning, as described in Ben Hur? . . . Instead of being the health resort of the nation, [the territory] will become the most abhorred and shunned locality we have." Urging all to recall the images of leprosy patients included in the 1902 Senate document, he suggested that no American would want them as neighbors, and supported the idea of sending mainland leprosy patients to one of the Hawaiian Islands instead.[72]

Rodey's celebration of the Southwest as a "health resort" demonstrated the ways in which policymakers accepted some diseases, such as tuberculosis, as "civilized," while relegating leprosy to the realm of the "primitive." Both diseases were communicable bacterial infections, though tuberculosis was actually more contagious. Medical health officials targeted the Southwest as an ideal site for a leprosarium due to the salubrious climate, sparse population, and accessible location—the same qualities that made Arizona and New Mexico ideal for tuberculosis sanatoria. Leprosy evoked different responses in the imagination of many Americans, however. Tuberculosis, while feared, remained associated with societies that Americans considered advanced, and many believed it was curable with appropriate rest in a healthful environment.[73] Its endemic nature bred familiarity and made tuberculosis less exotic and less frightening to many people. Members of Congress counted tuberculosis patients among their friends and associates, with one representative reminding his colleagues of a local businessman's once deathly-ill son who returned from an eighteen-month sojourn in Phoenix in vibrant health.[74] Leprosy, on the other hand, was associated with tropical climates that people perceived as primitive; politicians and medical officials alike discussed it as a foreign disease that had penetrated the United States. In addition, leprosy disfigured patients in ways that horrified the healthy, and doctors offered little hope of a cure. Representatives and dele-

gates who opposed the bill persuasively argued that establishing a leprosarium in the southwestern territories would only threaten the lives of the ill
who already flocked to Arizona and New Mexico to cure their tuberculosis
and other pulmonary diseases.[75] To territorial delegates and their supporters, the two diseases could not co-exist in the region, and tuberculosis patients won out as the more "civilized" and worthy sick.

This discussion also renewed congressional debate over the federal government's place in managing the health of the nation. While the surgeon
general and other federal medical officials sought to enlarge the authority of
an emerging national board of health, some politicians voiced concern that
such expansion threatened individual state autonomy.[76] Some members of
Congress recognized that enhancing federal medical authority had the potential to make certain states or territories the dumping ground for the
nation's ill. If the government assumed responsibility for all of the nation's
leprosy patients, they reasoned, what was to prevent them from nationalizing tuberculosis, or smallpox, or other diseases?[77] As most representatives
believed their states held few people with leprosy, they did not relish the
possibility of a national health board possessing the power to send patients
from throughout the United States to dwell in their home states, were a
leprosarium to be situated in their backyard. For many, health remained a
local, community concern and not an avenue for federal intervention.

Members of Congress who supported the bill countered that leprosy was
a national problem brought on by U.S. territorial expansion and therefore
the responsibility of the federal government. Representative Gilbert Hitchcock of Nebraska saw leprosy as one of the hardships the United States had
to face in its emergence as a world power: "It has not been brought upon us
by a single State, but it has been brought upon us by a national policy of
imperialism, and it is the duty of the nation having entered upon this policy
to deal with this evil in the best way possible." Such a view reinforced the
popular perception that the disease did not emerge naturally in the nation,
but arose as a result of U.S. intervention in such tropical areas as Hawai'i and
the Philippines. This notion persisted despite the fact that the 1902 leprosy
report included substantial documentation of the Scandinavian roots of the
disease in the Midwest that long predated the U.S. annexation of its island
colonies. Without providing any definitive data on the matter, Hitchcock
confidently and erroneously asserted that the disease had rapidly spread in
the country only since 1898.[78]

Those opposed to a national leprosarium on the mainland reasoned that if
the United States acquired leprosy when it annexed these new territories,

then people diagnosed with the disease should be placed in those "stepping-stones of the ocean," far away from the mainland.[79] The comments of these legislators reflected a disregard for the original inhabitants of these islands, as well as a lack of understanding or concern for how those residents lived, worked, and managed their land. Representative Albert Burleson of Texas suggested incorrectly that the entire island of Moloka'i already served as a "leper colony," and he concluded that patients should thus be sent there rather than New Mexico.[80] Representative John Williams of Mississippi concurred, offering Guam as an alternative site, as he claimed not to "know what else Guam is good for. It has no population practically." No opposing argument convinced a majority of legislators to support legislation that could potentially bring a dreaded disease into their communities. No legislators wanted a national leprosy institution within the borders of their state or territory, and many members of Congress opposed the idea of investing federal funds in a matter they felt individual states should handle themselves. Perhaps most important, legislators argued that the colonies provided the most suitable area for containing a tropical and uncivilized disease such as leprosy. They thus defeated the bill for establishing a federal leprosarium in 1905.[81]

Mr. Early Goes to Washington

Serious reconsideration of the establishment of a national leprosarium did not emerge again until 1914, when the Washington visit of John Early made the issue more pertinent to many members of Congress.[82] By placing himself in quarters where he had easy access to the political and social elite of the nation's capital, Early claimed he wanted to show how easily people with leprosy could circulate in American society. He did so with the intention of demonstrating the need for appropriate care for people who suffered from the disease and the social ostracism that accompanied it. Although his comments to journalists indicated that he thought he posed no threat to the public, as he was not contagious, he clearly recognized that his presence would cause a stir and send a "lesson" to members of Congress. Early explained, "That is why I chose the Pullman car, why I slept at the best hotels, ate in the best restaurants. No one cares what happens to the poor. If I had kept to the slums in my travels, the agitation would have been little."[83] He recognized the class component of existing health regulations and how they worked to protect the propertied from the diseases of the masses. Having just removed himself from a federal quarantine station in Washington State that was never intended to handle people with his disease, Early advocated the establishment of a national home that would welcome leprosy patients from any state and would provide appropriate care and treatment for them.

Early was no stranger to the nation's capital, having gained notoriety on a previous visit to the city. He had traveled to the District of Columbia in 1908 to demand a military pension for his service in the Spanish-American War, only to find himself diagnosed with leprosy and relegated to a facility on the banks of the Anacostia River. He challenged his diagnosis and ultimately gained his freedom, though he was forced to travel out of the city on a baggage car. As physicians and public health officials publicly debated his condition and subjected him to a series of examinations, Early fled to the West Coast in 1910 to seek a more anonymous existence. After a long series of struggles to establish a living for himself and his family, the war veteran requested reinstatement of his pension. An examination by health officials once again resulted in a diagnosis of leprosy for Early. His wife, Lottie, appealed for aid to President William Howard Taft, and Early received the offer of a small pension and salary in exchange for accepting segregation and caring for other sufferers of leprosy at the Diamond Point quarantine station near Port Townsend, Washington.[84] Divorced from his wife and separated from society, Early reportedly became violent in segregation, and health officials declared him insane.[85] According to public health officials, he "deserted" the quarantine station on 15 May 1914, though they did not realize it for several days because his fellow residents concealed his escape. After announcing his presence in Washington, D.C., on 2 June, Early generated considerable consternation among local and federal health officials as they debated what should be done to contain him.[86]

Early's actions also generated a brief flurry of activity in the House, though members of Congress again failed to agree on an appropriate site for a federal leprosarium. On the afternoon in which news of Early's Washington trip appeared in the local papers, two competing measures reached the House floor, one advocating a site on an Aleutian Island and the other within the mainland United States. The following day, Congress debated a third measure that would provide federal funding for Hawai'i to accept leprosy patients from the continental United States.[87] Fearful that Early would be returned to Washington State and aware that the federal government had already sent additional leprosy patients to the federal Diamond Point quarantine station, Representative Albert Johnson of Washington showed particular interest in finding an alternative site outside of North America. Responding to one committee member's complaint that "no one wants them," Johnson concurred that "a leper nowadays is pursued as he was long before Christ. He has no chance. He must go away." To his mind, this meant shipping all citizens diagnosed with the disease to the Moloka'i settlement.[88] Once again, some members of Congress looked to the new U.S. territories as a place apart from the country, where the nation's unwanted could be stored.

None of the bills made any progress, but Early's actions shifted the focus of the debate from inhabitants of U.S. colonies to native-born residents of the U.S. mainland.[89] Another leprosy measure calling for the construction of leprosaria within the continental United States was introduced in December 1914.[90] Authors of a report accompanying the bill identified the ease with which people with leprosy moved from state to state, and they argued that nationalizing the disease would ensure the creation of a uniform policy that could contain those with leprosy in one central and isolated setting. At the same time, legislators emphasized a more humanitarian function, stressing the need to protect the sick from neglect and ostracism. The authors of the report referred to leprosy's "loathsome character" as a factor in arousing "great abhorrence on the part of the general public," and they suggested that a government facility would provide a humane sanctuary for people treated harshly or cast out by local communities.[91]

Despite the more even-handed nature of this report, which identified the existing numbers of leprosy patients as alternately 146 and 278, members of Congress were quick to inject a note of hyperbole into the proceedings. One representative urged passage of the bill to stem a raging tide of leprosy: "The country is filling up with lepers, and they go about from State to State and it has gotten so that we have about 4,000 lepers in the United States." Another member of Congress, concerned that the bill would give the federal government unlimited power to erect leprosaria wherever it pleased throughout the country, demanded that the bill specify that only one such institution be constructed, "out in the wild somewhere, where nobody lives within a radius of many miles and where nobody ever will live."[92] The measure passed the House with such an amendment, though the Senate failed to act on it.[93]

Members of Congress continued to bicker about the location of a potential federal leprosarium, but they came to appreciate leprosy as a by-product of a new U.S. empire. If the work of managing the colonies exposed native-born American citizens to disease, then the federal government had a responsibility to treat them, some legislators reasoned. Politicians and physicians supporting a federal leprosarium consciously reshaped the leprosy patient from a foreign intruder to an implicitly white American who merited assistance, anticipating that such a profile might better persuade reluctant members of Congress that the federal government should be involved.[94] The face of the leprosy patient became "American," men and women who served their country through the diplomatic corps, commercial enterprises, missionary work, or military duty. Such individuals, members of Congress argued, deserved appropriate—though still isolated—care. Photographs of white men and women with leprosy shared space with pictures from Moloka'i in a congressional report released in 1916. In his preface to committee hearings on a new bill to provide care for leprosy patients, Senator Joseph Ransdell of Louisiana explained how leprosy within the nation increased as Americans traveled abroad and brought the disease back home. He singled out soldiers such as Early who had served in the Philippines as particularly susceptible to developing leprosy years after their initial encounter with the disease.[95] Dr. Isador Dyer, dean of the Tulane School of Medicine in New Orleans, also attributed rising cases of leprosy to a "close intercommunication" with Caribbean and Pacific islands, adding that the U.S. government had a responsibility to care for those who contracted the disease while serving their nation.[96]

The 1916 report and subsequent congressional debates proved decisive, in part because the changing image of the leprosy patient corresponded with a growing emphasis on humanitarian motivations for establishing a federal facility that had been largely absent in earlier debates. Leprosarium advocates in the report supported a dual purpose similar to that which informed the construction of mental asylums in the nineteenth century: just as the public needed to be protected from the deviant, so the deviant required treatment and protection from a hostile world.[97] Physicians called to testify before the committee spent as much time emphasizing the strain placed upon patients who lacked adequate care as they did describing the threat posed to communities exposed to the carrier of a contagious disease. These patients deserved shelter, the best medical care available, and, most significant, protection from an ignorant public who ostracized them. In addition to the physical affliction the leprosy patient endured, Dyer explained, "he also bears the burdens of centuries of opprobrium which makes him psychopathically different from a patient suffering from any other disease. For that reason they [sic] need just that much more care." Howard Fox, a New York dermatologist, noted how people with leprosy were "fairly hounded from one State to another," spurred by "public hysteria." He argued that a coherent federal policy replete with a secured institution could protect leprosy patients from such ostracism.[98]

Leprosy patients would willingly flock to a federal institution to acquire protection from stigma if Congress provided them with such a facility, several physicians argued in the 1916 report. Dyer estimated that 80 percent of patients at the Louisiana Leper Home, a state facility administered by the Daughters of Charity, submitted themselves to care voluntarily, attracted by the cleanliness of the facility and freedom from the constant need to conceal their affliction from neighbors and authorities.[99] In a similar vein, Dr. George McCoy, former director of the U.S. Leprosy Investigation Station in Hawai'i, testified that some patients sought admission to a receiving station in Honolulu because they could find no job or source of support outside the facility.[100]

While Louisiana and Hawai'i had special institutions for leprosy patients, people outside those localities faced a grimmer fate. No one made this point as poignantly as John Early. Remaining in quarantine behind bars after his 1914 arrest, Early sent a letter to Congress (which the authors of the 1916 Senate report included in their study) to reiterate his plea for a national institution. Early noted that current public health measures threatened both the health of the patient as well as the public. "As soon as a leper is found," he wrote, "under present conditions, he finds himself out of a home and absolutely unwelcome in the jurisdiction where he is found. . . . Then, we ought, as a Christian Nation, make provision for him. Remember we are outcasts of society; yes, with human tastes and feelings."[101] Some members of Congress might have been struck by Early's suggestion that the country had a "Christian" duty to care for people with leprosy. If U.S. missionaries attended to "foreign lepers," then surely the United States should be willing to care for the sick within its own borders.

Legislators confronted with the case of John Early recognized that some leprosy patients had served the nation and that those with leprosy deserved more humane treatment, but public health officials felt the need to constrain their right to autonomy. Having knowingly entered Washington, D.C., as a leprosy patient without a permit, Early had violated a city ordinance and found himself held in a building enclosed by an eight-foot-tall barbed-wire fence. When one senator asked whether Early was being treated "practically as a wild animal," District Health Inspector William Fowler admitted, "Practically, I am afraid; we have to in order to keep him."[102] Politicians and physicians may have considered many patients "American," but they looked upon those with leprosy as tainted by their disease, occupying a liminal space between deserving citizen and foreign contagion, patient and criminal. A person who contracted leprosy assumed a new identity as "leper," a term that designated one as an "Other" to be feared and contained.

Perhaps no disease metaphor had gained such cultural resonance as the term "leper," recognized as synonymous with "outcast." Even Mary Mallon, who became stigmatized with the appellation "Typhoid Mary," decried her treatment in 1909 by asking, "Why should I be banished like a leper and compelled to live in solitary confinement with only a dog for a companion?"[103] Officials in the 1916 report and congressional debates claimed that anyone with the disease violated American notions of appearance, hygiene, and civilization and therefore required isolation. The severe disfigurement common in the latter stages of the disease marked leprosy patients as deviant and threatening. One physician explained how leprosy transformed a young Louisiana patient from "a beautiful specimen of girlhood" into "a horrible and loathsome object," while another explained that "if you have ever seen a single leper in the terminal state of the disease . . . you will realize how needlessly the public is menaced" by allowing them to mingle freely with healthy people.[104]

Images of Americans with leprosy became entangled with orientalist characterizations of Asian and Pacific regions, which had emerged in earlier debates and recurred in 1916. Medical professionals continued to speak of leprosy as a disease of the tropics that was antithetical to a modern nation such as the United States. Health reformer Frederick Hoffman, for instance, attributed the high concentration of leprosy patients in tropical climes to an essentialized "native" spirit that shunned hard work, clean living, and a varied diet.[105] He claimed, "Under tropical conditions, where life is so much easier and where the people are more apt to ignore hygienic precautions it can be readily understood why leprosy should be more common and less easily eradicated than in temperate zones." Hoffman connected the disease to behavior, contrasting the nature and habits of the inhabitants of tropical regions with those of the "more active, industrious, and robust populations" of the United States.[106] Such comments called into question the practices of Americans who did contract the disease overseas, suggesting that they had "gone native," sacrificing civility and citizenship and suffering the consequences.

While the new U.S. possessions might be blamed for increasing the numbers of leprosy patients on the continent, they also provided the nation with experimental sites for learning about the disease and developing management practices that could be applied back home. Policymakers turned to the work of U.S. doctors in the Philippines and Hawai'i for guidance on how to build and manage a mainland leprosy facility. Physicians discussed treatment options based on experiments conducted on Filipino patients, presented the elaborate examination record used by the Hawai'i Territorial Board of Health as an appropriate form to use in the continental United States, and cited Hawaiian leprosy segregation laws and policing practices as effective tools for containing the disease.[107] The broad powers allocated to medical officials within the territories provided a precedent for expanding the powers of the Public Health Service on the mainland. These suggested models proved highly significant in the establishment of a federal facility. Using leprosy policies in the colonies as a foundation would allow public health officials to experiment on patients, to require extensive physical examinations and family medical histories of those suspected of carrying the disease, and to force patients to remain within an isolated facility under duress.

Not all physicians recommended compulsory segregation as the best model for a federal leprosarium. Dr. W. C. Woodward, the health officer of the District of Columbia, doubted that patients would willingly consent to being removed to a location far from their family and friends. He went so far as to suggest that patients should be allowed to remain isolated in their homes, if possible, questioning whether they posed such a threat to community health to warrant removal to an isolated facility.[108] Even W. C. Rucker, assistant surgeon general of the U.S. Public Health Service, claimed that "there are a great many people who are lepers who would hardly need to be admitted to such an institution."[109] His contention that some people possessed the "intelligence" and "means" to care for themselves reveals the ways in which the poor and other marginalized groups remained most vulnerable to institutionalization. Indeed, legislation for a national home never mandated that all leprosy patients be detained; instead, the proposed leprosarium would be open to any patient who voluntarily sought admittance, or who violated U.S. quarantine acts, or whom state or territorial health authorities consigned to the facility.[110]

This combination of worry about diseased and primitive "others," fear for U.S. citizens bringing infection home from imperial possessions, and confidence in public health expertise gleaned from colonial institutions provided the final impetus for the creation of a national leprosy institution. The bill for a federal home, which authorized $250,000 for the provision of care and treatment of leprosy patients, aroused limited interest when it came to a Senate vote in 1917. Although one senator suggested that more important matters should take precedence, supporters argued that the matter gravely concerned many states and would take only a short time to discuss. The sole opposition to the bill came from Senator Charles Thomas of Colorado, who voiced his concern that the federal government lacked the power to establish an institution for the care of any particular disease. He argued that it would set a dangerous precedent to create similar facilities for other afflictions, causing the government to assume responsibilities better left to individual states.[111] Despite this objection, the measure passed.[112]

President Woodrow Wilson signed the bill creating a national leprosy institution into law on 3 February 1917, but controversies over its location prevented a facility from taking shape until after World War I. Earlier debates had revealed that members of Congress could agree upon the necessity of establishing a federal leprosarium as long as it stood outside each representative's own jurisdictions. As soon as federal health officials targeted a site as appropriate for the care of leprosy patients, community activists from the area in question voiced their objections and tabled the plans. Ultimately, the Louisiana Leper Home, which had previously been declared in congressional debates to be insufficient for the needs of a federal institution, became the designated site. Members of the Louisiana congressional delegation not only failed to muster sufficient political muscle to prevent their state facility from becoming a federal repository for the nation's leprosy patients, but they also extracted little more than one-fourth of the original appropriation from Congress, receiving only $72,000 for the land and buildings at Carville.[113] Once legislators decided to fund an institution, they left it in the hands of federal health officials to make the Louisiana home like the Hawai'i settlement.

Conclusion

The debates surrounding the creation of a federal leprosarium demonstrate how the creation of an overseas American empire shaped public health policy on the mainland. Politicians did not consider leprosy a national issue until the acquisition of territories in tropical climates led them to suspect that interaction with locales they saw as exotic and primitive would dramatically increase the incidence of the disease within the states. Although members of Congress initially rejected calls for a national leprosy facility as unnecessary, even suggesting that unwanted "lepers" could always be shipped off to the colonies, they came to recognize that management of the new territories required a close interaction between the mainland and the colonies that would potentially result in U.S. citizens bringing the disease back to the mainland. Initial congressional testimony in the 1890s and 1900s evoked images of island "natives" hopping from newly annexed territories to the continent, or of unwanted immigrants slipping through medical examination stations to infect the nation. Members of Congress increasingly heard in the 1910s of men like John Early who had served in the U.S. military and acquired leprosy in the Philippines, or Cuba, or Hawai'i. Early's surprise 1914 visit to Washington raised politicians' fears about their own vulnerability to leprosy even as they increasingly felt compelled to offer some humanitarian protection to their own citizens who had contracted it. Public health officials persuaded members of Congress that their experience in managing leprosy in colonial contexts gave them the expertise to run a mainland federal institution that would both contain a threat to the nation's health and fulfill a national responsibility to care for the sick. The delay in finding a home for this institution, however, demonstrated the ongoing uneasiness among politicians over the seeming dangers posed by establishing a permanent facility for leprosy within the continental United States.

Testimonials to the charitable nature of a federal leprosarium disguised the colonialist assumptions embedded in the policies that demanded its construction. As physicians and public health officials learned about leprosy through their experiences in the territories, they adopted management practices designed to contain and control what they perceived to be uncivilized "natives" and transferred these policies to the mainland. In the process, they created a policy that labeled some Americans unfit to live among their friends and relatives, subjecting them to lifetime incarceration within an isolated facility in southern Louisiana. The very concept of a segregated facility designed expressly to isolate all people diagnosed with leprosy was grounded on the colonial practices of the Moloka'i settlement. Rather than recommending the development of a policy that would educate state and local health administrators about how to handle the disease within their own communities, public health officials urged the government to take an unprecedented step into the national management of a disease.

CHAPTER TWO

Creating a Colonial Disease

U.S. understandings of leprosy emerged in a colonial setting from contests that unfolded among political officials, physicians, and patients. For Western settlers of the Hawaiian Islands, the disease came to represent both a physical and symbolic "native" threat to the process of civilization. These colonials found in medicine a useful tool both for combating the perceived threat of leprosy and for implementing imperial policies through the categorization, management, and containment of Hawaiians. Public health policy in Hawai'i provided Euroamericans a means of ameliorating the possible danger that arose daily from the cross-cultural contacts in marketplaces, plantations, and villages, among presumably healthy white settlers and potentially diseased Hawaiians. Identifying and removing people with leprosy became centrally important to the economic stability of Euroamerican business interests and to the political success of their efforts to establish themselves as the appropriate leaders of the islands. For Hawaiians, leprosy policies became emblematic of Western efforts to dominate their society and erase indigenous practices. Many Hawaiians rejected the idea that people who contracted leprosy should be isolated from their communities, and they opposed regulations that worked to divide families and restrict patient autonomy. Colonials interpreted such resistance as a further demonstration of native inferiority and claimed that the rapid spread of leprosy throughout the islands demonstrated the presumed primitivism of Hawaiians. By casting the disease as a threat to civilized progress, as well as to the survival of Hawaiians, Western officials justified their intervention in Hawaiian domestic arrangements and community organization.

Examining the sites where Euroamericans and Hawaiians clashed over leprosy, however, reveals the limitations of colonial leprosy policy, and the provisional and contingent nature of Western rule.[1] The late 1800s marked a critical moment in the ongoing struggle over who would rule the Hawaiian Islands, as westerners gained political ascendancy by imposing the "Bayonet

Constitution" on an unwilling monarchy in 1887 and overthrowing Queen Liliʻuokalani in 1893. It was during these years that Euroamerican officials consolidated their control of all important administrative posts, including those overseeing public health in the islands. Westerners interested in the material and strategic benefits of the Hawaiian Islands viewed leprosy as a threat to the region's economic and social development. Their control allowed them to determine how to identify people with leprosy, where to place them, and how to treat them. By isolating all those with leprosy within the Kalihi Receiving Station in Honolulu and the leprosy settlement on Molokaʻi, Euroamerican authorities sought to impose Western notions of civilization on native Hawaiians. Although Euroamerican health officials commanded considerable power in removing people with leprosy to isolated centers far from their communities, Hawaiians drew on community networks for assistance to counter Western ambitions. Their resistance to Western regulations and their ability to carve out autonomous lives for themselves within expanded leprosy reservations indicate that officials failed to convince Hawaiians that Western—specifically American—governance was necessary or desirable. Paying attention to the creation and manipulation of medical policy in Hawaiʻi thus enriches our understanding of U.S. imperialism before and after the watershed year of 1898, directing attention to colonial mechanisms outside strictly diplomatic and military arenas and showing points of continuity in Western colonizing efforts before and after U.S. annexation of the islands.[2]

In embracing a policy of strict isolation, colonials often drew on religious concepts of both the "heathen native" and the "sinful leper." An examination of leprosy policy, therefore, reveals how religion and scientific medicine intersected to shape and bolster a colonialist agenda within the Hawaiian Islands. Scholars of the history of medicine tend to view religion as operating within a separate sphere from medicine or serving as an outmoded system of belief that medicine worked to replace.[3] Yet the creation of a leprosy policy mandating strict incarceration for all those who had the disease both reveals the ways in which physicians and religious leaders worked together and also illuminates the ways in which a Christian missionary ethic shaped Western political administration in Hawaiʻi. Public health officials mapped medical calls for segregation onto an older religious tradition of leprosy separation, but they changed the rationale supporting this policy to meet the needs of an imperialist agenda. Religious demands for humane treatment of leprosy coincided with Western administrators' interest in creating an isolated setting for the containment of people with leprosy and for the scientific study of the disease. In the context of these new understandings of leprosy, the model of the medieval Christian lazaretto was resuscitated as a Western imperial medical institution.[4]

The Road to Isolation

Leprosy became intimately identified with the Hawaiian Islands by the late nineteenth century, even though it was not indigenous to them. Brought to Hawai'i sometime after Captain James Cook established Western contact in 1778, leprosy slowly emerged in the hands of foreign advisers and legislators as a justification for intervening in the administration of the islands. Euroamerican health officials recognized that the Hawaiian population had decreased precipitously in the hundred years following Western contact, due in large part to diseases brought by outsiders. Officials chose, however, to interpret this decline as evidence of Hawaiians' inability to adapt to the rigors of "Christian civilization."[5] Foreign administrators condemned Hawaiians' acceptance of people with leprosy and their willingness to live among them. Such acceptance contrasted sharply with Western religious traditions of separating and stigmatizing people with leprosy in their communities. European and American colonizers interpreted Hawaiian failure to adopt these Christian practices as a cultural weakness that left Hawaiians vulnerable to extinction. In addition to what they characterized as this misplaced island spirit of aloha, Euroamerican health officials claimed that such Hawaiian practices as sharing a common poi bowl, sleeping on grass mats, and wearing unlaundered clothing spread leprosy. Although doctors recognized that tuberculosis, influenza, cholera, venereal diseases, and smallpox posed greater threats to Hawaiian lives, by 1865 leprosy nonetheless inspired the most attention and the most extreme method of containment: the compulsory removal of people with leprosy to an isolated settlement on the island of Moloka'i.[6]

The increasing dominance of European and American colonizers ensured both the spread of leprosy throughout Hawai'i and heightened awareness of it. During the first half of the nineteenth century, the sandalwood trade and whaling industry brought the islands' residents into contact with Asian and European merchants and sailors who probably introduced the disease to Hawai'i. American Protestant missionaries who arrived in the 1820s recorded Hawaiian living conditions and social practices, including perhaps some of the earliest cases of leprosy. Upon his arrival in Honolulu in 1823, the Rev.

Charles Stewart wrote in his diary about inhabitants suffering from "opthalmia, scrofula, and elephantiasis."[7] Religious colonizers such as Stewart connected health with spirituality, and they therefore viewed physical deformity as a sign of sinful action, "the curse of a God of purity."[8] Accordingly, they considered leprosy evidence of the need to inculcate Western cultural sensibilities and religious values in those whom they perceived to be heathens and savages.[9] Within such a mindset, a diagnosis of leprosy implied moral as well as physical weakness. When a Western physician definitively recognized leprosy in a bodyguard of the Hawaiian monarch Kamehameha III in 1840, Euroamerican colonists regarded it as another sign that Western management and scientific practices were needed to help protect the kingdom.[10]

Political and economic changes instigated primarily by British and American colonists brought new cases of leprosy to Hawai'i and ensured its spread throughout the islands. Kamehameha III embraced a constitution and a Western-style legal system in 1840, in part to gain the recognition of the United States and European nations, but the new government afforded white settlers in the islands increased power and authority.[11] English-speaking advisers gained influential access to the king and enabled foreigners to take long-term leases on, and eventually own, Hawaiian land.[12] Western landowners, many of them descended from British and U.S. Protestant missionaries, turned from proselytizing to profits as a result. They found sugar a lucrative crop and employed the land-intensive practice of plantation agriculture to best exploit its economic potential. The expansion of these plantations, along with the declining Hawaiian population, prompted foreign investors to stimulate immigration. They imported workers from around the globe, settling on China in the 1850s as the best source for labor.[13] Rising numbers of immigrants from such areas where leprosy was endemic brought additional cases of the disease to Hawai'i. When government officials took notice of the disturbing spread of leprosy among native-born Hawaiians in 1863, the number of Hawaiians had already been significantly diminished from a variety of Western diseases. Hawaiians had also lost significant control over their own land and government.

Western administrators, missionaries, and businessmen worked intimately with the Hawaiian monarchy to establish a leprosy policy that marked the disease as an unusually virulent threat to the community. Concerned about the rapid decline in the numbers of native Hawaiians, Kamehameha IV turned to his Western advisers in an effort to contain the effects of foreign diseases. He established a Board of Health in 1850 to investigate cholera; however, the predominantly Euroamerican membership proved more interested in pursuing the problem of leprosy. Upon the death of the king, his brother assumed the throne and heeded the advice of Western physicians who encouraged him to isolate all people with the disease. In 1865, Kamehameha V urged the legislature to pass "An Act to Prevent the Spread of Leprosy." The law strengthened the power of the Board of Health by granting its members the authority to treat those with the disease, establish places to isolate them, and create a system that authorized the arrest and inspection of any person "alleged to be a leper."[14]

Although the law mandated that any person found to have leprosy would be isolated, its actual implementation fell most harshly on native Hawaiians. Accustomed to handling disease within their own communities, Hawaiians discovered that the new regulations required them to send friends and relatives away to one of two areas established under the law to hold "lepers."[15] The Kalihi Hospital and Detention Center occupied a twelve-acre shorefront parcel two miles outside Honolulu. This site served as a treatment center for less-advanced cases of leprosy and a sorting station to determine which cases should be removed to a more remote locale. The board purchased 800 acres on the isolated Kalaupapa peninsula of the island of Moloka'i for all those who were "in an advanced state of the disease, and liable to endanger the health of others who may come in contact with them by spreading the contagion"[16] (Map 1). Of the 141 people sent to the Moloka'i settlement in 1866, 139 were Hawaiian.[17] In the following six years, the board sent on average 100 patients to the settlement annually, almost all of them Hawaiian and all showing physical manifestations of the disease.[18] Health officials provided residents of the settlement with limited food and supplies, intending them to become self-sufficient once they established themselves with a village and arable fields on the peninsula. During the 1870s, however, settlement residents complained of insufficient housing and food and objected to what they viewed as the foreign administrators' poor management in creating a settlement and failing to support it properly.[19]

The manner in which Western businessmen attempted to impose stricter measures on leprosy following the passage of the 1865 law reveals the close interconnections between colonial power, economic interests, and health policy. Plantation owners worried that the spread of leprosy jeopardized their workforce, while Euroamerican merchants in Honolulu feared that Western consumers might begin to associate leprosy with Hawaiian products. These white colonials found in King Lunalilo (the successor to Kamehameha V) a monarch willing to brave Hawaiian opposition to the leprosy policy in order to bolster a shaky economy that had grown dependent on

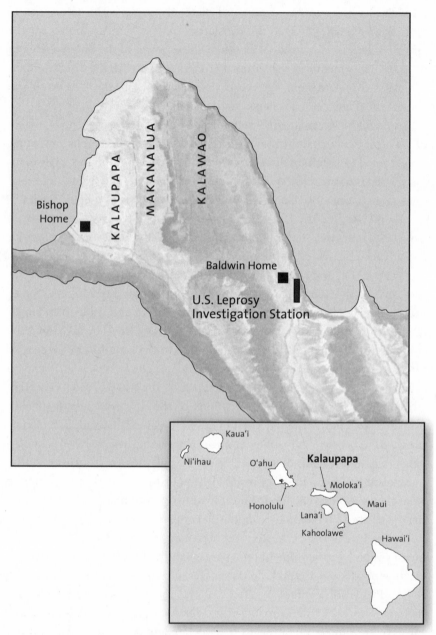

Map 1. The leprosy settlement on Moloka'i. Residents lived primarily in two portions of the peninsula: on the western side in Kalaupapa, also the site of the Bishop Home for women; and on the eastern side in Kalawao, also the site of the Baldwin Home for men. Based on a map in Mouritz, *Path of the Destroyer*.

Western—particularly American—support. They urged Lunalilo to act on health officials' proposals to round up people with leprosy more systematically. The king acquiesced to these demands in 1873 as part of an effort to ensure the negotiation of a sugar treaty with the United States favorable to Hawai'i.[20] In that year, the number of admissions to Moloka'i jumped to 487, up from a mere 105 in 1872.[21] The new group of patients even included a member of the Hawaiian nobility, Peter Kaeo, demonstrating the monarchy's commitment to segregation.[22]

The year 1873 also marked the arrival at the Moloka'i settlement of Father Damien, who dramatically influenced the ways in which the Western world would come to understand the Hawaiian model of strict segregation for people with leprosy.[23] Ironically, Damien's depiction of the dilapidated state of the settlement and the poor condition of its residents did not suggest to concerned Americans and Europeans that the concept of the isolated leprosarium was flawed; rather, the public took it as evidence of Hawaiian helplessness and need for the compassionate assistance of westerners. In the process of seeking to gain the trust of settlement residents and to create a large Catholic community, Damien worked to improve conditions and to garner worldwide attention for his mission. He disparaged the settlement upon his arrival, noting the shabby state of the wharf and the simple shelters of the patients. He further condemned the activities of the residents, noting how men and women of all ages and degrees of illness intermingled and "passed their time with playing cards, hula (native dances), drinking fermented ki-root beer . . . [and] home-made alcohol."[24] His depictions of settlement life proved flattering neither to the Board of Health nor to the patients he came to assist, but they did succeed in raising significant funds from both Catholics and Protestants throughout the Western world for settlement residents.[25] The money helped bring the kind of material improvements to buildings and supplies that settlement residents had long demanded from the monarchy and Euroamerican health officials. After years of living intimately among the patients and nurturing a Catholic community, Damien was diagnosed as having leprosy in 1884 and died in 1889.[26]

Hawaiians' refusal to comply with leprosy segregation laws frustrated physicians and health administrators, who used the fact that Damien contracted leprosy as evidence of the dangers of contagion. The settlement's resident physician, Arthur Mouritz, complained that Hawaiians' acceptance of people with leprosy remained the most significant obstacle to containing the disease. Medical officials such as Mouritz used contemporary medical research into leprosy to bolster medieval religious traditions of segregation, and they condemned Hawaiians for failing to follow Western moral and medical advice. Relatives and friends hid those with leprosy from health investigators, while people sent to Kalihi or the Kalaupapa settlement frequently escaped from those sites to transact business or to contact loved ones on "the outside." Mouritz predicted that "until such time as the Hawaiian mind is impressed with the necessity of social ostracism being practiced toward all lepers . . . the true advantages of public segregation in chosen sites" would not be seen.[27] Edward Arning, a German physician who worked within the Hawaiian leprosy facilities, viewed Damien's illness and death as a warning to those grown too accustomed to the presence of the disease. According to Arning, the example of Damien united religious and medical workers and "should teach us a lesson, and cause us all to work harmoniously and united for the one good end, to confine the dreaded leprosy to its closest limits, and to help and support the poor afflicted ones with the best of our will and skill."[28] For Western medical officials like Arning, this meant pursuing a rigid policy of surveying the islands and removing all people with leprosy to the established facilities at Kalihi and Kalaupapa.

Everyone to Their Proper Place: Contests over Segregation

Efforts to round up additional leprosy "suspects" intensified as westerners increased their control over the Hawaiian government. In 1887, a group calling itself the Hawaiian League, composed primarily of foreign businessmen and the descendants of missionaries, forced King Kalākaua to sign the Bayonet Constitution. The resulting government effectively removed power from the Hawaiian monarchy and placed it in the hands of westerners—mainly Americans—determined to protect their own property and business concerns.[29] With a new legislature came new appointments to the Board of Health and changes in the bureaucracy that improved the board's ability to round up those they suspected of having leprosy.[30] Lorrin A. Thurston, a leader of the Hawaiian League, assumed a position on the board, along with Bishop Bank head Samuel Damon.[31] Through their positions, board members such as Thurston and Damon could enhance Euroamerican political authority and ensure that medical policies would support their economic interests. Segregation of leprosy patients remained the centerpiece of the Board of Health's policies, and the number of people incarcerated for having the disease rose dramatically. In 1888, 579 people diagnosed with leprosy entered the Moloka'i settlement, compared with 220 in

1887 and only 43 in 1886, a year when only 590 people with the disease lived in the settlement. That number almost doubled in seven years, reaching 1,155 by the end of 1893.[32]

By rigorously enforcing leprosy laws, wealthy sons of prominent Protestant missionary families hoped finally to eradicate leprosy from the islands and thereby further justify their right to rule in the name of "Christian civilization" and "progress." Three years after the Hawaiian League imposed the Bayonet Constitution, Board of Health president J. H. Kimball drew upon both medical authorities and missionaries to assert the contagious nature of leprosy and the need for a rigid policy of isolation. He contended that "complete, thorough, and absolute segregation" provided the "only safe-guard" against the disease, one that would prevent the loss of "thousands of precious lives and untold treasure." Attempting to dispel notions that such a policy worked only to further Western interests, Kimball stated that segregation worked for the good of all and assured the legislature that public health authorities had "the welfare of our fellow citizens of the Hawaiian and the white races equally at heart."[33] He pointed to Hawaiians with leprosy who voluntarily submitted themselves to medical officials for examination as evidence that those "conversant with the facts" recognized that people in the leprosy settlement experienced better care than those "of their class" elsewhere on the islands.[34]

In the process of instilling a Christian loathing of the disease among Hawaiians, Kimball and other health officials in effect criminalized and stigmatized leprosy in the islands. Examining the design of the Kalihi complex and its regulations reveals, first, that individuals suspected of having leprosy were considered to have the disease until proven otherwise and, second, that having the disease was akin to engaging in criminal or immoral activity. Health officials emphasized that leprosy had no place in the civilized, Christian, economically prosperous nation that Hawai'i was becoming. In 1888, the Board of Health closed the old leprosy hospital near the entrance of Honolulu's harbor and opened a new complex the following year that was further away from the city, four miles west (Map 2). The urban setting had made it easy for escaping residents to find hospitable accommodations among Hawaiians in Honolulu and had allowed city residents easy access to their friends in the hospital. The new and more isolated Kalihi Leper Hospital and Receiving Station held all "suspects" sent by district health agents throughout the islands until a medical panel could determine who had the disease. Officials placed those diagnosed as "incurables" on the next available ship to the Moloka'i settlement. Physicians selected some

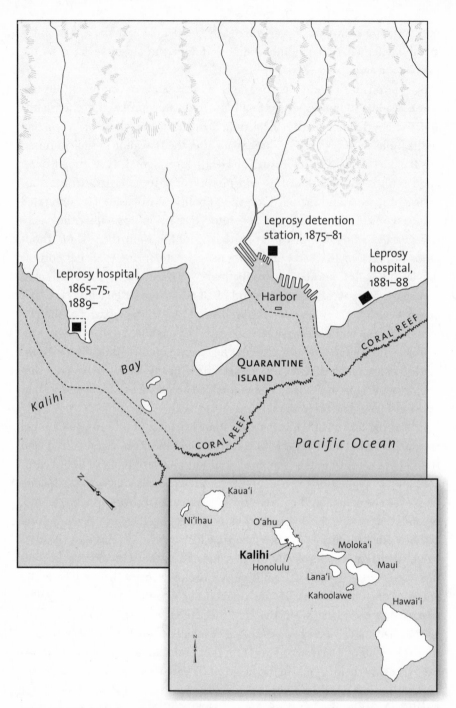

Map 2. Honolulu and environs, showing the changing location of the leprosy hospital. The Kalihi Receiving Station stood in the location identified as the 1889 hospital. Based on a map in Mouritz, *Path of the Destroyer*.

people in the early stages of the disease as "treatable" cases who remained at Kalihi for experimental purposes.[35]

Though health officials denied the charges by some Hawaiians that physicians treated people with leprosy as convicts, "suspects" brought in for medical evaluation had good reason to find parallels between medical and criminal detention. Two fences, each eight feet high and spaced eight feet apart, surrounded the Kalihi compound. Anyone brought to the facility as a potential or actual sufferer of leprosy had to remain unless health authorities granted them permission to leave.[36] All confined at Kalihi mingled together in common living areas until a specially designated panel of three Western physicians arrived for an examination, a process that occurred when the manager of the site felt a suitable number of suspected cases had arrived to warrant such an undertaking. As health officials and Hawaiians both recognized, this meant that some people later determined not to have leprosy would spend at least one week or possibly longer in close contact with people in different stages of the disease. The very language used to label the various categories reflected a sense of moral judgment that entered each determination: those determined free of the disease were identified as "clean" and released; "suspects" were kept under surveillance until their symptoms vanished or became more pronounced, as if held under suspicion for criminal activity; while those labeled "lepers" were contained until the next scheduled bi-weekly boat sailed for the settlement on Moloka'i.[37] In the 1888–90 period, the panel examined 1,090 people suspected of having the disease. Of these individuals, 154 were declared "not lepers" and released, while 789—of whom 778 were Hawaiian—were sent to Moloka'i.[38]

Officials initially intended the leprosy settlement on Moloka'i to be a self-sustaining colony in which residents would learn self-governance under the benevolent watch of Western health officials and religious workers. The site consisted of approximately 1,000 acres on a fairly isolated promontory separated from the rest of the island by high cliffs and surrounded on three sides by the ocean. Portions of the peninsula grew quite chilly by early afternoon when the sun fell behind the cliffs, but the area had a temperate climate and offered fresh water and land capable of sustaining taro fields. Health officials envisioned a settlement in which all people with leprosy would live in houses gathered around a central post, containing a common cook house and dining hall. The board welcomed a variety of religious workers who established Catholic, Protestant, and Mormon congregations within the settlement; health officials viewed their presence as another means of instilling Western self-discipline, communal responsibility, and order. Catholic priests, brothers, and sisters in particular worked closely with Protestant board officials in the administration of two gender-segregated complexes within the settlement.[39] Whether within these complexes or living independently in their own houses, all able-bodied residents were required to work communally in taro fields to produce crops for all residents.[40] Built with the idea of saving the territorial government money, such an institutional design also had the potential effect of disrupting traditional Hawaiian settlements, in which families established their own independent households and owned the crops they produced.

Contradictions of Imperialism: Creating a Hawaiian Community

With such a high percentage of Hawaiians sent to Kalaupapa, the board actually helped to create a particularly Hawaiian community at a time when displacement and disease caused the indigenous population outside Moloka'i to shrink at an alarming rate.[41] Of the 1,159 patients who lived within the settlement as of 31 March 1890, the superintendent identified 96 percent (1,114) as native Hawaiians. Chinese patients represented the next largest contingent with about 2.5 percent (28). Europeans and Americans composed a tiny minority of 1 percent (12).[42] The sheer numbers of Hawaiian residents within the settlement afforded them a place where they could command a clear majority, assert their autonomy, and make many decisions about the ways in which they lived.

Patients recognized and attempted to exploit the contradictions embedded in a settlement administration that sought to create both a self-sufficient colony and a Western-regulated community. They argued that since the government forced them into the settlement, it should support them "as a partial compensation for depriving [them] of [their] liberty."[43] The government thus institutionalized what it had hoped would be a temporary measure of providing patients with food and other supplies.[44] To offset the limitations of strictly regimented rations, patients added variety to their diets in creative ways. While residents proved unwilling to work in the fields under order from administrators, many grew gardens, cultivated taro, and raised hogs or chickens to supplement their rations. Furthermore, they earned money by selling their excess to the board (for use within the settlement) or to other patients. Many residents maintained contact with friends and relatives on the "outside," receiving money via the boats that regularly transported new patients to the settlement.[45] Insisting that the board give them their clothing ration in funds rather than materials, patients found another way to circumvent the intentions of health officials. With the $10 annual clothing allotment to purchase whatever they wanted from the Board of Health store, some patients used significant portions of their stipend to purchase sugar, which they then used to make their own liquor.[46]

Health officials attempted to inculcate in settlement residents Western notions of appropriate ways of living, but the majority of patients exercised considerable autonomy in shaping their lives. More than 80 percent of the patients lived independently in their own cottages, with most of them situated either at the village of Kalaupapa on the western part of the peninsula or the village of Kalawao on the eastern side.[47] While the Board of Health owned almost half of the cottages occupied by patients, more than 200 of them were built and owned by patients themselves.[48] Residents determined with whom they lived, and some even managed to re-create a semblance of their former familial life by bringing in a spouse to live with them as a kōkua or helper. Through this practice, healthy men and women could enter the settlement with loved ones to nurse them and help maintain their households.[49]

Although health officials initially looked upon the kōkua practice as a reasonable method of limiting costs while providing basic care to people with leprosy, they came to view kōkuas as representative of a Hawaiian refusal to accept the seriousness of the disease. Arguing that it was "wrong to expose the healthy to the disease," the board sought ways of limiting the number of people admitted to the settlement who did not have leprosy.[50] In an 1892 review of the 168 kōkuas who lived in the settlement, board members concluded that few patients really needed these helpers, and they went so far as to accuse those who volunteered to come of attempting to contract the disease so they could gather rations and live off the government's largesse.[51] Kōkuas generally stayed in the settlement after the death of the persons they came to care for, and they often married other patients. In this way, officials feared the perpetuation of a dependent class of citizens who flouted warnings about leprosy's contagious nature. That few of these kōkuas actually contracted the disease further confounded officials.[52]

Strong local ties among "healthy" Hawaiians and those with leprosy further demonstrated Euroamerican health officials' utter failure to convince Hawaiians of the danger of leprosy and the necessity of segregation. Despite the height of the cliffs (2,000–4,000 feet) separating the Kalaupapa peninsula from the rest of Moloka'i, able-bodied patients climbed them and produced a regular traffic to and from the settlement. Some scaled the cliffs to escape, and a few patients made it to Maui before health agents caught and returned them, but most of these residents used the opportunity to meet friends at the top of the cliff, purchase supplies, or simply enjoy some freedom from their restricted living area.[53] Just as some patients left the settlement, some Moloka'i residents entered it, including schoolchildren "who [went] there to meet their leper friends."[54] More troubling still to administrators was the interaction between those with leprosy and the kama'āinas (original residents) on the Kalaupapa peninsula who chose to remain on their land when the government brought them new neighbors with a disease. Although they technically resided in a separate area from the villages occupied by patients, their land lay adjacent to the settlement property at sea level and provided what board president David Dayton called a "neutral ground" where visiting relatives could set up covert meetings with their segregated loved ones. The kama'āinas themselves entertained patients and conducted business with them, leading health officials to make the purchase of their land and their removal from the Kalaupapa peninsula a top priority.[55]

Settlement residents also sought their own methods of treating the disease in ways that sometimes conflicted with those recommended by Western health professionals, who protested that patients neither appreciated nor took advantage of the medical care afforded them.[56] The resident physician complained that once Hawaiians arrived at Moloka'i, they felt no compunction to comply with Western medical professionals and sought the advice of a resident kahuna (healer) instead.[57] Board members regularly expressed their concern about residents' refusal to enter the settlement hospital, which they attributed to the Hawaiians' aversion to "confinement."[58] Resident physician Sidney Swift offered a less popular explanation: he opined that the ineffectiveness of all treatments offered to patients in the hospital undermined the authority of Western doctors. Swift followed this perceptive remark, however, with the more common Euroamerican assumption that many Hawaiians did not want to be cured.[59] In many ways, the settlement hospital served the same role as hospitals on the U.S. mainland for much of the nineteenth century: a place of last resort for those who lacked friends to care for them.

Those with leprosy confined to one of the settlement's religious-administered institutions made famous by Father Damien fell under more direct Western supervision. Catholic brothers, priests, and sisters oversaw the administration of the Baldwin Home for boys and men in the village of Kalawao, and the Bishop Home for girls and "unprotected friendless females" at Kalaupapa. Initially created to offset what Damien viewed as the immoral and wanton living of the native Hawaiians, these sex-segregated institutions remained after his death to protect those considered vulnerable to exploitation by the strong and unscrupulous. In 1890, the Baldwin Home contained 105 men and boys and the Bishop Home held 95 girls and women, constituting 17 percent of the patient population between them.[60] Health agent R. W. Meyer expressed his concern to the provisional government that some young girls and boys remained outside of the Bishop and Baldwin homes, "falling prey to immorality and licentiousness." He recommended that the board assume legal guardianship of all minors without parents at the settlement and place them under the care of the sisters and priests to give the children proper moral and religious guidance. He charged those Hawaiians who came forward to adopt parentless children as self-interested or worse, suggesting they acted solely "to obtain a portion of their rations and labor, if boys, other considerations possibly, if girls."[61] Meyer believed that Hawaiians, in other words, threatened to exploit and corrupt their own young. The rhetoric and policies regarding the care of minors in the settlement revealed strains of Western paternalism, as some health administrators argued that religious administrators could provide the kind of moral authority lacking among the Hawaiians in the settlement population.

These more regulated sites, which sought to impose Western schedules, clothing, religious practices, and living conditions upon their residents, still failed to establish total control. In 1890, the boys of the Baldwin Home staged an uprising when Superintendent T. E. Evans ordered them to move their quarters to a new site in Kalaupapa. They prevented carpenters from tearing down their old houses and tied up Evans. The residents of the Baldwin Home eventually released the superintendent, who had the supposed "ringleaders" arrested and jailed on the premises; the boys did successfully prevent the destruction of the Kalawao complex, however, and brought about the resignation of the beleaguered Evans.[62] Health officials sought to downplay the significance of such activities in their reports to the legislature, yet uprisings and other forms of resistance revealed the limitations of a leprosy policy designed to contain Hawaiian residents and to reshape their lives along Western lines.

The "Sad Experience at Kalalau"

The year 1893 marked the decisive moment when Euroamerican administrators seized control of the Hawaiian government and thereby acquired the means to enforce leprosy policy more strictly. The subsequent struggles between Board of Health officials and Hawaiians revealed both the growing strength and the enduring limitations of Western rule. Although Board of Health officials had approved of the establishment of the Moloka'i leprosy settlement in 1866, they lacked the ability at that time to direct police officials, which meant they could not forcibly compel Hawaiians to notify public health authorities about leprosy cases. Hawaiians' differing conception of where and how the sick should be treated proved increasingly challenging to the Board of Health's power to relocate those with leprosy. Recognizing that shipment to Moloka'i generally meant a lifetime sentence, people with leprosy and their family members saw little reason to comply voluntarily with notification regulations. In some communities, Hawaiians with the disease carved out small, relatively hidden enclaves where they could remain in contact with loved ones and beyond the reach of health officials.[63] In this way, relatives and friends could visit and provide food and other necessities. The Board of Health contented itself with periodic raids on such leprosy "strongholds," which its members saw as both a threat to public health and an affront to Western authority. Because friends and family members also warned those with leprosy when health agents planned to investigate an area, these raids were usually unsuccessful. The power structure shifted dramatically in 1893, when Queen Lili'uokalani attempted to wrest control of the kingdom back from her Euroamerican ministers, sparking a confrontation that allowed a group of Americans to depose her and declare Hawai'i an independent republic under the control of white settlers.[64] With the establishment of a new provisional government dominated by westerners, health officials gained the power and access to legal officials necessary to root out these pockets of people with leprosy.

For the new provisional government, public health policy became a useful tool for displaying and exercising moral and civil authority. The fact that Board of Health president William O. Smith also occupied the position of attorney general under the new regime was a visible consolidation of medical and civil authority, enabling health policy to serve as an avenue for maintaining order and gaining control over Hawaiian bodies. Health agents dispatched to various localities throughout the islands worked with local police to identify, collect, and incarcerate those suspected of having leprosy. In some cases, they were also now granted policing authority themselves, as when the local health agent concurrently held a law enforcement position. Such was the case with health agent and deputy sheriff Louis H. Stolz, who in May 1893 requested an extension of his territory on the island of Kaua'i to incorporate the Kalalau Valley, a site where numerous people with leprosy remained in hiding. Believing in the necessity of strict segregation for the regulation of public health and the maintenance of order under the new government, Stolz vowed to peaceably "round up" all people with the disease who had been evading the law and bring them to the Moloka'i settlement.[65]

The efforts undertaken by Stolz and other health officials illustrate the degree to which medical policies embodied the missionary goals of their ancestors.[66] As one newspaper editorial phrased it, the leprosy policy of strict segregation needed to be enforced in the "interests of public health and morality."[67] For the Western board, issues of disease containment and sanitation were inextricably linked to notions of civilization and Christian living. Demanding compliance with existing leprosy laws formed part of their self-imposed duty to enlighten the Hawaiians and save them from their supposedly self-destructive ways. In the months following the removal of Queen Lili'uokalani, Board of Health members renewed their commitment to this mission, supported by one English-language newspaper's call for vigorously pursuing the "wise and humane policy" of leprosy segregation, which it believed the board would "undoubtedly carry out in a kind yet firm manner."[68]

Reaction to Stolz's plan among Kalalau Valley residents tempered the health agent's initial confidence that Hawaiians with leprosy would indeed succumb to the "kind yet firm" hand of the board. After gaining permission to proceed, Stolz reported that he had placed the valley under quarantine to weed out the "leprous" from the "non-leprous" residents and had begun to estimate the expense of removing those with leprosy from the island. His efforts to encourage people with leprosy to leave their homes and move to the Moloka'i settlement met with mixed success. Some people offered to go, others proved less willing, and the younger and stronger—those most capable of physically resisting health officials' decrees—openly challenged him. The board offered to send in troops to force the removal of resistant Hawaiians with leprosy who headed deeper into the valley to escape incarceration, but Stolz insisted that he wished to handle the matter "peacefully."[69]

Hawaiians did not consider forced removal from their families and lifelong banishment at the Moloka'i settlement a peaceful undertaking, but Euroamerican officials convinced of Hawaiian passivity did not anticipate strong opposition to the round-up and deportation. Identifying a cowboy foreman named Ko'olau as the ringleader of the resisters, Stolz planned an ambush to capture the Hawaiian. Ko'olau saw through the trap, shot and killed the deputy sheriff, and escaped deep inland with his wife, son, and other Hawaiians with leprosy.[70] Ironically, on the same day that officials in

Honolulu learned of Stolz's death, the *Daily Pacific Commercial Advertiser*, the Euroamerican paper most supportive of the Board of Health's enterprise, reported that Hawaiians in Kalalau Valley would pose no serious objection to forced removal. Characterizing Stolz's actions as "negotiations," the paper contended that only "two or three" residents showed "any disposition to resist the orders" and confidently asserted that "there will be little or no trouble in effecting their removal."[71] The underestimation of the number of residents opposed to the colonial directive displayed Euroamerican blindness to the strength of the community and familial ties that connected individuals such as Koʻolau to broader networks of resistance.

In the wake of Stolz's death, the new government struggled to legitimate its authority with a strong show of force. Republic president Sanford Dole proclaimed a state of martial law in the Kauaʻi districts surrounding the Kalalau Valley and ordered all those suspected of having leprosy to "surrender" within twenty-four hours. He also dispatched a brigade of thirty-five armed men to the Kalalau beach. Although the *Advertiser* announced Dole's intention "to remove the lepers without further bloodshed," it also made clear the government's commitment to "clean out every leper from the valley either dead or alive."[72] Thus, a policy that ostensibly aimed to provide humane treatment became wedded to a colonial drive to cleanse the islands of the menace of leprosy by forcible and potentially violent removal. To the provisional government, the shooting incident bolstered the perception that every person with leprosy who refused removal was a criminal on the run, a threat to public health and safety until detained by the state. By sending troops to hunt down Koʻolau and to round up all people with the disease, Dole and his provisional government asserted their commitment to solidifying Western authority and morality and ensuring that the leprosy laws were strictly obeyed.

Coverage in the *Daily Bulletin* indicated, however, that not all Euroamericans supported the stringent measures toward leprosy taken by the new Board of Health.[73] While the paper condemned Koʻolau as a cowardly criminal who should be brought to justice, it ran an editorial criticizing the board for its ruthless and costly determination to send all people with leprosy to Molokaʻi. The editorial spoke approvingly of past administrations that "silently and tacitly acquiesced" in allowing people with the disease to use Kalalau Valley as an "asylum," where they could "end their days in peace, and at their own and at their friend's expense, without charge to the taxpayers, or danger of contagion to the community." In a rare display of compassion for Hawaiians with the disease, the editorial expressed sympathy for "the unfortunate lepers, hunted and harried like brute game," and demanded that all except Koʻolau be allowed to remain.[74]

The *Advertiser* highlighted the fissures in the Euroamerican community further by labeling the *Bulletin*'s coverage as "royalist" and its readers as covert supporters of the deposed queen. Castigating the *Bulletin* for blaming Board of Health officials for Stolz's death, an *Advertiser* editorial firmly linked a reinvigorated leprosy policy with progress and its detractors with the outmoded policies of the previous administration under Liliʻuokalani. In calling for support of strict segregation, and implicitly the new provisional government, the editorial charged that the *Bulletin* and all its followers were clinging to a "policy of national retrogression, which so clearly marked and stamped the decline and termination of native rule in Hawaii." According to the editorial writer, "every respectable citizen of these islands who would keep the contamination of leprosy from his family threshold" should support Dole's efforts to use force as a necessary action for freeing the islands of a dangerous contagion.[75]

Hawaiians were also divided, and the Kalalau Valley incident demonstrated that some saw economic and political benefits in supporting the new provisional government and its rigid leprosy regulations. Stolz, for example, was able to enlist the assistance of several local residents who served as guides in the unfamiliar valley terrain during the search for the renegade band. Two other Hawaiians housed Stolz and his officers during their mission to the valley. In fact, English-language papers identified one of Stolz's supporters as a Hawaiian hero for paddling fifteen miles to the nearest telephone to contact a law enforcement officer after hearing the gunshots that killed Stolz. The white settler press portrayed Koʻolau and other resisters as acting against the interests of all who lived in the islands, going so far as to claim that many Hawaiian taro growers in the valley resented the presence of people with leprosy, accused them of stealing produce and livestock, and welcomed their removal as a chance to improve the quality of their own lives.[76]

Despite this limited support, the Board of Health recognized the Kalalau Valley incident as a challenge to its authority. Board members viewed the shooting as an extreme act of resistance and a sign that some Hawaiians still failed to grasp the grave risk that leprosy posed to their islands. In their public statements, health officials attempted to portray the incident as the hostile action of a lone man, but they could not long ignore the fact that Koʻolau and the other resisters had the cooperation of a community whose members aided their escape and generally refused to assist Western officials by providing information on their whereabouts.[77] One newspaper account admitted that in the Kaua'i district of Hanalei, "it was difficult to get any information regarding Kalalau or the movements of the murderous lepers." Officials arrested a Hawaiian identified as "Wahinealoha" for supplying the resisters and refusing to disclose their location.[78]

As days passed without the surrender of Ko'olau or the other resisters, the government response assumed a more pointedly militaristic tone. The small army sent to Kaua'i enlisted several Hawaiians to contact the renegade group and warn them that if they did not surrender within two days, "war would be declared on them." At the mouth of the valley, soldiers set up military quarters, which they christened "Camp Dole." The threat of armed violence convinced other Hawaiians with leprosy to capitulate to authorities. Board of Health members Dr. C. E. Cooper and Dr. C. B. Reynolds conducted an impromptu examination of thirty local residents, diagnosing eight of them with leprosy. An additional eight people with leprosy who had been hiding from the health authorities agreed to turn themselves in, as long as they were protected from the soldiers.[79] However, the increased military threat solidified Ko'olau's resolve to remain at large, because he claimed that he feared for his life and those of his wife and son. Soldiers responded by firing shells at the base of the cliff where the family remained hidden. Five other valley residents with leprosy escaped into the Hanalei mountains, where troops were dispatched to track them down.[80]

Euroamerican politicians and businessmen characterized the resisters as dangerous outlaws and labeled leprosy a "national curse" that threatened the future of the young nation if left unchecked. Reporters for the *Advertiser* portrayed Ko'olau and his family as an army unto themselves, claiming that they possessed 3,000 rounds of ammunition and identifying each member, including the nine-year-old son, as a skilled sharpshooter.[81] Such exaggerated portrayals of the threat posed by Ko'olau and other Hawaiians with leprosy helped to justify the extraordinary steps taken by the provisional government in the Kalalau Valley. On 4 July, fifteen soldiers moved up the mountain toward the location of the sequestered family. As they approached, Ko'olau shot and killed two soldiers, and a third accidentally shot himself in the melee.[82] Placing the blame for the bloodshed squarely on Ko'olau rather than the military intervention that precipitated the confrontation, one editorial writer declared that the incident only demonstrated the need for the new "re-established and purified" government to conduct a full-scale effort to locate and remove all people with the disease.[83] The account drew upon what Warwick Anderson has referred to as the "poetics of pollution" to cast uncooperative Hawaiians as dangerous contaminants who needed to be quarantined and subjected to medical discipline.[84]

Despite such press accounts, the provisional government came to realize that total segregation could never occur without the full consent of the Hawaiian population, and full consent it did not have. After learning that Ko'olau and his family had escaped the shells that blasted their position on the cliff, officials suspected that the resisters continued to have the assistance of local relatives or friends.[85] The fact that five other resisters from Kalalau Valley surrendered to authorities did not offset the humiliation of losing Ko'olau or of facing opposition from Hawaiians in raids on other Kaua'i communities. When Dr. Reynolds and a company of soldiers inspected all houses in Hanalei, residents claimed that people with leprosy had left without telling friends or neighbors where they intended to go. Reynolds, who claimed he "knew the natives were lying," threatened to punish residents and destroy their property if they failed to turn over those with leprosy by noon. Some of the men retorted, "If you want the lepers, go and find them." Although the government was willing to display additional power by arresting selected residents to elicit information regarding the whereabouts of people with the disease, such tactics failed to produce useful results. The local deputy claimed that his Hawaiian officers were "useless" and hampered the removal effort.[86] Ultimately, the government called off the search for Ko'olau and returned to Honolulu.

In the months following Ko'olau's resistance, the board attempted to recover from the embarrassment of what it termed "the sad experience at Kalalau" by portraying itself as a noble army engaged in a crusade against a dangerous enemy. Except for the elusive Ko'olau, the executive officer claimed that board members could "congratulate themselves on the fact that the Islands have not been so free from known lepers at large for the past ten years as at present." Speaking of people stricken with a disease as armed guerrillas, he pointed to health agents' success in removing people from the Kalalau and Wainiha valleys on Kaua'i and on the more remote islands Ni'ihau and Lana'i, "places that have been undisturbed strongholds of lepers for many years." Health officials identified 60 leprosy patients in these areas, in addition to 280 others from more traditionally regulated portions of the islands. Many islanders viewed this as an unnecessarily harsh targeting of native Hawaiians, but the executive officer of the board termed it an "impartial and thorough segregation" crucial to eliminating leprosy from the region.[87] Still, the roundup of other Hawaiians with leprosy could not offset the reality that Ko'olau had successfully slipped away into the forests of

Kauaʻi with his family and had inspired a widespread tale of Hawaiian resistance to the board's authority. He died three years later, still free.[88]

Regulating the "Colony": New Rules for the Molokaʻi Settlement

Even as agents of the Board of Health tried to pry Koʻolau off Kauaʻi, board members moved quickly to consolidate the authority of the provisional government within the Kalaupapa settlement by imposing Western patterns of behavior and by punishing Hawaiian ones. At their 7 July 1893 meeting, board members approved a new set of twenty-three rules to govern both patients and kōkuas living at the Molokaʻi settlement.[89] Just as Koʻolau's successful effort to elude capture demonstrated the degree to which Euroamerican health officials failed to convince all Hawaiians of the necessity of segregation, so did the impact of the new regulations demonstrate the limits of board control. Hawaiians within the leprosy settlement continued to reject Western conceptions of leprosy as a dangerous contagion that threatened all who came into contact with it. With the institution of the provisional government, however, health officials hoped to create a legal apparatus that would assist them in their efforts to curtail behavior they considered conducive to the spread of leprosy within the islands.

Intent on tightening the level of isolation imposed by life in the settlement, the board enacted these new regulations to sever ties between patients and those who did not have the disease and to reiterate the board's insistence that only strict segregation could eliminate leprosy in the islands. New rules reiterated that "lepers" had to remain in the settlement and refrain from scaling the palis (cliffs) unless permitted by the superintendent. Punishment for attempts to leave ranged from a $25 fine to a month's imprisonment in the settlement jail. The new regulations also spelled out a ban on patients interacting with the kamaʻāinas and imposed punishments on any patient who entered the kuleanas (parcels owned by these original residents) or attempted to live there.[90] Under the new provisional government, the Board of Health could at last use "legal" means to force those individuals with legitimate claim to lands on Kalaupapa off the peninsula. It successfully lobbied the new legislature to pass a law that transferred ownership of all land on the peninsula to the territory and delegated control to the Board of Health. The law gave owners only sixty days' notice to present their claims to the government, which then reimbursed them with a "fair value" for the land and gave them some time to vacate the premises.[91] The board hailed the legislation as a measure that would help ensure that the "disturbing element will cease and the enforcement of the law of segregation will be easier."[92] By 1895, health officials had removed all kamaʻāinas from the region.

The board also attempted to use the 1893 regulations to introduce new housekeeping practices to settlement residents.[93] Health officials required residents to keep the area surrounding their homes clean and their houses whitewashed. This stipulation reflected not only officials' efforts to control the conditions in which patients lived but also their attempts to apply Western notions of cleanliness within the settlement. Restricting the practice of allowing debris to accumulate around homes and demanding that homes be painted both inside and out were both common strategies in Europe and the United States to combat disease. The newly emerging germ theory and older conceptions of disease such as the belief in miasmas accommodated the idea that dirt spread sickness and that proper hygiene and domestic cleaning could keep it at bay.[94] In this way, descendants of Protestant missionaries drew on scientific knowledge to reinforce links between moral behavior and cleanliness that had deep roots in Christian thought.

Those within the settlement's specialized homes and hospital had to conform to more direct oversight by religious personnel and public health administrators, but the board also established broad rules to regulate the activities of those who chose to live independently in Kalaupapa. Patients could build their own houses and select their own sites—provided they received clearance from the superintendent—but the board now claimed the right to move any house if it required the land for other purposes, and no patient was allowed to own more than one house. Patients could use designated land for their own agricultural use, but no one could neglect their property or obtain more land than he or she could cultivate.[95] These restrictions not only reminded patients that they lived on their land at the board's discretion, but also served as an attempt to limit the kinds of households that patients could create and to place their dependence on the board rather than on each other.

The regulation of kōkuas represented the final area in which the board endeavored to assert its authority over settlement residents. Attempting to tighten control over who could be admitted to the site under the pretense of becoming a kōkua, the board stipulated that only those who obtained written permission could live at the settlement in such a capacity.[96] This allowed health officials to weigh the moral and physical fitness of potential kōkuas, though they sometimes seemed to make their decisions based on political or fiscal concerns. For example, the board honored the request of two Hawaiian women to accompany their husbands in January 1895, provided that the superintendent "grant their petition at such a time as not to attract too much attention." Officials in Honolulu seemed more worried about whether their approval would provoke a flood of additional requests than about the merits of these women's requests. At its next meeting, the board delayed making a decision on another woman's petition to assist her husband. The members wanted her to demonstrate that relatives would care for her children who remained at home so that they would not become a drain on the republic's taxpayers.[97]

The policy of allowing kōkuas into the settlement presumably saved the government money by providing unpaid caregivers for the sick, but several of the regulations revealed the board's belief that many people who entered the settlement as kōkuas sought to exploit the generosity of the government. Refusing to accept that caring for a sick individual with a chronic disease could be a full-time occupation, board members stipulated that kōkuas had to perform additional work at the superintendent's request. Though they would be paid "fair wages" for such services as agricultural work, carpentry, or butchering, kōkuas had to pay for any food they consumed.[98] Without such restrictions, the board contended, parasitic individuals would enter the settlement under false pretenses for the benefit of gaining free food and lodging. To prevent the number of people without leprosy from dramatically increasing, the regulations also stated that kōkuas had to leave the settlement within two weeks of the death of those they had tended, after proving to the settlement physician's satisfaction that they had not contracted the disease during their tenure. As a further precaution against the spread of leprosy, kōkuas could not leave the settlement without written permission from the superintendent.[99]

The rising number of children born to people with leprosy and their kōkuas posed a new set of problems for health officials. Settlement Superintendent R. W. Meyer's adverse reaction to these births suggests that administrators often saw immorality and vice as by-products of the disease, at least when leprosy patients lived together in such an unrestricted environment as at Kalaupapa. He found particularly troubling the idea that children born to at least one parent with leprosy would be raised among those with the disease, the "clean" with the "unclean." Not only did this represent a threat to children's physical well-being, Meyer argued, but it threatened their moral health as well. Though they might not contract the disease, he feared that such children would be influenced by what he considered the lax morality of the settlement: "They will grow up probably a lawless and dangerous element. . . . There is no work for them, they have learned nothing, they have seen little else than idleness, drinking and gambling, and whatever else [would make] hoodlums and tramps."[100] While such pastimes may have been deemed acceptable for those hopelessly condemned to leprosy, Meyer feared that public health policy might produce an entirely new immoral and dependent class. His comments also reinforced the civilizing and Christianizing mission embedded in public health policies directed toward patients and their kōkuas. In other words, he worried not only that these children might become infected with leprosy, but also that they might succumb to behaviors Euroamericans increasingly identified as Hawaiian.

The board also severely restricted visits from relatives and friends, further intensifying the level of isolation that settlement residents experienced and reinforcing the idea that having leprosy required imprisonment. Those wishing to visit friends or relatives at Kalaupapa needed to request permission from the board and await its decision, which could take weeks. For many, a visitor's permit would give them their first opportunity to spend time with a family member in three, ten, or even fifteen years. For others, the visit represented a last chance to see their loved ones alive, as one list of those requesting access to the settlement duly noted the physical condition of many of the residents as very old, sick, or weak. Even then, the numbers allowed into the settlement were limited. Out of 192 people who asked to visit the settlement in July 1899, the board's leprosy committee granted permission to little more than 25 percent.[101]

Heartfelt appeals and political connections proved two effective means of gaining permission to visit the settlement, further demonstrating the paternalistic attitudes of board members and the close connections between business interests and health policy. Luki Wila addressed her request in 1899 to Board of Health president C. E. Cooper with a letter explaining her desire to see her grandchildren at the settlement once more before she died. Asking Cooper to recognize the tragic elements of a leprosy policy that separated families, she wrote, "You are Father perhaps yourself. . . . Think for a moment if circumstances should remove them far from you! How intense would be your desire to be reunited to them and for them to press you upon their heart, if it should be for but a few hours!"[102] One Hawaiian by the name of Kiaaina successfully managed passage by getting another health official to intervene on his behalf. Board member and business magnate W. R. Castle requested in 1899 that Kiaaina be allowed to visit his son at the settlement to attend to important business matters. Castle intimated that the board could profit from Kiaaina's visit to the settlement, suggesting that in return he would influence Hawaiians in Waikiki "to revise their opinions with regard to the present state of affairs and their relations to the ex-queen."[103] At a time when Euroamerican businessmen and politicians sought to smooth the road toward territorial status for Hawai'i within the United States, health officials found it useful to grant favors to Hawaiians in exchange for their support of Western government officials.

Conclusion

As colonials gained greater control over the political and economic management of the Hawaiian Islands, from the imposition of the Bayonet Constitution in 1887 to the overthrow of Queen Lili'uokalani in 1893, they constructed a powerful legal structure for containing people with leprosy. Leprosy policy in Hawai'i thus increasingly served to bolster the authority of the Western government as the bulwark of order and "Christian civilization," both by policing native Hawaiians and by shoring up support among white settlers. Government officials justified the extreme provisions of their strict segregation policy by portraying it as a humanitarian arrangement that employed the benefits of Western medicine, religion, and civilization to save what they viewed as a primitive and irresponsible Hawaiian "race" from extinction. More practically, they saw the policy as a means of protecting Western business interests from the taint of leprosy and of exerting physical and moral control over Hawaiians.

Hawaiians thwarted the goal of total segregation, however, and thereby revealed the tenuous nature of colonial authority. As the story of Ko'olau demonstrates, many Hawaiians resented Western leprosy policies and refused to comply with them. Viewing the policy of strict segregation as an unjust and unnecessary colonial enterprise that destroyed their communities, they often assisted friends and relatives with leprosy in hiding from health officials. Hawaiians outside the former ruling class both challenged the necessity of the segregation policy and actively worked to improve the lives of those sentenced to Kalaupapa and Kalihi. In the process, they called into question the legitimacy of foreign intervention as a whole. Even after the Western-dominated Board of Health sought to strengthen its authority through the passage of new rules and regulations, Hawaiians found ways to recognize and manipulate fractures in the system to suit their own ends and to challenge foreign dominance.

Rather than viewing this period as the Hawaiians' last stand against a dominant and ultimately triumphant Western presence, the final decade of the nineteenth century should be seen as the beginning of a new phase in an ongoing conflict between colonizer and colonized. Writing in 1916, former settlement physician A. A. Mouritz professed to having heard Hawaiians "of the better class" remark, "Hawaii is our country, it belongs to us, or at least it did until the haole [white foreigner] got possession of most of it. If the haole is afraid of leprosy let him go back to where he came from."[104] While Hawaiians could neither eject westerners nor prevent the incorporation of their islands into the United States by the end of the century, they did continue to undermine leprosy policies by evading health officials, escaping incarceration, or manipulating institutional rules to suit their own purposes. Within the Kalaupapa settlement, they also created a distinctly Hawaiian community that would remain at odds in a territory that became more diversified and Americanized throughout the twentieth century.

The colonial project in Hawai'i also had a direct impact on the conduct of public health policy within the mainland United States. Western physicians and medical administrators encountered leprosy in the islands and developed institutions for the incarceration of those found to have the disease, and these public health officials helped the idea of a specialized leprosy institution gain credence on the mainland. As the U.S. Congress debated the merits of a national leprosarium, local physicians, politicians, and religious workers established and managed a specialized leprosy institution in Louisiana. The emergence of this facility further demonstrates the connections between religion, medicine, and imperialism, as the members of the religious order who managed the Louisiana Leper Home saw themselves conducting the same spiritual and corporal mission as their Catholic colleagues in Moloka'i.

CHAPTER THREE

Sacred Duties, Public Spaces

Workers on the Mississippi River levee in New Orleans paused briefly on 16 April 1896 when four Daughters of Charity approached the steamboat *Paul Tulane*. As they boarded, according to a reporter with the *Daily Picayune*, onlookers murmured "in hushed whispers the words which sealed their fate, 'They are bound for leper land.'" These Catholic women had agreed to work as administrators and nurses at the Louisiana Leper Home, a state institution established in 1894 on an isolated bend of the Mississippi River. The newspaper coverage depicted the sisters' mission as one of otherworldly nobility and sacrifice, suggesting that only women who had already "left all to follow Christ" could so willingly work among "the loathsome diseased beings whom the world had shunned." The reporter cast the sisters as "heroines, every one of them . . . taking up with willing hands and of their own volition a work at which the heart of the strongest man might quail." He also emphasized the reputation of the religious order as able and devoted caregivers, whose presence—it was hoped—would convince people with leprosy to voluntarily submit themselves to the institution. A state health official acknowledged, "The very name of the Sisters of Charity [*sic*] implies confidence—and that is what we need in our work. The [Leper Home] Board alone could not inspire this."[1]

The Daughters of Charity of St. Vincent de Paul (often mistakenly called the Sisters of Charity) played an instrumental role in the development and the preservation of the Louisiana Leper Home, a role that complemented the aims of state public health officials and medical practitioners. State officials enlisted the Daughters of Charity to assume administrative authority over the institution in 1896, and the sisters imposed upon the home a moral and religious framework that continued to shape the institution even after it became a federal facility in 1921. The sisters sought to endow medical treatment with a religious sensibility that ultimately would improve conditions for patients.[2] Their efforts meshed with those of state administrators who sought knowledgeable but affordable care for a group of patients whom few wanted to treat. Together, public officials and religious workers devised, implemented, and defended a public health policy that brought together religion and medicine to provide care for leprosy patients. Correspondence with state officials reveals how the sisters actually shared many of the public health advocates' beliefs regarding the contagious nature of the disease, the need to segregate patients, and the desirability of locating the institution close to an urban setting.[3] This combination of medical practice and religious work ironically legitimized the stigma attached to leprosy and justified the decision to segregate these patients in institutions far removed from mainstream society.

The account of the sisters' departure to the Louisiana Leper Home reflects popular images of the disease as both an exotic scourge and a religious concern. The sisters who embarked on their seventy-five-mile journey from New Orleans to Iberville Parish were viewed as potential martyrs comparable to Father Damien in Moloka'i. The sisters themselves saw parallels between their mission to the leprosy patients in Louisiana and that of their Catholic colleagues at Kalaupapa, though they viewed their own home as a uniquely American institution where they could enforce a strict moral code among "civilized" patients. The religious connotations of leprosy, coupled with a tradition linking religious workers and health care in Louisiana, allowed the state to enlist avowed Catholic workers as administrators of a secular, state-run institution.

The gendered and religious nature of these Catholic women's mission proved fundamental to their selection as caregivers for the leprosy patients. The majority Catholic population in Louisiana acknowledged the Daughters of Charity as skilled nurses and medical administrators, as demonstrated by their work in such institutions as Charity Hospital in New Orleans. As women, they commanded authority as both moral guardians and nurturing caregivers.[4] The public could view their very public role as administrators of a state institution as a gender-appropriate extension of the domestic sphere. At the same time, their religious role afforded them the ability to renounce the traditional roles of marriage and motherhood to assume the hazardous position of caring for people viewed as having a dangerous disease.[5] These Catholic sisters commanded respect and appreciation for their willingness to provide humane care to the afflicted, and they could also tap into the economic and administrative power of the Catholic Church at a time when the state government provided limited funds and managerial support for the home.

Yet their position as women also left them vulnerable to challenges to their authority. The contract negotiated between the state and the Daughters of Charity placed them in a compromised position, forcing them to defer to male politicians, lay health officials, and doctors. Patients in particular learned to use this vulnerability to their advantage, turning to authorities outside the home when they disagreed with policies enacted by the sisters. While many patients expressed their appreciation for the material efforts of the sisters, some questioned institutional rules requiring sexual segregation within the facility and rigid containment from the outside world. Ultimately, the Daughters of Charity grew frustrated by lackluster support from state officials and the repeated challenges to their authority by patients. The sisters came to see the federal government as their best hope for providing the kinds of doctors, economic capital, and administrative authority necessary for establishing a more modern, efficient health care facility for patients. This openness to federal medical authority ultimately enabled them to remain patient caregivers once the Louisiana Leper Home became the U.S. National Leprosarium, thus ensuring that many of their religiously inspired regulations would remain intact.

Building a Home for "Lepers"

The initial establishment of a state leprosy institution in 1894 emerged because of the converging interests of two groups: New Orleanians who feared the presence of people with leprosy in their community and Louisiana physicians intent on enlarging public health programs. Leprosy was not new to Louisiana; records from Charity Hospital in New Orleans reveal the presence of leprosy patients from its earliest extant records in 1857 through the 1890s.[6] However, U.S. imperialist ventures raised the profile of the disease during the late nineteenth century and heightened public anxiety about the potential of leprosy to spread throughout the nation. Following a series of muckraking articles on the condition of a New Orleans pest house in 1891, the Orleans Parish Medical Society recommended that the state legislature isolate all people with leprosy and provide them with proper medical care under a qualified practitioner. Designed to bring attention to the overcrowded condition of the facility and the poor care provided to its residents, the articles instead made New Orleanians aware of leprosy in their midst.[7] Acting on the medical society's recommendation and the public outcry, the legislature created the Board of Control for the Leper Home to shape and oversee a state facility in 1894. In August of that year, the governor appointed the board's members and placed them under the leadership of Dr. Isadore Dyer, a key proponent of quarantine measures for contagious disease.[8]

Dyer initially envisioned a modern medical facility that could facilitate scientific experimentation and serve as a model for other state public health institutions, but he found it impossible to realize his vision. The New Orleans City Council, comprising the same kind of business-minded individuals who had helped keep news of an 1887 yellow fever epidemic out of the press, thwarted an effort to establish the institution within the city.[9] Unable to situate the facility within close proximity to an urban area, the board settled on a five-year lease of a dilapidated plantation, Indian Camp, located on an isolated bend of the Mississippi River approximately seventy-five miles northwest of New Orleans in Iberville Parish. Health officials sent the first contingent of four patients on a barge from New Orleans in late November. The group traveled by night, ostensibly to keep their arrival in the community as inconspicuous as possible. Contrary to the claims of the public health officials who pressed for the creation of the Louisiana Leper Home, most state physicians failed to find evidence of a growing epidemic of the disease in their localities and sent few people with leprosy to the new institution. Only through "personal persuasion, through individual voluntary inclination, and, in some instances, by legal action," did the number of patients increase to twenty-six by the end of its second year.[10]

The new facility had little to recommend it. Patients occupied ramshackle cabins that had formerly housed the enslaved African Americans who had worked the land during its days as a plantation. The institution lacked running water, much less heated water, a fact resident physician L. A. Wailes complained interfered with patients' ability to bathe themselves regularly. Wood-burning stoves provided the only sources of heat, which posed a particular risk for leprosy patients whose nerve-damaged extremities left them prone to burning themselves without realizing it when sitting too close to a stove.[11] The location and climate of the home also interfered with the treatment of patients. Wailes blamed the swampy region for causing several of his patients to display "malarial symptoms" and noted that others felt the winter cold acutely. The warmer months proved even more conducive to ill-health; in June, Wailes predicted that rising flood waters would bring additional sickness to the home.[12]

The stigma attached to leprosy and the home's limited funds resulted in a tiny staff that further constrained the success of the institution. Wailes served as the sole official residing on the grounds, and he was supported only by a nurse, cook, and general handyman. In addition to his medical duties, therefore, Wailes was responsible for ensuring that meals were cooked and served, clothing laundered, rooms cleaned, necessary buildings constructed and maintained, gardens tended, and supplies ordered and fetched. These tasks became more difficult when he discharged the cook and steward for repeated instances of drunkenness and disorderly conduct. Although he managed to find a new hire to prepare meals, able-bodied patients assumed some tasks to help keep the home in operation.[13] Few workers could be lured to the home without the promise of decent wages or assurances of adequate protection from disease; the board provided neither.[14]

Patients responded to the poor conditions and loose oversight by attempting to forge their own program of treatment. While each demanded particular remedies developed by physicians, believing to some degree in the curative power of medical science, they refused to passively accept medical instruction handed down by the resident doctor. Wailes complained to the Board of Control that his patients did not fully obey his orders. He expressed particular annoyance with patients' tendency to follow their own course of treatment: "I find that each individual has a preconceived idea as to what medicine or course of medicine has come to be the most beneficial in his particular case." Where one patient insisted on pure chaulmoogra oil, another preferred "iodine of potash."[15] Others refused particular treatments that they believed harmed them.[16] Wailes found the behavior of the patients another obstacle to his ability to provide appropriate medical care, and requested that the board provide additional medical support to help enforce treatment programs.

The lack of response from the Board of Control demonstrated the degree to which the state offered limited resources for the support of its leprosy institution. In November 1895, Wailes welcomed a new nurse, cook, and laundress. The board also managed to staff at least one position—that of nurse and matron—with a patient, known as Miss Saunders. Still, the resident doctor had little faith that the state would ever provide the kind of financial and managerial support necessary to realize its original intention of creating an efficient medical institution. After serving one year as resident physician of the home, Wailes offered to resign.[17] Agreeing to remain at the home until a replacement could be found, he left the institution in April to accept a public health position in Central America.[18] Board member E. M. Cooper replaced him in that capacity on 1 May 1896, but the board recognized that the home could not continue to function without a dramatic change in the administrative structure of the facility.[19]

Bridging Church and State: Contract with the Sisters

Concerned about the potential viability of the institution, the Louisiana Board of Health requested that the Daughters of Charity administer the home, providing nursing and basic care for the patients consigned there. The appointment of the sisters made good economic and political sense at a time when the future of the Louisiana Leper Home remained clouded by financial troubles, low patient admissions, and insufficient medical provisions. The state obtained, for limited money, health care providers who were long recognized in Louisiana for their humane and skilled service in caring for the ill (since the sisters had already "left all to follow Christ," they required a negligible salary). Economic considerations aside, the sisters offered the kind of care and symbolic capital that could ensure the success of the institution. The Daughters of Charity provided a very new type of state intervention into the health care of Louisiana residents that also had links to a tradition of Catholic medical care.[20] Most Louisiana residents accepted religious sisters as health care workers and administrators of hospitals, particularly those established to care for patients who lacked the resources or family members to provide their own treatment.

Despite this tradition, the order was not willing to send a contingent of its members to a facility totally devoid of shelter and sanitation, and the sisters demanded at least minimal improvements before committing to the task. Sister Agnes Slavin, sent by the Mother Superior from Charity Hospital to investigate the Louisiana Leper Home, drew particular attention to its inaccessibility and the deteriorated condition of the rooms in which the sisters would live. The grounds consisted of twenty-two acres enclosed by an eight-foot fence. Each of six former slave cabins could hold six to eight patients, with two slated for men, two for women, one for the kitchen, and the other, Sister Agnes suggested, for a chapel. The former plantation mansion, then in considerable disrepair, could house the sisters. Even a person accustomed to privation felt it necessary to comment to the Mother Superior, "On the whole I could not imagine anything so uncomfortable—there is only a single floor and when you are under the house you can see through the crevices. I would not think of letting the Sisters live in this house—they would lose their health."[21] She recommended that the sisters refrain from coming until sanitary conditions and the water supply improved.

Sister Agnes's letter, however, indicated that she believed patients at the home needed both the spiritual guidance and physical assistance her order could provide. For the sisters, enforcing patient adherence to a strict moral code was as necessary to their well-being as fulfilling their needs for appropriate shelter, food, and medical care. As they set about improving the material conditions of the home, therefore, they also paid attention to providing an environment in which the patients could focus on their spiritual development, as defined by the Catholic Church. Slavin expressed concern that in the short period of the home's existence, patients had adopted questionable habits. In particular, she worried that men and women associated with each other "even at night," which left them vulnerable to sexual temptation or at least impure thoughts. She also noted that no one was attending to the religious needs of the patients. In response to her inquiry as to whether one seriously ill patient had seen a priest, he replied, "Oh, no, Sister, they won't come here." While acknowledging that the patients appeared clean and comfortable, considering the rudimentary condition of their surroundings, Sister Agnes insisted that the Daughters of Charity could improve conditions for them. She also recognized that such improvements demanded a certain financial commitment from the state: "It is not nice now but could be made so by money."[22]

After brief negotiations, the Board of Control of the Lepers' Home of Louisiana and the Mother Superior of the order devised a contract that closely linked church with state. In addition to accepting responsibility for the "domestic management" of the institution and the nursing of all patients, the sisters also were "entitled" to "inculcate good morals among the inmates, without interfering with their religious belief; to maintain proper decorum, good order and discipline; and to enforce the rules now in force, or to be hereafter adopted on these subjects." The contract afforded the sisters a great deal of authority within the facility while still leaving the power of allocating finances and establishing rules with the state. Both parties accepted a convergence of corporal and moral treatment, and found it appropriate that the state should subsidize such care. Although it offered no salary for their services, the board did contract to provide accommodations for the sisters, room for a chapel, the services of a priest, and a $100 annual allowance to each sister for clothing and personal necessities.[23]

The contract placed the sisters within a complicated web of authority comprising political, medical, and religious strands. Although charged with the management of the facility, the sisters answered to the state Board of Control, which approved all financial budgets and handed down regulations regarding the administration of the facility. The contract also placed them under the direction of the resident physician in providing medical treatment and requisitioning medical supplies.[24] At the same time, the sisters remained under the jurisdiction of their Mother Superior, and decisions regarding the nature and duration of a "mission" to the home came from the hierarchy of the order. Within the Catholic Church, the bishop of the diocese acted as their ultimate authority. The fact that the sisters viewed their mission of saving souls as their primary duty and religious authorities as their principal source of direction would cause some degree of controversy among patients, physicians, and state officials in later years.

The vagueness of the contract and the limited amount of medical oversight at the home left most of the daily responsibilities for patient treatment in the hands of the sisters. Sister Beatrice Hart, who served as the first de facto administrator of the home, saw herself periodically assuming a new role, "playing Doctor," by giving patients "what they need in the way of lotions, tablets, tonics, etc."[25] Her statement reveals that the kind of treatments available to patients with leprosy during the late nineteenth century did not necessarily require a physician's supervision, a fact that helped bolster the sisters' position as superior providers of succor and care. Physicians possessed no cure for leprosy, so the doctor's care of patients remained limited to treatment of associated ailments and any experimental remedies they could induce patients to try.[26] The sisters resided on the site and provided daily care that met patients' needs—everything from changing bandages and applying salves, to assisting those who required help with feeding, to counseling those overwhelmed with the emotional strain of having the disease. The sisters claimed to have a better ability than doctors to respond to the physical and emotional concerns of patients.[27] In one letter to the board, Sister Beatrice reminded members that the patients frequently commented on how much they appreciated "the untiring efforts of the Sisters to make their lives as comfortable and pleasant as possible."[28]

Even as they assumed unexpected responsibilities in the medical arena, they found their administrative actions circumscribed by a Board of Control concerned about finances. What the sisters might view as an action necessary to the upkeep of the home, the board might see as a breach of the proper chain of command.[29] The sisters rapidly learned that their belief in providing the best care possible for the patients would not always be matched by state officials who most desired a tight rein on expenditures. While the isolation of the facility afforded the sisters a degree of freedom to administer the institution free of daily intervention by either lay or medical authorities, it also limited their ability to quickly obtain money from the board or to exert personal pressure on board members to act on requests in a timely fashion. The board required that the sisters direct all bills to the treasurer, who would grant them only a small allowance for discretionary spending.[30]

Sister Beatrice nevertheless demonstrated that she was quite willing to ignore the board's miserly financial provisions for the home when she felt the situation warranted such action. Owing to the deteriorated state of the institution and the limited funding provided by the state, this occurred quite frequently. Unlike Dr. Wailes, Sister Beatrice did not wait for funds to come to her before embarking on much-needed repairs; she asserted her authority to oversee expenditures as the administrator of the institution and expected the board to respect her decisions and pay the bills. Pointing out that the patients profited from her judicious spending, Sister Beatrice justified a large lumber bill by informing the board that much of the wood was used to seal the walls of patient quarters. As she explained, "It does one good to go into them and find them warm and clean."[31] With the closest store a ferry ride or a journey over a rough road away, the sisters worked to improve the institution's ability to provide some fresh food on site. Enlisting the assistance of able-bodied patients, the sisters used additional lumber to construct a poultry yard to provide eggs for patients.[32]

Such efforts on the part of the sisters brought considerable improvements to the institution, but in the end they did little to increase the state's expenditures for the home. Sister Beatrice requested an increase in state funding, but she also expressed doubts that legislators would properly provide for the home. "I am watching very closely the proceedings of the Legislature to see how we will fare. I hope they will be liberal in their views and generous when the time comes to deal out the appropriations, but we must wait and see."[33] Quite frequently, local establishments who trusted that billed items would eventually be paid supported the institution for months at a time, while the sisters sought additional funding from generous philanthropists and more modest donations.[34] In this regard, the sisters' affiliation with the Catholic Church and their historical association with health care provision granted them the means to keep the facility operating at a time when public health officials could not do so alone.

Making a Home: The Formation of a Religious Medical Institution

The sisters' initial efforts to improve the quality of care for patients revealed their interconnected desires to offer them physical comfort and to make religious devotion a part of the facility's daily regime. One of their first acts as administrators was to attend to patients' physical needs by requisitioning sheets, underwear, and other clothing. They then quickly set about providing for patients' spiritual needs. The sisters offered instruction in catechism and established a nightly ritual in which the chaplain, Father Colton, led all patients in a recitation of the rosary and short meditation.[35]

The sisters expressed both their belief in the germ theory of disease and in the need for religious worship when they created what they considered an acceptable chapel for the home. Upon selecting a cabin to serve in that capacity, the sisters covered the ceiling with white sheeting, both to improve its appearance and "to keep the microbes, spores, and all belonging to the Bacteriology behind the cloth."[36] Cleanliness of body and of soul became closely interlinked in the mission of the Daughters of Charity at the Louisiana Leper Home.

The patients could not help but notice the ways in which religion influenced the administration of the home. Soon after the sisters arrived, the archbishop of New Orleans came to visit the facility to examine the site and approve the sisters' mission. Patients were outfitted in their newly purchased Sunday clothes, and the archbishop praised their cleanliness and that of their cabins. One of the patients thanked the archbishop for sending the sisters to them. While the contract might have been made between the order and the Board of Control, the patients—all but one Catholic—understood that the archbishop held the ultimate authority over the new administrators of the site. They also learned that the sisters would insist that they practice their faith. Sister Beatrice duly noted in an early letter to a fellow sister in the order that among the Catholic patients, all had complied with church attendance but one. She characterized the holdout as "a little stubborn in the matter of resistance" but expressed her hope that "he will think better of it before it is too late."[37] Such a comment suggested that while the majority of patients embraced the arrival of the sisters, those unwilling to accept the religious component of care might face a more difficult time. Whether welcomed or not, proselytizing remained an important duty of the sisters. Sister

Beatrice eagerly reported in August on their first patient convert to Catholicism, a nineteen-year-old boy. He became part of a small class of students preparing to make their first communion.[38] The following January, the archbishop of New Orleans visited the home to administer the sacrament of confirmation to four boys and two girls.[39]

One could assume that as Catholics, many of the patients shared the sense of the sisters that they had a right to practice their faith in ways that had been denied them before the arrival of a priest, particularly in rituals surrounding death. When the first patient died under the sisters' administration, they provided all the ceremony that normally accompanied a Catholic death. One sister prepared the body for a wake, using tables, sheets, and tree boughs to arrange a bier, decorated with flowers and lit by candlelight. The following day, the resident priest said a high mass, in which the patients participated, followed by burial of the deceased "as a Christian."[40] The care and respect the sisters paid to the body must have resonated with the patients who had witnessed previous deaths dealt with quickly by an overworked doctor and his limited staff.

In addition to the religious component of their oversight, the sisters had a distinctive approach to the patients that combined a humanitarian belief in the dignity of the individual with a sense that their charges were children with simple needs and sensibilities. Sister Beatrice declared the patients a happy group, "if you can judge by their always being ready to sing or laugh, or jump, or swing." In purchasing new clothing for the patients, the sisters took particular care to avoid creating a "uniform" that they felt would label the patients "paupers." In describing the patients' delight in receiving such clothing, however, Sister Beatrice recounted that each patient eagerly "held them up, and tried them on and showed them to each other, as children might."[41] Recognizing the need to offer patients the kind of humane care that recognized their status as human beings, as the previous haphazard arrangement of incarceration failed to do, the sisters nevertheless viewed the residents of the home as less than adult, a view that fit comfortably with their insistence on providing a new regime of strict discipline and order.

The sisters recognized, in ways that the state administrators seldom discussed, that most of the patients were relatively well and mobile, and the rundown, remote former plantation offered little in the way of activities or amusements. Although Sister Beatrice did not mention the Kalaupapa settlement by name, its proximity to the ocean provided Hawaiian patients the kind of diversions she identified as missing at Indian Camp: fishing, sailing, bathing.[42] Though the home was situated on the Mississippi River, a wall, road, and levee blocked patients from this potential source of exercise and entertainment. The sisters attempted to find other activities for patients, but these pastimes tended to emphasize industry and instruction more than amusement. In the spring, the sisters distributed seeds to the patients and encouraged them to plant their own gardens.[43] According to Sister Beatrice, "in the intervals of sunshine both men and women are busy in the gardens, the latter getting ready to cultivate flowers, the men busy on the vegetables. . . . I notice the greatest change in them since they have become so interested in the outdoor work."[44] She also considered religious and academic coursework suitable activities for diverting patients' attention from their disease. By the fall of 1897, Sister Beatrice reported that the patients' time was "so happily divided between work and prayer, study and necessary relaxation that they do not have much to devote to the consideration of their problems or forlorn condition."[45]

Although the sisters prided themselves on providing patients with the best care possible at the Louisiana Leper Home, they insisted that they could do a better job if the state moved the facility to a more appropriate locality. As early as August 1896, Sister Beatrice had begun urging the board to seek a new site, going so far as to identify potential alternatives. She found, for instance, some land outside of New Orleans in Covington available for $3,000 and recommended that the board make the purchase. "Those who think [Indian Camp] is just the place ought to come here and live and feel their wants before they talk so loud," she complained about the existing site.[46] For some of the sisters, the mission to Louisiana, with its subtropical climate and accompanying insects and reptiles, represented an exotic colonial assignment. Sister Beatrice declared that she would "expiate all my sins here, just by putting up with the mosquitoes, frogs, lizards, and all sorts of things of that kind, jumping at me."[47] Indeed, the location on a swampy bank of the Mississippi did pose health problems for the sisters, their staff, and the patients, all of whom faced the threat of malaria during their first summer at the home.[48]

When Sister Beatrice learned that the owners of the land on which Indian Camp stood offered to sell the property to the state, she urged the board not to acquire it. "I am praying with all my might that nothing will induce you to make the purchase," she wrote. "Believe me, the work will never prosper here. I am speaking from experience acquired during our eighteen months of residence in the place."[49] She also pressed her point with state legislators and was gratified when Louisiana adopted an act in 1898 authorizing the purchase of new land for the construction of a leprosy facility. Though heartened by the action, she also recognized that such a move would require another community to allow the placement of a leprosy institution within its borders, an unlikely prospect. As Sister Beatrice noted, "So great is the horror inspired by the leprosy, that no one would be reconciled to have the dread disease even within the limits of the neighborhood."[50]

Community understandings of leprosy remained shrouded in fear, a fear that prevented residents of Iberville Parish from embracing the presence of the home. U.S. congressional investigations into the question of leprosy during the late nineteenth century heightened local residents' awareness of the home and its residents. Rather than assuring the local community that the state institution protected public health by containing people with leprosy, congressional debates about the need for a national leprosarium only fueled the perception among area residents that the Louisiana Leper Home directly threatened them. In particular, certain residents were concerned that people associated with the home actively mingled with members of the local community and thereby posed a health hazard. James Ware, owner of Belle Grove and Celeste Plantations in the neighboring town of White Castle, wrote the governor to complain of "inmates . . . permitted to deal at the gate with peddlers," as well as a "priest and attendants crossing the river to this side" where they interacted with community members. Ware specifically criticized the priest for going directly to his tenant's sick wife after a visit to the home "without even changing his clothing." The original founders of the home may have wished to create a very new institution from the urban asylum it replaced, but to local residents, the home still operated as "a pest house."[51]

Resigned to the fact that the state seemed most intent on leaving the institution in its isolated environment, the Daughters of Charity worked with limited means to improve the home and its public reputation. The sisters assumed the state hired them not only to nurse the patients but also to provide the same kind of administrative order and institutional discipline they brought to the hospitals they staffed and managed. In other words, they intended to develop a legitimate medical institution, as they envisioned one. This involved reorganizing the Louisiana Leper Home to properly reflect their spiritual and medical mission. With physical improvements to the buildings and grounds underway, they focused their attention on developing an institutional hierarchy that would provide them with control within the home, even as they still deferred to state and board officials outside of it.

The sisters considered themselves open to scientific medicine, and they combined their brand of spiritual and material comfort with any medical treatments and practices that could improve the condition of patients. They also recognized the necessity of having a doctor associated with the facility, and they consistently asked the board to hire one who would visit regularly or reside on the premises.[52] In fact, it was generally Sister Beatrice rather than the visiting doctor who complained that insufficient state funding prevented the home from becoming a more effective medical facility. She voiced support for the patients' demand for an oculist, for example, agreeing that their disease caused severe eye problems that necessitated the expertise of a specialist.[53] Sister Beatrice also commented on the rapidly deteriorating condition of many of the patients, suggesting that the "mixing up of the patients in the various stages of the disease" was partially responsible. Her words echoed the convictions of some public health officials at the time who believed patients should be segregated by the degree of their affliction. She blamed the lack of sufficient room and conveniences for this state of affairs.[54]

Struggles for Authority

Despite their best intentions, the Daughters of Charity often found their authority within and over the Louisiana Leper Home compromised by their precarious position as religious women. They constantly had to negotiate the conflicting social roles that on the one hand afforded them power as moral guardians and caregivers and on the other insisted they defer in decision making to their male superiors. The Board of Control valued the sisters' affordable care but resisted their efforts to take financial matters in their own hands. It also refused to grant the sisters complete jurisdiction over the governing of patients, forcing the sisters to constantly call on board members to intervene on their behalf in patient disputes. The Daughters of Charity became experts in playing their roles in ways that maximized their ability to run the home as they saw fit. The actions of state officials and patients, however, regularly reminded them of the contingent nature of their power.

Board members continually sought to minimize the costs of the home, viewing budgetary overruns not as a sign of underfunding but as evidence of the sisters' spendthrift ways. The Board of Control, charged with dispensing funds, attempted to limit expenses most frequently by ignoring requests for additional money. At other times, the board treasurer would issue a check along with a sharp reminder that the sisters needed to operate within a budget. Such messages embodied the gendered relationship that emerged between the female administrative head of the home and the male provider of funds. In one exchange, the board treasurer assumed the role of a husband chiding an extravagant wife, explaining that one of the sister's pleas for funds required him to overdraw the board's account. He objected to what he saw as excessive food purchases, advised her to spend only what was appropriated, and announced that the "whole board has been hoping you would manage to provide the lepers with everything that was really necessary" on $900 a month.[55] Such a budget failed to account for the material refurbishing of aging buildings, however, much less for the construction and outfitting of new quarters for a growing population base. While the board might claim that the sisters had trouble economizing, the facility's endurance under their administration demonstrates the considerable degree to which the sisters knew how to stretch meager funds to keep the home operating.

The sisters found that patient resistance posed one of the greatest and most persistent challenges to their position as appropriate administrators inside the home. In their role as institutional administrators, the Daughters of Charity dealt with patients on a daily basis and served as the mediators between disgruntled residents and the board. As representatives of the state, the sisters often heard the first hints of any resident dissatisfaction and found themselves in the sometimes uncomfortable position of enforcing discipline. Sister Beatrice informed the board of "some cases of discontent among the patients," expressing concern about the "friction between us and them." Patients sometimes bridled at the directives of the sisters, perhaps not sharing the same sense as Sister Beatrice that "a little discipline is necessary to govern the place with credit to ourselves and equal justice to all."[56] Convinced that the previous administration had complacently accepted behavior ruinous to the health and morals of the patients, she decided that official regulations were required.[57] Once established, she framed and hung copies of the regulations "in the most conspicuous places" throughout the facility in June 1897.[58]

Issues of sexual segregation emerged as a significant point of contention between patients and sisters. The Daughters of Charity considered the separation of men from women crucial to creating both a modern medical facility and a moral religious home. They viewed their policy as an extension of the kind of organization found in other medical facilities. Where hospitals and mental institutions had separate sleeping quarters for men and women, the sisters expanded the directive to ban all association between the sexes, including chance encounters on the grounds.[59] Not surprisingly for women who took a vow of chastity, they viewed abstinence from all sexual thoughts and activities essential to spiritual well-being. Initiating a strict policy of sexual segregation, therefore, was one of the first policies established by the sisters upon their arrival at the home, and one they guarded most vigilantly.[60]

For their part, patients resented the increased level of surveillance and attempted to circumvent such rules. Finding little opportunity to freely mingle during the day when the sisters roamed the grounds, some patients took to sneaking out at night to visit companions in other cabins. In an attempt to thwart such plans, Sister Beatrice and Sister M. Thomas took to sleeping within the enclosure set aside for patient quarters, an arrangement that worked—temporarily.[61] As the patient population rose from twenty-six to more than fifty, however, it became more difficult for four sisters to track every patient. In February 1898, Sister Beatrice reported to the board that a core group of six patients regularly violated the restrictions. Loosening the boards in the fence that divided the women's quarters from those of the men, three men regularly slipped through late at night to visit the women. While these patients viewed their action as a means of asserting their dissatisfaction with the regulations prohibiting "the visiting of one sex to the other," Sister Beatrice considered it a challenge to her ability to manage the home, and she requested assistance from the board to enforce the rules. Even in recognizing this act of resistance, however, Sister Beatrice couched her criticism of the patients in terms a parent would use toward wayward children: "Poor deluded people do not know how well off they are."[62]

The manner in which Sister Beatrice portrayed the situation to the board revealed the extent to which the sisters recognized their vulnerability as managers of the facility. Though seeking assistance from the board, she sought to convey the sense that the sisters were fully capable of keeping patients in line. Sister Beatrice hastened to explain that patient discontent regarding sexual segregation was not causing any serious problems, "nothing like a quarrel between them and us." Increased surveillance had been effective in thwarting the efforts of renegade patients. She explained, "We have simply been more vigilant never leaving them alone. . . . Now they are surprised at all hours to see some one of the sisters going in different directions so that they cannot plan." She intimated, though, that the sisters might not be able to manage them in this manner without further assistance.[63]

The confrontation between the sisters and residents revealed divisions over the degree to which patients should be granted autonomy in the conduct of their everyday lives. Sister Beatrice's correspondence revealed that patients believed they were only pursuing rights that ought to be theirs as adults. "They feel that they are deprived of their rights as men and women by being shut up here when so many others similarly affected are at large and enjoying home and friends," she related. More pointedly, the patients informed the sisters that the original administrator of the home had not enforced such stringent regulations, and they called the new rules "a species of tyranny."[64] The sisters chose to address patient complaints by intensifying the level of scrutiny under which they lived, leaving residents alone only during their own half-hour meals.[65]

Patients refused to accept such a rigid policy of sexual segregation without debate and eventually appealed directly to the Board of Control, requesting that it accept an alternative plan. Patient Walter Abrams wrote a letter directly to board member Albert Phelps, asserting that the sisters imposed unnecessarily rigid regulations that essentially criminalized ordinary behavior and compounded the burden of living within a remote facility: "It's bad enough we have to [be] isolated here from the outside world for humanity['s] sake without wanting to take such means that may make our living more miserable than what it is already." He protested that his action of sitting and talking with a woman on the porch of her quarters did not cause anyone harm. More significant, his rhetoric suggested that he found the sisters overstepping their boundaries of caregivers by regulating moral behavior: "Now I didn't come here to join the church nor any Christian society but to be treated as an American citizen should be treated." His willingness to write directly to the board revealed his ability to use one of the few weapons accorded to patients, and he promised Phelps that he would seek to sway the opinions of the broader public if the board did not instruct the sisters to change their ways.[66] When Abrams found no support from Phelps on this matter, however, he employed another method of protest employed by patients dissatisfied with life inside the home—he packed his bags and left.[67]

The sisters, receiving neither assistance nor censure from the board, took additional steps to end nightly visitations between some men and women. Sister Benedicta Roache ordered the clearing of a cornfield behind one of the women's quarters, which had afforded male patients cover, and installed two lampposts to illuminate the area. Still, some patients continued to complain about the separation of the sexes, prompting Sister Benedicta to marvel, "You could hardly credit the many ways the sexes, that is a few on both sides, have resorted to keep up on intercourse with each other." She planned to add additional lamps and a watchman in the future to assist the sisters in bringing an end to these practices.[68]

Contesting the sisters' claim that patients could not demand the same freedoms as healthy adults, some patients tried to negotiate with board members and the sisters to alter the unwanted regulation. A committee of four patients elected a chairman from their ranks to question Sister Benedicta about the rationale behind the ban on social interaction among men and women. She replied that the board had made the decision, and the sisters therefore enforced it. Sister Benedicta provided her own accounting of the event to the board and requested that it send "a few lines" reiterating the need for patients to "continue to hold their recreations in their respective enclosures and quarters," each with sufficient amusements "for sick people sojourning at the Home for medical treatment."[69] The committee of patients, however, petitioned the board directly to reconsider its regulations regarding the strict separation of the sexes. Appealing to the board members' "sense of justice in the matter," they requested that men and women be allowed to gather "under the Oaks" on Sunday afternoons between one and four P.M.[70]

When the board did not send a timely response to their inquiry, committee members followed up with a new letter. John Drew, secretary for the new patient committee, reminded board member Phelps that he previously had informed the patients that if they directed "reasonable" requests to the board through an organized committee, they would be granted. The petition to socialize on the grounds of the home represented such a request, according to the patients. "We are not asking the board for anything that will cost them a great outlay of money for us," Drew maintained. "No! All that we are asking of your honorable body is to give the men, women, and children of our Camp, only a few hours of innocent pleasure and amusement on each Sunday afternoon." He reminded the board of the great suffering they normally had to endure as people with leprosy and claimed that the granting of this request would help them "bear the burden of our sorrows."[71]

Drew demanded that the male patients be accorded the honor due southern gentlemen, and he subtly suggested that the current regulations insulted the men who resided at the home. Recognizing that the ban on interaction among men and women stemmed from concerns regarding potential sexual activity, he addressed the issue directly, insisting that the patient request would not allow for any illicit behavior. He pointed out that a Sunday outing would bring men and women "together in the broad daylight, once a week, under the keen eyes of as many chaperons or sisters as the board may see fit to have among us (even though I do not think there would be any need for them)." He invoked the spiritual practices of the patients as evidence of their upright behavior. "Why," Drew demanded, "do you think our beautiful little Chapel and all our religious services and church going would do us any good if we have such little morals that we cannot be in the presence of ladies once a week and then with the Sisters as chaperons, without acting as rowdies or hoodlums?" He reminded Phelps of the southern masculine code of honor. "I know Mr. Phelps if you were present and could answer this question orally, you would say: 'No boys I have too much respect for you all, to think that any of you would forget yourselves, or not act as perfect gentlemen when in the presence of the ladies.' "[72]

Despite this entreaty, the board upheld the ban on the "intermingling of the sexes" while establishing a new body to enforce discipline at the home. The new committee, to comprise four board members plus the resident physician and sister superior of the home, would have the power to adopt any rules intended to maintain proper discipline and uphold existing regulations at the home.[73] This action did not resolve the ongoing difference of opinion between patients and administrators over the issue of segregating the sexes. Some patients would continue to protest this regulation as a fundamental violation of their humanity, while the sisters remained adamant in their belief that it represented the linchpin of administrative order and moral control. The board's support of the directive demonstrates the degree to which the state, and later the federal government, agreed that such a regulation helped maintain a sense of discipline among the patients appropriate to a modern medical facility. Religious morals, medical values, and institutional order were closely linked.

Racial segregation remained an equally significant though less outwardly debated aspect of institutional organization. White and African American patients were rigidly separated. Unlike the issue of dividing men from women, racial segregation had been part of the organizational framework of the institution since its inception. Such a division was so commonplace in medical institutions that it did not emerge as an issue very frequently in the correspondence between administrators and the board.[74] The Daughters of Charity enforced racial divisions as strictly as sexual divisions, informing the board of available space in quarters assigned to each race.[75] The increasing patient population sometimes called for makeshift arrangements to ensure that white and black patients could not mingle. When the number of African American male patients grew too large for the existing dining hall allocated to them, the sisters railed off a section of the white male dining room to accommodate them. The sisters urged the legislature to approve funding for new dining hall buildings for male and female African American patients "so as to entirely separate the races."[76]

Any attempt to deviate from the order of a segregated community met with harsh rebuke. One African American patient, Joe Albien, rebelled against orders to remain in his quarters. This prompted a letter from Sister Benedicta to the board, in which she related that "I explained to him firmly that he was not to go outside his own precinct, that is, in and around the colored cottages, and galleries," yet "he went yesterday three or four times around the dining room." She insisted that "this man must be restricted to his own negro quarters," asserting that in the past he had been punished for "his bold and persistent effort to get into communication with colored female inmates by climbing on separation fences, boring holes in fences, and going on [the] road in front of [the] colored house."[77] The board acted on this complaint, writing a letter to the father of the patient and telling the sisters to advise Albien "that if he continues to violate the rules some other provision will have to be made for his welfare which may not be as pleasant as his present surroundings."[78] In the Jim Crow South, such a threat no doubt served as a particularly menacing warning to the patient and his family.

The possibility of miscegenation posed a grave threat to the order and discipline of the home in the sisters' view and prompted the suggestion of harsh punishment. One young white male patient, Bourgois Robeaux, had been reprimanded after being caught in the quarters of an African American patient, Eva Lyge. The sisters notified the young man's father, who "came to the Home and gave his son the called for reproof." Despite threatening to remove the patient to his father's care if he again ventured into the enclosure set aside for black patients, the sisters discovered that he had once more "been frequenting [the] colored enclosure of [the] female department." Sister Benedicta insisted that such activities interfered with the sisters' efforts to care for the sick. "If the sick patients are determined on this way of doing they will have to be transported to some other place," she insisted, "even at the expense of shipping them to the U.S. leper possession at Molokai."[79] Such a comment strongly implied that Sister Benedicta found such interracial relationships more appropriate to the less restrictive regulations of the Hawaiian facility. The board had another kind of action in mind, and informed Bourgois Robeaux that if his "misconduct" occurred again, the police of Iberville Parish were instructed "to take such measures as will stop all further infractions of the rules."[80]

Gun-toters, "Absconders," and Other Tales of Resistance

When patients failed to negotiate a workable compromise over the rules with the sisters and the Board of Control, they resisted their authority through the only methods at their disposal: leaving the facility, flouting regulations, and even threatening the sisters with physical harm. The Daughters of Charity argued that they enforced the regulations to ensure the physical and spiritual well-being of patients, but some patients argued just as strenuously that such regulations had little to do with health and everything to do with the personal and religious interests of the administration. Patient resistance proved to be a powerful, albeit not always an entirely successful, tool. As people with leprosy, patients realized that the state had expressed its intention both to contain and care for them. Although the sisters may have wished otherwise, patients could not be discharged for bad behavior, nor could they receive any kind of punishment that might jeopardize their already fragile health. They recognized that the sisters could not take extreme measures to enforce discipline without the consent of the board. Even when board members eventually acted to support the sisters' decisions, they reminded the sisters of their subordinate role in overseeing the home.

The issue of patient violence, though rare, revealed the vulnerability of the sisters and the ways in which an often unresponsive board could undermine the authority and safety of the religious women it placed in charge of the facility. In November 1904, a patient entered the dining room with a loaded gun, prompting the sisters to ask for regulations banning firearms. No regulations were forthcoming. Months later, the same patient attempted to hit one of the sisters with an iron rod. Several of the male patients came to the aid of the sister and contained him, and the sisters threatened to keep him locked in a barred room if he disrupted things again.[81] Sister Benedicta could not forget the incident, and she reminded Board of Control president J. F. Pollack of it three years later when she related to him the story of a Daughter of Charity who was shot and killed by a patient at a Milwaukee hospital.[82] Combined with patient resistance to existing regulations, armed patients presented a formidable challenge to the authority and safety of the sisters.

Sister Benedicta reported any activity regarding firearms to the board as a potential threat to the stability of the institution. When she noticed that one patient received four boxes of shells in the mail in November 1907, she confiscated the materials and intended to hold them until the board officially determined whether patients could have access to ammunition. She reminded board members that while they had given her permission to secure firearms from all male patients in the institution after the 1904 incident, they had failed to accede to her request for a committee of men to handle the task. The sisters did not want to attempt to wrestle guns from the male patients on their own, so they remained armed. The patients, for their part, claimed that they kept the guns merely for the purpose of amusement, to hunt for wild fowl and game. Sister Benedicta argued that even the recreational use of guns violated institutional rules, as patients tended to sneak away from the facility to find the best hunting grounds. Some patients also used the threat of violence to expedite their escape from the home; the night watchman reported that several patients threatened "to do him in" if he pursued them.[83]

Sister Benedicta's frustration over patient firearms reflected her broader concern that the Board of Control failed to provide the sisters with the support they needed to properly contain the patients. The sisters viewed the quarantine of people with leprosy as a critical medical function of the home, and considered any violation of that regulation a threat to the public's health. Sister Benedicta reminded the board that the sisters found it difficult to care for patients who were regularly "roaming around the country all night." In relating a recent incident in which male patients had turned the framed copy of the rules to face the wall, Sister Benedicta reminded the board that such patient infractions represented not just a threat to the sisters, but a challenge to the authority of the Board of Control as well.[84]

The sisters encouraged the board to authorize new punishments that might discourage violations of institutional rules. After a series of patients such as Walter Abrams and John Drew escaped from the home, the sisters requested that the board issue a statement warning patients that anyone who left the home without a medical discharge would be "advertised as [a] menace to the public." Such action posed a nasty threat to the patients who, Sister Benedicta knew, often sought protection from public notoriety within the walls of the home. Most patients who fled the institution displayed few obvious physical signs of the disease, and they expected to live in society without the public learning they had leprosy. Within one month during the summer of 1903, three patients "in good condition" left the home, and the sisters demanded action from the board to thwart their efforts. "When they take on themselves to discharge themselves," threatened Sister Benedicta, "the penalty will be publicity."[85] Patient Harry Zimmerman protested this policy, claiming that publication of the names of patients affected not only the person fleeing the facility, but his or her family as well. After reading about three escaped patients in the *New Orleans Times*, Zimmerman claimed to speak for the majority of patients when he objected to the release of any surname to the public. "If the Almighty in his wisdom seen proper and fit to place such an affliction upon us," he explained, "let us have the burden alone, for it is no fault of the loved ones that we left behind."[86]

The threat of publicity did not prevent some patients from attempting to leave the home when they could. Some enlisted the assistance of relatives, such as one successful patient escapee who used a visit from her husband as an opportunity to leave the premises. Others managed to escape after nightfall, using the cover of darkness to distance themselves from the home.[87] Many of these patients quickly found themselves back within the confines of the home, either returning of their own accord or by means of people who learned of their patient status. One African American patient, denied admission on a train, was quickly identified and returned to the home. The law enforcement officers of the neighboring town of White Castle regularly sent bills to the home for transportation costs incurred by authorities bringing unwilling patients back to the institution.[88] Other patients left the home for brief visits to family members or to obtain materials they could not get within the facility, and they generally returned voluntarily.[89] Sister Benedicta resented the fact that such patients were allowed back into the facility without penalty and asked that the board take steps to help the sisters improve security measures to prevent escapes and to punish those who "absconded."[90]

When news of patients leaving the home reached members of the Louisiana Board of Health, they demanded some explanation as to why a Board of Control responsible for keeping patients with leprosy away from the general public had failed in its duty. In a letter to the state health board, Phelps maintained that reports of runaway patients had been greatly exaggerated. He argued, contrary to the views of Sister Benedicta, "there have been few violations of our rules requiring patients to remain within the Leper enclosure." Attempting to preempt any suggestion that patients may have been leaving due to unpleasant conditions, Phelps contended, "Our patients are only too glad to remain quietly at the Home and there should be no reason for them to wish to wander away from it." Still, he did take the opportunity to try to wrestle additional state funding for the Board of Control to provide suitable fencing and additional guards for the facility.[91]

Perhaps the Board of Health's concern encouraged the Board of Control to show greater support for the sisters' efforts to punish unsanctioned leave from the facility. Harry Zimmerman received a letter from the president of the Board of Control informing him that future violations of the regulations would necessitate his placement in solitary confinement.[92] Zimmerman's response reveals how many patients did not see themselves as threats to the community and consequently considered their periodic leave-taking from the home as harmless excursions. He resented being threatened with a punishment "usually delt [sic] out to murderers" and objected to the board singling out his actions and making him "a scapegoat for the acts of ¾ of the inmates of this home." He contrasted his brief trips to a local store for "eggs, sardines, cheese and crackers and a couple of bottles of porter" with patients who left the home for weeks at a time before returning. Calling into question the effectiveness of the board's threatening letter, Zimmerman promised, "When I leave the enclosure again, it will be to leave the Home, the Parish and the entire State of Louisiana."[93]

Concerns expressed by the communities surrounding the Louisiana Leper Home offered the kind of pressure for board action that the sisters could not inspire. Twelve residents of Iberville Parish, along with the local health officer, sent a letter to the Board of Control in 1907 complaining of how "the inmates of the Leper Home are daily roaming, hunting, and trespassing our fields." The letter provides an interesting insight into the ways in which the general public continued to view leprosy as an extremely contagious disease that could be transmitted through even indirect contact with people who had it. The local planters complained that patients had been seen in neighboring cotton fields, "placing their hands upon cotton balls, which our laborers necessarily must pick, consequently causing them to come in direct contact with disease." The residents also asserted that sewage from the home emptied directly into the bayou and into their fields. "We wish to state that we consider this an injustice, that you yourselves are doing," the local landholders complained, "worthy at least of criminal prosecution."[94] The petition moved the board to remind patients that possessing firearms and leaving the home to hunt constituted "a gross violation of the rules and regulations at the Home and of our orders and an insult to this Board." The board instructed patients to hand over their guns or face action from the legal authorities of Iberville Parish.[95]

Debates over who had the responsibility and the authority to maintain discipline continued to frustrate the sisters' efforts to establish a stable and efficient home. The rising numbers of patients admitted to the facility (the population stood at sixty-two in July 1909) made caring for the patients increasingly challenging, even without the added burden of dealing with those who flouted institutional rules.[96] Board members acted as though issuing strongly worded messages represented sufficient action on their part and held the sisters responsible for regulating patient behavior. The sisters insisted that their duties focused on nursing and caring for the patients, not in service as police officers. When patients took it upon themselves to trespass on neighboring properties, Sister Benedicta insisted, "it was up to the Board of Control and State authorities to remedy the situation and protect our neighbors' property." She requested that the board take further action against those patients who refused to turn over their firearms, as well as those who continued to leave the premises.[97] The board secretary, however, insinuated that it was the job of the sisters, as on-site administrators, to ensure that patients obeyed public health regulations.[98]

Ongoing congressional debates over whether to establish a federal leprosarium gave Sister Benedicta new ammunition of her own to pressure the board to enforce patient discipline. Referring to an American Medical Association report on leprosy written by Louisiana physicians William Hopkins and Isadore Dyer, Sister Benedicta reminded board members that quarantine officials in other states who failed to create leprosy institutions were not alone to blame for the continued "evil" spread of leprosy. "Your Board knows too well the number of cases yearly absconding from this institution to California, New York, Missouri, Tennessee, Texas," she stated. Invoking the rationale of scientific medicine, she argued that the home's mission to protect public health was not being met as long as the mostly male patients who escaped from the institution "in septic condition tramp their way into other states, thereby germinating this disease through the states." Sister Benedicta urged the board to address the governor and general assembly to provide the home with greater security and to penalize more harshly those who escaped.[99]

From State to Nation

As the Louisiana Leper Home gained national attention in the debate over whether to establish a federal leprosarium, the Board of Control grudgingly granted the Daughters of Charity additional authority to contain patients within the facility. The persistent efforts of the sisters, along with the rising numbers of escaped patients tabulated in the annual reports, spurred the board to pass a resolution calling for stricter controls on patient behavior. At a November 1913 board meeting in New Orleans, members passed a resolution calling for the construction of an iron fence around the perimeter of the institution's grounds and the appointment of four watchmen to guard the premises.[100] Although the state legislature generally ignored frequent requests for additional funds, it did authorize the hiring of security guards. The following July, four night watchmen and two day guards went on duty.[101] More significant, the board passed a resolution in January 1914 that afforded Sister Benedicta "complete control of and authority over the Leper Home, including authority to make rules and regulations governing inmates of the Home and the authority to enforce such rules and regulations."[102] No longer would the Sister Superior need to write board members to enforce rules; this action invested the sisters with the power to regulate patient behavior themselves.

The Daughters of Charity took advantage of their new authority to establish what amounted to a prison within the institution, sending a message that the sick could and would be punished if they refused to accept the rules of the home. When Sister Benedicta decided that locking patients deemed "unruly" in "detention cells" was necessary to enforce discipline, the board supported her decision. Having formerly turned to the local authorities to assist the home in enforcing order, the board now supported Sister Benedicta's contention that the institution needed to attend to its own. "It is up to the Leper Home to maintain order and confine its inmates," the board proclaimed. "We must hold [patients] in the institution by such means as will accomplish the result."[103] In the view of at least one patient, this amounted to the state placing the institution "under martial law, surrounded with armed guards."[104] Although some patients continued to leave the home, they faced harsher penalties upon their return. By December 1916, the sisters had in place a policy by which all "returned abscondees" were placed in a detention building constructed for the purpose of holding patients who violated institutional rules. Such patients remained in the holding cell twenty days for the first offense, with the punishment increasing in increments of twenty days for each additional violation.[105]

While the sisters gained additional authority to enforce the containment of patients, they still faced a difficult battle in gaining necessary funding, a situation that helped stimulate their support for transforming the home into a federal leprosy institution. As congressional debates over the need for a national leprosy facility gathered momentum in the 1910s, the sisters came to believe that the U.S. government would provide the kind of material support necessary to care for the patients. Monetary concerns escalated as the patient population increased from 1915 to 1917. Throughout these years,

Sister Benedicta faced mounting pressure from creditors increasingly upset by the failure of the administration to pay its bills.[106] As the letters from area shopkeepers and service providers grew testier, Sister Benedicta stepped up her demands for increased funding to cover expenses. The situation intensified in January 1917, when the president of the Board of Control threatened to resign if Sister Benedicta "interfere[d] in the finances of the Home." In a letter to the Louisiana governor, Sister Benedicta defended her actions, claiming she only sought information regarding how the board allocated the home's maintenance fund because August, September, and October bills had gone unpaid, leaving her "much embarrassed in purchasing supplies."[107] The continued failure of the Board of Control to elicit sufficient funding from the state helped convince the Daughters of Charity to attempt to win financial support from the U.S. government by transforming the Indian Camp location into a federal facility.

The sisters had previously argued that the home should be moved due to its insalubrious environment and poor location, but they now played up the benefits of the site in order to convince the federal government that it could serve as an excellent national leprosarium. In a letter to the Louisiana State Board of Health, the new superintendent, Sister Edith, glossed over her predecessor's warnings about the threat of malaria arising from the home's swampy locale and claimed instead that the only risk of spreading infection lay with patients absconding. She argued that the federal government would be more capable than the state in preventing such actions. She also argued that since most of the patients were native Louisianans, building a national institution in another area would remove them to a distant state or territory and deprive them "of the sole consolation left them—the occasional visit of relatives." Sister Edith downplayed earlier concerns about the hostility the facility faced from area residents to assert instead that many neighboring communities supported the home, as it improved property values and brought jobs to the region.[108] Though she stressed most strongly the needs of the patients, her assertion that area residents accepted the home appeared to carry the most weight. The national committee that was authorized to select a site for the new federal leprosarium did not initially view the Louisiana Leper Home as an ideal location, but its members eventually recognized that the Louisiana government and Iberville Parish specifically were the most open to having a facility for leprosy patients in their locality.[109]

As the U.S. Public Health Service and the Louisiana State Legislature debated a purchase price for the home, the sisters worked to ensure that they would have a place in the new administration. Dr. Oswald Denney, the U.S.

public health official who would assume the position of Medical Officer in Charge (MOC) of the National Leprosarium, met with Sister Edith in August 1920 to discuss future arrangements. Having worked with sisters in the care of leprosy patients in the Philippines, Denney had no difficulty in retaining the Daughters of Charity as the nursing staff when the federal government gained control of the home. Sister Edith asked the superior of the order how to negotiate the specifics of the new arrangement, intimating, "The way it stands now, I think they imagine it will continue the same as it is."[110] Other sisters remained less sanguine about the future and suggested that their position needed to be clarified. One sister informed the superior of the order that Sister Edith was not up to the task of negotiating the new contract, claiming "she is quite willing to turn everything over to the Doctor." While welcoming federal control and the concomitant lifting of responsibility for the entire administration of the facility, she argued that "the patients would profit by the retention of some of the rights or privileges the State accorded us."[111]

The Daughters of Charity ultimately conceded their recently acquired regulatory authority, however, to better ensure their ability to maintain and reinforce what they viewed as their more important roles as the physical caregivers and moral guardians of the patients. Although the U.S. government assumed administrative oversight for the institution when it became the U.S. National Leprosarium in 1921, the contract drawn up by Denney made clear that the sisters would remain a critical part of the personnel.[112] The six sisters working at the Louisiana Leper Home became classified as civil service employees. In addition to a salary, the government provided the sisters with quarters and laundry service and granted them permission to retain their private chapel.[113] They also composed the nursing staff, which allowed the sisters to maintain the kind of close daily interaction with patients they had experienced for a quarter of a century and to ensure that the moral code they had woven into the regulations overseeing patient behavior remained intact. In a letter to the archbishop, Sister Edith expressed her confidence that the Daughters of Charity could continue and even improve their ministry to leprosy patients under the new federal administration. Recognizing the superior resources and commitment of the U.S. government compared to that of Louisiana, she wrote, "With the larger financial aid thus secured and the prestige attached to works undertaken by the United States Government, we hope to make life much brighter for our charges."[114] Patients would continue to contend with the restrictions they had resented in the facility's days as the Louisiana Leper Home, but they would now have to direct their complaints not only to the sisters but also to a new administration of federal public health officials and physicians.

Conclusion

When the U.S. government established the national leprosarium at Carville in 1921, it built upon more than two decades of public health initiatives and leprosy care by state officials and the Daughters of Charity in Louisiana. Constructed in 1894 during a period when U.S. territorial expansion increased public anxiety about leprosy, the state opened the Louisiana Leper Home to contain and segregate what initially amounted to a tiny number of people with the disease. When its isolated setting and limited funding threatened the institution, the Daughters of Charity assumed administrative control over daily operations and the care of patients. Public familiarity with Father Damien in Moloka'i, as well as the sisters' tradition of health care in Louisiana, made the religious administration of a state institution for leprosy patients acceptable to state residents. While the sisters considered themselves experts in medical care and embraced scientific medicine, their religious mission of providing spiritual comfort and moral guidance to their patients became intricately intertwined with that care and shaped many of the regulations that continued to govern the institution even after it became a federal facility. Furthermore, the visible alliance the sisters forged between state and religious health workers also had the unfortunate side effect of buttressing the stigma attached to leprosy patients in the popular imagination, in which patients appeared as social outcasts, attended to only by those willing to face martyrdom.

Patients recognized and protested both how religious workers unintentionally revitalized the notion of leprosy as a disease of the "unclean" and how their moral discipline became institutionalized as public health policy in the facility. Patients mounted a consistent challenge to the authority of the sisters, and thereby to the authority of the state that imposed restrictions upon them as necessary to the protection of public health. While many patients appeared generally grateful for the care and assistance they received, differences over what constituted appropriate conduct for home residents frequently erupted. These challenges to authority reminded both the sisters and members of the Board of Control that they could not contain people with leprosy without some measure of consent on the patients' part, whether that consent was wrested from them by force or willingly granted.

This lesson would prove instrumental in the development of leprosy institutions in both Hawai'i and Louisiana. Health officials learned that patient cooperation was necessary to the success of their medical and public health initiatives, but racialized understandings of the majority native Hawaiian patients in the Moloka'i leprosy settlement and the majority white population in Louisiana would shape different public health policies in the two institutions. Despite the protests instigated by the Louisiana patients in the early 1900s, health administrators viewed them as more willing and able to comply with the medical discipline they saw as necessary to the workings of scientific medicine. Health officials had greater difficulty learning to negotiate with a largely Hawaiian population in developing a research center in the Moloka'i settlement.

CHAPTER FOUR

Institutionalizing American Leprosy

At the beginning of the twentieth century, the Hawaiian leprosy institutions at the Kalaupapa settlement on Moloka'i and the Kalihi station on O'ahu stood at the center of international debates regarding the treatment and research of the disease. At Kalaupapa in particular, health officials strove to create a state-of-the-art facility for investigating and applying Western medical techniques. The settlement's predominantly Hawaiian patients and their allies, however, organized to assert their right to participate in shaping treatment and experimentation. The contests that unfolded reveal the degree to which the definitions of appropriate care and necessary research could differ dramatically between patients and medical practitioners. When U.S. health officials established an experiment station at the settlement, patients refused to participate in its activities, forcing the facility to close in 1913. These responses to Western medicine compelled public health officials to reconsider their assumptions about who made the most reliable research subjects and what location fostered the best environment for medical investigations.

After watching the U.S. experimental station fail in Kalaupapa, federal public health officials turned their attention to the mainland facility at Carville, Louisiana. Experiences in Hawai'i still proved useful, as physicians and public health officials applied knowledge generated in the islands to the new national leprosarium. In Louisiana, they instituted bacteriological testing protocols, chaulmoogra oil treatments, and rigid regulations for stricter separation between medical personnel and patient living areas—all of which were earlier developed at Kalihi and Kalaupapa. Health officials also learned in Hawai'i that patient mobility and loose administrative oversight could result in patients having the autonomy to refuse medical treatment and experimentation. They thus designed a more structured campus layout and more comprehensive techniques to control patients at the U.S. National Leprosarium in Louisiana.

The interrelationship between the two institutions poses a challenge to traditional views of the colony as laboratory and of colonial subjects as passive research subjects. Physicians and administrators came to believe that the residents of the Louisiana facility would prove more amenable to stricter medical discipline than their Hawaiian counterparts. Racial and gendered assumptions regarding the behaviors of Hawaiians and Euroamericans, and of men and women, were grounded on an imperial foundation and resulted in two distinct sets of regulations concerning the management of patients. The institution at Carville complemented the colonial settlement at Kalaupapa as a site of investigation. When Hawaiian patients with leprosy actively drew upon political and social networks to question the efficacy of medical techniques and suggest alternatives, public health officials chose to interpret this as a sign of Hawaiians' failure to adapt to the rigors of modern Western medicine. Administrators looked instead to Carville's mainland patients as possessing a properly pliant attitude toward medical professionals.

The Politics of Leprosy: Patient Power and Political Strategy

Western health officials tightened surveillance over Hawaiian residents with leprosy after the United States incorporated the islands as a territorial possession in 1900.[1] They made the identification and incarceration of those suspected of having leprosy a top priority, instructing government physicians to inspect all "suspects" and deliver their names to local sheriffs or deputies for apprehension. In addition, doctors received instructions to inspect schools for evidence of any contagious or infectious diseases, including leprosy.[2] As surveillance intensified and became increasingly bureaucratized, health officials reassured the public that improved bacteriological testing guaranteed that only those people actually infected with the leprosy bacilli would be sent to Kalaupapa.[3] Such a pledge implicitly admitted what Hawaiians had long realized, that in the past doctors had mistakenly diagnosed people with the disease and sent them to the Moloka'i settlement for incarceration often lasting a lifetime. Members of the territorial Board of Health thus hoped to bolster their reputation among Hawaiians by emphasizing their command of medical technology. By tightening control over leprosy, public health officials sought to assert their authority to categorize and manage the island population.

Health officials sought to curtail contact between people with leprosy who lived at the Kalaupapa settlement and friends and relatives on the "outside."

Settlement administrators thought this intermingling posed a threat to public health, which they blamed on Hawaiians who lacked a proper fear of the disease. In an attempt to reinforce the idea that people with leprosy were dangerous contaminants who required rigid segregation from the healthy, officials worked to foreclose all personal contact between those with the disease and their visitors.[4] Of the eighty-eight people who received permission to visit Kalaupapa from July 1901 to December 1902, forty-nine had to "remain in corral," which meant that they had to stay within a fenced area that prevented them from physical contact with their loved ones confined at the settlement. Administrators expected that white visitors, such as religious missionaries and medical personnel, would naturally avoid close contact with settlement residents who had leprosy; they did not "remain in corral" when visiting.[5]

Euroamerican settlement administrators claimed that they bore the responsibility of caring for and uplifting Kalaupapa's residents, whom they portrayed as lacking the civilized virtues of sacrifice, discipline, and cooperation. Health officials in the early 1900s sought to impose stricter institutional discipline upon residents at Kalaupapa by adopting new regulations and enforcing existing ones more stringently. New restrictions included bans on the use of firearms and on the consumption of "spiritous liquors" by patients.[6] Resident Superintendent J. D. McVeigh cracked down on what he termed the "beer makers, drunkards and law breakers" soon after his appointment in 1902. Settlement residents found that violations of the law could now result in significant penalties. During his first year, McVeigh brought fourteen residents before a Moloka'i judge on charges of assault and battery; all were found guilty and received punishments that varied from fines of twenty-five dollars to imprisonment for two months in the settlement jail. Resident entrepreneurs convicted of either manufacturing or selling liquor received sizable fines of one hundred dollars, while three residents convicted of drunkenness received fines of two or three dollars. Other violations resulting in convictions included trespassing, disturbing the peace, larceny, leaving the settlement without a permit, violating Sunday Laws, and keeping a disorderly house. One woman charged with solicitation was "severely reprimanded and discharged," while a couple who pleaded guilty to the charge of fornication avoided punishment by agreeing to marry.[7]

Despite such cases of illicit patient behavior, the superintendent sought to portray the settlement to the public as a generally peaceful community filled with law-abiding citizens. In a 1904 report, McVeigh expressed doubt that other communities the size of Kalaupapa could match its record of orderliness, an achievement made all the more impressive by "the fact that our people are segregated from their families and friends."[8] Resident administrators such as McVeigh attempted in the early 1900s to convey to the Board of Health and the territorial legislature the sense that officials at Kalaupapa were effectively developing a malleable and appreciative patient body. The superintendent went out of his way to describe the "splendid good-feeling that exists among our people," exemplified by patient efforts to help each other. "Very little is now seen of the small 'clique-fights,' which have been the curse of this place in the past. . . . The people realize," McVeigh concluded, "that the Board of Health and the Superintendent are doing everything in their power to promote their comfort and welfare."[9]

McVeigh's depiction of a contented and grateful community notwithstanding, Hawaiian patients found much to criticize, and they challenged regulations they found restrictive by making use of their political clout. With the passage of the Organic Act in 1900, Hawaiians regained the right to vote for local representatives.[10] Unlike in Louisiana, patients in Kalaupapa did not lose this right upon entering the settlement. These residents used their voting power—201 of 311 eligible voters at Kalaupapa cast their ballots in the November 1900 election[11]—to lobby politicians in the territorial legislature. Territorial politicians who hoped to capture the votes of those living within the settlement, along with those of any friends and relatives those residents might influence, added Kalaupapa as a stop on their campaign trail. Though not allowed to enter the settlement without permits from the Board of Health, candidates could deliver their speeches from boats moored close to shore.[12] Residents of Kalaupapa knew that their disease had a high political profile, meaning their lives and concerns could generate public attention. As a result, Western public health officials discovered that what they believed to be straightforward medical questions reserved for medical professionals could become the subject of contentious political debates among doctors, patients, and community members.

When political candidates chose to visit the settlement and campaign for patients' votes, health officials objected to the disruption and public attention. Members of the Board of Health in 1904 protested that such "political agitation" negatively influenced the patients and administrators at Kalaupapa. The board attempted to thwart candidate visits, arguing that such practices would be unthinkable at other kinds of hospitals and institutions.[13] Board administrators and political candidates both realized, however, that patients at Kalaupapa occupied a unique position. While considered terminally ill, many were highly mobile and engaged in issues affecting their community. Most recognized that they would spend the rest of their lives at the settlement if existing policies continued, and they therefore felt they had a great deal at stake in political questions regarding their fate. Politicians also appreciated that the creation and maintenance of Kalaupapa was fraught with social controversy, and they attempted to elicit votes from patients and their families by promising that they would pay greater attention to their concerns than their opponents would.

The Board of Health could not prevent politicians from attempting to use the issue of leprosy to their political advantage, but it did successfully end candidate visits within the boundaries of Kalaupapa. Board members claimed that they based their decision to deny entry to politicians solely on "scientific and personal consideration for the patient, as well as protection of the public from infection." Politicians countered that the board used its permit-granting power not to protect patients or the public, but to keep out candidates critical of board actions. Nevertheless, a federal court in 1904 upheld the Board of Health's right to regulate who entered the settlement, effectively affirming the legal authority of board members to screen out visitors they found undesirable.[14]

Limiting contact with politicians, however, did not resolve other disputes within the settlement, particularly those concerning medical treatment. Officials such as Superintendent McVeigh had insisted that patients cheerfully deferred to territorial administrators, but in reality, residents did not automatically assume that Western medicine was benign or useful. This attitude frustrated Euroamerican doctors, who frequently attributed such skepticism to the ignorance of their non-Western charges. Patients' suspicion of Western medical practice, however, resulted not from a lack of knowledge of these techniques but from their familiarity with it. Clinical encounters often induced discomfort or pain, and some patients made connections between medical treatments and the onset of other physical ailments. For example, many residents balked at the use of a hypodermic needle to inject sodium cacodylate, one experimental and painful treatment attempted by resident physician W. J. Goodhue. An outbreak of "swollen head fever" (a complication of leprosy that caused painful inflammation of the glands in the head and face) followed this procedure and further confounded the experiment, as many patients drew a direct link between the outbreak of the disease and the uncomfortable treatments.[15]

Despite such patient aversion to certain medical practices, Goodhue insisted that Kalaupapa residents at the turn-of-the-century exhibited more openness to Western medicine and less reliance on traditional Hawaiian healing practices than they had in previous decades. He wrote that he had witnessed a "marked change . . . in the disposition of the native toward the medical and surgical treatment of his common ailments and intercurrent disease, which he does not neglect as he did before." Goodhue claimed that patients still called kahunas (Hawaiian healers) when they were ill, but they increasingly did so only "in deference to traditionary [sic] customs and usages." More remarkably, he found that patients consulted with kahunas "without discontinuing, or modifying, the more rational [Western] treatment."[16] While the resident physician viewed such actions as indicative of the residents' growing acceptance of Western medicine over traditional practices, he actually provided no evidence to suggest that Hawaiians viewed one approach as more effective than another. For many patients who availed themselves of treatment from territorial doctors and kahunas, the promise of a cure proved worth pursuing, regardless of its source.

In actuality, patients most readily submitted to experimental treatments by physicians such as Goodhue when they lived within carefully circumscribed environments and had little choice in the matter. Under such conditions, control provided an adequate substitute for cooperation, as it allowed Goodhue and other medical personnel to pursue their work among patients they considered properly pliant. At the Bishop Home in Kalaupapa, for example, the Sisters of Mercy closely scrutinized the activities of all the women under their care. In this environment, Goodhue rhapsodized, "results could be watched, and diet, administration, cleanliness and the necessary attention to the elimination through the various emunctories would be guaranteed by the unceasing care and conscientious attendance of the Sister nurse."[17] Residents in the Bishop Home lived under stricter regulations than those who occupied individual cottages in the settlement. Women and girls generally lived at the home when they had no other settlement relatives or friends to support them, and they were expected to defer to the sisters who served as both nurses and administrators within this facility. The institution imposed this deference on its residents, but doctors portrayed it as a sign that patients were beginning to accept Western medical models of treatment.

Though public health administrators touted the importance of cooperation between patients and doctors in the quest to identify new treatments leading to a cure, most offerings at Kalaupapa were purely symptomatic. Cold sponge baths, antiseptic dressing of lesions, and the administration of "some appropriate tonic to sustain the vital powers" proved the most frequently administered treatments. Still, Goodhue contended that the restrictive territorial leprosy policy of segregation helped those sent to Kalaupapa, claiming that 98 percent of new residents showed improvement. Better hygienic conditions and a good climate, he argued, combined with "complete relief from anxiety and self-imposed restraint of the suspect at large," brought tangible health benefits to those suffering from the disease. Goodhue also claimed that the territorial administration provided high quality beef, salmon, and pa'i'ai rations and took steps to ensure that all patients received equitable allotments, an argument designed to offset criticisms about the kinds of foods provided to patients.[18]

Goodhue attempted to portray the relationship between patients and physicians positively, but some residents expressed considerable distrust of medical professionals, whom they viewed as potentially deadly. One patient alerted Board of Health president S. E. Pinkham that several Kalaupapa residents intended to write their legislators to complain about Dr. H. T. Hollman, an assistant physician, and to demand his removal.[19] Residents had concluded that Hollman was a bad doctor, going so far as to suggest that he brought about the untimely deaths of those unfortunate enough to receive his ministrations. In one case, Hollman prescribed treatments for a patient fully capable of moving about; soon after, they contended, this patient was "confined to bed and death follow[ed]." The patient reporting on these complaints professed to support Hollman, but he also mentioned that his friends warned him that writing to Pinkham might anger the resident doctors and cause them to poison him, "as has happened before."[20] The letter revealed how fear of Western physicians affected even some of those residents who claimed to support these doctors.

Board president Pinkham responded to this complaint and took the opportunity to convince at least one Hawaiian resident of Kalaupapa to trust in the superiority and generosity of American medical practitioners. He sought both to encourage such reports of patient discontent to the Board of Health and to provide a lesson on the impartiality of Western medicine. Pinkham assured the patient that no harm would befall him for his efforts, claiming that "physicians educated in the medical colleges of the United States and Europe are taught to do all the good they can for everybody whether they like them or not." He contrasted this tenet with that of Hawaiian medical practitioners, suggesting "it has been stated that kahunas have in past times revenged themselves on those they dislike." Driving home the point that Hawaiians were slow to recognize how Western medicine drew on beneficent scientific principles rather than potentially vengeful superstition, Pinkham explained, "The Hawaiian people have not yet got over their old ideas and think white doctors act the same as the old kahunas did." He further instructed that a wise patient "follows the advice of his physicians and does not attempt to dictate with his uneducated and inexperienced mind and will."[21] The letter exemplifies territorial officials' understanding of medicine and patient relations: Hawaiians could raise questions, but ultimately they should defer to Euroamerican directives and trust in the inherent superiority of Western practices over indigenous ones.

The J. Lor Wallach Case

Despite confident administrative assertions about patient acceptance of Western authority, Hawaiians continually pursued their own treatment agendas. Willing to entertain almost any type of therapy that seemed to offer the strong possibility of a cure, patients mobilized in 1907 to bring J. Lor Wallach, a self-proclaimed South Asian herbalist with a cure for leprosy, to the islands. Administrators balked at the suggestion that Wallach be allowed to treat patients at the settlement, arguing that he failed to meet the criteria established by the territorial Board of Health for medical practitioners. Patients then turned to sympathetic leaders in the territorial legislature to force the administration's hand. The Wallach incident highlighted the failure of health officials to create a submissive patient community willing to defer to Western medical authority.

Western health administrators found it difficult to contain the political activism of patients, whose mobilization in the Wallach case threatened their authority to run the facility and regulate courses of treatment. Publicizing himself as an "Indian Herbist [sic] and Manufacturer of the Famous Indian Remedies," Wallach had distributed handbills throughout Honolulu that promoted the curative powers of his medicines. In an advertisement placed in the 9 August 1906 *Evening Bulletin*, Wallach declared, "I cure leprosy," and offered $100 to anyone who brought him a case of "leper spots, leper sores, leper swelling, or scale or loss of feeling in flesh caused by leprosy . . . which my Indian Remedies can not absolutely cure in from 4 to 6 months." He further boasted that he had "cured cases of 30 years' standing" and promised strict confidentiality.[22] Such pronouncements caught the attention of people with leprosy, along with their friends and relatives, who urged the Board of Health to permit Wallach to treat patients in the territory. A petition with 500 names of "American citizens of the Island and County of Oahu" requesting that Lor Wallach treat people with the disease at the Kalihi Receiving Station in Honolulu reached the board in April 1907.

The petition, written in both English and Hawaiian, further asked that the Indian herbalist be allowed to care for patients of his choosing, suggesting that patients from Kalaupapa could be moved to Honolulu for treatment if he deemed it appropriate.[23] In support of this public petition, both houses of the territorial legislature requested that the Board of Health permit Wallach to treat patients at Kalihi.

By fighting for the Indian herbalist, Hawaiian residents challenged the board's authority to determine who could practice medicine within Hawai'i generally and at the leprosy institutions of Kalihi and Kalaupapa specifically. The incident emerged in the wake of a failed effort by several Hawaiian territorial legislators to amend public health laws in a way that would have enabled nonlicensed healers to practice in the territory.[24] Members of the Board of Health had helped defeat this legislation, defending their medical monopoly on the grounds that they held superior knowledge regarding the ability to recognize and treat contagious disease. They explained that while a patient might "contend it is his right to employ an intangible practitioner, possessed of an intangible education and intangible experience, to make an intangible diagnosis and attempt an intangible cure, the Board of Health holds a different opinion." As a matter of public safety, they explained, the board had the obligation to regulate those who wished to treat the sick. Moreover, they accused anyone "of high or low degree, who, on sentiment, theory or intangible belief, seeks to weaken the laws, and thereby the vigilance and authority of the Board of Health," of seeking "to weaken every sound interest pertaining to the Territory of Hawaii."[25] Public health officials asserted that proper scientific training and medical experience was necessary to combat disease and protect the economic well-being of the islands.

Although these public health officials believed they had the final word in whether to accept or reject Wallach, politicians and patients challenged their authority. The Board of Health refused to accept Wallach as a credible medical practitioner and denied the petition in April 1907. The board members sparked further dissent by informing the legislature they could not honor its request. Board president Pinkham pointed out that Wallach offered no medical qualifications, nor could he explain "by what means, tangible or intangible, such cure can be effected." Concluding that Wallach was therefore not "a fit and proper person to trust with the treatment of any disease, leprosy or otherwise, of wards of the Territory," he and his fellow board members denied the request.[26] Some members of the legislature condemned the Board of Health for its "insulting and disrespectful" refusal. The territorial House and Senate passed a resolution urging the board to recon-sider. Their actions testified to the political strength of Kalaupapa residents and reflected a growing commitment among Hawaiians and some white settlers to consider any type of remedy that might offer a cure for a disease that continued to confound the Western medical community. The legislative resolution described the board's action as "unjustifiable, arbitrary and des-potic, uncharitable, and in utter and merciless disregard of the desire of those unfortunate persons to receive such treatment, and their hope thereby to find for themselves and for those likewise afflicted a cure for the afore-said disease."[27]

Residents of Kalaupapa, for their part, tried to gain access to Wallach and his cures by incorporating them into the existing medical system. They at-tempted to make his treatment more palatable to Board of Health members by suggesting that Wallach's remedies be administered under the watchful gaze of resident physician Goodhue. Board president Pinkham received a letter signed by a "Committee of Seven" whose members had been charged by the residents of Kalaupapa to speak on their behalf. These seven patients, undeterred by Wallach's lack of a medical license, pronounced themselves willing to receive the proposed treatment. They suggested that his remedy be given a "fair trial" of six months, during which time Goodhue could oversee the dosages and conclude whether or not the medicines had any effect. Reminding Pinkham that the territorial Western medical establishment, for all of its certifications and laws, had provided no useful alternative to Wal-lach's South Asian treatment, the letter stated, "Dr. Goodhue does his best for us, many a life he has saved, many a sufferer he has relieved, but he tells us that he is sorry because he cannot find a cure for us." All that the patients wanted, these seven insisted, was a proper trial for Wallach's treatment.[28]

To allow both sides the opportunity to debate the merits of their position publicly, Hawaiian territorial governor Walter F. Frear held hearings to con-sider the petition of Lor Wallach to treat the disease. Demonstrating the degree to which the case had become a political matter, Charles Notely, self-proclaimed leader of the Home Rule Party, spoke on behalf of Wallach and efforts to allow him to administer his medicines. Notely and his party stood for the right of native Hawaiians to govern the territory; they took particular interest in the predominantly Hawaiian residents at Kalaupapa. In the hear-ings, Wallach decried the tensions between doctors and patients, and he expressed doubts that the board and its doctors would provide him a fair hearing. He also defended himself against charges of fraud and attempted to distinguish himself from hucksters by pointing out that he did not accept money for his cures. Wallach also insisted that he used only organic materials, including nothing that could be poisonous to his patients.[29] Pinkham, however, remained unconvinced, contending that in failing to reveal the exact contents of his treatments, in treating people without a license, and in failing to produce anyone who had actually benefited from his treatment, Wallach had demonstrated himself to be a fraud.[30]

This debate over what constituted legitimate medical practice in Hawaiʻi occurred as the American Medical Association sought to strengthen its authority on the mainland by establishing strict regulations against medical fraud. The AMA proved largely successful in its efforts to eliminate patent medicines and to criminalize the individuals who promoted them within the mainland United States, in part by finding support among muckraking journalists and Progressive legislators.[31] The Hawaiian context proved more complicated. Territorial health officials might have viewed Wallach as an obvious huckster, but Western physicians lacked the cultural authority and professional dominance necessary to convince legislators and patients to accept their medical knowledge as superior. Indeed, at a time when Western physicians still commonly administered a South Asian remedy—chaulmoogra oil—as a treatment for leprosy, they faced a difficult battle in persuading people to accept their contention that an Indian herbalist was inferior to American doctors.

Kalaupapa residents remained firm in their insistence that the board allow them access to Wallach's treatments. An October 1907 petition signed by 527 settlement residents requested that the board either allow Wallach to treat patients within Kalaupapa or let him select fifteen cases to receive treatment in Honolulu.[32] The letter writers conceded that the "Honorable Board has the discretionary power to permit any person whether . . . a regular licensed physician or not, to engage in the treatment of lepers or of persons supposed to have leprosy." Since Wallach had testified to the veracity of his claim of cure, however, the petitioners requested that the board accept his sworn statement and allow him to practice his treatment. Home Rule leader Notely, along with fellow legislator Joseph K. Naukana, forwarded the petition to the board.[33]

In the midst of the furor surrounding the Wallach affair, Pinkham published an illustrated pamphlet on the history and workings of Kalaupapa that sought to defend the position of the Board of Health. Ostensibly created to inform interested parties "both at home and abroad" about the settlement, the publication devoted considerable space to justifying the board's authority over territorial leprosy policy, particularly the policy of segregation, and its policing of nonprofessionals claiming to offer cures. Pinkham criticized those who believed in the promises of men such as Wallach and those who denounced the board for refusing to give pseudo-physicians (as he saw them) the opportunity to demonstrate the capability of their medicines. He explained that people claiming to have discovered a cure for leprosy appeared often, and some of them were "reputable scientific men." Pinkham insisted that the board had to proceed cautiously to ensure the safety of the patients in its care. The board would be sure to make "any reliable discovery" known, he assured his readers. Taking more explicit aim at those involved in the Wallach incident, Pinkham wrote, "There is a class of fakirs who are trying to make money by claiming they have secret remedies for the disease." He explained that the board customarily requested references and treatment details from such individuals. When such individuals refused to comply, Pinkham explained that he and his fellow medical administrators "safely concluded they are adventurers seeking only to take a chance at making money."[34]

Politicians in the legislature, however, saw Kalaupapa residents as voters with rights rather than simply patients under the jurisdiction of the Board of Health. Several legislators again asked board members in October 1907 to allow Wallach to treat three to five people from Kalaupapa at the Kalihi Receiving Station and to provide him with food and accommodation for the six months required for his experiment. The members of the territorial congress pointed out that "from time immemorial Leprosy has been recognized as one, if not the greatest, ill flesh is heir to," and they reminded the board that any effort to try to alleviate such an ill would be warmly received by the voting public. Senators and representatives pointed out that Wallach's claims had convinced a number of people and that "a great deal of dissatisfaction" would ensue "if . . . Wallach is not permitted to have an opportunity to demonstrate what he and his so-called cure can do." Perhaps trying to indicate to the board the political benefits of allowing Wallach to attempt his cure, the legislators noted that "any step which your Honorable Body can take to alleviate, if not cure, the said disease with which about a thousand of friends, relatives, and acquaintances are alleged to be afflicted . . . would be an act of humanity."[35] By emphasizing leprosy's status as a stigmatized disease with no known cure, legislators indicated that it would be difficult to convince a stricken community that it was not worth pursuing all treatment options.

Both supporters and detractors of Wallach invoked claims about honor and healing experience to bolster their position. Euroamerican health officials and physicians defended their honor as men of education and good sense who protected the public good when they refused Wallach. Pinkham explained to patients that "it is not in my power to induce members of the board to throw away their judgment and manhood on demands based on the assertions of a man who had disclosed such a lack of character as . . . Lor Wallach."[36] At the same time, board members felt comfortable dismissing Wallach as a quack based on his lack of medical licensing and training, as well as his inability to produce relevant medical research indicating the healing properties of his medicines. Politicians who supported Wallach, along with the Kalaupapa residents who sought his alleged cure, saw no reason to disallow his experiments on such criteria. For them, his word and his willingness to attempt the cure provided sufficient reason to proceed. Patients presented yet another petition in support of Wallach to the board in November 1907; this one highlighted the personal testimony of several friends of Kalaupapa residents who vouched for the effectiveness of Wallach's treatments. The patient committee considered this example of the community's trust as a sound basis on which to build a case for Wallach's credibility: "Whatever may be the opinion of others as to the ability and character of J. Lor Wallach, we cannot but believe our friends have told us the truth concerning these cures, as it would be a great crime to deceive us."[37]

This final statement seemed to impress upon Pinkham the firm resolve of the patients, as he worked to devise a compromise solution that would grant Wallach permission to treat some people with leprosy. The debate over Wallach also revealed the degree to which Euroamerican health officials and Western administrators more generally had failed to win the faith of their constituents in Kalihi and Kalaupapa. Wallach's actions suggest that he was every bit the charlatan medical officials thought him to be: he provided no evidence of individuals cured by his medicines, he refused to disclose the composition of his treatments, and he offered no substantive explanation of how his treatment worked. Still, the board was hard pressed to explain to patients how Wallach's proposed treatment differed in nature from any of the failed cures attempted by Western medical practitioners. Efforts directed at preventing the Indian herbalist from even attempting his cure gave the appearance that Euroamerican administrators would try to prohibit any course of action that might grant Kalaupapa residents eventual freedom. It was perhaps this awareness that ultimately led Pinkham to issue a statement that granted the patients' request while maintaining the Board of Health's position that Wallach was a fraud. The board president declared Wallach to be "juggling with the political schemes of certain politicians, . . . imposing on the credulity of Hawaiians, . . . [and] extracting such sums of money as he can from Hawaiians." He concluded that the herbalist would "at no distant day unmask himself and expose his own chicanery."[38] Believing that the residents would never recognize Wallach for what he was unless they learned from firsthand experience, the board granted the petition. Members agreed to let twelve people with leprosy journey from Kalaupapa to receive Wallach's treatment at the Kalihi Receiving Station.[39]

Residents at Kalaupapa, however, never received the opportunity to try Wallach's medicines. Pinkham informed them, through the patient-appointed Committee of Seven, that Wallach had refused in early 1908 to agree to the "Terms and Conditions" established by both the board and the patients. Wallach would therefore not be allowed to treat anyone with leprosy. In words perhaps more hopeful than factual, the board president stated, "The Board of Health considers the matter as forever terminated and dismissed."[40] The members of the Committee of Seven responded in kind, thanking the Board of Health for its efforts and expressing "their feeling of regret to realize that the hope which existed within us and the 527 petitioners should thus be extinguished."[41] Wallach's actions were further circumscribed after he fell under charges of fraud later that year.[42]

The conclusion of the Wallach affair did not end patient challenges to the authority of the territorial Board of Health. Having shown itself willing to question the board's authority on questions of treatment, the Committee of Seven further determined to challenge Pinkham and the board on the issue of segregation. Territorial laws regarding leprosy clearly established the power of the Board of Health to segregate any person whom an authorized physician had determined to have the disease and to be capable of spreading it.[43] Pinkham could point to the law to support his position, but such power did not translate into acceptance from the Hawaiian population. At a general meeting at the settlement on 11 April 1908, Hawaiian residents objected to the potential reappointment of Pinkham as president of the Board of Health, terming him "a political trickster." His actions regarding the Wallach case convinced many of them that he did not "want to lessen the number of lepers at the Settlement, so as to insure a large appropriation, and we Hawaiians as a class to form the base of supply for his unfortunate victims." Patients suggested that the Hawaiian residents of the islands paid considerable taxes to support the settlement, which they believed to be both unnecessary and the cause of great suffering to families whose members were separated against their will. Ultimately, they requested that Pinkham not be reappointed unless he pledged to "allow a free and open trial of the Wallach remedy at the Settlement," so that both the petitioners and the public at large could be convinced that "the utmost has been done to relieve them without regard to any objections of scientific isms or fine-spun theories."[44] Pinkham had the board and the law on his side, but he had lost the respect and support of Kalaupapa's residents, and he resigned his post soon after the meeting.[45]

The Rise and Fall of the U.S. Experiment Station

As Hawaiians with leprosy learned to exercise their political clout to challenge territorial officials over questions of treatment, U.S. medical officials worked toward establishing their own experimental medical facility within Kalaupapa. In contrast to their objections to J. Lor Wallach, Board of Health members gave full support and assistance to the U.S. Public Health Service when it made plans to conduct research on leprosy and to develop experimental treatments at the Hawaiian settlement. In 1908, the *Hawaiian Gazette* heralded the coming construction of a new federal Leprosy Investigation Station on Moloka'i as a demonstration that "treatment is to be considered of more importance than segregation, and that segregation is to be incidental only to treatment, an almost complete reversal of the policy which has been in force in these Islands for the past forty-three years."[46] This perceived shift in position partly reflected a philosophy that many settlement residents had long encouraged board members to adopt: namely, placing a higher priority on the treatment of patients than on their segregation. Treatment required a segregated population base, however, and it would be firmly grounded in a sense of Western scientific superiority that allowed little place for Hawaiian contributions or debate. In fact, territorial officials hoped they could use the new facility to quash a local political drive to end the practice of sending patients to the settlement on Moloka'i.[47] The new investigation station would become a miniature colonial outpost within the settlement.

The plan to allow national medical officials into the settlement had its roots in the territory's 1904 request for additional federal funding. Members of the U.S. Congress had proven reluctant to assume primary responsibility for the care of Hawaiians with the disease, but they did appropriate $100,000 in 1905 for the construction of a U.S. Public Health Service hospital station and laboratory in Hawai'i to study leprosy.[48] The territorial legislature agreed to give the federal government one square mile within the Moloka'i settlement for this facility. A committee of U.S. public health officials selected a site within the Kalawao portion of the settlement, near the religious-run Baldwin Home and Catholic Church but removed from the more densely settled and more autonomous patient community on the western portion of the peninsula. The U.S. Public Health Service appointed Dr. Walter R. Brinckerhoff to direct the new laboratory when it opened and Frank L. Gibson, a public health service pharmacist, to serve as the on-site equipment manager and administrative officer.[49] Although territorial government officials welcomed this planned facility as helpful to their broader effort to eradicate the disease from the islands, Kalaupapa residents worried that the federal government viewed this Hawaiian settlement as a useful laboratory with the patients as the experimental subjects.

The actions of the U.S. Public Health Service did nothing to alter residents' distrust of the new facility. Patients discovered that the new institution would force some of them to relocate their homes when Brinckerhoff announced that all people living on the newly designated federal land had to vacate it before 31 July 1906.[50] The bulk of the construction at the new medical complex, however, occurred largely in isolation from the rest of the Kalaupapa community. Indeed, the siting and design of the institution emphasized its removal from the broader settlement and established clear divisions among the staff residences, the administrative offices and research space, and the hospital.[51] Historian A. O. Bushnell described the buildings as "bureaucratic-baroque": large structures with high ceilings and wide porches supported by slender pillars, "a mainlander's idea of a southern planter's mansion transplanted to the sunny, languid tropics." A double fence surrounded the compound, which was declared off-limits to all settlement residents, except those who agreed to accept treatment in the forty-bed hospital.[52] Although residents observed the construction of the federal facility with curiosity, it was not designed to encourage their participation in its functions or to make them feel welcome.

The U.S. Public Health Service designed the new laboratory and hospital to be the most modern and well-equipped facility for the study of leprosy in the world, but its location hampered this mission even as it highlighted the colonialist underpinnings of the enterprise. The practically inaccessible Moloka'i settlement on the Kalaupapa peninsula may have been better than the Kalihi Receiving Station in Honolulu for containing people with leprosy, but it was also difficult to import construction materials, livestock, and laboratory instruments to the site. Every item needed to be shipped by steamer to the island, where it was floated ashore or transported by small craft to the peninsula's landing or shipped down the pali trail by mule.[53] Emma Warren Gibson, who accompanied her husband in his on-site administrative duties, related that "Uncle Sam furnished us with the best of everything," from fine linen to electric lights to a staff of thirty-two Chinese workers.[54] The government sought to supply its personnel with every modern convenience from the mainland while protecting them from the surrounding residents and their culture.

Fears of the disease and of settlement residents themselves further constrained open relations between medical administrators and patients, highlighting the colonial nature of the experiment station. The site building contractor brought Emma Gibson a pistol and trained her how to shoot, believing she might need it to defend herself until the double fence surrounding the station was completed. Her presence as the lone white woman at the settlement, he feared, made her vulnerable to the supposed licentiousness of Hawaiian men with leprosy, "as sufferers ravaged by the disease were not always entirely accountable for their acts."[55] Such fears reflected mainland myths of racialized men of color raping white women, but they also evoked colonialist concerns of interracial mixing.[56] The isolated setting of Kalaupapa further heightened white colonial anxieties, as Hawaiian men with leprosy posed the threat of both racial and medical contamination. The notion that a healthy white woman might be ravaged by a diseased Hawaiian man proved particularly repulsive to American health officials and perhaps provided another motivation for the broader policy of strict segregation within the settlement.

Federal health officials worked to establish clear boundaries between the private lives of U.S. personnel and Hawaiian patients even as they found it necessary to have both groups work together within the settlement to best learn about the disease. Emma Gibson described the mission of the federal facility as one of "discovering a cure for one of the most dreadful diseases with which mankind has been afflicted," but it was a mission that officials would conduct while having as little contact as possible with the residents of the settlement.[57] Though "choked with pity" when patients came to serenade her at Christmas, Gibson avoided any contact with the residents, taking care not even to look directly at the "bad cases."[58] Such an attitude stood in marked contrast to the religious personnel who regularly worked among and associated with the residents. Tellingly, when Dr. Donald H. Currie officially opened the new federal facility at Kalawao on 24 December 1909, he invited only the staff and their families to a small ceremony. Residents of

Kalaupapa had to observe the flag-raising ceremony from a spot beyond the double fences.[59]

To the surprise of federal health officials, the facility failed to attract a sufficient number of patients necessary to conduct proper experiments on leprosy. Administrators agreed only to take volunteers, in part to offset the Hawaiian perception that U.S. officials planned to use Kalaupapa residents as hapless guinea pigs. Only nine people with leprosy submitted themselves for treatment at the research station. The officials praised the merits of the facility, including the fact that each patient could have his or her own room in the new hospital. They failed to understand how the requirement that patients had to remain within the institution during experiments could hardly be welcomed by residents accustomed to pursuing their own independent lives within the broader confines of the settlement. As Emma Gibson recalled, "Unused as they were to the restrictions of hospital life, they had little liking for it and proved uncooperative. They rebelled against the rigor of the treatments and the confinement of living within the grounds after the unlimited freedom offered at the Settlement."[60] Rather than consider an alternative to their residency requirement, such as working with patients to design an experimental regime that would allow them to have a more independent lifestyle, federal officials decided to close the Kalawao station. After the final patient left and the facility closed in 1913, only four years after it had opened, health officials in Washington ended scientific work at the settlement and moved all research to Kalihi. Gibson expressed the general sentiment of Euroamerican officials, who placed blame for the failure of the facility squarely upon the Hawaiians. "After all the expense and trouble of building and equipping these buildings, it was a sad blow that human nature, as shown in the happy-go-lucky Hawaiians, could make or break a human project."[61] Between their enthusiasm for Wallach and their suspicion of the Kalawao facility, Hawaiians demonstrated themselves to be poor patients in the eyes of territorial and federal health officials.

The actions of Kalaupapa's residents do not support the contention that they disavowed all Western medicine, however, or that they lacked the willingness to enter a medical institution and submit to treatment. From June 1909 to June 1910, the resident physician at the Moloka'i settlement reported 17,882 medical and surgical cases treated at the Kalaupapa dispensary, including 490 operations.[62] The residents' refusal to participate in the research conducted at the U.S. Kalawao investigation station suggests instead a deeper distrust of experiments that took place behind tall fences, required extended stays, and limited visits from friends and family. Reports that Euroamerican scientists intended to use patients as research animals to benefit federal careers and national interests rather than to help Hawaiians with leprosy increased the skepticism of some settlement residents. The behavior of federal officials themselves proved most damaging to their own cause. Sturdy barriers between the quarters of medical and administrative personnel and those of patients; the double fences that divided the station from the rest of the settlement; and limited social contact with residents exacerbated poor relations and perpetuated a vision of Western medical professionals as interlopers who were autocratic and indifferent to the needs of Hawaiians.[63]

Jerrold M. Michael views the closing of the U.S. investigation station at Kalawao as an "opportunity lost" for a potential early discovery of an effective leprosy treatment. He contends that an "emphasis on technology without a concomitant emphasis on the important human dynamics of communication, patient education, and behavior change led to wasted resources and inadequate treatment." This conclusion, however, still interprets the incident as a case of white scientists failing to properly explain the merits of Western medicine to an indigenous population. Michael treats the federal annexation of the Hawaiian Islands and U.S. public health officials' annexation of the Kalawao lands as causing an "overlay of resentment" in "many islanders," suggesting that better communication between Euroamerican scientists and Kalaupapa residents could have dispelled such misunderstandings.[64] This reading ignores the very real colonialist thread that connected federal health policy to the U.S. acquisition of the islands, and it also slights the degree to which Hawaiians properly understood the U.S. Kalawao station's mission as a nationalist and colonial enterprise that had little to do with their concerns.

The remains of the station stood idle for many years, a testament to federal health officials' indecision regarding the best approach to the medical investigation of leprosy. Officially, the U.S. Public Health Service moved its research facilities to the more comfortable and accessible Kalihi Receiving Station on Oʻahu, where Brinckerhoff had initially worked while the Kalawao complex was under construction. Federal officials occasionally sent foraging crews to bring back equipment from the Kalawao site. The facility that both the federal and territorial governments had hoped would set a world standard for leprosy research became a decaying embarrassment that symbolized the failure of Western medical practitioners to overcome the mistrust they had engendered among Hawaiians and other island residents with leprosy. After years of abandonment, a bill authorizing the transfer of the federal land at Kalawao back to the territory of Hawai'i came before Congress in 1922. In defending the bill, Representative Charles Forrest Curry of California blamed the siting of the facility, rather than poor relations with Kalaupapa's residents, for the closing of the station. He explained that officials learned after its construction that "it was not in the proper location, the climate was bad, the winds were high, and it was not a good place for lepers to be treated in a sanitarium." Curry further stated that the "Molokai leper settlement is in the neighborhood of this tract of land," as if the location of a site for the study of leprosy close to a place where people with leprosy lived might undermine research efforts. He concluded his remarks by explaining that the site could no longer serve any use to the government as the remains were "contaminated by being inhabited by lepers."[65] The House and Senate both approved the bill without amendment, and President Warren G. Harding signed it into law in September 1922.[66]

Constructing a Modern Leprosarium on the Mainland

As federal health officials dismantled operations at the failed investigation station on Moloka'i, the U.S. Public Health Service quietly shifted its attention to the new leprosy hospital taking shape in Carville, Louisiana. The government had provided funds in Hawai'i primarily for scientific research rather than patient care, believing the treatment of patients in the islands to be a territorial rather than a national concern. On the mainland, however, politicians and health officials sought to upgrade the facilities at the U.S. National Leprosarium in the 1920s to provide better treatment for patients. Initial debates over the future of the Carville facility did not include proposals for an experimental laboratory, though health officials and physicians gradually came to appreciate the research potential both of the facility and of its patients.

Members of Congress used the rhetoric of both fear and national pride to generate support for appropriations that would increase the capacity of the U.S. National Leprosarium. In November 1921, Representative James O'Connor of Louisiana raised the disturbing possibility that 150 people with leprosy would roam about the United States unless the national facility could provide the necessary housing to accommodate them. He accused the U.S. government of being "so frugal, so economical, so cheap and parsimonious, niggardly, and miserly" that it failed to provide shelter for "those that are, after all, however penalized by nature . . . our blood, our kith, and our kin . . . American men and women . . . whose path we have at least once crossed." He reminded members of Congress that the U.S. government had assumed responsibility for the Carville institution the previous spring, but it had not provided the means to transform it into a proper medical facility. He concluded, "In its present state [it] is no credit to the United States of America."[67] Congress earmarked $80,000 in the U.S. Public Health Service budget for the U.S. National Leprosarium, but others continued to press for a bill that would authorize the distribution of funds directly to the site.

Representative Richard Elliott in 1923 again conjured visions of homeless leprosy victims tramping across America to win support for new construction at Carville. Perpetuating the idea that the current conditions at the national leprosarium left people with leprosy wandering in the streets, Elliott claimed that as many as 1,000 such individuals lived outside the bounds of the institution, with some "running around over the country . . . [a] short time ago they found one running an elevator in New York City." Elliott also reminded members of Congress of the earlier sojourn to Washington by patient John Early and concluded, "The fact is that there is not anybody in this country who wants to associate for one minute with a leper, and if you let the information get out in a community that a leper is loose . . . it would start more of a commotion than if you were to start a smallpox scare."[68] Elliott supported an increase in funding to make the U.S. National Leprosarium, in the words of Treasury Secretary Andrew Mellon, "a modern plant for the care of persons suffering from leprosy." Mellon estimated that it would cost $650,000 to upgrade the facility, which would entail increased bed capacity, "first-class professional facilities" for leprosy treatment, recreational facilities, an updated kitchen and dining halls, and a modernized power plant. More pointedly, Mellon noted that Congress had created the national leprosarium to segregate and care for all people with leprosy in the United States and that such a purpose could not be achieved when applicants seeking to enter the facility were turned away because there was no room.[69]

One reason that these early 1920s debates did not discuss the possibility of making Carville a research center was that members of Congress themselves did not hold out much hope for the discovery of a cure for leprosy. When asked if the development of a cure was possible, for example, Elliott discounted it. "The whole idea seems to be that if you can get them all segregated into one spot and keep them there until they die the disease will die with them," he explained. Representative Fritz Lanham of Texas hastened to put a more charitable spin on the institutional enterprise, asserting that doctors had made some progress in treating leprosy. He added that "by proper diet, proper sanitation, [and a] proper environment that makes for a cheerful mood[,] much may be accomplished for these people." Lanham contended that under such conditions, some patients might even be "cured," by which he meant that the leprosy bacillus would be "so arrested that it is safe for the patients to be returned to their normal conditions of life and to mix and mingle with their friends and those who are dear to them."[70] Despite this occasional optimism, many members supported the renovation of the national facility because it would remove people with a seemingly incurable and communicable disease from their districts. The measure for additional funds passed.[71]

As Congress debated how much financial support it would provide a national leprosy institution, health officials and medical practitioners discussed what form such a facility would take. Hopes that the U.S. Public Health Service would bring immediate, tangible, and beneficial improvements to Carville proved overly optimistic, as the new administrators had not even been aware of the moment in 1921 when a congressional mandate had given them the leadership of what formerly stood as the Louisiana Leper Home. Sister Edith, the Daughter of Charity who served as the final superintendent of the institution during its state-administered years, notified Louisiana officials in February 1921, "It will no doubt surprise you as it surprised all of us—including Major Denney—to know that the Home passed into the hands of the Federal Government on the third of January." Indeed, U.S. Public Health Service physician Oswald E. Denney learned that he was the superintendent of the facility "only . . . through a casual allusion made to it in an official communication."[72] Officials first raised the U.S. flag over the institution on 1 February 1921, thereby making the institution a U.S. Public Health Service facility, henceforth to be identified as U.S. Marine Hospital No. 66.

Patients who had bristled under the regulations instituted at the Louisiana home by the Daughters of Charity were disappointed when the U.S. Public Health Service adopted and codified these same restrictions by the end of the year. Some patients had hoped that the federal acquisition of the institution might curtail the type of discipline enforced by the sisters, and Denney's early decisions to remove a fence dividing men from women and to hold a dance allowing fraternization between the sexes bolstered their expectations.[73] When Denney published "Regulations for the Apprehension, Detention, Treatment, and Release of Lepers," however, he invoked the language of incarceration and reinforced the idea that the facility served first as a place of segregation and containment and only secondarily as one of care. The new superintendent reiterated in the new list the most contested regulations under the sisters, including the ban on any patient excursions beyond the confines of the institutional grounds and restrictions on inter-actions between male and female patients.[74]

Officials expected mainland patients would be more willing than Hawai-ians to submit themselves to medical discipline, and they enforced contain-ment and rules governing patient conduct strictly. Specifically, patients in Louisiana had to submit to a routine system of medical surveillance. All people with leprosy at Carville were required to undergo clinical examina-tions and to accept physician-prescribed treatment. Under a standardized protocol for possible discharge from the institution, each patient had to have an annual bacterioscopic examination. If such an exam revealed no trace of the leprosy bacillus, the patient would be kept under observation for an additional six months, submitting to monthly tests throughout this period. If the tests remained negative, the patient would move to "that portion of the reservation set aside for special observation purposes" for another year of monthly examinations. After such a year of "special observation and isola-tion," if the patient showed no signs of the disease, a panel of three medical officers would convene for a final analysis. At that point, the panel could "recommend the discharge of the patient on probation as either 'cured,' 'arrested,' or 'latent,' and 'no longer a menace of the public health.' "[75] Many patients willingly accepted regular medical surveillance as part of the terms that could lead to a possible discharge. The annual examination came to be viewed as a potential means of release from the institution. Some patients, however, refused to accept that measuring the mere presence of bacilli could serve as a suitable measure for determining whether they constituted a true "menace" to the public.[76] Patients at Kalaupapa did not have to submit to such annual exams, but this also decreased the already slight possibility that they might someday win release from the facility on Moloka'i.

Differences in the regulations of Hawai'i and Louisiana stemmed in part from differences in the laws governing admission to the institutions. In Hawai'i, territorial law mandated that all those determined to have the disease submit to isolation at Kalihi or Kalaupapa, but no federal law re-quired all people with leprosy on the mainland to enter the facility at Car-ville. Some people might enter the U.S. National Leprosarium involuntarily, either because they had been "apprehended under authority of the United States Quarantine acts" or because they were sent to the institution by "the proper health authorities of any State, Territory, or the District of Colum-bia."[77] Still, health officials liked to portray admission to the institution as voluntary, with administrators accepting anyone with the disease "who presents himself or herself for care, detention, and treatment." Once they entered, however, patients had to stay. As Denney rationalized, "Once a leper is in detention . . . it is a crime against society for him to abscond and subject his fellow human beings to the risk of contracting a malady that is practically incurable. To restrain such an individual is for the public good."[78] Such reasoning also comfortably supported the idea that once inside the facility, patients had to submit to any medical examination deemed neces-sary by medical personnel.

Denney portrayed the rules regulating patient behavior and maintaining patient containment as necessary public health measures that afforded ap-propriate care to U.S. citizens who had leprosy, while at the same time they protected the nation from contamination. Where territorial health officials accused Hawaiians with leprosy of failing to appreciate the threat they posed to others, Denney credited Carville residents for understanding their poten-tial to contaminate the national body. Patients who entered the U.S. Na-tional Leprosarium could gain comfort from the "full realization of the fact that they are no longer a menace to the health and contentment of their fellow beings."[79] Asserting that "segregation of all lepers is essential to the complete eradication of the disease," he implicitly contrasted the United States with other nations and areas that lacked "adequate legislation for the complete isolation of lepers." Denney had experience working with leprosy in the Philippines, where health officials had difficulty "breaking strong social ties and the customs of lepers" and lacked the necessary "expenditure of tremendous sums of money with which to maintain the segregation." The United States had made a good start at the Louisiana facility, according to Denney, but if it were to rid itself of leprosy properly where other nations and societies had failed, it needed to continue making financial commit-ments and regulating patients closely.[80]

To reassure those outside of the institution that Carville's residents re-ceived the best care possible, medical practitioners emphasized the modern nature of the federal leprosarium in their reports. Even before Congress had granted funds for improvements, health officials touted plans in the early 1920s to modernize the former Louisiana Leper Home by remodeling old buildings and constructing new facilities. Noting the chronic nature of lep-rosy, health officials sought to provide hospital accommodations for those in the acute stages of the disease and cottages of a less institutional nature for the living quarters of the more mobile majority.[81] By 1926, Denney could boast that Carville had newly constructed cottages that provided each patient "a room and surroundings which might be considered as his home." Each cottage contained twelve private rooms, a recreation room, bathroom facilities, and screened verandas; each structure had all the modern conveniences of steam heat, indoor plumbing, and electric lighting. Covered and screened walks linked all patient buildings.[82] In describing conditions at Carville, Denney emphasized the homelike accommodations, spacious grounds, and superior medical attention available to patients.

Denney failed to mention that the U.S. Public Health Service also upheld the institutional practice of segregation, with separate structures allocated to African American, Asian, and white patients. While discussions of separate housing did not enter into annual public health reports, two nurses at Carville offhandedly mentioned the custom in their discussion of the national leprosarium for a national nursing journal. "As almost every nation is represented," Sister Martha and Sister Catherine explained, "an effort is made to segregate the races."[83] Including such information in an article that praised the quality of care provided to patients as generous and up to date, the nurses presented the separation of patients based on racial differentiation as a medically approved and modern practice.

Medical practitioners promoted the national leprosarium as a site of enlightened care, a place where patients could lead fulfilling lives with the hope that science might provide them with a future free of the disease. Sisters Martha and Catherine chronicled a typical "day in the life" of a composite leprosy patient: "John Doe, American citizen, a ward of Uncle Sam's." They wrote that Doe enjoyed the benefits of a furnished private room, abundant food, fulfilling work, and engaging entertainment. According to the article, his most pressing problems included rushing to the "well lighted, airy" cafeteria in time to snag a healthy portion of pork sausage and biscuits; escaping the tortured noise produced by the amateur patient band while they practiced their instruments; and attempting to gain the notice of a newly admitted "fluffy haired girl from Texas." The nurses explained that most able-bodied patients held jobs that earned a monthly salary of $15 to $40 and assisted in the general operations of the institution by helping the orderlies, groundskeepers, and nurses. More entertaining diversions included sports, pool, movies, concerts, and club meetings. Still, the nurses did not slight the medical aspects of institutionalization. They discussed Doe's visits to the hospital, the laboratory, and the X-ray room as moments of optimism about the possibility of future treatments for leprosy.

The patients' baseball team at the U.S. National Leprosarium, Carville, Louisiana, from the 14 May 1926 issue of *Public Health Reports*.

The article concluded with Doe warmly assuring his "fluffy haired" Texas companion, "*Sure* you'll get well."[84]

In contrast to the colonialist assumptions that Hawaiians with leprosy were ignorant creatures who failed to appreciate the advantages of Western medicine, mainland medical practitioners depicted Carville's patients as eager recipients of modern science. For instance, the composite character John Doe viewed a trip to the laboratory as a festive occasion, one requiring his best clothes. After offering a skin or blood sample, he left the medical officer "whistling happily." Why? As the nurses explained, "If one is down in a hole, it's mighty good to know that those above ground are working with might and main to get you out."[85] By promoting the idea that patients could be released if their condition improved, such assertions helped to convince patients to cooperate with the routine of regular physical and bacterioscopic examinations, as well as to submit to experimental treatments.

Indeed, although not emphasized in congressional debates over funding for the national facility, experimental treatment efforts increasingly became a significant aspect of Carville's mission in the later 1920s. Efforts to update and modernize facilities at the national leprosarium included the construction of a "clinic set aside for experimental treatments."[86] Reports that health officials in 1925 discharged four patients from Carville as arrested cases spurred belief that medical science as practiced at the new institution might provide a cure for leprosy.[87] One newspaper flagged the Associated Press account of the patients' release with the headline, "Science Wins Again," heralding the defeat of leprosy as another triumph for modern medicine.[88] Annual reports provided information on the progress of various forms of therapy and suggested that patients willingly acceded to experimental treatments with the belief that they might improve their condition. While Denney admitted that chaulmoogra oil treatments, for instance, afforded "no spectacular results," he explained that "definite improvement has followed in a sufficiently large percentage of cases to encourage the patients in the continuation of treatment."[89] He also publicized the development of newer methods of physical therapy involving X-rays, ultraviolet light, and hydrotherapy, as well as new medicinal treatments. Acknowledging that none of these methods had yet yielded positive results in more than a select number of patients, he intimated that "a specific remedy may result" from the flurry of scientific research devoted to leprosy treatment.[90]

The construction and use of a "well-equipped laboratory" available for "research purposes," as well as the increasing numbers of medical visitors and publications, helped to establish the national leprosarium as a premier site for investigating leprosy and developing treatments by the end of the 1920s.[91] Denney increasingly promoted the investigative function of the institution over its function as a site dedicated to the care and containment of people with leprosy. For example, he reported in 1927 on the development of a collection of clinical photographs, the study of bacilli isolated from patient blood and skin samples, and even the observation of a select group of Carville patients injected with the smallpox virus to determine its possible therapeutic benefits.[92] In his survey of world leprosaria, Brazilian physician H. C. de Souza-Araujo praised the Louisiana institution as "well-adapted to serve as a school of leprology," with "all conveniences for the study of any branch of leprology."[93] In 1927 alone, 93 medical students, 110 physicians, and 32 nurses visited the institution, which had begun to identify itself as a facility "available for undergraduate and postgraduate instruction in leprosy."[94] Such accessibility to visiting medical practitioners and its availability as a site of medical education helped solidify Carville as a research institution distinct from Kalaupapa and other leprosaria, which continued to exist primarily as sites of containment.[95]

As a result, by the end of the decade operations at the national leprosarium differed markedly from those at Kalaupapa. Denney commented on the "hopeful outlook of a considerable proportion of the patients," an optimism he felt had been steadily increasing in the years since the United States assumed control of the facility in 1921. Nineteen patients were paroled as arrested cases in 1928 and 1929, bringing the total to forty-eight cases in just under ten years.[96] "Parole" was not an option for residents of Kalaupapa, who could at best seek a transfer to the more accessible location of the Kalihi Receiving Station. As U.S. public health officials on the mainland heralded the benefits that promising laboratory experiments and medical and surgical services at Carville could provide to its patients with leprosy, territorial and federal health officials confronted the fact that Kalaupapa had failed to emerge as a world center for the study and treatment of leprosy. A territorial Board of Health survey concluded in 1929 that "the Settlement has for years been merely an asylum" and vowed to develop an improvement plan "laid out on progressive lines."[97]

U.S. public health officials and medical practitioners, however, had already determined that the future of their most innovative work on the treatment and investigation of leprosy resided on the mainland. Having developed their initial strategies of leprosy containment in the colony, they moved the center of their operations back to the site where they believed that patients would prove more willing to accept the promises and premises of Western medicine, along with the system of surveillance and institutional discipline that public health officials believed it required.

Conclusion

An examination of early-twentieth-century U.S. leprosy policies in Hawai'i and Louisiana demonstrates the reciprocal nature of the relationship between mainland and colony. Kalaupapa certainly served as a colonial laboratory in many respects, generating knowledge about the disease and its treatment that physicians and medical administrators incorporated into practices on the mainland. In a very literal sense, however, it also failed as a laboratory. As federal health officials came to believe that patient resistance at Kalaupapa would thwart their efforts to establish the settlement as an international research site, they turned their attention and hopes back to the mainland in order to develop a medical institution with more submissive patients at Carville. Believed to be better versed in the benefits of medical science and more willing to subject themselves to the kind of discipline it entailed, mainland patients emerged as the preferred experimental subject for medical professionals. In fact, much of what would be learned at Carville in the following decades would be transferred back to Kalaupapa. Still, physicians and health officials did not completely abandon the idea that Hawai'i could provide a valuable site for the study of what they still considered to be a uniquely tropical disease, a view reinforced by territorial politicians and officials. Dialogue between the two facilities remained an ongoing feature of the development of U.S. medical policy for treating people with leprosy throughout the twentieth century.

CHAPTER FIVE

Leprosy and Citizenship

Patients and officials in both Hawai'i and Louisiana recognized that questions of American identity and citizenship lay at the heart of leprosy regulation. Ideas about how those questions should be addressed, however, differed considerably at the two locations, revealing the degree to which imperialist beliefs and attitudes continued to influence medical policies at both Kalaupapa and Carville throughout the 1930s and 1940s. As the early decades of leprosy management had revealed, medical officials at each institution regularly looked to the other for approaches on how to manage and treat the disease, but they also assumed that the mainland and the Hawaiian Islands contained two very different kinds of patients. The patients themselves, particularly at Carville, challenged the right of these officials to shape leprosy policy unilaterally, but their arguments had the unforeseen consequence of further dividing the two communities.

Health officials in Hawai'i perceived the management of leprosy as an avenue for demonstrating their ability both to contain the threat of contamination posed by an undisciplined Hawaiian population and to groom their charges as future citizens of a full-fledged U.S. state. They portrayed themselves as selfless stewards of the Hawaiians, whom they coached in proper Western attitudes toward the disease. At the same time, they tried to show how they effectively policed and controlled "deviant" Hawaiian bodies, bodies that threatened to reproduce both themselves and the disease and thus create a new class of dependents who would burden the state. Conceptions of citizenship proved more problematic for U.S. public health officials at Carville. On the one hand, officials embraced the notion that mainland patients could be expected to conform to the discipline of a modern U.S. medical facility in ways that Hawaiian patients could not. On the other, the need for surveillance and order at a modern medical institution and the mental and physical incapacitation that presumably accompanied the leprosy bacillus made them reluctant to accord Carville's residents the same rights as those on the "outside."

Patients at Carville, however, drew upon their status as U.S. citizens to challenge their image as enfeebled dependents and to publicize public health regulations as unjustified restrictions on their freedom.[1] Recognizing how Americans in the 1930s continued to view leprosy as a disease of the deviant and uncivilized, they worked to portray themselves as ordinary U.S. citizens who posed no threat to the broader population. During World War II, they deployed wartime rhetoric to demand their civil liberties and freedom from incarceration. They also embraced advances in scientific medicine in the form of sulfone drugs, which both promised to improve their physical appearance and give them the opportunity to position themselves as partners to physicians in advancing a medical breakthrough. These tactics granted patient activists at Carville some success at relaxing regulations. Yet their assertion of citizenship as a reason for change reinforced the idea that it was leprosy in other lands—"foreign leprosy"—that threatened U.S. public health and that those who resisted scientific medical treatment forfeited certain rights.

Patients at Kalaupapa could not invoke their rights as Americans to protest their treatment. Labeled as the colonized "others," they found it difficult to challenge policies of segregation and restrictions on family formation. Nor was inclusion in the United States necessarily something to which they aspired, as it implied complicity with a colonialist agenda. Many Hawaiian patients instead worked toward attaining what they viewed as their natural rights as human beings. They remained aloof from Euroamerican attempts to incorporate them into a modern U.S. medical program and formed a Hawaiian enclave within Kalaupapa in the face of increasing Americanization throughout the rest of the islands. Martial law and other World War II contingencies of the early 1940s further created conditions that labeled patients more indelibly as non-Americans. Their containment and isolation afforded them greater latitude to shape a distinctly Hawaiian community that would criticize and challenge U.S. intervention and medical administration.

Modernizing the Settlement: Citizenship and Civilization in Hawai'i

When President Herbert Hoover appointed Lawrence Judd as governor of Hawai'i in 1929, the new leader made an evaluation of the territory's leprosy

Aerial photograph of the Kalaupapa settlement, Moloka'i, Hawai'i, ca. 1931. Photo courtesy of the Bishop Museum.

policy a top priority of his administration. Judd wanted to showcase Hawai'i as a potential future state, and he viewed leprosy as an obstacle to his plan. A desire to improve the public image of the territory, as well as a long-term fascination with Kalaupapa and a concern for the welfare of its residents, motivated him. Significantly, Judd's first action during his three-month transition period was to form a leprosy advisory commission to investigate conditions at Kalaupapa. This action preceded his appointment of commissioners to overhaul the territorial educational system and criminal code, displaying the significance of the management of disease to the colonial state. The leprosy commission included such powerful community business leaders as W. H. McInerny, J. P. Cooke Jr., and Mark A. Robinson, with former U.S. Army engineer Harry A. Kluegel selected to conduct the official survey of the leprosy institutions.[2] Only three physicians designated as "medical advisers" served on the ten-member commission, suggesting the degree to which Judd viewed the disease as a political and business issue, to be handled by those individuals who recognized how existing policies hampered efforts to depict the territory as worthy of its "American" status.

Through its care of leprosy patients, the Judd administration demonstrated the territorial government's commitment to instilling Western values in its Hawaiian charges. The Euroamerican leadership realized that the racial composition of the islands raised fears on the mainland about the territory's ability to assimilate as a state. The presence of leprosy heightened the perception of Hawai'i as an uncivilized tropical outpost that could contaminate the nation. Under Judd, leprosy facilities emerged as laboratories where the administration could demonstrate that it was capable of managing the presumed threat and where the government could impose its vision of the tenets of U.S. citizenship—self-discipline, sexual control, proper middle-class gender roles and lifestyles—on their racially diverse charges.

To accomplish its goals, the territorial government needed to overhaul the existing leprosy institutions. Special investigator Kluegel surveyed the territory's leprosy facilities and concluded that the Kalaupapa settlement on Moloka'i was in a disgraceful state of disrepair and neglect. Serving both as the home for more advanced cases and as a detention center for patients deemed unruly by public health officials, Kalaupapa had earned a reputation among Hawaiians and other residents of the territory as a site of horror and lifetime banishment. Members of the Judd administration feared that such beliefs highlighted their deficiencies as stewards of the Hawaiian Islands, demonstrating both their inability to teach proper "American" ways of behavior to leprosy patients and their failure to contain threats to mainlanders and their interests. Kluegel's report of his investigations spurred plans to improve the Hawaiian leprosy program. The administration would then use these changes to show U.S. mainlanders how it used modern medicine and public health regulations to inculcate in the Hawaiian population an appreciation of Western science and proper Western behaviors. As Kluegel explained, "Any civilization is as strong as its weakest link. Until we have more adequately met this grave responsibility in these Islands the sum total of our progress is greatly retarded."[3] Failure to handle the leprosy problem effectively would reflect poorly on a territorial government struggling to convince Congress that Hawai'i was well on the path to statehood.

Business and political leaders in the territory had seen little need to expedite the process of becoming a state in the years before 1930, but congressional responses to nativist fears about Asian immigration to the U.S. mainland and the economic hardships of the Great Depression changed their attitudes. After the United States accorded the territory incorporated status through the Organic Act of 1900, members of the white elite controlled the legislature and exercised considerable influence over the territorial governor and other key administrators appointed by the U.S. government. As long as

Congress acknowledged Hawai'i's right to become a state eventually and supported Western business interests, the territorial legislature endorsed the rhetoric of statehood while reserving for itself the right to determine when the territory would be ready to make such a transition. Congressional moves to restrict the mainland importation of Filipino laborers during the mid-1920s (many of whom had first come to Hawai'i) and to reduce Hawaiian sugar exports to the United States in the early 1930s, however, prompted many of the white business elite to initiate a more formal statehood campaign. These leaders came to recognize that without representation in Congress and the full economic and political rights accorded to states, their personal power and monetary strength could be decimated anytime by the federal government.[4]

As Euroamerican territorial leaders pressed the cause for statehood, however, they found their efforts to portray themselves as stewards of an ethnically diverse populace undermined by a shift in Hawai'i's public image among people on the mainland. Extensive press coverage of a linked pair of rape and murder trials in 1931 led many people on the mainland to conclude that Hawai'i was less of a tropical paradise and more of a hotbed of racial tension and violence. Unlike other territories acquired by the United States during the late nineteenth century, Congress granted Hawai'i the same incorporated status that had been given to territories in the American West, thereby placing Hawai'i on the path toward eventual statehood. This prospect made some mainlanders uneasy in light of the racial composition of the islands' population. By 1930 Caucasians represented less than one-quarter of the territory's residents, while residents of Japanese descent numbered more than one-third.[5] Supporters of Hawai'i portrayed it as a site of racial harmony, as well as a prosperous U.S. territory that offered exotic allure and economic and military benefits to the nation. Others interpreted increasing labor tensions in the cane fields and other plantations as a sign of racial unrest.[6] These negative portrayals of Hawaiian race relations intensified in 1931 when Thalia Massie, a white woman and the wife of a U.S. naval lieutenant, accused five Hawaiian and Japanese men of sexually assaulting her. The case ended in a mistrial, with all jury members of color deciding on a not-guilty verdict; after the trial, Massie's husband and mother, along with two accomplices, murdered Joseph Kahahawai, one of the suspects. A jury found them guilty of manslaughter, but Governor Judd commuted their sentence to one hour. As the trials and their aftermath attracted widespread media attention, national papers decried what they saw as criminal and judicial chaos in Hawai'i.[7] Congress threatened to impose a commission-style government on Hawai'i, which would have essentially stripped residents of their voting rights, while territorial politicians struggled to present themselves as most capable of keeping the diverse population in line.

Enacting a humane and progressive leprosy policy afforded the Judd administration an opportunity to address questions about the white elites' ability to prepare the island's non-Western population for statehood. In his report, Kluegel had recommended that "the best social and humanitarian conscience and intelligence in the Territory should be directed towards making [Kalaupapa] the Territory's model Institution," and he reminded administrators that it was one of only three leprosy settlements "under the American flag."[8] He further emphasized that providing care for the sick was "one of the services for which government is instituted" and noted that the manner in which the legislature handled the responsibility "will directly reflect upon the character of the Territory." The failure of pre-1930s policies to provide adequately for Hawai'i's leprosy patients demonstrated an inability to create a sufficiently progressive "American" society, according to Kluegel. "The physical and sanitary conditions [at Kalaupapa] are deplorable," he reported. "Any one driving casually through the Settlement would think it a very down in the heel Hawaiian village." Judd hoped to transform such "native" squalor into a model American community.

The report's emphasis on modernization linked with humanitarianism reveals the Judd administration's imperialist concerns with fulfilling its proper role in "civilizing" what it viewed as the most neglected Hawaiians in the islands. Part of this mission required that Western officials pay as much attention to moral behavior as to physical well-being. Kluegel suggested instituting an "up-to-date social welfare program" that would provide "more organized recreation to offset any glaring moral lapses" among residents at the Kalaupapa settlement. Carefully monitored recreation was "the twentieth century antidote" for immorality, according to Kluegel. "Enforced idleness—such as is too often the condition at Kalaupapa—should receive constructive treatment." To this end, he recommended close cooperation with the religious organizations already established in the community. He praised Catholics, Protestants, Mormons, and "a Japanese group" in the settlement for providing patients with a moral grounding. He urged the territorial government to give greater support to efforts by these religious groups; such a move would demonstrate how different races could work in harmony under the direction of the Western elite. Embodying the sentiments of nineteenth-century missionaries, his report suggested that to be considered a truly enlightened and modern society, the territorial government needed to accept its duty to uplift its "unfortunate and tragic wards."[9]

The goal of creating a better institution to contain people with leprosy in Hawai'i was closely intertwined with the desire to instill in patients a Western attitude toward health and disease. Such an understanding required inculcating in patients a range of beliefs, from the necessity of living in orderly rows of white-washed frame cottages to the need for compulsory medical supervision. In recommending physical improvements to Hawaiian leprosy facilities, Kluegel intended the changes to have a "psychological effect upon the patients" that would alter their conception of how they should conduct their lives. Making the entire settlement organized and neat would bring about "more orderly living on [the patients'] part, and an increased desire to receive medical and scientific attention, which, though available is in many instances now refused."[10] Administrators perceived Hawaiian leprosy patients' resistance to hospitalization as part of a broader refusal to accept Western authority. Territorial officials needed to overcome such reluctance if they were to succeed in teaching Hawaiians how to be proper U.S. citizens. Replacing individually constructed patient homes with evenly spaced and identically built sanitarium models served as an initial step toward this status, because it would teach patients to conform to the standards of Western institutional discipline and medical treatment. The humanitarian mission embedded in Kluegel's recommendations for physical improvements cannot be easily disentangled from the desire to impose a Western character on the largely Hawaiian community.

The advisory committee on leprosy created by Judd responded to Kluegel's survey in 1930 by recommending a radical overhaul of the entire leprosy program. Believing that a fear of lifelong banishment to Kalaupapa prevented patients from coming forward, the committee suggested improving facilities at the settlement while promising all territorial residents that no one would be forced to go there, which was a significant departure from then-current practices. The plan was to allow the population to shrink naturally and eventually to abandon the site altogether in favor of expanding facilities at the Kalihi hospital in Honolulu. The committee concluded that two additional steps were crucial for eliminating the disease in the islands: first, undertaking a thorough epidemiological survey of the disease in Hawai'i; and second, developing case histories of all residents in leprosy facilities. These case histories would "furnish a means of determining 'backwards' the previous exposure—hereditary, familial contact or others—and 'forwards' the individuals, familial or otherwise, who have been exposed to leprous infection and who in the future should be observed for the earliest signs of the disease."[11] The committee's recommendations reflected both a confidence in the ability of scientific research to identify a solution to the leprosy problem and a sense that modern public health practices entailed the close surveillance of populations deemed to harbor disease.

The committee's report reflected the dual aims of the Judd administration's leprosy policy, which were to create a more open approach to leprosy to eradicate fear of the disease and to correct a "lack of understanding of the seriousness of the disease" among the territory's non-Western residents, especially Hawaiians.[12] Judd's intention of establishing a more humane policy reflected in part a desire to counter the perception among mainland Americans that leprosy was a disease of the uncivilized, a perception that could hamper efforts to portray Hawai'i as a modern U.S. territory poised for statehood. At the same time, the rhetoric of the report suggests that the committee expected to find most of the incipient cases of the disease among the nonwhite residents of the islands, those who demonstrated an "absolute lack of fear of the disease" and needed to accept that they posed a threat to healthy members of their communities.[13] Both goals of this new leprosy policy aimed at incorporation. The first, by decreasing irrational fears among westerners, attempted to open the way for Hawai'i's entry into the community of states. The second, by instilling respect for Western medicine and inculcating a sense of self-discipline, aimed to increase the civic maturity of non-Western territorial residents and prepare them for citizenship.

The committee report used Kalaupapa as a symbol of the difficulties the Judd administration faced in trying to compensate for the failures of earlier leprosy policies. The committee's long-term plan to close Kalaupapa stemmed in part from its conviction that the settlement could never attain the standards "of first class hospitals." The report explained that residents had been living too long under the relaxed village plan whereby the majority "set up housekeeping in their own way" and decided on their own whether to "avail themselves of facilities provided for their care and treatment." Committee members condemned such a system and affirmed the modern practice of caring for people with communicable disease through hospitalization. The report concluded, however, "that any effort to create new customs and new traditions at Kalaupapa under a system diametrically opposed to that one which has been in operation for 65 years, will result in failure from lack of cooperation on the part of the inmates, and would create a hiatus of mental unrest, something that should be carefully avoided."[14]

Clearly, the freedom that Kalaupapa's residents had enjoyed in shaping their own treatment convinced the committee it would take years of unstinting efforts to develop the pliant patient population it envisioned as appropriate to a modern hospital.[15]

To signal a dramatic shift in leprosy policy, the Judd administration in 1931 separated all supervision of the disease from the territorial Board of Health and placed those responsibilities with a new Board of Hospitals and Settlement headed by Kluegel. The governor also persuaded the legislature to allocate a biannual budget of $375,000 for the construction of new facilities at Kalaupapa and Kalihi, with an additional appropriation of $870,460 for operating expenses. The territorial government hoped to use both the structural changes and the financial commitment to encourage people with incipient cases of leprosy to submit themselves to medical authorities and to improve the morale of those people with the disease already under the care of health officials.[16] Newspaper coverage reflected the new tone of optimism and openness toward the disease, with one daily announcing the changes under the headline, "New Day Ahead for Kalaupapa Colony People."[17]

Under Kluegel's leadership, the new board embraced the idea that leprosy policy provided a critical arena in which the territory could prove itself a distinctly American political entity capable of humanely containing and treating a disease viewed across the world as a marker of an "uncivilized" society. In the board's first report to the legislature in 1932, Kluegel declared, "The fight for the control of leprosy in Hawaii should be the greatest collective effort that Hawaii has ever undertaken. There can be no standing still. The world moves on. We in Hawaii must advance, accept progressive adjustments." As colonial authorities, the Western board envisioned "Hawaii" as the political and social body formed by Western concerns. The rhetoric Kluegel employed detailing the territory's "responsibility" for treating people with leprosy embodied a missionary spirit of helping those who could not help themselves, "a brotherly spirit of devoted service and cooperation for our afflicted fellow citizens."[18] This colonial sense of paternalistic intervention, however, embodied a racial sensibility that saw citizenship as a process. Board members displayed a genuine commitment to providing the kind of improved care that could eradicate the very real suffering of people with leprosy, but they also saw their "fellow citizens" with leprosy as not yet ready to accept the rights and duties of full citizenship.

The missionary spirit inspired humanitarian concern for those with the disease, but it also reinforced the stigma that underpinned segregation mandates, reflecting the degree to which medical and religious practices remained intimately intertwined in twentieth-century leprosy policy. In its 1932 report to the legislature, board members quoted approvingly an 1873 Hawaiian Evangelical Association resolution that called for "strict, thorough separation from us [of] all infected persons, not only established lepers, but also all who are reasonably suspected. If we obey God's leadings and follow this rule our nation will be saved. If we do not we are doomed to an early and shameful death."[19] The board used this quote to assert the ongoing spiritual and medical benefits of strict isolation of people with leprosy. Board members tied notions of Christian responsibility to their conception of citizenship and cast themselves as the appropriate judges of who could be "reasonably suspected" of having the disease.

The board report further employed racial assumptions to explain why the disease continued to exist in the territory and why strict segregation of all people with leprosy served as the only appropriate means to halt its spread. The report explained that the policy of segregation had been implemented "largely because of the habits and customs of the Hawaiians" and their susceptibility to the disease, noting that the "power of resistance is not as strong in Polynesians as in the people of northern latitudes. . . . [Hawaiians'] characteristics and customs render them more liable to contagion or inoculation." Board members criticized practices that produced "terrible tragedies in the lives of many Hawaiians" and conceded that segregation would inspire resistance, but they did not question the racial stereotypes or the stigma that underpinned segregation.[20] They blamed settlement residents' continued practice of following their "racial customs in diet" for interfering with proper treatment of leprosy and made "improvement in personal hygiene" a priority under the new administration.[21] They further targeted the broader Hawaiian and non-Western community outside of the settlement, establishing an "anti-leprosy education" plan that intended to instill "proper living conditions, proper diet, proper exercise and the removal of fear of hospitalization and treatment" in all residents of the islands. Officials hoped to have people internalize standards of sanitation and hygiene; teaching these "less advanced" races to police themselves lay at the heart of the Euroamerican plan to impose citizenship from above. Contending that leprosy had died out in "countries where there is the greatest advance in sanitation and hygiene," health officials worked to make the territory of Hawai'i such a "civilized" state by stopping the spread of the disease.[22]

Introducing Western architecture served as a visible representation of the transformation health officials intended to orchestrate in the leprosy program. Using the money slated for new facilities at Kalaupapa, health officials planned to replace patient-constructed dwellings with Western homes and create a more suitably modern medical institution on the Moloka'i peninsula. Board members took great steps to eliminate buildings that violated Western institutional sanitation and safety standards. New patient cottages constructed with board funds gave visible evidence of the ongoing efforts to modernize the facility, improve care, and instill proper Western values of home maintenance and indoor plumbing in Hawaiian patients. Resident Superintendent R. L. Cooke reported in 1932 that he oversaw the construction of twelve new two-bedroom patient cottages fully equipped with modern toilets, bathtubs, and sinks, as well as electric lighting. He spoke with pride of the way many patients chose to use their own money to purchase home furnishings that would compare "very favorabl[y] with any standard home in Honolulu." Other patients put in fencing and tended to lawns. The board spared some older patient dwellings from demolition and outfitted them with indoor plumbing.[23] Health officials also sought to modernize the settlement by constructing a new fifty-bed hospital and dispensary, encouraging Kalaupapa's residents to seek medical treatment under the supervision of the staff physician.[24]

Board members viewed leprosy patients' acceptance of medical treatment within the confines of a hospital as a vital step toward improving their care and bringing them in step with up-to-date methods. Beginning in 1931, Kalaupapa resident physician L. F. Luckie started presenting films and lectures on health and sanitation to settlement residents. He hoped to encourage patients to trust health professionals and voluntarily enter the facility's medical clinic for consultation or its hospital for treatment. Luckie credited the educational program, along with "kindly advice and psychology," for increasing the number of consultations within the settlement to 15,393 in the 1931–32 year, an increase of more than 5,000 from the previous year.[25] Health officials claimed that people with leprosy throughout the islands also were learning to accept and seek medical treatment, citing thirty-one voluntary admissions to Kalaupapa during the 1931–32 period.[26] Hospital admittance remained a matter of patient choice at Kalaupapa, so physicians worked to make a stay attractive to patients in order to gain their patronage. Hospital attendance increased throughout the 1930s, in part because physicians offered various therapies, such as infrared lamp and UV ray treatments, massage, sun baths, hydrotherapy, and medicinal inhalations, that patients could not provide for themselves.[27] The increasing willingness on the part of Kalaupapa residents to seek a doctor's advice or enter the settlement hospital was viewed not only as a symbol of the success of the leprosy program, but also as a symbol of Hawaiian acceptance of Western ways. It also challenged the earlier conclusions reached by federal health officials, who had contended in previous decades that Kalaupapa's residents would not consent to Western experimental medical practices.

The territorial government sought to display its fitness for U.S. statehood by coordinating its localized reforms with a broader international leprosy eradication effort. The Judd administration intended Hawaiʻi to play a leading role in the move to bring the United States into full participation with other colonial powers on the proper management of "tropical disease" within their empires.[28] The 1932 board report invoked the international leprosy conference held in Manila the previous year to connect the territory's reformulated policy to a global "offensive" unleashed upon the "world disease."[29] Under the heading "Prevention and Cure: The American Fight Against Disease," the board outlined what it considered to be "Hawaii's Responsibility" in eradicating leprosy: providing appropriate treatment for patients and attending to their welfare and that of their families; establishing proper measures of protection and prevention in the territory; cooperating with the international movement to control and eliminate leprosy, as well as to identify a cure for the disease; and directing adequate public funds toward these efforts. By working toward "simultaneous progress on all sectors of this battle line—scientific, social, and economic," the territorial government would demonstrate its ability to carry out a distinctively American mission and present the Hawaiian Islands as a territory properly managed by its Western stewards.[30]

The financial demands of these leprosy reforms strained the resources of the territory and prompted the legislature to call upon the U.S. government for financial assistance with Hawaiʻi's leprosy program. Even as it sought to obtain congressional aid, however, the predominantly Western territorial government wanted to establish clear divisions between direct and indirect federal intervention. While money for leprosy programs was welcome, federal oversight was not. In this regard, its posturing was not unlike that of a state seeking to keep out an intrusive national presence while profiting from federal funding. In the process of requesting aid for Kalaupapa and Kalihi, the territorial government promoted its image as a humane political body spending a great deal of money to care for the outcasts of society, while subtly indicating that they had more expertise and experience than the federal government in knowing how to contain non-Western peoples with leprosy and keep them from contaminating the islands and the nation as a whole.

The territorial legislature carefully crafted its request for funds to portray itself as a U.S. territory worthy of certain rights and financial support, based on its generous and humane provision for its most unfortunate residents. V. S. K. Houston, Hawai'i's nonvoting delegate to the U.S. Congress, urged Governor Judd to invoke a 1920 federal statute allowing any state or territory to ask the federal government to pay for the hospitalization of people with leprosy. Congress had passed the law to open the U.S. National Leprosarium in Carville, Louisiana, to all citizens, but Houston felt the territory should use it to request a federal financial contribution to Hawai'i's leprosy program "in lieu of Federal hospitalization."[31] In April 1931, Judd approved a legislative joint resolution to request federal aid to support the territory's segregation and treatment of those with leprosy, and Houston introduced a U.S. House resolution in December of that year to provide Hawai'i with such federal assistance.[32]

In a calculated ploy designed to force the hand of Congress, Judd also wrote a letter asking Surgeon General Hugh Cumming whether the U.S. National Leprosarium could accommodate 700 leprosy patients from Hawai'i. Judd used the letter to remind Congress that the Hawaiian Islands were a U.S. territory whose residents were eligible for care and treatment at the U.S. National Leprosarium. When Cumming responded that "facilities at Carville are sufficient only for leprous patients from the continental United States and Alaska," he provided the territorial government with leverage to argue that the federal government lacked the resources and expertise to assume direct responsibility for Hawaiians with leprosy. Since the territorial government had the necessary experience and facilities to care for its residents with leprosy, Judd believed that the proper role for the federal government was to provide financial assistance in their efforts.[33]

Congressional debates over funding for Hawai'i's leprosy program forced U.S. legislators to examine the territory's relationship to the United States, but they also produced less money and more oversight than territorial officials desired. During House debates over his resolution, Houston explained the Judd administration's plans for improving conditions within Hawai'i's leprosy institutions, noting that the territorial government was better suited to oversee the changes as its members had a better understanding of those "unfortunate people" than the mainland public health service.[34] In an attempt to find a less costly alternative to Houston's proposal, Representative Claude Parsons proposed that the U.S. surgeon general should conduct a thorough survey of the leprosy situation in Hawai'i before committing the government to any large outlay of funds.[35] In debates over Parsons's measure, Representative William Stafford argued that since leprosy was an extensive health problem unique to Hawai'i, the territorial administration had the responsibility for dealing with it and should not ask the federal government to "assume exclusively State functions."[36] Such an argument implied that Hawai'i possessed certain self-governing capabilities that put it on more equal footing with mainland states, a suggestion that Houston and other Hawaiian statehood-minded people welcomed. Houston pointed out that "Hawai'i unfortunately has not yet reached that exalted position," though it "would like nothing better than to be a State." Having paid close to $8 million for treating and segregating people with leprosy since annexation, however, the territory sought the same kind of financial provision for leprosy patients that the federal government provided to the states.[37] The majority of congressional members proved more comfortable looking upon Hawai'i as a struggling territory that needed oversight, and they committed only enough funds for the U.S. Public Health Service to conduct an investigation of leprosy and its treatment within the territory.[38]

Territorial officials, then, failed to receive an immediate infusion of funds while attracting precisely the kind of federal oversight they had hoped to avoid. Their request for assistance inadvertently succeeded in making Congress recognize that the treatment of leprosy in Hawai'i provided another avenue for federal intervention into a territory whose relations to the mainland remained ambiguous. Congressional hearings demonstrated the degree to which health officials and politicians continued to view Hawai'i as different, a place apart from the rest of the United States. When Representative Parsons asked about the racial composition of patients at the Carville leprosarium, Dr. George McCoy, director of the National Institute of Health, responded that they were "very largely our own people; very largely white stock."[39] Patients in Hawai'i, by inference, were not primarily Caucasian, not lawmakers' "own people." Incidents such as the Massie rape and murder trials had underscored for white Americans how dangerous racial mingling could be.

Controlling Leprosy, Controlling Sexuality: Family Policy in Hawai'i

Racial anxieties and beliefs continued to justify different policies for leprosy on the mainland and in the territory, with patient sexuality emerging as a key marker demonstrating the different ways that administrators managed the lives of patients in Kalaupapa and Carville. The congressional debates over funding for Hawaiian leprosy patients had raised the point that health officials in Hawai'i allowed marriages within Kalaupapa, while U.S. public health officers forbade them in Carville.[40] Regulations in Hawai'i represented a concession to the realities of cultural difference in the eyes of Western elites, who believed that Hawaiians' presumed tendency toward promiscuity made it difficult to impose strict abstinence upon the men and women at Kalaupapa. During the 1930s, territorial administrators struggled to balance their desire to modernize conditions and reform regulations at the settlement with the sense that they needed to retain certain practices required by the unique cultural traditions and racial composition of their leprosy institutions. In the process of crafting policies to maintain this balance, health officials revealed their view that modern efforts to control and eradicate leprosy in the territory required the social engineering of patient families.

Judd administration officials at the Kalaupapa settlement continued to allow open interaction among men and women, but they attempted to draw distinct lines between what they considered "legitimate" and "illegitimate" interaction, particularly with regard to cohabitation. Believing that Hawaiian men and women would more willingly accept their confinement if allowed to live together, administrators condoned a village design for the settlement that allowed couples to share the same home. Adultery concerned board members, and they made obtaining legal marriage as simple as possible. Encouraging such unions connected contemporary practice to older Christian missionary traditions that encouraged marriage to advance social harmony and moral progress. The 1932 board report stated, "Marriage is encouraged whenever possible for moral reasons." In the 1931–32 fiscal year alone, twenty-one marriages were performed.[41]

Allowing married couples to live together, however, meant that some patients bore children, a situation the board identified as "the gravest problem of all."[42] Territorial health officials considered several remedies to the problem posed by childbirth among Kalaupapa's residents, including the sterilization of patients. Eugenicists had been suggesting for several decades that mentally and physically "defective" people should not be allowed to reproduce because it would burden the state.[43] Such propositions resonated with territorial officials concerned about the cost of caring for the children of people with leprosy. This argument justified the sterilization of an increasing number of "feeble-minded" patients on the mainland throughout the 1930s and provided a public health precedent for territorial officials.[44]

Most territorial physicians had discounted the theory that leprosy was a hereditary disease, but they also believed that children who lived among people with leprosy had a greater risk of contracting the disease and creating a new generation of people who would require the expense of treatment and supervision by the territorial government. If no children were born, they reasoned, the spread of leprosy could be contained. A Governor's Advisory Committee on Leprosy recommended in a 1931 report that patients be "convinced" to undergo "voluntary" sterilization.[45] Board members decided to pay for the procedures, allocating $20 for vasectomies and $50 for salpingectomies.[46] Territorial health officials discussed no other method of birth control, suggesting that they did not believe non-Western patients were capable of taking any steps to control their fertility that would require sexual restraint or planning.[47] No record of the number of sterilizations exists in the Board of Health records, but published oral histories reveal that some patients felt pressured to undergo these operations, particularly if they sought temporary, physician-approved leave from the facility.[48]

When board members failed to prevent patients from having children, they placed extraordinary restrictions on their parental rights. Allowing men and women to live together increased the likelihood of children and raised expectations among settlement residents that they could keep and raise them. Public health regulations, however, required pregnant women to give birth within the settlement hospital and instructed the medical staff to remove children from their parents immediately and transfer them to the nursery. Generally within a month of birth, the board sent infants born to Kalaupapa residents to Honolulu.[49] In 1931–32, ten children were born at Kalaupapa.[50] After physicians determined that the children had not contracted leprosy, they placed them with foster families or in the two territorial institutions designated for their care: the Kapiolani Girls' Home and Kalihi Boys' Home, both in Honolulu. By isolating these children in specialized homes, health officials virtually guaranteed their stigmatization, even labeling them "children of leprous parents."[51] Board members kept parents and their offspring separated even when a patient's child contracted leprosy, underscoring the racial and gender norms that shaped policies ostensibly created to protect public health. The decision to keep such children away from their parents revealed the degree to which public health officials saw Hawaiians with leprosy as inherently incapable parents and viewed Kalaupapa as a poor environment in which to raise children, even those who had contracted leprosy.

The Great Depression intensified concerns that possible offspring would strain public resources and prompted a reevaluation of the comparatively liberal policy governing patient helpers who potentially helped to produce such offspring. Health officials had initially decided to maintain the tradition of allowing some healthy friends and relatives to enter Kalaupapa and live with patients as kōkuas, as long as they had no dependent children at home. Throughout the 1930s, however, territorial health officials increasingly refused requests by friends and relatives to join their loved ones as caregivers in Kalaupapa. Dr. Eric Fennel, a member of the board who had proven receptive to patient requests for kōkuas, remarked in 1933 that the offspring resulting from kōkua-patient relationships made it increasingly difficult to persuade health officials to admit new helpers. Such concerns had more to do with the burdens that such children placed on the territory than with a concern for the health and well-being of the kōkuas or the children themselves. Fennel admitted, for example, that he could probably gain permission for one Hawaiian male to come to Kalaupapa if he could convince the board that the potential kōkua was sterile.[52] Restricting the admittance of new kōkuas provided another avenue by which medical officials sought to control familial relations among settlement residents.

Board members also imported from the mainland social welfare programs designed to surveil and shore up poor and nonwhite families, and they fitted them with colonialist trappings.[53] The territory's Social Service Bureau, for example, provided pensions for any dependents of a male patient entering a leprosy facility in Hawaiʻi, basing the policy on white, middle-class assumptions that men acted as breadwinners for the family. Such a policy collided with Hawaiian practices of having family members care for one another during times of illness. In November 1933, Elizabeth Stone asked to enter Kalaupapa as a kōkua to her husband. Welfare worker E. V. Paris recommended that the superintendent of the Board of Hospitals and Settlement deny her request because Stone had three young children at home. Paris wrote that "the Board did not approve of a mother with young children going to Kalaupapa. She would be doing a greater service to the community by maintaining a home for her children."[54] As the Social Service Bureau had been paying rent and electricity for the Stones, the social worker claimed the state had a particular investment in this situation, thereby ignoring Elizabeth Stone's investment in caring for her family. All women accepting money from the bureau endured regular visitations and judgments from social workers to ensure that the family continued to function properly.[55] Such policies positioned the territorial government as a steward for the families of Hawaiians with leprosy, and suggested that they made dubious candidates for parent-hood because of their disease and their ethnic heritage.

The case of the Kupele family demonstrates how settlement residents challenged territorial officials' familial policies and resisted efforts to allow a disease to define them as incapable parents. In 1934, David and Annie Kupele demanded the transfer of their eight-year-old son William—diagnosed with leprosy—from the Kalihi leprosy hospital in Honolulu to Kalaupapa so the family could live together. The couple portrayed themselves as an ordinary mother and father, concerned for their son's well-being and desiring to provide him with a home most conducive to his proper spiritual and physi-cal development. The petition drew not on their status as citizens, but on their Christian beliefs and their humanity. The Kupeles argued that having their son with them in Kalaupapa "would improve his moral welfare, health, and education in every respect according to the laws of GOD as well as the laws of mankind."[56] They added a medical note, asserting that since the boy already had leprosy, the parents posed no health risk to the child. The board denied their petition, ignoring arguments about their human rights and spiritual imperatives and insisting instead that the hospital could provide better care than the parents.

The Kupeles contrasted their own parental concern for their child with what they viewed as the scientific self-interest of Kalihi public health offi-cials who used their son to test a variety of medical treatments. Their argu-ment implied that Kalaupapa officials had less interest in teaching patients how to be good parents and citizens and desired more to use such patients to further their own medical education. U.S. doctors and hospital administra-tors commonly sought parental consent for surgical operations on minors by the early twentieth century, but Kalihi officials clearly saw no need for such permission. Treatment of children whose parents had leprosy suggests that the racial and class beliefs of physicians and administrators led them to view such children as orphan subjects. The Kupeles charged that their son had been "regarded as a species for experimental purposes" without their consent.[57] The couple contended that on the occasions when the board al-lowed children to be transferred from Kalihi, they did so "solely on the ground that no further need could be made of them for experimental pur-poses." To their minds, such evidence belied health officials' contentions that children received superior care at the Honolulu leprosy hospital.[58]

When the couple challenged the board's refusal to return their child, Hawai'i attorney general W. B. Pitman countered with the assumed superiority of Western medicine to argue that the Kupeles' son should remain separated from his parents. Pitman accepted the judgment of Board of Health chairman F. J. Pinkerton, who contended that at Kalihi, William Kupele received the best medical care and educational opportunities, enjoyed a healthy diet, and was "happy and lives as normal a life as could be."[59] Pinkerton did not explain that the intradermal and diathermic electric treatments applied to William's skin lesions and feet were, in fact, in their experimental stages and provided no hope of a cure. Accepting the advice of the board, Pitman concluded, "We appreciate the attitude of the parents and deeply sympathize with them, but as I have said we can only look to the best interests of the child and must not be swayed by our sympathy for the parents."[60] Embedded in his decision was the conclusion that the Hawaiian diet, lifestyle, and values of the Kupeles at Kalaupapa would not provide the best parental guidance for a new generation of Hawaiian Americans. This kind of guidance was the duty of the Euroamerican elite, already well schooled in teaching their non-Western charges the rights and responsibilities of citizenship.

Kalaupapa residents had to contend not only with public health officials but also with a Euroamerican public that shared the board's conclusions that people with leprosy made unfit parents. Indeed, members of the public believed that greater steps could be taken to contain the sexual behavior of Kalaupapa residents. The comments of journalist Ernie Pyle revealed that some Americans believed the general public should have a stake in keeping people with leprosy in Hawai'i from having children. He claimed that only one thing shocked him during his 1937 visit to Kalaupapa: "That leprous patients—even those scourged to the very door of death—are permitted to reproduce themselves. . . . Patients marry, and re-marry, and don't marry at all—and babies keep coming."[61] Pyle's outraged rhetoric revealed two interconnected but not uncommon assumptions among Euroamericans: first, that Hawaiians with leprosy had sex and reproduced frequently and indiscriminately; and second, that the reproductive lives of certain people could and should be controlled. Pyle saw nothing good emerging from a policy that allowed people with leprosy to have children. "What is the use? What is the gain? There can be no parental affection," he insisted, "for the babies are taken away at the very moment of birth, and the parents usually never see them again. And even though they may avoid leprosy, the children are doomed either to imbecility or unnatural loneliness."[62] He never questioned the policy that mandated the immediate removal of children at birth, failing to entertain the possibility that both parents and children could thrive in an environment that allowed them to live together. For Pyle, the children of leprosy patients existed as a social burden, an inferior group condemned to either mental retardation or emotional anguish. Non-Western patients at Kalaupapa such as the Kupeles found their voices diminished by outraged denunciations from white Americans who believed that such behavior marked them as inferior and unfit parents.

Patient Activism and Representation at the National Leprosarium

People with leprosy in Hawai'i had limited power in the 1930s to alter restrictive public health policies, much less affect the stigma that shaped American views toward people with the disease, but patients at the U.S. National Leprosarium in Carville found themselves better situated both to influence medical policy and to create alternative public images of leprosy. Carvillians drew on their status as American citizens to challenge their treatment. The white majority of patients at Carville sought to portray their community as composed of capable Americans who had lost their status as citizens through no fault of their own. They therefore mounted an educational campaign to enlighten the public, to encourage medical research on treating and curing leprosy, and to end their enforced isolation.

The ways in which patients mobilized at Carville during the Depression and war years posed potential problems for any larger effort to forge ties with patients at Kalaupapa or any other territorial or international facility. By staking a claim to U.S. citizenship as their means of resistance, Carville residents also implicitly supported ideas of racial difference upon which their understanding of citizenship rested. Kalaupapa residents had been isolated partly for their care and partly in the belief that they were not really Americans at all. Hence, by laying claim to a universalizing discourse of U.S. civilization and democracy, Carville patients presented themselves as people who did not need the policing practices of a Kalaupapa because they were not "natives," but Americans.

To publicize their situation, patients at the U.S. National Leprosarium made effective connections with organizations outside the facility for financial assistance and political clout, and the most influential of these groups were veterans' organizations. The American Legion, the American Legion Auxiliary, and the Forty and Eight served as links to the outside community and provided advocates for patients' needs. Initially, most of the work of these veterans' groups naturally consisted of providing amenities to Carville residents who had served in the military. Their interest in improving the care and treatment of war veterans, however, drew them into broader debates on patient care. In 1931, the Louisiana State Commander of the American Legion, Sam Jones, visited a group of twenty-three World War I veterans at Carville to listen to their demands for an improved infirmary, a new recreation hall, and more contact with "the outside world." Jones agreed to intervene on the veterans' behalf and also helped them establish their own post within the Carville facility. Carville resident and veteran Stanley Stein later recalled how impressed the patients were that "such a huge and powerful organization should take an interest in just a handful of men." He asserted that "there could be no doubt of their sincerity, for there was surely no political or personal advantage to be gained from espousing what had for centuries been an unpopular cause."[63]

The Legionnaires, however, did see that they had something to gain by championing the cause of these veterans. Veterans were the beneficiaries of the largest federally sponsored and funded hospital system in the country.[64] Both veterans and leprosy patients had a strong interest in maintaining and expanding their influence over federal health policy. The American Legion had formed in part to ensure that the federal government provided appropriate benefits and pensions for service-related disabilities. The Legionnaires saw the plight of this small group of Carville veterans as an example of government neglect. By calling attention to the situation of the patient veterans, the Legion could thereby generate broader sympathy for veteran rights.

Patients at Carville found that this connection to the national veterans' association brought them enhanced public influence and improved facilities. At the American Legion national convention in Detroit in 1931, the Legionnaires adopted a resolution requesting that the government build a "permanent hospital" at Carville to replace the existing one. By the early 1930s, the nineteenth-century plantation structures were deteriorating, and the replacement structures had proved inadequate. Legionnaires, responding to complaints by resident veterans, argued that a new facility would provide more appropriate care for all patients and urged the U.S. Public Health Service (PHS) to take action.[65] Over time, such publicity had a positive impact. In 1935, a new fireproof infirmary opened, and a 1939 PHS inspection of the facility prompted its multi-million-dollar renovation. During the 1939 inspection, the national organization helped arrange a meeting between local Legion post members and the visiting inspector, at which the Legion-

naire patients protested the loss of evening visiting privileges and the halt-
ing of beer sales at the patient canteen.[66] The inspector recommended
changes in these policies, a result that suggests that the influence of the
national organization provided the veteran patient group with the kind of
political capital that could prove useful to the broader patient community.
Indeed, patients viewed the influence of the American Legion as critical to
the federal government's renewed financial commitment to improving the
facility in the 1930s.

The successful alliance with the veterans convinced some patients that
they could make more far-reaching changes in the administration and medical policies at Carville. Stanley Stein's activities in the Carville American
Legion post inspired him to use a patient newsletter as a tool both to mobilize the patient community and to educate the public about the most current
medical understandings of the disease. In 1940, Stein asked Dr. H. E. Hasseltine, then medical officer in charge (MOC), for permission to publish a small
monthly patient newspaper that would be independent of the administration.[67] In order to avoid the possibility of censorship, he intended to finance
the paper through subscription fees and assured Hasseltine that he would
use no government funds.[68] Hasseltine supported the idea of a patient publication in principle, but he was uncomfortable with the idea of any paper
leaving the facility without his review and approval. He presented his concerns to the assistant surgeon general, expressing uneasiness with Stein's
emerging activism.[69] Hasseltine left Carville in 1940, however, and his replacement, Dr. Guy Faget, proved more sympathetic to Stein's journalistic
endeavors and allowed him to publish the paper without censorship by PHS
officials.[70]

To work as effective activists, however, some patients had to grapple with
the manner in which they themselves had internalized many of the social
stigmas and prejudices associated with leprosy, particularly those grounded
in assumptions that people with the disease violated racial and gender
norms. Betty Martin, a white Louisiana society woman diagnosed with leprosy and incarcerated at Carville in the 1920s, recorded her experiences in the
memoir *Miracle at Carville*. Martin wrote that she initially refused to accept
the news that she had leprosy because her self-image did not match her own
conception of a "leper." Martin speculated that leprosy "might exist in lands
far away, in India perhaps, or China, but surely leprosy could not exist here, in
our own United States, and surely not in me."[71] Though she came to accept
her diagnosis, the society in which she lived could not. The disease and the
medical response to it eventually brought an end to her engagement to a

young New Orleans doctor and brought about her isolation at Carville.[72] Leprosy radically redefined her as a foreign body, an external threat to the social and civic communities to which she previously had belonged.

Inside Carville, Martin became one of a group of patient activists who joined Stein's efforts to challenge images of unclean and highly contagious "lepers," images which they themselves previously had accepted. Patients sought to alter people's conception of their disease by renaming it. Although former MOC Hasseltine had dismissed Stein's mission to abolish the term "leper" as an "obsession,"[73] patients believed that names mattered. Whereas "leprosy" continued to conjure biblical or medieval associations of the "unclean," patient activists hoped that referring to it as Hansen's disease (HD) would simply identify a nonthreatening medical condition. Named for the Norwegian physician who first identified the bacillus in 1873, Hansen's disease was intended to serve as a more medically precise term, one that lacked any stigmatizing associations.[74] Patients therefore sought to portray people with Hansen's disease as ordinary, all-American individuals who held the same interests as men and women on the "outside" and who consequently deserved the same rights.

The development and distribution of *The Star* in the 1940s proved invaluable to their campaign. With its first publication in 1941, the newspaper not only served to inform and entertain the patient community but also to educate the public about "the real facts concerning Hansen's disease."[75] The paper circulated to almost a thousand civic groups and institutions across the nation. An initial staff of fifteen patients prepared stories, proofread copy, typed columns, drew illustrations, and mimeographed each issue of ten to twenty pages. While the group that produced the paper was small, evidence (in the form of letters to the editor, for example) suggests that many of the residents at Carville agreed with the paper's educational mission and its efforts to reform regulations.[76]

Carville patients who produced *The Star* used medical knowledge to advance their own interests by challenging the notion that such knowledge was the exclusive domain of the medical profession. Some scholars have emphasized how scientific knowledge has been used by medical professionals to disempower and exclude patients,[77] but other historians of medicine have demonstrated that patients can challenge the authority of such knowledge by resisting medical definitions of illness, uniting with other patients to undermine institutional policies, and using legal means to challenge medical authority.[78] Such findings demonstrate that members of the patient communities within medical institutions can develop the sense that they have the right and the duty to police the manner in which other people employ scientific knowledge about their disease. Patients at Carville began a campaign in the 1940s to ensure that both the public and medical professionals had a proper understanding of their disease. In its first issue, *The Star*'s masthead promoted the far-reaching goal of "Radiating the Light of Truth on Hansen's Disease." They worked to alter public views of the disease as virulently contagious. The November 1941 issue, which commemorated the anniversary of Carville's opening, pointed out that none of the facility's employees or medical staff members had ever contracted Hansen's disease, despite prolonged exposure to patients. One editorial inquired of its readers, "Can such a record be cited for any other disease which is considered even feebly contagious?"[79]

MOC Faget offered his support to the public education campaign, suggesting that the patients could enlist the assistance of physicians themselves, at least when their needs meshed with those of public health officials. He contributed an article to the December 1941 issue that encouraged the public to recognize Hansen's disease as a "germ disease, just like tuberculosis," rather than a punishment to sinners or the result of unsanitary habits. He maintained that just as the public had lost its fear of tuberculosis and eliminated the use of the term "consumptive," so might the "unwarranted hysterical fear of leprosy also pass away, and the word 'leper' lose its evil meaning and also become obsolete."[80] Faget demonstrated a greater willingness than his predecessor Hasseltine to encourage patient activism that aimed to reduce public fears of the disease; however, he still saw the need for a policy of strict segregation for patients who tested positive for the presence of the leprosy bacillus. This practice united administrators in Hawai'i and Louisiana and displayed the limits to any alliance between patients and medical officials.

Carville activists used the discovery of new forms of treatment in the early 1940s to challenge the policy of containment. They used the rhetoric of medical advancement to argue that new drugs would eventually allow them to live outside Carville by masking the more disfiguring aspects of the disease. Patients at the U.S. National Leprosarium proved eager to participate in experimental drug trials, demonstrating that despite their challenges to conventional medical assumptions about Hansen's disease, they ultimately had faith that scientific medicine would provide them with a cure. In 1941, Faget initiated a series of investigations into the effectiveness of Promin, a sulfone drug initially developed as a treatment for tuberculosis. He conducted experiments on a volunteer control group of nine patients, and after six months he reported a clearing of the patients' skin ulcers.[81] The November 1941 *Star* mentioned these experimental results and suggested that conditions might soon improve for Hansen's disease patients.[82]

Medical officials wished to proceed cautiously and limit the amount of publicity surrounding early results of new sulfone drug treatments, but patients promoted the drugs vigorously as an effective innovation and used them to initiate their own optimistic public health education campaign. When U.S. public health officials and Carville physicians proved less forthcoming about later results of research, patients found the information from other sources and printed it within the pages of their newspaper. By 1944, staff physicians had conducted a number of successful experimental treatments, and Faget pronounced Promin a "valuable drug in the treatment of leprosy." More significantly, he announced that a patient had been "paroled" in 1944 after two and a half years of treatment with Promin had apparently eliminated all traces of the Hansen's bacillus from his body.[83] Carville PHS officials printed these results within their 1944 annual report, but Faget did not reveal any of this information in his regular column in *The Star*. Patients, however, located the information in an issue of *The Military Surgeon* and published it for the benefit of their readers.[84] Patient activists incarcerated at Carville were willing and capable of sifting through the available medical literature to educate themselves and others about Hansen's disease. For doctors, the results of these treatments offered no compelling reason to change regulations at Carville; *The Star* staff, on the other hand, thought such results provided ample evidence that there was no longer any need for incarceration. Such treatments offered the hope that patients might alter public perceptions of Hansen's disease and regain their rights as citizens.

The Star staffers were determined to provide the public with contemporary insights into the disease, maintaining that a clearer understanding of the biological aspects of Hansen's disease would eradicate superstition and stigma and demonstrate that medical treatment rather than social isolation could more effectively manage the disease. In December 1942, patients began printing in every edition of the newspaper the recommendation from the 1938 World Conference on Leprosy that "any scheme for the control of leprosy will depend for its success on an educated public opinion." They also included a brief list of "Facts You Should Know About Hansen's Disease," which outlined the limited nature of the disease's communicability, the simple precautions taken by the medical staff to avoid contagion, and the freedom of outside guests to visit the facility.[85]

Patients drew on their alliances with outside groups to gain material support for their newspaper and thereby to expand their publicity campaign to reach a national and even international audience. The newspaper staff called on national veterans' groups in particular to help them muster the financial support necessary for *The Star* to remain independent of the Carville administration and to increase its circulation. Organizations such as the American Legion and its Women's Auxiliary cooperated in part because they could use the publicity about Carville patients to call for broader recognition of veteran rights. Another veterans' group, the Louisiana Forty and Eight, contributed a printing press and equipment to *The Star*, while Legionnaires throughout the country supported the paper through subscriptions.[86] Patients also increased circulation by instituting exchange programs with other hospitals, particularly with tuberculosis sanatoria. In this manner, *The Star* staff hoped to broaden their educational movement by enlisting the support of other patient groups with similar concerns. The February 1942 issue of *The Star* included an expression of solidarity from a patient at a tuberculosis sanatorium in Verona, New Jersey. Later issues featured correspondence from English-speaking patients at leprosaria throughout the world.[87] Such letters described conditions at these HD facilities and often revealed differences in policies that added momentum to the Carville patients' drive for change, strengthening their belief that many HD policies, particularly segregation, served social ends rather than medical ones.[88]

As they came to understand that publicizing medical studies alone would not alter public opinion, Carville activists devoted considerable attention to changing social perceptions of their disease. A crucial element of the patients' campaign entailed representing themselves as attractive, heterosexually active, and able to fulfill their roles as men and women, all deliberate attempts to eradicate representations of "lepers" as physically repulsive deviants who violated social conceptions of femininity and masculinity. *The Star* gave its outside readership glimpses of a patient community engaged in "typical" masculine and feminine endeavors. The sports page regularly featured stories of men performing athletic feats on the baseball diamond or golf course, while the woman's page showed Carville women to be concerned with fashion, beauty, home decorating, and gardening. In the September 1944 issue of *The Star*, one columnist credited male patients with keeping the community operating smoothly. They took jobs to earn money for their families; operated such Carville businesses as a barber shop, a bicycle repair shop, and a laundry; and served as volunteer firemen.[89] The same issue sported a new masthead for Ann Page's "The Ladies" column, which featured sketches of female patients engaged in such traditionally feminine pursuits as sewing, gossiping, cooking, and reading romances. Page explained that these images "vividly bring out with a few strokes of the pen what I've been trying to impress on our readers for three years now, namely that our girls can do most anything."[90] By "anything," Page meant those pursuits connected with the activities of American middle-class women.

Patients in Hawai'i contended with medical policies premised on the belief that they could not contain their sexual desires, but patients in Carville faced regulations that required them to suppress their sexuality. Federal public health officials continued the practice of separating men and women, a practice initiated by the Daughters of Charity during the institution's days as the Louisiana Leper Home. Officials drafted rule 6(b) in 1921 to mandate that "patients shall, on no account, visit the quarters allotted to, or hold communication with, patients of the opposite sex, unless authorized to do so by special permission of the medical officer in charge." This restriction further explained that men and women could visit each other only in established places at established times.[91] The alliance between patients and veterans' organizations had helped win extensive renovations at Carville in the 1930s and 1940s, but health officials refused requests from patients to alter regulations concerning the mixing of men and women. In 1943, Faget wrote a column in *The Star* explaining his belief that the rules remained necessary for the protection and health of Carville patients and reasserting the administration's authority to enforce the rules when necessary.[92] Patients understood this to be a veiled threat to strengthen the ban on men and women spending time together.

Faget's action surprised Carville's residents, as patients had been evading rule 6(b) since the federal government established the institution. They had grown accustomed to certain tacitly accepted violations: men and women visited each other's quarters, prepared and shared meals together, and engaged in various social activities.[93] A select group of patients with the ability or money to build cabins did so, and the rear of the 385-acre grounds came to be known as "Cottage Grove," or "Suburbia." In these tiny houses, patients of both sexes could freely mingle, dine, and entertain.[94] Faget's reassertion of the regulations in 1943, however, reminded patients that administrators could choose to enforce the rule strictly if they wanted. *The Star* staff responded to Faget's column with a call to revoke the old regulations, including those that restricted interaction between men and women. They asked instead for the kind of humane treatment that they felt reflected current medical understandings of the disease and that were more appropriate to a "modern leprosarium."[95] Only by eliminating the written restrictions, patients argued, could they break down Carville's institutional atmosphere and live their lives as ordinary men and women.

Patients particularly criticized an unwritten but rigidly enforced ban on marriage that they saw as an unjustified restriction on their civic and religious rights. A 1944 editorial noted that some patients managed to evade this prohibition by marrying while on sanctioned leave or by escaping through the "hole in the fence," an actual opening in the enclosure surrounding Carville's grounds that patients used as a route to the "outside." However, once couples returned, "They [must] live in separate quarters . . . and the higher and more elevating phases of the marital relationship, those provided by a home and joint interest, are totally unprovided for."[96] Betty Martin's memoir highlighted the predicament of patients who saw themselves as honest citizens forced to break the law in order to marry. After Martin lost her first fiancé, she found love within the institution with patient Harry Martin. She agreed to escape from the facility with him, married him, and enjoyed six years on the outside while the two evaded health officials. When Harry's condition worsened, the couple returned to Carville for treatment, where they endured the punishment of thirty days' isolation—he in the facility jail, she in the barred-window cottage reserved for the mentally ill.[97]

The fact that U.S. health administrators in Hawai'i allowed men and women to live together at the Kalaupapa settlement was not lost on Carville patients, who demanded that they receive the same treatment.[98] Patient activists distinguished Carville from other institutions, however, based on the different racial and ethnic characteristics among the populations of HD facilities around the world. Officials in Hawai'i originally allowed cohabitation because they believed Kalaupapa residents lacked the ability to restrain their sexual passions, but activists at Carville claimed the same right because of their status as U.S. citizens who could be trusted to control themselves. Hence, patient activists in Louisiana did not often directly link their condition to that of people with Hansen's disease in other parts of the globe. Activists claimed a common identity as Hansen's disease patients, a medical category that could potentially unite all people with the disease throughout the world, but they often consciously distanced themselves from patients in other territories and countries out of fear that such associations would reinforce the perception that leprosy was a "foreign" contagion and would perpetuate the exaggerated imagery connoted by this designation.

Patients used *The Star* to challenge assertions that the population at Carville differed from other ordinary American middle-class communities. An April 1942 *Star* article, for example, criticized missionary magazines for focusing on their work with leprosy among "primitive peoples." The staff writer complained that "for the patient in the United States, the picture of the foreign sufferer is so vividly overdrawn that the reader's conception of, and attitude toward, all victims of leprosy is prejudiced by the highly colored reports of the disease in distant lands." In the same article, the writer hastened to correct Victor Heiser's assertion in his best-selling memoir, *An American Doctor's Odyssey*, that most of Carville's residents were not native-born whites. "Of course, this is misinformation—it is not true, and never has been," contended the *Star* reporter. "Asiatic and West Indian negroes constitute a very small percentage of our patient population."[99] The writer implied that residents at Carville looked and behaved like "average" Americans who were portrayed as white and of European descent.

Such comments relegated the nonwhite patient population to the margins of the Carville community and undermined the activists' own efforts to create a common identity of "Hansen's disease patients" that could incorporate patient experiences from a variety of backgrounds. While technically the article correctly identified Asian and West Indian patients as a "small percentage" of Carville's population, it neglected to mention that approximately one-third of the patients were born outside of the United States, with an additional 10 percent coming from U.S. territories.[100] *The Star* regularly marginalized non-Anglo patients. It rarely acknowledged the existence of the community's Mexican Club, for example, aside from its annual celebration of Mexican independence, nor did it include the activities of its African American patients, for whom the term "segregation" meant more than isolation within a leprosarium. While segregated facilities were not mandated by law when the federal government assumed control in 1921, the custom of separate quarters continued.[101] Patient activists downplayed the diversity within their own ranks to construct a narrow and misleading public image of Carville's community as composed of middle-class, white, native-born American men and women. Such a move subtly suggested a difference between the behavior and attitudes of American Hansen's disease patients and those of "foreign lepers" and allowed the public to assign any patient of color to the latter category.

Patient Patriots: Citizenship and Rights in Wartime Carville

The need to distinguish themselves as "American" rather than "foreign" took on particular urgency during World War II, as patients cultivated an image of themselves as patriotic and capable U.S. citizens willing to make sacrifices for the national war effort. The January 1942 cover of *The Star* pictured Uncle Sam with a Red Cross emblem on his lapel and the headline "Meeting the Emergency" emblazoned across the bottom. Each issue that followed reported on Carville's local Red Cross campaign and its defense war stamp and bond drives to provide monetary support for the Allied cause. The patient who served as Carville's librarian asked *The Star*'s readers to stop sending donations of books and magazines to the Louisiana facility and direct them instead to "our boys in the Armed Service." The woman's page explained how Carville women followed Department of Agriculture bulletins on proper canning techniques, and it provided tips to its readers on the proper cultivation of Victory Gardens.[102]

Carville's patients drew on the rhetoric of wartime patriotism to argue that the institution's policies contradicted American democratic principles. Betty Martin, then a seventeen-year resident at Carville, wrote an article that revealed patient efforts to improve their conditions by pointing out the contradiction between the nation's fight for world democracy and the restrictions placed on U.S. citizens within its borders. Entitled "Why Am I Not Free?" and published in the July 1945 issue of *The Star*, the piece challenged medical policies that kept Martin incarcerated in a federal institution, revoked her right to vote, and labeled her with the stigmatizing term "leper." Drawing on the rhetoric of U.S. democratic ideals, Martin asked, "Why am I, an American, denied my rightful heritage—Liberty, Justice, and the Pursuit of Happiness, when my only crime is being sick?" She concluded with a request: "Please, someone, somewhere, give me rational answers to my rational questions, or else set me free."[103]

This essay appeared in the Independence Day issue of *The Star*, which the newspaper staff used to emphasize the contradiction between the nation's fight against tyranny and the unjust incarceration of U.S. citizens within the walls at Carville. The cover highlighted the irony of a quarantined patient community celebrating independence. It featured a patient looking out of his window at a fluttering American flag, which waved from a pole standing near the facility fence topped with barbed wire.[104] Martin's essay reminded readers that patients within the facility had served their country in past wars. She asked, "Why should I stand silently by watching some of our boys who have gone through the inferno of the European and Pacific wars being condemned by One Little Word to this institution and years of another kind of inferno in their own country?"[105]

Martin unwittingly echoed the sentiments of African Americans' Double V

Cover of the July 1945 issue of *The Star*, illustrating the contrast between the American ideal of freedom and the reality of patients' incarceration.

campaign. She called on the public to recognize the contradictions embedded in policies that restricted the rights of citizens even as the government asked those citizens to make wartime sacrifices.[106] She did not decry the racial segregation in Carville, however. While African Americans struggled for victory against fascism abroad and racism at home, Martin voiced no awareness of the links between her own forced separation from society and the segregation of patients of color within the community at Carville. Nor did she discuss the situation faced by those in Kalaupapa, who found their isolation intensified during the war. Despite its soaring rhetoric, Martin and other white patients at Carville hoped to use the war to achieve the specific and limited goals of amending federal policies governing Hansen's disease.

The Carville American Legion post reprinted Martin's article and directed it to the attention of several members of Congress, an act that helped initiate a focused campaign to amend the National Leprosy Act of 1917. In particular, patient activists intended to eliminate the ban on patient cohabitation and marriages, to end the forced incarceration of patients, and to encourage more lenient leave policies and the development of out-patient care. The post brought these issues to the attention of the national American Legion to generate more widespread publicity in Washington. At its national convention in 1945, the Legion recommended that Surgeon General Thomas Parran establish a national advisory committee to study management of the disease in the United States. Watson B. Miller, an ally of the veterans and the recently appointed head of the Federal Security Agency (which included the Public Health Service), also pushed for the creation of such a board. By May 1946, the surgeon general had appointed a committee consisting of federal and state public health officials, representatives from secular and religious Hansen's disease organizations, physicians and medical attendants, and other advisers, such as Claude A. Brown, national field secretary of the American Legion.[107] Patients recognized that the committee was only a small step forward, but they hoped it would serve as an influential conduit between their own recently formed Patients' Committee for Social Improvement and Rehabilitation and the federal public health officials in Washington who held the power to alter national HD policy.

The patients' efforts to assert their rights as citizens suffering unjust treatment and to direct national attention to policies and conditions at Carville received an unexpected postwar boost from the publicity surrounding the case of Hans and Gertrude Hornbostel. In May 1946, Major Hans Hornbostel, a World War II veteran and survivor of the Bataan death march, publicly announced that his wife, Gertrude, had contracted Hansen's disease and that he intended to live with her at the national leprosarium at Carville. Gertrude Hornbostel—who had been imprisoned in a Japanese concentration camp in the Philippines until the end of the war—had received a diagnosis of Hansen's disease a year after her return to the United States.[108] Although her doctor could have quietly provided her with sulfone drug treatments on an outpatient basis and thereby avoided notifying public health officials, she decided she could receive better treatment at Carville, where doctors were most familiar with the disease and its treatment.[109]

Initial accounts of the story presented it as a lurid melodrama, thereby seemingly undermining the patients' educational campaign. The Hornbostels had decided to publicize Gertrude's decision to seek treatment at Carville to generate sympathy for the couple and to gain permission for Hans to live at the facility with his wife. Instead, the media crafted a sensationalized tale of romantic sacrifice that did little to generate public acceptance of the disease or to alter national HD policy. Newspaper accounts presented portraits of leprosy sufferers as loathsome outcasts and spread inaccuracies about the facility and the disease. The *San Francisco Call-Bulletin* ran a front-page banner headline announcing "San Francisco Wife Leper: Army Mate Begs to Share Isolation for Life."[110] An editorial in the *Springfield (Mass.) Union* related that "Major Hornbostel is ready to leave the outside world with its accustomed comforts, its safety, its cleanliness behind him to enter that dark place which brings to mind that ominous word 'unclean.' To be with his wife, he is ready to run the risk of himself becoming a leper."[111] Such publicity failed to convince public health officials to allow Hans access to the facility outside the regular 7 A.M. to 7 P.M. visiting hours.

Patients complained that these accounts spread misinformation about Hansen's disease, but *The Star* staff realized that the publicity also provided an eager audience for the patients' reeducation campaign. Martin recalled in her autobiography, "As an incorrigible optimist I sincerely believed we could turn the affair to a good advantage, since it was bringing a hush-hush subject into the open and making the nation leprosy conscious."[112] *The Star* acted as a news bureau. Its staff sent the United Press reporters information pertaining to medical research conducted at Carville, to the recovery of patients due to sulfone drugs, and to the limited likelihood of Major Hornbostel's contracting the disease. They also urged the U.S. Public Health Service to send corrections to newspapers that printed medically inaccurate accounts.

The presence of the Hornbostels and the visits they attracted from interested parties and journalists energized the patient community and its reform campaign. The September 1946 cover of *The Star* featured a cartoon sketch of patients leading multiple tours through an active facility filled with smiling, productive people. One visitor exclaims, "Why doctor they look just like real people." Another asks her guide, "But aren't you afraid to work here?" and receives the reply, "I'm a patient." A third individual identifies himself as a representative of the New York Legion post and is introduced to the local adjutant.[113] Gertrude Hornbostel became a magnet for visitors and fan mail, and she used her contact with the public to advance the patients' educational campaign. She joined the staff of *The Star* and frequently wrote columns highly critical of Carville's medical staff and federal public health officials. In one *Star* article, Hornbostel urged the PHS to put an end to patient segregation and to take a more active role in improving conditions for patients who sought treatment. "I would like to see everyone who suffers from Hansen's disease get treatment with the new sulfa drugs, but it must be voluntary," she insisted, claiming that the "'traditional segregation idea' should be abandoned." She further stressed the need for a "thorough educational campaign for the public through the country's press, the radio, the schools and the use of public clinics for treatment."[114] Hans Hornbostel, too, became a vocal advocate for Carville's residents. He initiated a successful campaign to amend the Louisiana law that had stripped patients of their right to vote, and he joined the Carville chapter of the American Legion, providing the post with a member who could leave the facility freely and serve as a spokesman for their demands.[115]

The patient strategy of redirecting the publicity surrounding the Hornbostels toward their public education efforts worked. In the months following the couple's announcement, members of the press frequently toured the facility, interviewed patients, and wrote less sensationalized accounts of life at Carville. Reporters from Chicago, New Orleans, and St. Louis all made visits to the facility and wrote extensive feature stories on Carville for their respective newspapers.[116] These articles not only promoted a more educated view of HD patients; they also criticized the public fear and official policy that detained patients at Carville. One *St. Louis Post-Dispatch* editorial pointed out the implications of the language used by officials at the facility: "The 'inmates' are 'guarded' against 'absconding' until they are 'paroled.' The very terms speak of imprisonment." The editorial condemned such treatment as "inhumane" and "senseless" and called for a more enlightened policy that would encourage the estimated 2,000 to 5,000 people with Hansen's disease outside of the facility to come forward and receive treatment free of the threat of humiliation and confinement.[117]

The Star staff used such reporting to compel the PHS to change the way its officers managed Carville. A patient committee working closely with members of *The Star* developed a list of recommended changes, the most pressing being a call for an end to mandatory confinement.[118] The patients sent a copy of their petition and recommendations, signed by 312 members of the community, to each member of the National Leprosy Advisory Committee, which the PHS had formed in 1946. This committee subsequently recommended a more open containment policy, an effective system of treatment centers throughout the country, and housing for married couples.[119] Patients and *The Star* staff pressed the Public Health Service to implement these and other suggestions, an effort that would eventually yield results in the following decade.

Still, the Hornbostel case had unforeseen consequences relative to the Carville patients' ability to form a coalition with HD patients at Kalaupapa. The fact that Gertrude Hornbostel contracted her disease in the Philippines only heightened public perceptions that Hansen's disease represented a foreign disease that threatened the American population. Her efforts to change American perceptions of the disease seemed to extend primarily to changing people's ideas of what should be done with those accepted as true American citizens who had the disease. This allowed people to continue to view Hawai'i, with a population composed primarily of Asians and Pacific Islanders, as a separate entity requiring a different set of standards.

The Other Americans: Resistance and Isolation in Hawai'i

As Carville activists on the mainland mobilized their status as citizens to demand a voice in their treatment, residents of Kalaupapa resisted the attempts by health officials to impose their vision of proper civic behavior from above. The experience of war only exacerbated racial tensions and further isolated the residents of Kalaupapa. After Japan bombed Pearl Harbor on 7 December 1941, Hawai'i became the strategic linchpin for the United States in its war against Japan. In these circumstances, territorial residents found increased opportunity for presenting their home as a potential state and positioning themselves as worthy American citizens. At the same time, however, federal officials underscored the lack of democracy in Hawai'i by placing the islands under martial law. Statehood efforts came to a halt as mainlanders grew more suspicious of the loyalties of the territory's majority nonwhite population, particularly those of Japanese descent, and Euroamerican officials concluded that constraining nonwhite bodies was even more crucial in their effort to maintain authority.[120] As considerable attention was directed toward the war effort, the Board of Hospitals and Settlement worked to minimize the needs of HD facilities while still keeping patients tightly constrained.

The disruptions of the Second World War altered the fabric of life in

Kalaupapa and Kalihi in a way that would have long-term reverberations. Where once Kalaupapa was held to be a punishment for patients too unruly to be held in Kalihi, or as the site to send the most helpless cases who could not benefit from the medical advancements in Honolulu, during the war it became the primary site for the care of HD patients. By January 1942, the board arranged to transfer patients at Kalihi to Kalaupapa, with the understanding that the more isolated island of Moloka'i represented a safer environment for the sick than Kalihi's vulnerable O'ahu harbor location.[121] By 15 May 1942, all but twenty Kalihi patients were relocated to Kalaupapa.

Where the protests of individual parents in the 1930s had failed to gain sympathetic publicity or to move health officials to transfer children with leprosy to their parents at the settlement, the threat of additional Japanese raids on O'ahu convinced the Board of Hospitals and Settlement to bring the children of Kalihi to Kalaupapa. Forty-two children between the ages of nine and eighteen suddenly made the settlement their new home.[122] Their presence changed the composition of the community and mandated the creation of institutions deemed appropriate for their well-being and civic education.[123] To that end, the board established Kalaupapa Boy Scout Troop No. 46, which began awarding merit badges in 1942, and followed with a Girl Scout Troop the next year. Board members authorized the construction of a new school at Kalaupapa, which opened in October 1942 with equipment from Mt. Happy School at Kalihi. Instruction in "an appropriate program of academic, domestic science and vocational work" began for these children in the new environment of Kalaupapa.[124] After the war, however, the policy toward children reverted to the pre-Pearl Harbor standard. No children were allowed into the settlement; by spring of 1948, only sixteen patients under the age of sixteen remained at Kalaupapa.[125] The wishes of such families as the Kupeles to raise their children played no part in the board's decision to bring children to Kalaupapa, and they failed to prevent the board from reversing its decision with the war's end.

Yet the board's actions may have strengthened the Hawaiian community at Kalaupapa by forcing its members to turn inward. In certain respects, military contingencies made the Kalaupapa settlement more isolated from the rest of the islands. With inter-island transportation considered an extravagance, regular weekly freight and passenger steamer service ended in 1942. The U.S. Army also canceled all flights to Kalaupapa Airport. Administrators focused attention on transporting necessary food and supplies to the facility, contracting with locally owned sampans and the occasional military craft to carry necessary materials to the settlement.[126] While these alternative methods provided sufficient goods to keep the facility in operation, they could not replicate prewar conditions in a way that encouraged close communication between the Kalaupapa community and other islands. Relatives could no longer visit, nor could letters and packages arrive every week for patients seeking words from home or materials that could not be found in the small, isolated environs of Kalaupapa.

The war thus effectively drew the territorial administration's attention away from the settlement and reinforced among many Kalaupapa residents a strong sense of community and Hawaiian identity. Obtaining the full rights of American citizenship became more clearly seen by some settlement residents as a particularly Euroamerican enterprise that would not provide a particularly useful tool for Hawaiian patients to demand improved conditions. Depicted both by territorial officials and to some degree by Carville patients as "foreign lepers," they could not draw upon the same notions of U.S. citizenship as did patients at the U.S. National Leprosarium. During the war, they developed a sense of solidarity as Hawaiians instead. Residents would struggle to maintain this identity in the years following World War II, however. Territorial administrators renewed their statehood and modernization efforts, a goal that required the Euroamerican elite to portray the territory's diverse populace as ready and willing to assume their roles as citizens. At the same time, public health officials again separated families and divided the patient community in Hawai'i between the Kalaupapa settlement and Honolulu.

Conclusion

Examining the ways in which public health officials, politicians, and patients employed different notions of citizenship to support different conceptions of how leprosy should be regulated reveals critical distinctions in the way people conceived of the disease in Hawai'i and Louisiana. Public health administrators viewed both Kalaupapa and Carville as operating "under the American flag," but ideas about racial, ethnic, and colonial difference shaped different policies at each institution. In Hawai'i, Euroamerican administrators used leprosy policy as a means of demonstrating their ability to act as proper stewards to a society unschooled in notions of Western medicine and order. They attempted to transform Kalaupapa into a modern medical facility that would teach its Hawaiian and Asian population how to be good American citizens and how to adopt to proper American lifestyles while keeping these men and women rigidly segregated from the rest of society. Euroamerican health officials and legislators hoped this would perform a second function by showing people on the mainland that the territory was entirely capable of controlling threats to the prosperity and health of "American" bodies, thereby strengthening the case for eventual full inclusion of Hawai'i in the nation as a state.

Hawaiian patients found little room to maneuver within this Euroamerican conception of citizenship, though they challenged the health authorities in the Judd administration when they could. Seldom able to communicate their own conception of the disease to the public, they instead focused on building a community that challenged the government's attempt to label them as inferior or needing Western oversight. This effort gained momentum from the settlement's enforced isolation during the war years. Even as health officials sought to create a model American medical institution at Kalaupapa, patient segregation led to the creation of a uniquely Hawaiian space that stood in sharp contrast to Euroamerican visions of Kalaupapa as a laboratory for Americanization imposed from above.

Health officials in Louisiana shared many of their territorial colleagues' notions about the threatening character of leprosy and sought to contain patients who had the disease, but activists at Carville managed to turn the rhetoric of U.S. citizenship to their advantage. During the Great Depression, they formed alliances with outside groups to challenge U.S. public health officials on the questions of how to treat people with their disease properly. World War II provided an opportunity for Carvillians to contrast Americans' willingness to fight for freedom abroad with the government's insistence on restricting the freedom of people with Hansen's disease at home. Indeed, they presented themselves as willing to sacrifice for the war effort and therefore just as worthy of civil liberties as those Americans without Hansen's disease. Whereas Hawaiian patients looked askance at Western medical policy, viewing it as another American colonialist effort to alter the fabric of life in their community, patients at Carville sought to draw on and reshape a medical discourse to support their own needs and goals. To some extent, they proved successful, using wartime rhetoric and medical knowledge to force public health officials to reevaluate how they would understand and respond to Hansen's disease.

The white majority at Carville, however, glossed over the racial and ethnic diversity that existed within their own institution and reinforced the colonialist rhetoric of U.S. public health officials who associated the disease with "uncivilized" areas and peoples. They distanced themselves from their fellow HD patients in tropical climates, such as Hawai'i, fearing that such an association could undermine their efforts to depict themselves as self-reliant, ordinary, and nonthreatening American citizens. Patients at Carville based their claim to loosened restrictions on a notion of citizenship based on racial distinctions that barred their fellow patients in Hawai'i from participation; furthermore, they unwittingly invoked a language that territorial officials had long used to defend their right to segregate people with Hansen's disease in Hawai'i. Ultimately, they did force a partial public reconception of their disease, but they also inadvertently strengthened connections between "leprosy" and foreign bodies as threats to American citizens' public health.

CHAPTER SIX

Negotiating an End to Segregation

Carville patient activists prodded doctors to publicize the beneficial effects of sulfone drugs in the years following World War II, hoping to use them as a tool toward ending segregation. Dr. G. H. Faget, Carville's medical director, instead saw these promising treatments as a means to lure new patients to the institution while maintaining a policy of mandatory confinement and isolation. In the September 1946 issue of *The Star*, he hailed Promin, Diasone, and Promizole as "helpful drugs in the treatment of Hansen's disease" that could—"with time"—"restore the health of many patients." Faget's appeal blended enticing images of the facility with sober preaching about the risk of contagion. After depicting Carville as a hospital with "all the comforts of a first-class hotel," he admonished prospective patients that they "should realize that they are a menace to their families." For Faget, drug therapies and institutional isolation were inherently linked. "In this hospital alone will you find all of the facilities for the administration of the sulfa drugs that combat Hansen's disease," he wrote. "You will be given the advantage of all that modern medical science has to offer you. Come and your hope will be born anew!"[1] If the postwar era offered new promise for people with Hansen's disease, that promise still depended upon institutional confinement, according to medical administrators such as Faget.

The questions of what "modern medical science" could offer patients and where it would be offered proved crucial to defining HD policy in the postwar era. It is tempting to view the development of HD drug therapies as the key to ending the segregation of patients with Hansen's disease, but drugs alone did not loosen or terminate this policy. Rather, the reverse was true— innovations in treatment initially intensified institutional control over patients. As Barron Lerner has shown in his study of Seattle's Skid Road tuberculosis patients, institutions in the postwar era simultaneously became the focus of disease eradication efforts and emerged as the best places to monitor patients undergoing drug therapy.[2] Physicians and hospital administrators in Carville and Kalaupapa worked to keep HD patients confined at their institutions because they saw it as the best method for dispensing treatment, observing the results, and controlling the patient population. For physicians and public health administrators, the initial success of sulfone drugs presented a new reason to uphold a policy of isolating and institutionalizing patients with Hansen's disease: only in the institution could the patient receive the most modern and closely regulated treatment for the disease. People with the disease in both Hawai'i and Louisiana experienced a greater degree of surveillance within institutional walls after 1945 as administrators increasingly adopted the kind of bureaucratic discipline found in U.S. general hospitals.

Patients, for their part, used the new therapies to demand greater freedom and to remind health officials forcibly that new drug trials and regimens required the cooperation of patients. Carville residents effectively utilized a rhetoric of medical progress to portray themselves as collaborators in the quest for the most scientific and effective treatment of Hansen's disease and to characterize the policy of strict segregation as a throwback to less enlightened times. Postwar pressure from patients and their allies ultimately improved conditions at the facility and brought about the lifting of the segregation mandate. By the later 1950s, patients could receive treatment at local outpatient clinics, and they no longer needed to abandon friends and family to reside in an isolated institution. Such policies also dispersed the patient community, however, and ultimately weakened their efforts to eliminate the cultural stigma surrounding their disease. In particular, patients relied on a medical discourse that had long characterized those who failed to embrace scientific understandings of disease as uncivilized and barbaric, and this discourse perpetuated divisions between mainland patients and some of their fellow HD sufferers in Hawai'i.

Patients in Hawai'i, meanwhile, fractured between those supporting outpatient programs and those seeking to retain a uniquely "Hawaiian" community within Kalaupapa. As Hawai'i moved toward becoming a state, some Hawaiians with Hansen's disease positioned themselves as part of the national body to counter perceptions that linked "leprosy" with savagery and foreignness. Some residents remaining at Kalaupapa, however, were not anxious to abandon the settlement. They sought the right to leave the peninsula when they desired, but they also wished to retain the community they had forged over many decades. They used their isolation to create a vibrant interethnic Hawaiian identity and to challenge a Western medical policy that first sought to contain them and later to disperse them.

Aerial photograph of the U.S. National Leprosarium, Carville, Louisiana, situated on the banks of the Mississippi River. Photo courtesy of the United States Public Health Service and the National Library of Medicine.

The years after 1945, then, proved instrumental for devising new treatments and meanings for Hansen's disease. Patients and public health officials confronted and attempted to reconcile the differences in HD policies in Hawai'i and Louisiana. Patients called for institutions that could operate under less restrictive regulations while still serving as state-of-the-art medical treatment facilities. Doctors often sought to create more orderly institutions that would also act as useful scientific research sites. In the process, both groups recognized the need to eradicate the stigma associated with leprosy, which had been reinforced by the U.S. history of incarcerating people with the disease. Such a history threatened the sense of scientific promise that doctors, patients, and public health officials hoped to embody with more modern HD institutions. The process of defining a containable, treatable, and "American" Hansen's disease at Carville, however, depended upon the continuing existence of a threatening, chronic, and "foreign" leprosy within Kalaupapa.

Educating the Public: Patients versus the PHS

Debates over how HD policies should change in response to such scientific medical advancements as sulfone drug therapies motivated patient activists at Carville to heighten their campaign against the existing segregation mandate after World War II. While they welcomed Faget's discussion of the benefits of Promin, Diasone, and Promizole, they disagreed with his argument that HD patients outside of the facility were a "menace" to their families. Activists feared that such a view only reinforced notions that the disease was highly contagious. Patient Stanley Stein responded to Faget's 1946 article in an editorial that criticized existing policies enforced by health officials, contending that "under the regulations now in effect, leprosy is regarded more as a disgrace than as a slightly communicable, bacterial disease." He suggested that Faget could succeed in having more people come to Carville voluntarily if patients did not lose their freedom upon entry. Only when policies toward HD more closely resembled those toward tuberculosis, Stein argued, would people with the disease report for early treatment.[3]

Gertrude Hornbostel wrote a more scathing rebuttal to Faget's article, in which she both criticized public health policy and charged Carville doctors with advocating the continued practice of patient containment to advance their own interests. Faget had suggested that patients should consider receiving care at Carville a "privilege," but Hornbostel rejoined, "It seems to me that the doctors in this hospital are the 'privileged,' as they are the only ones in this country who have the opportunity to experiment on patients with Hansen's disease." The segregation of patients at Carville placed knowledge of new treatment primarily in the hands of the few physicians in Louisiana. Challenging Faget's argument that patients lived free of charge in a facility comparable to a "first-class hotel," Hornbostel claimed that patients would rather pay for treatment than give up their freedom, particularly when few amenities accompanied confinement. While not wishing to dissuade people from seeking the new drugs, she emphasized that patients should come with a clear recognition of the kinds of conditions they would face upon arrival. She pointedly concluded that "segregation is not the solution, but for a medical experiment station for the Health Service, it is perfect."[4] Hornbostel's critique reveals an underlying sense among some patients that the segregation mandate served more to promote the research and professional agendas of doctors than to protect the public health.

Carville patients identified economic interests as the motivation behind efforts by both the hospital personnel and neighboring communities to retain the policy of strict segregation. Patients who used current medical knowledge to publicize Hansen's disease as only slightly contagious jeopardized the hazard pay that both attendants and physicians received for working in the leprosarium. In his memoir, Stanley Stein recalled that some employees at Carville feared that their 25 to 50 percent salary bonuses might be cut if the government became convinced that they were not at risk from infection.[5] Hospital personnel who wanted to continue the policy of segregation sought support from members of the surrounding Louisiana communities of Carville, Gonzales, and St. Gabriel. One *Star* article noted that residents who had once resisted efforts to establish a federal leprosarium in their backyards had now grown to appreciate the economic benefits of such a facility. Local merchants welcomed the money of facility visitors, while politicians worked to retain the "juicy plum" that brought federal dollars to the region.[6] All these groups resisted patients' efforts at policy reform. Hospital workers and leaders of Carville's neighboring communities attempted to stifle patient activists by asking the American Legion to withdraw its support for the recent federally appointed National Leprosy Advisory Committee, arguing that it did not represent the wishes of the entire patient body.[7]

In contrast to what local economic interests wanted the public to believe, the patients at Carville unanimously supported an end to mandatory confinement and other revisions in HD regulations. Every able-bodied patient— 312 in all—signed a petition advocating a fifteen-point list of recommended changes, with a call for an end to segregation as the first item.[8] The list of demands demonstrated a patient consensus that concrete measures would alter the nature of treatment and life within the facility, increase research funding for Hansen's disease, and eliminate the stigma surrounding the disease.[9] Patients understood that changes in all these areas were necessary to improve the quality of life for people who had Hansen's disease in the United States.

The Carville United Patients Committee actively sought to influence the politically appointed National Leprosy Advisory Committee to adopt its recommendations. Patient activists sent a copy of their petition to each member of the national committee and encouraged them to visit the facility for additional consultation with the patients, who were well versed in the current medical findings concerning Hansen's disease. At its December 1946 meeting, the advisory committee agreed with patient recommendations for the establishment of a more liberal leave policy, an effective system of outpatient treatment centers throughout the country, improved recreational facilities, and housing for married couples.[10] Patients welcomed the suggestions of the advisory group, but they also pressed for a firm commitment from the U.S. Public Health Service (PHS) that it would actually make these and other changes. In particular, patients wanted PHS officials to agree to move quickly on a specific recommendation regarding revisions to the "outmoded regulations" governing patient activities within the leprosarium.[11]

Patient activists found an influential ally during their campaign in a prominent Army veteran, Col. G. H. Rarey, the national vice president of the American Federation of the Physically Handicapped. Rarey first became acquainted with leprosy while serving in the Philippines from 1899 to 1911. In 1946, he published a manifesto in *The Star* outlining how the public could "help rid the world of leprosy." His five-point plan required research, education, an end to the segregation policy, rehabilitation, and the establishment of a treatment center in a cooler and drier climate.[12] He brought the article to the attention of two congressmen, who had the piece read into the *Congressional Record*. Following the announcement of the National Leprosy Advisory Committee's recommendations, Rarey argued that such efforts only focused on minor concerns and failed to address the central problems of stigmatization and isolation that the patients encountered.[13] He proved instrumental in generating additional congressional support for legislation designed to improve the situation of people with Hansen's disease. Although a bill introduced in the House in 1948 by Representative Charles J. Kersten died in committee, a Senate subcommittee held hearings on a revised National Leprosy Act in May 1949.[14]

This act of focusing congressional attention on their demands represented an extraordinary achievement for the relatively small group of HD patient activists segregated at Carville.[15] The proposed new National Leprosy Act drew extensively from the patients' original fifteen-point list of recommendations and demonstrated their ambition and commitment to spreading medical knowledge about the disease in order to change its social meaning. The first article in the bill—and for the patients, one of the most crucial— called for the creation of a national HD education campaign, which would help in "fostering a spirit of tolerance and understanding upon the part of the public."[16] Patient activists believed that eliminating the stigma attached to Hansen's disease would help the public accept people who had it, which would make possible both outpatient care and an end to segregation. The bill also called for expanding research on the disease, another significant patient demand. Carville patients placed a great deal of trust in the medical system and believed that a strong financial commitment to scientific investigation could only yield benefits for those who suffered from the disease.

The bill also reflected the concerns of the patients' most powerful allies, the veterans' groups that championed the Carville patient activists. As of 1947, the Carville facility contained thirty-two World War II veterans, and public health officials expected the number to rise as doctors made additional diagnoses of Hansen's disease among those who had served in the Pacific theater.[17] Rarey and other veterans' group leaders saw the PHS's handling of the disease as an example of the government's failure to provide proper care for those who had sacrificed their health to defend their country. These leaders effectively instigated material changes to the facility and brought patients' demands to the attention of federal lawmakers. The National Leprosy Act's emphasis on such expensive programs as providing federal financial support for families of HD patients and giving hiring preferences to discharged Carvillians, however, proved unpalatable to public health officials and, ultimately, to Congress.

U.S. Public Health Service officials, fearing that such a law would weaken their control over HD research and treatment, did not accept many patient recommendations. PHS representatives testified that the National Leprosy Act was unnecessary because its provisions would either duplicate existing programs or undermine the service's efforts to protect the health of patients and the public. J. Donald Kingsley, acting administrative head of the Federal Security Agency, argued that the disease remained somewhat communicable and therefore required the forced detention of certain patients, a position that placed the PHS firmly in opposition to the movement to end segregation. Other comments by Kingsley revealed deeper tensions between the PHS on one side and veterans' groups and Carville's patient community on the other. The PHS was wary of provisions in Title II of the bill that failed to define clearly which agency had the responsibility for the care and expense of treating veterans. The Veterans' Administration (VA) already managed health care for former military personnel. Kingsley feared that the new law would force the PHS to pay the expense for HD patients who sought care in VA hospitals, while giving the service no oversight in treatment. At the same time, the situation at Carville would grow more complicated under the proposed law because the VA would gain authority over those veterans who remained at the Louisiana facility. Finally, the PHS resisted provisions for vocational training, hiring preferences, and financial assistance that offered special treatment for HD patients. PHS officials turned patient arguments about medical advancements in Hansen's disease research against the bill's proponents, suggesting that "new knowledge of this disease seems to weaken, rather than strengthen, the case for singling out it and its victims for such special consideration as S. 704 [the National Leprosy Act] would provide."[18]

If the bill aimed to bestow special rights on HD patients, proponents argued that it did so only to counter the negative effects that arose from the PHS's years of singling out the disease for special discrimination and isolation. Senator Claude Pepper, who introduced the bill, challenged the PHS's record in managing the disease over the previous decades. He pointed out that a lack of proper knowledge of the disease among most medical practitioners had led to misdiagnoses and improper treatment for many patients before they were correctly identified as having contracted Hansen's disease. Furthermore, the fifty-year policy of containment had failed to control or eradicate the disease in the United States. It had instead contributed to people's decisions not to seek treatment at Carville. Doctors at the institution had proven unable to identify how individuals contracted or transmitted the disease. While the PHS continued to argue that Hansen's disease required segregation due to its communicability, patients repeatedly pointed out that not one staff member had ever contracted the disease after working at the National Leprosarium. Pepper supported instead an initiative by the New York Health Department, which had ended a policy of compulsory segregation in the 1940s and allowed Hansen's disease patients to seek treatment at any New York hospital and to live among other citizens between treatments. He concluded his assessment with a statement echoing the patients' demands for education and innovation: "If we profess to be an enlightened democracy, surely we can do no more than change our ideas and practices in treating the victims of this dreaded disease."[19]

Where Pepper called on the democratic ideals of the nation to defend the bill, other proponents used the rhetoric of veteran sacrifice to convince the Senate committee of the need for a revised national leprosy policy. Paul Strachan, president of the American Federation of the Physically Handicapped, spoke of the many military personnel who might have exposed themselves to the disease "while on duty in the steaming jungles or rice paddies of the Orient," arguing that those "disabled heroes who fought to preserve our country" deserved more than "a mere gesture of good will or a pious hope on the part of Congress."[20] The bill's supporters offered as an example the story of "Pancho," a former GI from California who suffered in isolation in the Los Angeles County Hospital's communicable disease ward before the American Legion secured passage to Carville for him. *The Star* publicized his case as an example of an inefficient national policy that failed to provide effective care for all patients diagnosed with Hansen's disease.[21] Patients and their allies also recounted Gertrude Hornbostel's imprisonment in a Japanese concentration camp and the efforts of her World War II veteran husband to accompany her into Carville.[22] The patients' statements pointed out that veterans at Carville did not even receive the rehabilitation or educational benefits guaranteed by the GI Bill of Rights.[23] Though supporters of the bill mobilized stories of selfless soldiers to gain acceptance for those with the disease, their emphasis on Hansen's disease as a hidden danger lurking in Asian locales also continued to underscore the perception of the disease as a foreign contagion.

Advocates of the bill faced other obstacles, as Hansen's disease simply did not generate the widespread impact and interest of other illnesses. In seeking to reassure PHS officials that the bill would enlarge the service's authority, not impinge upon it, Pepper attempted to draw comparisons between Hansen's disease and other medical conditions. Similar laws instituting the National Heart Institute and the National Cancer Institute had also included seeming duplications of authority, he explained, but they instead produced further progress in the investigations of those health issues.[24] Despite the active support of national veterans' groups, however, the level of public interest for devoting additional funds for Hansen's disease did not match that associated with heart disease and cancer. Those diseases were looked upon as sicknesses of progress and civilization that national officials and medical professionals needed to fight in order to improve modern living for U.S. citizens.[25] While patient activists and their supporters sought to transform understandings of the disease, in part by referring to it as Hansen's, the bill that was meant to address their concerns still called it "leprosy." The older term evoked a disease that most Americans viewed as a stigma redolent of other times and regions, not an American disease that required national funds or attention. Despite attempts to work out differences between the bill's supporters and PHS officials, the National Leprosy Act died in a congressional committee. Rarey repeatedly tried to revive the bill until his death in 1954, but it never passed.[26]

Drugs and Institutional Discipline in Postwar Hawai'i

Debates over the proper administration of leprosy[27] during the postwar era proved even more divisive in Hawai'i, as fractures emerged not only between patients and medical administrators, but also among public health officials. Whereas Carville administrators could tout their on-site development of drugs with the potential to cure Hansen's disease, medical researchers in Hawai'i saw their scientific resources actually diminish as the federal government closed its investigation station at Kalihi during the war. Some physicians hoped to reinvent Kalaupapa as a world-class disease research and treatment facility after 1945, while others sought to develop a new approach to leprosy treatment in the islands by establishing a less isolated institution on the outskirts of Honolulu. Both alternatives meant that health officials would consider ending the practice of sending new patients to Kalaupapa. Some patients feared that this change in policy would result in the disruption or even destruction of what they viewed as an autonomous Hawaiian community. As administrators drew links between drugs, research, and scientific progress, patients who did not display a willingness to participate in new medical regimens became cast once again as threats to the future of the territory.

Territorial health officials saw the postwar era's promise of improved medical treatment and technology as an opportunity to eliminate the stigma attached to leprosy by emphasizing treatment over isolation. In other words, they hoped to depict Kalaupapa as a place where people with leprosy went to improve their condition rather than as a place where the sick went to die. Even before the war ended, the medical staff at the settlement urged the Board of Hospitals and Settlement to initiate a public health education campaign that could tell people of the "joys of life at Kalaupapa." By eliminating the "hush-hush attitude" that surrounded discussions of leprosy, medical personnel hoped to overcome patients' hesitancy toward revealing their disease, to make life easier for patients' families, and to improve conditions for "parolees" who returned to their homes.[28]

As Faget had at Carville, Hawai'i's health officials intended to use the promise of sulfone drugs to change the nature of treatment within the settlement. Since Kalaupapa lacked the funding for medical personnel, research, and resources that Carville possessed, legislative support became a top priority for Kalaupapa physicians. They sought funding for additional research, particularly for the "clinical and laboratory study of patients and how to improve their condition, not investigation of rats and hamsters."[29] Drugs that had been favorably tested on patients at Carville during the war years did not find their way to Hawai'i until 1945, when six patients began using Promin. Resident physician Norman Sloan expressed his frustration with the limited nature of the drug therapies. "We would like to extend their use to all patients who desire them; but until we have adequate facilities for care of patients and laboratory control, we must move very slowly. Many of the patients are growing impatient—and who can blame them?" Financial difficulties also limited hiring and curtailed necessary upgrades to buildings and equipment. Having managed to make do throughout World War II, officials grew frustrated that the end of the war failed to bring about renewed investment in the leprosy program. Sloan complained, "Although the war is over, we have been forced to struggle through another year with too few nurses, and with no action on the urgent regulations which were submitted to the Board over a year ago."[30]

Sloan hoped that further testing of the drugs in the Kalaupapa community would both benefit the patients and draw positive attention to the settlement's medical program, results that would thereby stimulate additional funding. By June 1947, he reported 107 patients on Promin and 120 on Diasone and hailed the drug therapies as an "outstanding development" under which all patients improved.[31] He cautioned, however, that while 77 percent of Kalaupapa patients with active cases of leprosy received sulfone treatment, the settlement hospital lacked the space, the equipment, and the personnel for proper administration of the program. New drugs, he insisted, could not be merely handed over to patients without oversight. "There is another side to the picture," Sloan explained. "These drugs are definitely poisonous." Medical personnel needed to supervise their use and administer blood and urine testing. Sloan heralded the positive accounts that the drug treatment received in the local press, believing that the information would help educate the public and encourage patients to submit to treatment during the early stages of their disease, but he reminded the legislature that the program required more funding to ensure its success. "A new day is here in the history of leprosy," Sloan proclaimed. "A new and wonderful opportunity is in our hands. *And we are not prepared to meet it*."[32] Patients and doctors at Carville had the resources to debate the nature of different treatments, while officials at Kalaupapa struggled simply to provide them.

The medical staff at Kalaupapa compared their conditions with those at Carville and found the Hawaiian settlement wanting in many ways. Clearly envisioning the Louisiana institution as a model, medical personnel advocated separate grounds for patients and personnel, whereby "workers can live relatively normal lives and rear their families." Perhaps envying the tennis courts and nine-hole golf course available to doctors at Carville, the Kalaupapa staff suggested that the installation of a swimming pool in the settlement would provide beneficial leisure options. They also recommended quarterly leave and higher pay.[33] Sloan called attention to a more significant discrepancy between the two facilities when he visited Carville in 1948. The Louisiana institution boasted six doctors for four hundred patients and a laboratory with three full-time technicians and a blood chemist.[34] Kalaupapa had only two full-time physicians for approximately two hundred patients, and it lacked a separately staffed lab altogether. Reacting to further budget reductions in the late 1940s, Sloan argued that the time for wartime sacrifice in Hawai'i had ended and the time for "progress" had begun. He focused on the threat that low funding posed to the therapeutic programs, but he also highlighted the degree to which low salaries, isolation, and the lack of adequate housing and recreational facilities made it difficult for the board to attract properly trained workers to Kalaupapa.[35]

Physicians such as Sloan believed increased funding could transform Kalaupapa into a premier leprosy research and treatment institution because they found the settlement already superior to Carville in significant ways. He emphasized, for example, that the cottage system at Kalaupapa was "more to be desired than Carville's highly institutionalized layout," noting that Louisiana patients competed for the few individual cottages available. Sloan also found that patients in the mainland facility had more severe ulcerations than residents at Kalaupapa. He suggested that this condition might result because patients at Carville tended to be in a more advanced state of the disease when they first arrived for treatment.[36]

H. R. G. von Scorebrand, a visiting physician at Kalaupapa, argued that the Hawaiian legislature had an obligation to increase funding for the settlement and thereby make Hawai'i a world leader in the area of medical treatment for leprosy. Scorebrand contrasted what he viewed as the old Kalaupapa—a settlement whose residents were left only with religion and religious figures for succor—with the possibilities of a new settlement—a leading internationally recognized institution providing the most modern treatments in the Pacific. Since Kalaupapa had become only the second institution outside of Carville to test the sulfone drugs, a wide array of international scientists, politicians, and health administrators would turn to Hawai'i, according to Scorebrand. "We cannot deny any longer our responsibilities toward world medicine," he stated.[37]

Scorebrand also linked Kalaupapa's potential rise to Hawai'i's future as a state, suggesting that "we also should not overlook our opportunities to impress Hawaii upon the minds of people who may be influential in according to Hawaii the place which she claims should be hers." If territorial officials assumed responsibility for transforming Kalaupapa into a center for leprosy treatment, it could help Hawai'i on its rightful path to statehood. "Medical progress, modern means of communication, changes of global importance are metamorphosing the ancient Sandwich Islands into a full-fledged State in the Union. . . . We must raise our sights, if we are to fulfill our responsibility toward the future."[38] Improving Kalaupapa meant helping Hawai'i and the world.

Many patients at Kalaupapa also welcomed new treatments, but they showed more interest in improving their physical condition and obtaining the freedom to leave the settlement than in achieving greater glory for the territory. Officials in the first quarter of the century had found settlement residents unwilling to participate in experimental research programs, but by the 1940s, many Kalaupapa residents embraced innovative treatments and eagerly participated in the new drug trials. Those who did so experienced tangible improvements relatively quickly. Because territorial law required that only active cases remain segregated, patients eager to rejoin family and friends on the outside submitted to regular medical tests and examinations that allowed physicians to evaluate the status of the disease in the hope that the tests would show that the drugs worked. By January 1948, thirty-two patients had requested skin scrapings, the method by which physicians determined active cases of leprosy. Seventeen of these tests proved negative, which offered those patients hope of "parole."[39] In September 1948, the board granted temporary release to the inactive cases who applied for it.[40] For these individuals, modern drug therapies afforded them a clear path out of isolation.

While patients appreciated the benefits of treatment, they resented what they saw as Sloan's greater concern for the advancement of science than for improving their lives at the settlement. Stephen Dawson, a patient at Kalaupapa, started a petition calling for the removal of Sloan, accusing him of "negligence, disregard, and indifference." The petition claimed that the resident physician treated patients "as outcasts" and that he made clear his hostility toward paid patient workers, high patient allowances, and patients' right to vote. In particular, Kalaupapa residents resented Sloan's view of leprosy as highly contagious.[41] Indeed, when Sloan publicly promoted the positive results of drug trials at Kalaupapa in the press, he echoed Faget's argument at Carville that a strict segregation policy made such work possible. Sloan's public endorsement of segregation, along with his warning that no cure for leprosy yet existed, rankled patients at a time when they believed new medical understandings warranted a greater openness toward the disease.[42] The territorial Board of Health, however, approved of Sloan's approach and extended him a vote of full confidence in his position at Kalaupapa.[43]

Settlement residents also began to recognize that the medical culture surrounding drug treatment threatened the cohesive nature of their community by drawing clearer divisions between those who had leprosy and those who did not. Throughout the twentieth century, Kalaupapa's residents had mustered the political capital to lobby successfully for the admittance of kōkuas and for the right of people with inactive cases of leprosy to remain within the settlement if they wished. Residents thus managed to shape a community that extended beyond the boundaries of people having the disease to embrace wider groups with a shared sense of a local Hawaiian identity.[44] Politicians, however, had long viewed Kalaupapa residents who did not have leprosy as a financial drain on the territory. Kōkuas and inactive leprosy cases had persuaded reluctant legislators that their association with the disease made it difficult for them to leave the settlement. New drug therapies, however, held the promise of arresting the disease and allowing patients to be safely released to the general public. Political officials also used these new treatments to argue that the stigma attached to leprosy would decrease, thereby eliminating any reason to keep those without the disease at Kalaupapa. Hence, legislators supported administrative efforts to remove from Kalaupapa all residents free of the disease.

Government officials also defended settlement doctors' efforts to increase medical surveillance under the belief that such oversight would allow physicians to improve drug therapies and ultimately release more patients. Territorial Attorney General Walter D. Ackerman effectively undermined settlement residents' right to refuse medical intervention by claiming "cryptic language" in the Hawaiian law allowed doctors to examine patients without their consent "for the purpose of determining whether a particular patient is still affected with the disease." In this way, the board could eliminate from the settlement residents who did not have leprosy, as it was "under no legal obligation to provide for the continued support, maintenance and segregation of well persons."[45] Such compulsory examinations could quickly divide the healthy from the unwell, freeing doctors to transform the Kalaupapa settlement from a Hawaiian community into a strictly medical institution.

Patients who desired to preserve their local Hawaiian community at Kalaupapa proved less eager to embrace the new medical regimens than their counterparts at Carville did. Settlement residents voiced their fear that drug therapies followed by enforced examinations represented an effort to drive them from their homes.[46] To allay such concerns, C. V. Caver, newly appointed medical director of the settlement, held a meeting with twenty-three patients to assure them that the examinations were required solely to gain statistical information regarding leprosy. He also clearly implied that doctors would declare those found free of the disease to be inactive cases. Caver reported that although the patients accepted his assurances, they pointed out that being declared inactive offered no real benefits to a patient. Indeed, the board made clear in 1950 that such residents would lose their clothing and cash allowances.[47] Residents remained skeptical that board members would not at a future date attempt to remove such individuals from the community, and Caver was forced to admit that health officials might in the future require all individuals with inactive cases of leprosy to leave the settlement.[48]

Forging New Divisions under a Changing Regime

Medical personnel, politicians, and patients in Hawai'i all shared the sense that the postwar era should bring changes in territorial leprosy policies and treatments, but their visions for the future clashed. Doctors envisioned a disciplined and orderly patient body within a state-of-the-art medical facility. Territorial legislators sought to use the promise of a cure to scale back a leprosy program that they considered too expensive. Former Governor Lawrence M. Judd also took part in efforts to reform policies in the late 1940s and early 1950s, and he emphasized public health education and relaxed restrictions as the best approach to changing conceptions of leprosy and improving the care of patients. Kalaupapa residents initially embraced Judd's efforts, believing his approach could both preserve their community and give them more freedom to come and go as they pleased. Uneasy compromises among these groups would bring about by the 1950s the end of mandatory admissions to Kalaupapa, the abandonment of the receiving station and hospital at Kalihi, and the creation of Hale Mohalu, a new hospital in the former military barracks outside Pearl Harbor.[49] These efforts ultimately divided the patient community between those who embraced the promise of medical policies at Hale Mohalu and those who sought to maintain a protected community within Kalaupapa. It also created rifts between those officials who hoped to place leprosy policy more firmly under the control of doctors and those who continued to view the disease as a social problem requiring the expertise of politically savvy administrators.

When Judd requested the job of resident superintendent in 1947, he viewed the position as a natural culmination of his long career of territorial civil service and his special humanitarian concern for people with leprosy.[50] He had a vested interest in the Hawaiian leprosy policy, having initiated the reorganization of the leprosy institutions while governor in the early 1930s. As resident superintendent, Judd intended to institute the kinds of radical changes he believed never emerged from the 1932 reorganization. Just as settlement physicians looked to Carville for drug therapies, Judd also drew inspiration from the Louisiana institution. He, however, looked to its new rehabilitation programs and Carville patients' efforts to educate the public and to loosen regulations that confined them to the Louisiana facility. Judd also brought to the Kalaupapa settlement the same missionary zeal of uplift and reform that had informed his 1930s efforts. He saw Kalaupapa as a community mired in despair, and he believed that the inculcation of good moral habits would both raise morale and improve the general quality of life for all residents.[51]

By providing structured activities and instigating a general cleanup of the grounds, Judd attempted to eradicate habits he considered disruptive and unhealthy and replace them with wholesome pastimes that engaged patients in the community and elevated their spirits.[52] He considered the appointment of a recreational activities director a top priority, and later sought the advice of the newly hired director of community activities at Carville to bring Kalaupapa in line with the kinds of programs and recreational facilities available to patients on the mainland.[53] Judd oversaw the establishment of a Boy Scout camp on the abandoned U.S. Investigation Station flats in the Kalawao region of the settlement.[54] He encouraged the Kalaupapa Entertainment Club to put on dances, plays, and auctions. A Kalaupapa chorus and band formed, gaining enough proficiency by December 1948 to record a Christmas concert that aired over the Aloha radio network.[55] He also helped initiate a rehabilitation program, similar to that established at Carville, which gave patients job training to help them gain wage-earning positions once they left the settlement.[56]

Through these and other programs, Judd worked to connect a newly energized group of patients with broader communities outside of the settlement and to reduce the stigma of leprosy. Soon after his arrival, eighteen veterans asked to establish an American Legion post, and the resulting Damien Post No. 30 received its temporary charter in August 1947.[57] Judd invited residents of "top-side" Moloka'i (those living outside of the settlement, on the other side of the cliff that separated Kalaupapa from the rest of the island) to the first meeting of the Kalaupapa Lions Club in April 1948, calling them "fellow 'Molokaians.'" Reminding these guests that Kalaupapa was both "an integral part of Molokai" and the "most renowned portion of the island," Judd attempted to break down barriers between leprosy patients and those outside the institution. He saw greater openness as a means of educating the public about the disease and gaining greater acceptance for those who had it.[58] The Kalaupapa Entertainment Club occasionally staged activities that involved members of the broader Moloka'i community, such as having members of the local Community Center serve as judges for a Lei Day garden and flower display contest.[59] The Moloka'i Girl Scouts voted to help girls and women at Kalaupapa and worked to establish ties with the settlement chapter.[60] In addition to incorporating members of the Moloka'i community, Judd welcomed famous Americans to the settlement, including Edgar Bergen and Charlie McCarthy, Al Jolson, and Shirley Temple.[61]

Patients believed that the path toward eliminating the stigma of their disease had to be more bi-directional: not only did outsiders need greater access into Kalaupapa, the residents needed to be able to enter the outside world more easily. Unlike medical personnel such as Sloan—who sought to remove inactive residents while keeping a tighter rein on those who still tested positive for leprosy—Judd supported efforts to allow patients greater opportunities for temporary travel outside the settlement. Some officials worked to relax regulations regarding when and under what conditions patients could take brief trips out of Kalaupapa. For example, assistant health director Richard K. C. Lee recommended eliminating the extensive and demoralizing fumigation procedures that patients had to endure before leaving. Existing regulations required patients to submit all clothing and personal effects that they wanted to take outside the settlement for treatment with steam or a liquid disinfectant. Claiming that disinfection of personal belongings was not necessary as long as such items underwent thorough cleaning, Lee explained that the purpose behind the procedures had been largely psychological and designed to reassure those outside of the settlement: "I believe the time has arrived when public fear of a disease should be approached by other means." He advocated that patients be instructed in certain matters of personal hygiene, however, and he encouraged them to use their own items while on leave and to avoid "kissing and fondling" children.[62]

These desires to relax restrictions at Kalaupapa as a means to improve patient morale and foster a healing community did not sit well with territorial administrators who were eager to maintain strict control over leprosy patients. While Judd could alter conditions within the settlement without a great deal of criticism, territorial health officials questioned his attempts to allow patients greater freedom to move about the territory. In October 1948, Board of Health members objected to plane rides that Kalaupapa patients took to outside islands without prior approval from Board Superintendent Harry Kluegel. Judd viewed this objection as a direct critique of his administration and interpreted the statement as an effort to curb the level of authority he exercised as resident superintendent.[63]

Health officials contorted themselves into bizarre positions to give the appearance of flexibility and progressiveness while attempting to exert a greater degree of surveillance over leprosy patients. In the matter of flight visits, board member Charles Wilbar informed county health officers in 1949 that patients should be allowed to make short visits to their home islands, but only under closely monitored conditions. Patients would be allowed to land in an island airport, visit with friends or relatives for an hour, and then return to the settlement. While at the airport, a uniformed health department official would ensure that patients did not wander, drink from public water fountains, or contact children. Though Wilbar acknowledged that patients posed no direct threat to the people outside the settlement, he maintained that such restrictions were necessary "because of the present considerable fear of leprosy in the minds of the public."[64] This public fear, which Wilbar apparently found unnecessary to document, proved more powerful in shaping leprosy policy than appeals to humanitarianism and comparisons to Carville. He proved unmoved by Judd's assertion that he did "not know of any action that has contributed more to the joy of the patients concerned" than the plane visits. Equally unsuccessful was Judd's argument that Carville operated under a more liberal leave policy, in which there were no special conditions designed to monitor patient visits to their homes.[65]

Territorial officials increasingly saw Judd as a hindrance to efforts to scale back leprosy operations and keep costs in line. Upset over a board mandate to reduce his proposed budget by at least 20 percent, Judd defended existing spending by explaining to board members that the settlement had been severely underfunded for years.[66] The Director of the Bureau of the Budget, however, was not impressed by Judd's complaints that long-term neglect required an extensive investment in upgrades and repairs. He viewed Kalaupapa's operating deficit of $218,280 as a sign of either Judd's incompetence or his flagrant disregard for appropriations. He expressed his confidence that budget cuts would not prove critically damaging to Kalaupapa and "that the time is drawing near when we will have to reappraise the whole program of the Board of Hospitals and Settlement."[67] Territorial officials were more interested in cost-effective management of the leprosy program than in making the institution a humane, world-class treatment facility.

Judd's attempts to replicate in Kalaupapa the modern Western facility he had seen at Carville and his support for patients who wished to do the same mixed uneasily with the desires of other Hawaiian officials to keep those with leprosy safely contained and strictly separated from the rest of society. Health officials encouraged changes in policies that would maintain the ideal of segregation until a demonstrated cure could be found. In the spring of 1949, the legislature abolished the Board of Hospitals and Settlement and transferred the administration of the leprosy program back to the territorial Board of Health. Physicians and those with medical training gained more power within the Board of Health, while lay officials like Judd found their power diminished.

Although this dramatic shift of power to the territorial Board of Health took workers at Kalaupapa by surprise, Judd attempted to work with the new administration to move toward less restrictive medical policies for people with leprosy in Hawai'i. He suggested that the abolition of the Board of Hospitals and Settlement displayed the territorial legislature's advocacy of "a more modern, humane and efficient approach to the management of Hansen's disease."[68] To that end, Judd suggested, the Board of Health should direct more effort toward developing a public health campaign that would educate Hawaiians about the disease. The campaign would inform them that it was "simply one of the least communicable of the communicable diseases, that people can be 'cured' of it, that there is no stigma whatsoever attached to it and that people apparently cured should be able to live lives which are useful to themselves and to the community."[69] In effect, he advocated the same kinds of measures demanded by patient activists in Carville.

When territorial officials named Judd acting director of the Division of Hospitals and Settlement of the Board of Health on 5 July 1949, they initiated a period of change that heralded a dramatic shift in the management of Hansen's disease in the territory.[70] Judd put new policies and programs into effect, including new construction and the installation of new equipment at Kalaupapa. Most notably, he oversaw the closing of the Kalihi hospital and the opening of Hale Mohalu, a new facility at Pearl City on the outskirts of Honolulu. Kalihi's use over the years as a holding and examination facility and an "experimentation station" had given it an ambiguous legacy. After the U.S. Public Health Service closed its laboratory there in 1942, business and military leaders urged that the remaining territorial hospital personnel and facilities be removed from the site, which had become more populated during the 1940s. Health officials decided to abandon the aging facility and establish a new institution at Hale Mohalu that could provide more space, newer equipment, better housing, and more lenient policies.

The creation of this new facility, however, threatened the Kalaupapa community. Hale Mohalu attracted a great deal of attention and funding, and it emerged as the site that represented the future of HD policy in the territory. Some officials sought to use the opening of Hale Mohalu as an opportunity to close Kalaupapa, thus eliminating it as a stigma to the territory and a potential barrier to statehood. Many settlement residents had a very different idea of the role played by Kalaupapa, and some protested the idea that their existence should be viewed as an embarrassment to the broader community. Patients rejected Governor Ingram Stainback's 1949 call to the legislature to close Kalaupapa and particularly resented his statement that the settlement represented a "blot upon Hawaii's good name." Judge E. Bell, patient and settlement magistrate, wrote a letter of protest to Stainback on behalf of all patients, informing him that the residents of Kalaupapa opposed any action that did not consider the patients' viewpoint.[71]

Officials celebrated Hale Mohalu as a modern facility with more up-to-date medical equipment, housing, and amenities than could be found at Kalaupapa, but many patients sought more than medical technology and the accoutrements of modern living when deciding where they wanted to live. Nine patients, including Bell, had flown to the Pearl City site to consider moving there. He explained that eight of the nine found themselves unwilling to "relinquish the happy and near normal life now existent here in Kalaupapa, for what appears to be a life of confinement and misery." Some of them viewed relegation to a more regimented modern institutional facility as akin to "lead[ing] the life of a condemned criminal." As did patients at Carville, a significant number of Kalaupapa residents relished their relative independence and did not welcome the idea of leaving their individual cottages for the strictures of institutional life. Attempting to convey the considerable disruption such a move would cause, Bell explained that approximately one-third of the patients at Kalaupapa lived in individual homes, where they could "do all housekeeping, marketing, preparing of meals, [and] upkeep of the premises." They also furnished their homes, held jobs, led active lives in the community, and enjoyed driving cars about the settlement. The patients feared such activities might be eliminated at a new facility and urged that the governor defer any decision on whether to shift all operations to the new HD institution.[72]

Judd defended the settlement residents' efforts to remain at Kalaupapa, but he also devoted a great deal of attention to making Hale Mohalu into the kind of community he had witnessed at Carville. Acting on the Kalaupapa patients' behalf, Judd cautioned the president of the Board of Health that any move to abandon Kalaupapa should be tempered with consideration for those who still lived there, reminding health officials that some residents had been members of the community for fifty years.[73] At the same time, he supported the establishment of a less isolated facility and viewed Hale Mohalu as the showplace for publicizing the territory's enlightened perspective on Hansen's disease. He encouraged the creation of a patient newsletter, the *Halemohalu News*, which attempted to mirror the efforts of *The Star* in educating the public on the "Facts and Fallacies about Hansen's Disease."[74] Unlike *The Star*, however, the *Halemohalu News* remained an administration publication circulated within the institution and never emerged as an organ for patient activists. Judd served as a conduit between patients and the Board of Health, seeking to address patient desires for greater freedoms by altering the regulations he had the power to modify and appealing to the board on patients' behalf when he lacked the authority to make changes.

Board of Health officials proved somewhat open to Judd's entreaties, but they still believed Hansen's disease to be a significant threat to the public health and tried to maintain rigid controls on the mobility of patients with active cases of the disease. Efforts to allow a patient band to tour outside the institution highlighted this tension. Even health officials open to progressive reform expressed skepticism toward proposals that would allow patients to move about in public. When the administrator of Hale Mohalu suggested that the patient band could serve as musical ambassadors, playing Hawaiian and popular mainland tunes at public concerts, medical officials balked, claiming such concerts represented a health risk.[75] Chief of Medical Services E. K. Chung-Hoon claimed he supported "progressive advances" in the management of Hansen's disease, but he maintained that Hansen's disease was "a contagious disease" from which the public had to be protected. "It is my opinion that authorizing active, communicable cases to leave isolation to provide musical entertainment . . . is not compatible with the best interests of public health," Chung-Hoon wrote.[76] Quoting from the Board of Health's own pamphlet, "Facts and Fallacies about Hansen's Disease," Judd countered that "there is no evidence that the disease was contagious to such a degree as would warrant the drastic segregation measures practiced throughout the ages and even today in certain localities." Noting that the disease was difficult to transmit and required a long period of contact, he failed to understand why patients could not be granted broader liberties in moving about the territory.[77]

Board of Health members viewed the band debate as evidence that Judd lacked the proper medical education needed to develop Hansen's disease policies in the modern age, and they demonstrated a new commitment to place all medical matters in the hands of doctors. Since Chung-Hoon had stated that a danger of contagion existed, the board supported his decision to ban the public concerts, "desirable as it may be from a social point of view" to allow the patients to play.[78] Judd refused to relent, pointing out that medical professionals did not agree on the matter of the contagiousness of Hansen's disease and asserting that the board's decision conflicted with the "spirit and intent" of the territorial laws governing the disease. "It is an unnecessary and ill-conceived restriction of a liberty to which the patients may be legally and are reasonably entitled," Judd wrote, using language similar to that of Carville's patients in pressing for reforms. After years of vigorous effort on behalf of HD patients and repeated failures to alter the opinions of medical administrators, Judd resigned in frustration in November 1951.[79]

Judd may have viewed the Board of Health's intention to replace him with a medical professional as a sign of its resistance to a more open and humane public health policy toward Hansen's disease, but it also reflected a broader effort by territorial health officials to gradually sever ties with the old ways of dealing with the disease. For board members, these older ways were symbolized by the Kalaupapa settlement and its lay advocate, Lawrence Judd. Judd later left Hawai'i to serve as the colonial governor of American Samoa, while the territorial Board of Health worked to bring treatment of Hansen's disease in the territory in line with how public health officials handled it on the mainland.

Creating a Modern American HD Policy

As patients and health officials in Hawai'i and Louisiana debated how "scientific understandings of Hansen's disease" should shape public health policy, participants at each site looked to the other to gauge their progress. Patients in both locations pressed for a loosening of restrictions, while physicians and policymakers emphasized the need to improve institutional discipline, methods of medical examination, and controlled environments. Patients did gain some relaxation of restrictions, resulting in their ability to leave HD facilities for brief vacations or longer "temporary releases." Those remaining in the facilities, however, found that officials and medical personnel altered patient lifestyles to adhere better to the regimented order of medical institutions. In this process, patients, politicians, and health officials noted and sought to diminish distinctions in policy between HD programs in the territory and those on the mainland. Members of all these groups sought to establish more common procedures and policies for these institutions in Hawai'i and Louisiana by the end of the 1950s.

In Hawai'i, patients pressured territorial health officials to change existing regulations to better reflect what they considered the more modern and relaxed rules governing Carville. As early as 1947, a Kalaupapa patient protested newly enforced rules requiring visitors to bring their own food and linens, pointing out that Carville did not operate under such restrictions. Suggesting that the new postwar era should bring about greater freedom, he wrote, "We are living in a tomic [sic] age and you are still fooling around with our lives."[80] In response to requests from Hawai'i for information on how patients in Louisiana fared in their attempts to loosen restrictions, Carville patient activist Stanley Stein detailed mainland policies. He explained how the United Patients Committee at Carville had recently managed to increase the number of patients allowed to leave the institution for the holidays from about ten in the early 1940s to sixty in December 1948. In championing looser restrictions, Stein advocated policies that "would help abolish the present conception of institutional restriction and exile." To those who argued that authorized leave took patients away from necessary treatment, he countered that "no treatment as yet has been used here that in any respect compares with the therapeutics of a vacation—Home."[81]

Stein raised awareness among HD patients in Hawai'i that a universal policy toward the disease did not exist in the United States and its territories. He also suggested that pressure from patients could help bring about changes in regulations. Patients in Hawai'i received copies of *The Star*, which they in turn circulated to doctors and other public officials in the territory. Kalaupapa residents also addressed the territorial press, asking for an end to compulsory segregation laws, for suitable arrangements for outpatient care, and for the official substitution of the term "Hansen's disease" for "leprosy."[82]

Many of these patient concerns found their way into new policies governing Hansen's disease drafted by public health officials in Hawai'i, though new regulations also imposed a greater degree of medical surveillance. When the Board of Health assumed control over the HD program in 1949, territorial officials approved changes that would help them depict the treatment of people with Hansen's disease in Hawai'i as particularly humane and progressive. Legislators officially decreed that "Hansen's disease" would replace the term "leprosy" in the territory. Health officials also ended a policy of sending new patients to Kalaupapa, though individuals could elect to enter the settlement if they chose. New regulations passed by the Board of Health in 1950 heralded a new era of less restrictive rules governing Hansen's disease. Although any person who had the disease was still required to report to the board or other health officials, a diagnosis of Hansen's disease no longer automatically meant institutionalization at a remote site. Centers for treatment now included out-patient clinics. Those in the communicable stages of the disease still had to be isolated, but "under conditions satisfactory to the Board." Such provisions allowed for a broader interpretation that meant treatment would not always result in isolation at Kalaupapa. Noncommunicable patients at the settlement could become eligible for temporary release, and even "bacteriologically positive" patients could apply for "emergency release" and receive a one-week leave if the medical director concluded that it would not pose an undue risk to the patient's health or that of the public. However, these policies entailed mandatory physical examinations, treatments, and close observations of any patient seeking to enjoy the benefits of looser restrictions.[83]

As the numbers of incarcerated people with Hansen's disease declined, health officials in the territory found it harder to justify appropriating a significant portion of the Department of Health's funding for the disease. Once again, officials turned to the federal government for assistance, arguing that the territory had borne the full financial burden for all HD funding since the U.S. Public Health Service closed its receiving station at the Kalihi Receiving Hospital in 1942. Challenging perceptions of the disease as innately "Hawaiian," health officials incorporated a statement into a resolution that reminded members of Congress that "the people of the Hawaiian Islands originally were free from Hansen's disease" and that outsiders brought it to their shores. Health officials also took the opportunity to point out that "a large percentage" of people receiving care for Hansen's disease in the territory came from the mainland United States and "other places."[84] Board members attempted to emphasize that the federal government should not view the disease as a concern peculiar to the territory but as a responsibility of the entire nation.

As they did during the 1930s, territorial politicians once again attempted to use the issue of funding for Hansen's disease as an opportunity to demonstrate Hawai'i's preparedness for statehood. When recently named Hawai'i governor Oren Long testified before the Congressional Subcommittee on Territories and Insular Possessions, for instance, he sought to counter images of Hawai'i as a colony. He instead pressed for the territory's inclusion in the national body. Referring to his years of service with the territorial Department of Welfare, he explained that his contact with the people of Hawai'i had demonstrated to him "that they are thoroughly American in their understanding and their loyalties." Claiming that territorial residents "look forward to statehood," Long asserted "that we are mature . . . that we have had the experience, and that we are smart enough to carry on our own affairs just as the mainland States do." Long expressed gratitude to Congress for its assistance with the development of Hawai'i, but he also mentioned that residents of the territory "may have felt at times that we were a little neglected."[85] The fact that Long gave such testimony during hearings devoted to Hansen's disease in Hawai'i implied that Congress was not meant to view requests for funds to manage Hansen's disease as pleas from a subordinate but as a responsible application from a government that had demonstrated its right to stand as an equal among other states by its adept and humane management of Hansen's disease.

According to territorial officials, congressional neglect translated into millions of dollars, which was the amount of money the territorial government had spent for management of the disease. They believed the federal government should more properly share this burden, since it provided complete support to all patients at the U.S. National Leprosarium in Carville. Hawaiian Delegate Joseph Farrington proposed a bill in 1951 that echoed an earlier 1931 resolution also endorsed by Hawaiian officials.[86] Both bills pointed out that U.S. Public Health Service regulations stated that anyone afflicted with leprosy in the United States could be admitted to any PHS hospital equipped for handling such patients. Since HD patients in Hawai'i did not avail themselves of the facilities at Carville, officials contended the federal government should provide a sum to the territorial Board of Health equal to the amount of money required for their treatment at the U.S. facility in Louisiana. In this way, patients in Hawai'i would appropriately "be placed on an equal basis with patients suffering from this disease on the mainland of the United States."[87]

Without such assistance, territorial health officials argued that they could not proceed with research into new testing and treatment of Hansen's disease. They drew comparisons between their request for funds and the grants-in-aid that Congress provided states and territories for tuberculosis, venereal disease, and cancer. Just as those diseases posed a financial burden to mainland localities, so Hansen's disease taxed Hawai'i, consuming about one-third of the territorial health department budget. Because the territory of Hawai'i paid "its fair share" of federal taxes and because 376 of the 470 people registered as cases of Hansen's disease in Hawai'i held U.S. citizenship, Board of Health president C. L. Wilbar argued that residents of the territory should "receive full and equal financial and other benefits from our National Government as do the other major political units of the country."[88] Such benefits would include equitable funding for Hansen's disease, but they also implicitly staked a claim for Hawai'i's inclusion in the national body.

Farrington sought to draw distinctions between the current territorial government and its "primitive" Hawaiian predecessors, a contrast which helped him bolster his claim that Hawai'i should enjoy equality with mainland states. He concluded his explanations of the territorial position by declaring, "We in Hawaii feel a great obligation to do everything that is possible to relieve the suffering that has come from the impact of our civilization on native Hawaiian people." Such an "obligation," he stated, "very properly should be shared by the Federal Government."[89] Farrington's comments maintained the same colonialist stance assumed by earlier territorial officials, clearly positioning the more recently settled white residents as Americans and citizens of the true "Hawaii" who would properly attend to the poor unfortunates left in their care—the victims of "civilization," the native Hawaiian HD sufferers. Congress passed the bill, which President Harry Truman signed into law in June 1952.[90]

The hearings gave territorial politicians and health officials the opportunity to publicize changes made in the management of Hansen's disease in Hawai'i and to demonstrate how management of the disease in the territory closely resembled practices in the states. Reporting on his visit to Hawai'i, Frederick A. Johansen of the U.S. Public Health Service spoke approvingly of arrangements at Hale Mohalu. Alonzo F. Brand, regional medical director for the Public Health Service, affirmed Johansen's position. He praised the Board of Health's decision to admit all new patients to Hale Mohalu rather than confine them to Kalaupapa. In particular, he recommended the Pearl City location for its educational value, noting that its placement near a major population center helped instruct the public that "Hansen's disease can be treated like any other infectious disease."[91]

The attention that federal and territorial officials paid to Hale Mohalu, however, stirred apprehension among Kalaupapa residents about the future of their settlement. Health officials expressed puzzlement over residents' fears, commenting that medical administrators had expended great effort "to reassure them and gain their confidence." Kalaupapa patients, nevertheless, worried that the financial burden of maintaining the settlement might convince the territorial government to abandon it. When settlement health officials attempted to move all discharged patients away from Kalaupapa to the "outside," it did not help assuage such fears.[92] Patients aired their concerns during a 1951 visit to the settlement by members of the territorial legislature's Committee on Health. Kalaupapa residents complained that since management of the settlement fell under the jurisdiction of the Board of Health in 1949, health officials had demonstrated little concern for them. They saw territorial efforts to make Hale Mohalu into Hawai'i's premier HD treatment facility a diversion of funding and attention from their settlement and urged the legislature to protect patients' ability to live out their lives at Kalaupapa. Patients had success in convincing legislators that the settlement was not some remote and primitive prison, but rather a vibrant community with strong roots in the Hawaiian Islands. M. G. Paschoal, chairman of the committee, admitted after the meeting that "contrary to popular belief[,] Kalaupapa is not an isolated community," and he recommended that the settlement remain open.[93]

Residents at the Moloka'i settlement nevertheless found themselves increasingly characterized as a throwback to a less enlightened era. All the rhetoric associating leprosy with darkness, banishment, and isolation attached itself to Kalaupapa. A reporter for the Associated Press seeking to interview Judd in 1952 about Hale Mohalu explained that he wanted his article "to tell how Hawaii is pioneering in conquering the age-old stigma of what once was a disease of exile until death." The reporter, Lief Erikson, portrayed Kalaupapa as the repository of the stigmatized, weak, or craven, claiming, "Kalaupapa has an 80 year tradition of banishment from which there rarely was any escape but death." Erikson explained that the settlement "continues to tie and bind the 240 people still there with that concept." He highlighted the fact that eighty residents in the arrested stage of the disease could leave, but they chose not to either because they were "afraid to make the venture to care for themselves outside" or, in "old cases," could not care for themselves alone on the outside.[94] His depiction ignored the vigorous community life that continued to exist for many residents in the settlement.

Kalaupapa patients once again turned to their elected officials to gain support for their community. Kaneo Kishimoto, the territorial representative of Maui County, accepted an invitation from patients to visit the settlement in 1952. He wrote the president of the Board of Health after his visit to protest that "nothing very much has been done in the way of improvements" that would demonstrate that the board "is doing right by those people." Since Judd's departure, he claimed, restrictions had intensified while conditions had not improved. "Instead of restricting [the patients]," he asked, "why not open things up like before and make those 248 or so patients happy where they are?"[95] Although health officials characterized his comments as the "rantings" of an "irresponsible" politician seeking to gain votes by criticizing the administration, the letter demonstrated that Kalaupapa residents had allies in the territorial legislature, a reminder to health officials that any action taken to close the settlement, increase restrictions, or severely curtail funding could be met with government resistance.[96]

Seeing territorial health policies governing Kalaupapa as a throwback to older conceptions of the disease, Carville patient activist Stanley Stein pressured territorial health officials to grant certain freedoms to patients and bring Kalaupapa in line with Carville. Stein noted that health officials did not require visitors at Carville to have entry permits, as anyone arriving at the hospital could enter as long as they signed in at the gate. Such visitors could purchase food at the patients' canteen or eat with the patients in their living quarters; they could exchange gifts and wander the grounds without supervision, eliminating the sense "that they are being continually watched by a Gestapo." While admitting that the theater and ball park grandstand had reserved seats separate from the area where patients sat, "these reserved sections are used, for the most part, by members of the hospital personnel and their families. Patients' guests sit right with them." Unlike at Kalaupapa and Hale Mohalu, visitors to Carville could shake hands and dance with patients. They could purchase items from the facility store, and many "visiting consultants" stocked up on items like cigarettes when at Carville because of the lower prices. Stein contrasted these rules with the regulations governing visitors at the Hawaiian HD institutions, which he described as "a cleverly worded set of negative ideas which will sow the seeds of doubt, fear, and in short, 'leprophobia' into the re-educational plans for Hansen's disease."[97]

Even as politicians and patient activists from both the mainland and Hawai'i put pressure on Hawaiian health officials to loosen restrictions on HD patients in the territory, the Carville community faced its own crisis of autonomy. Along with greater opportunities to leave the institution came increased medical discipline over those who remained. In 1953, U.S. Public Health officials mounted a challenge to the existence of twenty-two privately owned and maintained patient cottages at the facility in Louisiana. They argued that the retention of the cottages prevented hospital administrators from properly overseeing the treatment of patients. Patients countered that the cottages provided housing accommodations for families that the government had failed to offer. They also contended that these buildings provided the only thing resembling "home atmosphere" that existed at Carville.[98] The controversy over housing highlighted the unintended consequences of postwar changes in HD policy, as improved drug therapies initially brought intensified medical oversight rather than an end to segregation.

Carville administrators developed plans that addressed patient desires for improved housing while still eliminating the traditional arrangement that offered at least some patients an autonomous space. For patients who had invested their own funds to construct and maintain the cottages, health officials requested funding from Congress to reimburse them for these dwellings, which they intended to tear down and convert to apartment complexes.[99] The plan did not mollify patients. They noted that the new apartments included only a small food preparation area with a refrigerator for every four rooms, an arrangement that offered no real substitute for the kitchens they once possessed. Of even greater concern to some patients was the loss of their own furnishings, gardens, and pets. A Baton Rouge newspaper quoted a patient as complaining that the new arrangement was "just cold-blooded efficiency . . . the human element doesn't enter into it at all anymore."[100]

Patient activists mobilized a strike to protest the changes, and they sought once again to use outside allies to intervene on their behalf. Local press coverage criticized the PHS officials for their insensitivity, and Representative Otto Passman of the House Appropriations Committee visited Carville to hear patients' protests. Patient efforts led to the removal of the medical officer in charge, Edward M. Gordon, and a redesign of the new patient apartments in order to afford greater privacy for patients. Patients lost their battle to retain their old cottages, however. In 1959, bulldozers razed the area known as Cottage Grove, eliminating the last vestiges of the old autonomous patient community.[101]

The elimination of the cottages came in the same year that Hawai'i became a state, and the destruction of these homes drew the "modern" HD facilities at Hale Mohalu and Carville closer into line with one another. It also widened the gulf separating these newer institutions from the settlement at Kalaupapa. Health officials in both Hawai'i and in the U.S. Public Health Service debated how to streamline HD policy in the wake of Hawaiian statehood in 1959, but enduring differences remained. Rather than bring

Hale Mohalu and Kalaupapa under the jurisdiction of the Public Health Service, health officials in Hawai'i opted to continue accepting an annual disbursement of federal funds that they could allocate as they saw fit.[102] Such a decision preserved two distinct systems of care toward Hansen's disease: the well-funded "scientific" establishments at Hale Mohalu and Carville, and the subsistence support of Kalaupapa. Within the new state of Hawai'i, HD patients welcomed the maintenance of both institutions as affording them humane choices. Younger patients and those with families tended to choose the treatments and discharges available at Hale Mohalu, while older patients accustomed to the freedoms and community of Kalaupapa generally selected the Moloka'i settlement as their lifetime home.

As patients, public health officials, and medical practitioners sought to develop a coherent HD policy with the inclusion of Hawai'i as a state, they implicitly acknowledged that a uniform system of HD regulation would not be immediately forthcoming. Congressional debates over the funding and management of the disease in Hawai'i reflected the degree to which both federal and territorial officials had a stake in maintaining a sense of Hawaiian difference, leading them to conclude that Hawaiian health officials should continue to manage the disease outside the jurisdiction of the U.S. Public Health Service. Such a policy could enable the humane practice of allowing Kalaupapa residents to remain within their community while creating a new space at Hale Mohalu, but it also perpetuated the idea that "leprosy" was somehow a distinctively Hawaiian disease.

Conclusion

The expanding use of sulfone drugs as a treatment and potential cure for Hansen's disease brought dramatic changes to HD policies on both the mainland and in the territory of Hawai'i in the postwar years. While patients at Carville attempted to exploit and publicize the drug therapies to transform public understandings of their disease and to demand improved conditions within the leprosarium, physicians and public health officials presented such drugs as illustrative of the benefits of modern medical science and a means to draw new patients to leprosy facilities. Rather than acquiesce to such patient demands as increased outpatient care and relaxed institutional regulations, medical professionals argued that the rigors of scientific experimentation and the administration of drug therapies required a more closely regulated patient population that could be monitored most effectively in a central and isolated setting. Carville patient activists effectively drew on veteran allies to publicize their concerns and ultimately lift the mandate of total segregation, but in the process, their daily lives came under stricter scrutiny. Health officials bulldozed patient-constructed cabins in favor of uniform apartments, and a kind of unregulated socializing that had evolved around the right to prepare one's own meals and entertain on one's own porch was hampered. Altering regulations transformed the nature of the community as well.

In Hawai'i, public health officials and patients also had different conceptions about the best approach to altering policies toward Hansen's disease in the wake of new treatments. Some medical professionals welcomed the opportunity to transform what they viewed as the outdated conditions of their facilities to accommodate new scientific protocols and to transform Hawai'i into a world center for HD management. Their goals meshed nicely with some territorial officials' efforts to present the islands as a progressive, humane, and innovative community deserving of statehood. Some medical and political administrators clashed, however, on determining the most appropriate means of modernizing HD policies. While some health officials such as Lawrence Judd sought to update facilities at Kalaupapa, invite greater interaction between patients and those who did not have the disease, and loosen regulations that governed the management of Hansen's disease, other territorial officials sought to close the Moloka'i settlement and establish more modern facilities outside the major urban center of Honolulu. Some physicians embraced the opportunity to make Hansen's disease a more strictly medical rather than a political concern, arguing that they were more qualified than lay officials to make determinations about health policy. Their efforts, however, often embodied similar kinds of colonialist assumptions about what was best for patients and the territory as a whole.

Patients in Hawai'i also found themselves divided, as some embraced new therapies and the new facilities at Hale Mohalu, while others feared a changing policy would destroy the lives and communities they had forged at Kalaupapa. For the latter group, prospective drug treatments did not mean a beneficial path to freedom so much as a threat to their autonomy. They resisted policies that could force the removal of anyone found not to have the disease and resented finding their home depicted as an impediment to Hawai'i's progress and a site of exile. While all patients welcomed efforts to eradicate the stigma associated with their disease, they differed over whether Kalaupapa represented a throwback to colonialist policies of banishment, or whether it stood as a testament to the residents' ability to carve a cohesive, interethnic community that could resist Western authoritarian rule. A compromise enabled Kalaupapa residents to retain their home, while those who preferred the more urban setting of Hale Mohalu could find treatment there.

Ironically, this concession to patient demands helped preserve images of leprosy that linked it to isolation and foreign contagion. By 1959, then, two things had become clear: first, patients had succeeded in undermining the policy of mandated segregation (though it would officially linger a few years longer); and second, not even the inclusion of Hawai'i in the U.S. body politic had succeeded in altering public perceptions of the disease. Leprosy in America was something to be contained, examined, treated, managed, and pitied—but it was not something that Americans would acknowledge as their disease.

Epilogue

By the 1950s, medical professionals and patients shared a common mission of developing better methods of treatment for Hansen's disease and of challenging its stigmatized nature. They achieved some remarkable successes in the first of these goals, but the second goal has proven much harder to realize. One important reason that leprosy has been so resistant to redefinition may be found in its tangled relationship with U.S. imperialism, which transformed conceptions of leprosy from a timeless and ancient curse to a contemporary foreign scourge that endangered a modern and civilized nation. Ideas for containing people with leprosy within a specific federal institution may seem to have their roots in European medievalism, but they did not gain currency until U.S. missionary ventures, economic expansion, and colonial acquisitions in the nineteenth century made leprosy a more visible and exotic presence. Colonial administrators in Hawai'i and other territories gained knowledge in managing, categorizing, and containing bodies perceived to threaten U.S. interests. Treatment and management of the disease emerged in a colonial setting, and this context has continued to inform public health practice and Americans' understanding of the disease throughout the twentieth century and beyond. Recognizing this imperialist influence allows us to understand how leprosy's stigma has endured even as its meanings have changed over time.

To argue that the history of leprosy in the United States cannot be understood without appreciating how U.S. imperialism informed medical practice and patient experience is also to invite further explorations into the ways in which the possession and cultivation of an American empire shaped broader understandings of medicine, disease, and public health in both "foreign" and "domestic" settings. In the case of leprosy, for example, public health officials and physicians regularly invoked the supposed superiority of Western medicine to justify intervention into the intimate lives of Hawaiians. Medicine was a so-called "gift of civilization" that improved conditions for poor unfortunates, in the view of these officials. At the same time, both the understandings of leprosy and the policies developed to treat it in a colonial context were circulated and applied back to the mainland institution in Louisiana, albeit in uneven and often unexpected ways. Leprosy thus serves as an example of how "empire haunts the everyday," in the words of Ann Stoler, as the disease came to represent a "foreign" danger that threatened to invade a vulnerable homeland and infect "American" bodies.[1] Reconceptualizing leprosy as an exotic contagion lurking in new colonial possessions not only caused Congress to take unprecedented steps by creating a national leprosarium, it also cast all those who had the disease as "different" and therefore menacing. This shift in public understandings of the disease updated leprosy's stigma for modern times and impelled the state to remove those who had the disease from the civic and social body.

Imperial policies also unintentionally helped create the circumstances that allowed patients confined in leprosy institutions to challenge the popular images and medical policies that surrounded this disease. Those consigned to restrictive facilities in Hawai'i and Louisiana refused to accept their situation passively. It is true that public health officials assumed the authority to remove individuals from their families and communities, divide parents from their children, and assert control over the sexual and domestic lives of patients. People with leprosy nevertheless managed to challenge their incarceration and treatment by carving out autonomous spaces within medical institutions, resisting the authority and practices of public health officials, and disseminating their own understandings of the disease. This activism transformed conditions for patients in both the U.S. Leprosarium at Carville and the Kalaupapa settlement on Moloka'i, but the changes did not always bring about the intended results of less institutional discipline, more enlightened understandings of the disease, or even a consistent set of regulations.

The different circumstances that patients faced in Hawai'i and Louisiana had resulted in distinct forms of community and patient activism, and the Kalaupapa settlement and Carville institution continued to follow different trajectories after the liberalization of Hansen's disease policies in the 1950s. Such differences grew not just from the legacy of imperialism, but also arose because of the composition of the respective patient populations and the differing state and federal policies that regulated public health. The decision to maintain the Kalaupapa settlement allowed patients who remained there to retain a community grounded in a unique social and cultural space, but it also ironically preserved and celebrated the legacy of colonization and the association of leprosy with an imagined and exotic Hawaiian past. The emergence of an international research institution at the U.S. National Leprosarium, renamed the Gillis W. Long Hansen's Disease Center in 1986, eventually eclipsed the patient community at Carville altogether. The divergent paths of the two institutions reveal much about why the stigma surrounding "leprosy" has endured, long after patients won their freedom from mandatory incarceration.

In Hawai'i, patients worked hard to keep the Kalaupapa settlement open after the new state focused much of its public health resources in other areas. Their efforts, however, had paradoxical implications. On the one hand, their work represented a victory for patient rights. After lifting the mandate requiring enforced incarceration in 1969, the Hawaiian Board of Health allowed some people at Hale Mohalu to transfer to Kalaupapa, where patients and former patients continued to live in an interethnic but significantly Hawaiian community. Hawaiians constituted about 60 percent of the 128 patients who remained at the settlement in 1979, while they represented less than 20 percent of the state as a whole.[2] During the 1960s, the patients also gained the right to offer guided tours of the settlement for profit.[3] This enabled some residents to gain a source of income through tourism while also providing them with a new avenue for public education, as they talked with visitors and worked to break down stereotypes of the HD patient as helpless, highly contagious, and physically repulsive. When patients feared that the state might close the settlement and force them to relocate, they turned to the federal government and helped spur the creation of what became the Kalaupapa National Historical Park in 1980.[4]

Promoting the settlement as a tourist attraction, however, curiously preserves notions of the disease as an emblem of an implicitly less "civilized" era in Hawaiian history and continues to set Kalaupapa apart from the rest of the state as a throwback to this earlier era. A highlight of the settlement tour comes during visits to Father Damien's church and gravesite, where visitors pause to hear the well-known narrative of how the priest rescued the settlement residents from neglect and divisiveness and ultimately became "one of them." Carolyn Strange has rightly argued that modern Kalaupapa residents have managed to reclaim Damien as a local hero and genuinely respect him for his work in drawing attention to the Moloka'i settlement, but these revisions of the priest's role and the meaning of his work have limits.[5] Settlement residents cannot fully control how others make use of this icon. While patient tour guides might offer a vision of a vibrant Kalaupapa community and discuss Damien as a former member of this body of humane and active people, visitors receive a competing vision from many of the books on the priest available at the settlement gift shop. Even the National Park Service (NPS) interpretive material, which generally seeks to commemorate the patient experience, gives pride of place to Father Damien.[6]

By highlighting the natural features of the park, the NPS further connects images of Kalaupapa to other visions of the Hawaiian Islands as an exotic locale, implicitly distinct from the rest of the United States. Visitors to the park can purchase coffee table books filled with both sepia-toned photographs of the settlement's earlier years and contemporary black and white images.[7] Such works serve to exploit the tourist's desire for a nostalgic reading of the past, combined with the lush landscapes of a present-day tropical paradise. The park also remains somewhat difficult to reach; no car can be driven into the settlement, so visitors must arrive either by plane or by hiking or taking a mule ride down a three-mile cliffside trail. The limited accessibility, as well as park restrictions on the number and age of visitors, helps ensure patient privacy, but it also contributes to the sense of isolation and separateness connected with popular stereotypes of leprosy. The sights and sounds of the visit encourage tourists to feel as though they are truly entering a place apart and that they will experience a sense of both the segregation felt by earlier settlement residents and the breathtaking beauty of an "unspoiled" Hawaiian landscape.

In Louisiana, patients continued to participate in promoting scientific research and treatment at Carville, where new medical understandings of the disease and improved drug therapies dramatically altered this institution. The patient community changed in response, partly because new therapies meant that newly diagnosed individuals with Hansen's disease no longer needed long-term treatment and partly because restrictions on patients' mobility and rights had eased in the 1950s. An increasingly diverse patient population entered Carville in the 1950s and 1960s, though, and their experiences and actions continued to shape the understanding and treatment of Hansen's disease. More work is needed to explore how these residents adapted to, shaped, and challenged the changing policies that emerged during this era. As the existing population aged and declined in number, however, the institution's staff increasingly devoted their time to research and training. The institutions at Carville emerged as the international center for scientific research on Hansen's disease. Its Armadillo Research Program, launched in 1968, generated new understandings of the bacillus and led to investigations of an HD vaccine, as well as new multi-drug therapies.[8]

This work, which patients in the 1930s and 1940s had so passionately hoped would correct misunderstandings of their disease, has had curious consequences that display the ongoing power of imperialism to shape public health. This research helped reinforce the idea in the late twentieth century that "leprosy" was a disease of poor and developing nations. As the limited number of residential patients declined, the center at Carville began to work closely with the World Health Organization (WHO) and to welcome international researchers and scientists who came to study the disease. Medical knowledge produced at Carville was disseminated internationally through conferences, on-site seminars, and professional journals. Medical professionals in the United States regularly refer to Hansen's disease, the patients' preferred term, when discussing the illness, but this usage has never caught on in the international medical arena. Much of the information and research disseminated by the WHO continues to label the disease as "leprosy" and focus attention on its continued presence in parts of Asia, Africa, and South America rather than in the United States and Europe. This observation is certainly not meant to criticize the U.S. role in assisting the WHO to eradicate or ameliorate diseases, including Hansen's, throughout the globe; their partnership has helped dramatically reduce the incidence of HD.[9] Rather, I wish to draw attention to the manner in which the narratives that shape understandings of this disease have shifted. Patients who told stories of their own struggles to present themselves as Americans with Hansen's disease, which circulated in such publications as *The Star*, largely have given way to stories of scientific medicine's triumph over illness, which erase the human dimension of experiencing disease and subtly reassert an older colonialist rhetoric that poses the West as savior to "less fortunate" regions.

As the international medical community has inadvertently reinforced the link between leprosy and "foreign" countries, the politics of health care funding have threatened to eliminate the last vestiges of an HD patient community in the continental United States. Health officials acquiesced to patient demands for expanded out-patient clinics in the 1980s, thereby decreasing the number of patients who frequented the Louisiana facility. Carville stopped admitting residents for extended care in 1986, and by 1994, the number of long-term residents fell to 132.[10] By having convinced the public that medical technology would make segregation unnecessary, patients left themselves vulnerable to cutbacks in state and federal funding. The center continued to serve out-patients into the 1990s, and its staff even began treating people with diabetes, who often suffered physical effects similar to those of HD patients. Federal officials eventually concluded, however, that the limited numbers of patients did not merit the expense of maintaining the facility. Agreeing to pay a stipend to residents who wished to spend their remaining days at Carville, the U.S. government sold the institution back to the state of Louisiana in 1999 and moved its base of HD research and outpatient care—now known as the National Hansen's Disease Programs—to Baton Rouge. State legislators considered transforming the facility into a state prison before deciding in 2000 to make it an institution for at-risk youth run by the Louisiana National Guard.[11] The institutional base for a patient movement has thus been disrupted, and the patients have been dispersed. As HD patients in the United States tend not to publicize their affliction, nor identify their disease as leprosy, many people have come to assume that the disease no longer exists on the mainland.

Exploring these diverse and sometimes fractured patient movements thus highlights certain difficulties in challenging restrictive public health measures through an ostensibly medical discourse or through community-building efforts that resist the totalizing authority of such a discourse. Medical language could be used to help sway physicians and public health officials to alter restrictive policies, but it had limited value in eradicating entrenched public understandings of the disease. Building autonomous patient communities also had the potential to reinforce perceptions of Hansen's disease as outside the national body. To some extent, changing the name from leprosy to Hansen's disease—an effort in which patients from Carville and Kalaupapa found themselves united—helped efface the disease from national consciousness. Leprosy remains an affliction associated in the minds of many U.S. residents with developing nations, the Middle Ages, or the Bible, while the term Hansen's disease provokes only blank stares, its use limited to some medical arenas and patient activists. But the stigma does not only surround the name itself, as patient activists in both Louisiana and Hawai'i ultimately discovered. Whether known as leprosy or Hansen's disease, the policies, treatment programs, and understandings of the disease were crafted largely by physicians, public health officials, and politicians in an imperial setting. Their perceptions of the disease as a distinctively foreign threat and their belief in Western medicine as the superior framework for understanding that threat continue to shape knowledge of the disease both at home and internationally.

These issues are not unique to leprosy. Examining the tangled relationships between imperialism and medicine casts light on more recent issues, such as debates over the links between behavior and the acquisition of HIV; over the desirability of forcibly institutionalizing migratory tuberculosis patients; and over the portrayal of non-Western nations as crucibles of such diseases as AIDS, Ebola, or avian flu. The fears of the foreign contagion born in the late-nineteenth-century colonial context continue to invite an increased official surveillance over certain individuals suspected of violating national norms. Such concerns have also led to policies that do more to stigmatize certain groups than to provide tangible public health protections. Rather than turning to policies of isolation or quarantine, educational efforts and what Howard Markel has called "partnership between those orchestrating the battles against epidemics and the people who experience them firsthand" are necessary both to control disease and to protect human dignity.[12] Recognizing how social expectations shape our understandings of why people get sick and how they should be treated can be the first step toward creating more just, humane, and effective medical policies.

Introduction

1. Paramount News, 25 May 1946, Paramount Pictures, Inc., Collection, National Archives and Records Administration, College Park, Md.

2. *Big Jim McLain*, dir. Edward Ludwig.

3. Two recent popular histories have addressed the history of leprosy in the United States. Tayman's *The Colony* provides a general journalistic narrative of the history of the leprosy settlement on Moloka'i, emphasizing the more sensationalist aspects of the disease and those who were forced into isolation on the settlement. In providing a biographical history of leprosy in the modern era, Gould's *Disease Apart* focuses on some prominent individuals associated with Kalaupapa and Carville, such as Father Damien and patient Stanley Stein. While Tayman focuses exclusively on leprosy in Hawai'i, Gould explores the management of leprosy throughout the world, placing American episodes within an international narrative. Neither work examines the active interplay between the Hawaiian and Louisiana contexts, an absence reflected in more academic treatments as well. Gussow has written the most comprehensive scholarly history of the disease in the United States, locating the source of exclusionary leprosy policies in U.S. fears of the "yellow peril." While this work does gesture toward the imperial history of the United States, Gussow treats U.S. colonial ventures as a mere moment in the late nineteenth century that imparts a legacy of racism that informs medical policy well into the twentieth century; see Gussow, *Leprosy, Racism and Public Health*.

4. Patient activists had argued persuasively that the term "leper" has been used to dehumanize those who have the disease. I therefore use this word only when quoting people, when I am referring to proper names that incorporate the term, or when I am invoking it as a trope that embodies the colonialist conception of people with leprosy as primitive and unclean. I do, however, use leprosy rather than Hansen's disease in much of this work, since that was the common usage by both patients and medical officials until the 1940s. In that decade, patients mounted a campaign to replace leprosy with the term Hansen's disease, and the territory of Hawai'i passed a law mandating this usage. Hence, when discussing events in the later 1940s and 1950s, I use Hansen's disease rather than leprosy.

5. Trautman, "Epidemiological Aspects of Hansen's Disease (HD)"; WHO/Leprosy

Today, "Leprosy Elimination," <http://www.who.int/lep/en/>; Coordinating Centers for Infectious Diseases, "Hansen's Disease (Leprosy)," <http://www.cdc.gov/ncidod/dbmd/diseaseinfo/hansens_t.htm>.

6. Brody, *Disease of the Soul*, 104–6; and Richards, *Medieval Leper and His Northern Heirs*. For a discussion of medieval therapeutic writings on leprosy, see Demaitre, "Relevance of Futility."

7. Douglas, in "Witchcraft and Leprosy," illustrates how charging individuals with the spread of an infectious disease could serve as a useful tool for controlling already marginalized "vagabound, beggars and heretics," drawing connections to the ways in which fears of witchcraft had been used as a method of social rejection.

8. For examination of missionary efforts to use religious understandings of leprosy to build support for imperial medical missionary projects, see Joseph, " 'Essentially Christian, Eminently Philanthropic' "; for philanthropic use of the stigma attached to leprosy within a national context, see Bernabeu-Mestre and Ballester-Artigues, "Disease as a Metaphorical Resource."

9. For a discussion of the popular currency of the germ theory of disease, see Tomes, *Gospel of Germs*.

10. Williams provided one of the earliest examinations of the ways in which U.S. citizens identified with, profited from, and justified an image of the United States as global peacekeeper, arbiter, and provider, in *Empire as a Way of Life*. As recently as 1993, Kaplan criticized the enduring interpretation of American exceptionalism that viewed U.S. imperialism as a discrete and anomalous late nineteenth and early twentieth century moment in " 'Left Alone with America.' " More recent work has not only recognized the United States as an imperial power, but has investigated ways in which imperialism informed national culture and domestic life. See, for example, St. George, "Introduction," in *Possible Pasts*; Jacobson, *Barbarian Virtues*; Hoganson, "Cosmopolitan Domesticity"; Wexler, *Tender Violence*; Renda, *Taking Haiti*; and Kaplan, *Anarchy of Empire*.

11. Stoler, "Tense and Tender Ties."

12. In this regard, comparisons can be drawn, for example, between the regulation of leprosy patients and their children in Hawai'i and the medical management of childbirth in the Belgian Congo and the regulation of child rearing in the Dutch Indies. See Hunt, *Colonial Lexicon*; and Stoler, *Race and the Education of Desire*, 149–64.

13. For examples of scholarship that explore colonial medicine within a European imperial context, see Lyons, *Colonial Disease*; Patton, *Physicians, Colonial Racism, and Diaspora*; Vaughan, *Curing Their Ills*; Arnold, *Colonizing the Body*; Levine, *Prostitution, Race, and Politics*; and Anderson, *Cultivation of Whiteness*.

14. See, for example, Stoler, *Race and the Education of Desire*; Cooper and Stoler, eds., *Tensions of Empire*; Joseph et al., *Close Encounters of Empire*; Stoler, *Carnal Knowledge and Imperial Power*; and Ballantyne and Burton, eds., *Bodies in Contact*.

15. This work is informed by scholars of European imperialism who have moved beyond the peripheries of empire to explore how a colonizing mentality became

intricately interwoven into the domestic cultures of Western nations. See, for example, Burton, *Burdens of History*; Thorne, "'The Conversion of Englishmen'"; Stoler, *Race and the Education of Desire*; and Burton, ed., *After the Imperial Turn*.

16. Cohn, *Colonialism and Its Forms of Knowledge*, 3–15.

17. For a critique of colonial medical history that fails to place studies of discrete colonies within their broader transnational imperial contexts, see Anderson, "Where Is the Postcolonial History of Medicine?"

18. For works of medical history that move beyond the unidirectional model to examine how new medical theories emerge in the colonial setting and work back toward the center, see Anderson, "Immunities of Empire" and "Excremental Colonialism"; Peard, *Race, Place, and Medicine*; Santiago-Valles, "On the Historical Links"; and Briggs, *Reproducing Empire*.

19. See, for example, Gussow and Tracy, "Phenomenon of Leprosy Stigma," and "Stigma and the Leprosy Phenomenon"; Kalisch, "Lepers, Anachronisms, and the Progressives"; and Waxler, "Learning to Be a Leper," 169–74.

20. This idea is most clearly articulated in Kalisch, "Lepers, Anachronisms, and the Progressives," 503, but the idea of leprosy's "exceptionalism" informs other works as well, such as Gussow's.

21. For interpretations of late-nineteenth- and early-twentieth-century disease management that challenge the idea of Progressive enlightenment, see Brandt, *No Magic Bullet*, on syphilis; Rothman, *Living in the Shadow of Death*; and Craddock, *City of Plagues*, on tuberculosis; Lunbeck, *Psychiatric Persuasion*, on mental illness; Leavitt, *Typhoid Mary*, on typhoid and Mary Mallon; Kraut, *Silent Travelers*, on the treatment of immigrants; Markel, *Quarantine!*, on typhus and cholera; and Mohr, *Plague and Fire*, on bubonic plague.

22. Accounts of Damien have been a regular cottage industry, beginning with the publication of his writings compiled by his brother in the year of his death: de Veuster, *Life and Letters of Father Damien*. Other popular accounts include Farrow, *Damien the Leper*; Dutton, *Samaritans of Molokai*; and Debroey, *Father Damien*. More academic biographies are less hagiographic in their treatment of Damien but still tend to portray Hawaiians as ignorant and helpless, requiring the assistance of Western guidance; see Daws, *Holy Man*.

23. Moblo, "Defamation by Disease" and "Blessed Damien of Moloka'i." Moblo has also demonstrated how histories of Damien have erased the political nature of leprosy politics by ignoring how Western imperialists tried to use the disease to justify intervention and how Hawaiian leaders opposed to Western rule used the issue to further their own political agenda in the 1800s, in "Leprosy, Politics, and the Rise of Hawaii's Reform Party." For an exploration of how residents of Kalaupapa have reclaimed Damien as a local hero in the twentieth century, see Strange, "Symbiotic Commemoration."

24. Rosenberg, "Framing Disease," xiii.

25. Treichler, *How to Have Theory in an Epidemic*, 4.

26. For a cogent analysis of the constructed nature of science broadly and of AIDS specifically, see Treichler, "AIDS, HIV, and the Cultural Construction of Reality." There is a rich historical scholarship that has examined the social construction of disease; see Rosenberg, *Cholera Years*; Brandt, *No Magic Bullet*; Rogers, *Dirt and Disease*; Leavitt, *Typhoid Mary*; Patterson, *Dread Disease*; Reagan, "Engendering the Dread Disease"; Patton, *Inventing AIDS*; Brumberg, *Fasting Girls*; Wailoo, *Dying in the City of the Blues*; and Craddock, *City of Plagues*.

27. Latour and Woolgar, *Laboratory Life*, 236.

28. Scholars in recent years have begun to address patient experiences of leprosy. For an African context, see Silla, *People Are Not the Same*; for Hawai'i, see Strange, "Symbiotic Commemoration," and Inglis, "'A Land Set Apart'"; for Louisiana, see Gaudet, *Carville*, and Fairchild, "Community and Confinement"; for a comparative perspective, see Moran, "Colonizing Leprosy."

29. Foucault's *Madness and Civilization* has been a germinal text in the historiography of the institution, offering one of the first social control interpretations of the asylum. Interestingly, Foucault finds the leprosaria of the Middle Ages repopulated with the newly designated madmen and madwomen of the sixteenth and seventeenth centuries. He asserts that "what doubtless remained longer than leprosy, and would persist when the lazar houses had been empty for years, were the values and images attached to the figure of the leper as well as the meaning of his exclusion, the social importance of that insistent and fearful figure which was not driven off without first being inscribed within a sacred circle" (6). For an example of the social control model applied to the U.S. context, see Rothman, *Discovery of the Asylum*. For a gendered Foucauldian interpretation of the Progressive Era mental institution, see Lunbeck, *Psychiatric Persuasion*. For internal studies of institutions that challenge the social control model and demonstrate that disease definition and treatment are negotiated processes among administrators, physicians, families, and patients, see Tomes, *Generous Confidence*; Dwyer, *Homes for the Mad*; Bates, *Bargaining for Life*; and Bryder, *Below the Magic Mountain*. These works still tend to depict patients as the least influential players in the process of negotiation, particularly once placed within an institution.

30. Recent scholarship in the history of medicine has begun to reclaim for patients a degree of human agency that strict social control models have obscured; see Reagan, *When Abortion Was A Crime*; Rothman, *Living in the Shadow of Death*; Leavitt, *Typhoid Mary*; Kunzel, *Fallen Women, Problem Girls*; and Schoen, *Choice and Coercion*. For examples of how communities could work to challenge racial and ethnic policies of exclusion enforced by a white medical establishment, see Fett, *Working Cures*; Smith, *Sick and Tired* and *Japanese American Midwives*; and Shah, *Contagious Divides*.

31. For an example of how feminists encouraged women to educate themselves about their health and challenge indifference, ineffectiveness, and condescension from the medical profession, see the Boston Women's Health Book Collective, *Our Bodies, Ourselves*. For a discussion of how patients have challenged the authority of medical professionals to set research agendas, test treatments, direct funding, and make medi-

cal policy, see Bix, "Diseases Chasing Money and Power." On AIDS activism, see Epstein, *Impure Science*; Treichler, *How to Have Theory in an Epidemic*; and Shilts, *And the Band Played On*.

32. Social movement theory provides a method for interpreting the kind of mobilization and activism undertaken by these patient activists; see Hall, *Poor People's Social Movement Organizations*. For an examination of efforts to complement traditional resource mobilization theories with issues of social psychology, see Morris and Meuller, *Frontiers in Social Movement Theory*.

33. Sontag argues that society must peel away all social and cultural meanings of disease to deal with it as a strictly biological entity. She explores the stigmatizing and marginalizing effects of disease metaphors and concludes that those metaphors must be "exposed, criticized, belabored, used up" in order to better and more humanely manage disease. In this effort, she fails to consider both the problematic nature of removing a disease from its social context and the pervasive influence of social and cultural forces on biological and medical constructions of disease. See her *Illness as Metaphor* and *AIDS and Its Metaphors*.

34. Lupton, *Medicine as Culture*, 129.

35. A binary opposition similar to the one conceptualized by Edward Said between Europe and the Mideast—the Occident and the Orient—was in operation in Hawai'i, as westerners viewed native-born Hawaiians as the "savage" against whom they measured their "civilization"; see Said, *Orientalism*. For explorations of U.S. colonialist imaginings of Hawai'i and the Pacific, see Eperjesi, *Imperialist Imaginary*; and Wilson, *Reimagining the American Pacific*.

36. Santiago-Valles, "On the Historical Links," 109.

Chapter 1

1. "Leper a Prisoner after Tour de Luxe," *New York Times*, 3 June 1914, 4.

2. As recorded in *Congressional Record*, 63rd Cong., 2nd sess., 1914, 51, pt. 14: 9823.

3. "Leper a Prisoner," *New York Times*, 3 June 1914, 4.

4. Early was eventually shipped to Carville, Louisiana, in 1918, but he would also make periodic return trips to Washington, including a surprise visit to a congressional committee meeting on a bill considering the creation of a national home. His obituary credited his actions as bringing about the federal takeover of the leprosy facility in Carville. See "John Early, Sensational Tar Heel Leper, Stricken," *Burlington (N.C.) Daily Times-News*, 28 February 1938, 1.

5. Hudson and Genesse, "Hansen's Disease in the United States," 999–1001.

6. Duffy, *History of Medicine in Louisiana*, 259–63; Gussow, *Leprosy, Racism, and Public Health*, 51.

7. Washburn, "Leprosy Among Scandinavian Settlers," 128–30.

8. H. M. Bracken, "Leprosy in Minnesota," *Philadelphia Medical Journal*, 17 December

1898, as reprinted in Senate Committee on Public Health and National Quarantine, *Prevalence of Leprosy in the United States*, 45–48. In this way, treatment of people with leprosy was consistent with the treatment of other sick people. Those with money and family to care for them often could avoid placement in institutions. See Rosenberg, *Care of Strangers*, and Rothman, *Discovery of the Asylum*.

9. Senate, petition of A. Berger, M.D., of Tampa, relative to the introduction of epidemic disease in the state of Florida, *Congressional Record*, 50th Cong., 2nd sess., 1889, 20, pt. 1: 553–54; Senate, petition of the Philadelphia Board of Health asking for one or more stations for the treatment of those suffering from leprosy, *Congressional Record*, 52nd Cong., 1st sess., 1892, 23, pt. 1: 236. There was limited precedent for federal intervention into the provision of institutionalized care, as Congress had created the Marine Hospital Service in 1798 to provide care for merchant seamen. Under a reorganization of the system initiated in 1870, the federal government assumed responsibility for constructing and operating hospitals to care for these seamen who traveled throughout the world. During the late nineteenth century, the Marine Hospital Service gradually assumed additional responsibility for preventive medicine, including the regulation of national and interstate quarantine laws, collection of medical statistics, and investigation of disease. See Leigh, *Federal Health Administration in the United States*, 81, 100–102.

10. Zachary Gussow has argued that leprosy became "retainted" during the late nineteenth and early twentieth centuries, in large part due to U.S. encounters with racialized bodies in such places as Hawai'i. He argues that racism directed against Asians led to hard restrictions on leprosy, thought to be a distinctively Chinese disease. I find that health officials and politicians interpreted "foreign" more broadly, to incorporate a wide spectrum of racialized bodies westerners met in their colonial encounters. See Gussow, *Leprosy, Racism, and Public Health*, 22–24.

11. For a discussion of the emergence of medical missionaries in the late nineteenth century, see Booty, "Anglican Tradition," 254–55, and Weber, "Baptist Tradition," 300–304; for a discussion of European missionaries and their "near monopoly" of care among people with leprosy, see Watts, *Epidemics and History*, 71–76.

12. Bailey, "Mission Work Among the Lepers," 455.

13. Bailey, "Lepers of Asia," 818–21.

14. For examples of these accounts, see Stevenson, "Father Damien, an Open Letter," 344–56; and Stoddard, *Father Damien*. For more on Damien's life and legacy, see Chapter 2.

15. Davis, "Leprosy in America," 448. Rebecca Harding Davis's discussion of leprosy in Louisiana originally ran in the *New York Independent* under the title "Plague Spot of America."

16. White, "Contagiousness and Control of Leprosy," in *Transactions of the Congress of American Physicians and Surgeons*, 132–33; 135. The Congress of American Physicians and Surgeons consisted of medical specialists from seven medical associations—the Association of American Anatomists, the American Climatological Association, the

American Dermatological Association, the American Association of Genito-Urinary Surgeons, the American Gynecological Society, the American Laryngological Association, and the American Neurological Association—who met every three years both to exchange ideas and to assert their disciplinary authority. The papers presented at this third triennial convention were modestly declared by the chairman of the executive committee to represent "the flower of American Medicine" (xvii).

17. "Paper by Prof. Joseph D. Bryant Upon Control of Leprosy," in *Transactions of the Congress of American Physicians and Surgeons*, 142–44.

18. Wyman, "National Control of Leprosy," in *Transactions of the Congress of American Physicians and Surgeons*, 148.

19. House, petition to appoint a special committee to investigate the prevalence of leprosy in the United States and adjoining countries, *Congressional Record*, 53rd Cong., 2nd sess., 1894, 26, pt. 7: 6387; House, petition requesting appointment of a commission to investigate the existence of leprosy in the United States, *Congressional Record*, 53rd Cong., 2nd sess., 1894, 26, pt. 7: 6389.

20. The MHS assumed responsibility for quarantine and containment of contagious disease after wresting control from the short-lived National Board of Health in 1882; see Furman, *Profile of the United States Public Health Service*, 184–97, 206–11. Fitzhugh Mullan also discusses the formative years of the MHS in *Plagues and Politics*. For a discussion of an expanding federal government role in public health, see Duffy, *Sanitarians*, 157–72. For a discussion of the U.S. quarantine laws and the immigrant experience, see Kraut, *Silent Travelers*, 50–57, and Markel, *Quarantine!*

21. The bill (S. 2904) for the investigation of leprosy was originally introduced by Senator Cockrell in December and was referred to the Committee on Public Health and National Quarantine, *Congressional Record*, 55th Cong., 2nd sess., 1897, 31, pt. 1: 290. Senator Gallinger from the Committee on Public Health and National Quarantine reported on the bill for the investigation of leprosy without amendment and submitted the report (S. Rep. 463), *Congressional Record*, 55th Cong., 2nd sess., 1898, 31, pt. 1: 717. Four days later, Gallinger asked for unanimous consent on the bill, prompting the comment from Platt, *Congressional Record*, 55th Cong., 2nd sess., 1898, 31, pt. 1: 862.

22. Furman, *Profile of the U.S. Public Health Service*, 220.

23. Letter from Walter Wyman to George G. Vest of the Committee on Public Health and National Quarantine, 13 January 1898, as published in S. 2904, reprinted in *Public Health Reports* 14, no. 10 (1899): 306.

24. The amended bill read, "Be it enacted . . . that the Supervising-General of the Marine-Hospital Service, under the direction of the Secretary of the Treasury, shall appoint a commission of medical officers of the Marine-Hospital Service to investigate the origin and prevalence of leprosy in the United States, and to report upon what legislation is necessary for the prevention of the spread of this disease; the expenses of this investigation not to exceed the sum of $5,000, to be paid from the fund for preventing the spread of epidemic diseases"; *Congressional Record*, 55th Cong., 2nd

sess., 1898, 31, pt. 1: 862. The Senate requested concurrence on the bill from the House; *Congressional Record*, 55th Cong., 2nd sess., 1898, 31, pt. 1: 933. In the House, Representative Hepburn introduced a bill (H.R. 5431) for the investigation of leprosy, referred to the Committee on Interstate and Foreign Commerce, *Congressional Record*, 55th Cong., 2nd sess., 1897, 31, pt. 1: 304. The bill was reported on (H. Rep. 1215) and sent to the Committee of the Whole House on the State of the Union; *Congressional Record*, 55th Cong., 2nd sess., 1898, 31, pt. 5: 4418. A second bill was introduced by Representative Johnson of North Dakota (H.R. 6262); *Congressional Record*, 55th Cong., 2nd sess., 1898, 31, pt. 1: 553.

25. Morrow, "Leprosy and Hawaiian Annexation."

26. Foster, "Leprosy and the Hawaiian Annexation."

27. House, Mr. John B. Corliss reports on S. 2904; bill and report referred to the Committee of the Whole House on the State of the Union, *Congressional Record*, 55th Cong., 3rd sess., 1899, 32, pt. 1: 728.

28. *Congressional Record*, 55th Cong., 3rd sess., 1899, 32, pt. 3: 2492.

29. Ibid., 2707. The passage of a 1902 law that reorganized the service as the "Public Health and Marine Hospital Service of the United States" ultimately afforded Wyman the authority he sought; see Furman, *Profile of the U.S. Public Health Service*, 248–49.

30. Furman, *Profile of the U.S. Public Health Service*, 269.

31. For a discussion of Robert Koch's discovery of the anthrax bacillus and the development of the understanding that certain diseases are spread by specific bacterial contagions, see Hudson, *Disease and Its Control*, 159–68. For the role of bacteriology in enhancing medical authority and changing the shape of public health, see Starr, *Transformation of American Medicine*, particularly 137–38, 181–91. For an incisive discussion of the debates that raged between advocates of the germ theory and their opponents, see Tomes, *Gospel of Germs*, 26–47.

32. *Congressional Record*, 55th Cong., 3rd sess., 1899, 32, pt. 2: 1526.

33. Ibid., 56th Cong., 2nd sess., 1901, 34, pt. 4: 3014–15.

34. See, for example, Dr. Washington M. Ryer's nativist pamphlet, *Conflict of the Races*, in which he asserts, "By the same power which compels the Pacific States to endure the Mongolian presence, all their vices and diseases are maintained in these States, and the rising generation, now children of great promise, are being corrupted by contact with moral and physical leprosy" (80); and Dr. Douglass W. Montgomery's discussion of "the difference in social conservatism between the Aryans and the Mongolians" in "Leprosy in San Francisco," 137. For a broader discussion of racial intolerance toward Chinese immigrants, see Takaki, *Strangers from a Different Shore*. For a discussion of how fears of Chinese "lepers" in California came to embody nativist fears of miscegenation, see Shah, *Contagious Divides*, 97–104.

35. Furman, *Profile of the U.S. Public Health Service*, 223, 238, 244, 269. For a discussion of the MHS's role in the bubonic plague outbreak, see Kraut, *Silent Travelers*, 84–96. On racial management of the plague by health officials, see Shah, *Contagious Divides*, 120–57. On a later outbreak, see Risse, "'A Long Pull, A Strong Pull, and All Together.'"

36. Furman, *Profile of the U.S. Public Health Service*, 220.

37. *Congressional Record*, 57th Cong., 1st sess., 1902, 35, pt. 4: 3179; Senate Committee on Public Health and National Quarantine, *Leprosy in the United States.*

38. See, for example, D. A. Carmichael, "Report on Leprosy in the Hawaiian Islands, November 29, 1898," *Public Health Reports* (20 December 1898), and L. E. Coffer, "Description of the Leper Settlement on the Island of Molokai," *Public Health Reports* (11 October 1901), both reprinted in Senate Committee on Public Health and National Quarantine, *Leprosy in the United States*, 95–119.

39. Senate Committee on Public Health and National Quarantine, *Leprosy in the United States*, 10.

40. Ibid., 7–10.

41. Ibid., 10.

42. "Report of the Secretaries of the International Leprosy Conference, Berlin, 1897," in Senate Committee on Public Health and National Quarantine, *Leprosy in the United States*, 43–44.

43. Senate Committee on Public Health and National Quarantine, *Leprosy in the United States*, 10.

44. Ibid., 7–9.

45. Worboys, "Tropical Disease," 512–13, 530–31; Anderson, "Immunities of Empire."

46. This process of categorization had clear racial implications, as Warwick Anderson explains. He contends that "framing disease, framing 'environment' and framing 'race' all were the same maneuver—with political and social consequences perhaps as profound as any military deployment"; Anderson, "Disease, Race, and Empire," 63.

47. Watts, *Epidemics and History*, 69.

48. Bracken, "Are National Leprosaria Desirable?" in Senate Committee on Public Health and National Quarantine, *Leprosy in the United States*, 69.

49. For a more detailed discussion of racial typologies in relation to disease, see Anderson, "Immunities of Empire."

50. A. W. Hitt to J. H. White, 27 September 1900, in Senate Committee on Public Health and National Quarantine, *Leprosy in the United States*, 80–81.

51. Carmichael, "Report on Leprosy in the Hawaiian Islands," in Senate Committee on Public Health and National Quarantine, *Leprosy in the United States*, 104–5.

52. Ibid.

53. Fox and Lawrence, *Photographing Medicine*, 25–27.

54. Senate Committee on Public Health and National Quarantine, *Leprosy in the United States*, plates between 82 and 83.

55. A. W. Hitt, "Leprosy," in Senate Committee on Public Health and National Quarantine, *Leprosy in the United States*, 85.

56. R. D. Murray to the Leprosy Commission, 15 November 1900, in Senate Committee on Public Health and National Quarantine, *Leprosy in the United States*, 94.

57. *Congressional Record*, 57th Cong., 1st sess., 1902, 35, pt. 4: 3179; *Congressional*

Record, 58th Cong., 3rd sess., 1904, 39, pt. 1: 430, regarding H.R. 16913 and H.R. 16914; the Senate considered a similar proposal in February 1905: *Congressional Record*, 58th Cong., 3rd sess., 1905, 39, pt. 2: 1818, regarding S. 7055.

58. Moblo, "Defamation by Disease," 208; C. E. Cooper, "Report of the Committee on Leprosy," Appendix F, *Transactions of the Second Annual Conference of State and Territorial Health Officers*, 82–87.

59. House Committee on Interstate and Foreign Commerce, *Care and Treatment of Lepers*, 1.

60. Ibid., 2–4.

61. Cohn, *Colonialism and Its Forms of Knowledge*, 3–11.

62. *Congressional Record*, 58th Cong., 3rd sess., 1905, 39, pt. 4: 3667.

63. Ibid., 3900.

64. Senate Committee on Public Health and National Quarantine, *Leprosarium for the Segregation of Lepers*, 1–2. See also House Committee on Interstate and Foreign Commerce, *Leprosarium for the Segregation of Lepers*, 1–5.

65. Senate Committee on Public Health and National Quarantine, *Leprosarium for the Segregation of Lepers*, 2–3.

66. The 1905 meeting of U.S. public health officers attested to the wide variations in leprosy management. In California, individual counties bore full financial responsibility for leprosy patients; Louisiana had constructed a state institution in 1894 that contained 100 people; Massachusetts quarantined a few patients at a facility in Boston Harbor; Wisconsin isolated a few cases on country farms; and no other state reported any measures for segregating people with leprosy. *Transactions of the Third Annual Conference of State and Territorial Health Officers with the United States Public Health and Marine-Hospital Service*, 10–17.

67. Senate Committee on Public Health and National Quarantine, *Leprosarium for the Segregation of Lepers*, 2–3.

68. For a discussion of the ambiguous status of residents of U.S. territories and its implication for understanding efforts to draw distinctions between the "domestic" and the "foreign" during the early twentieth century, see Kaplan, *Anarchy of Empire*, 1–12.

69. As stated by Representative William Hepburn of Iowa, *Congressional Record*, 58th Cong., 3rd sess., 1905, 39, pt. 4: 3908–9.

70. Ibid.

71. For further discussion of the nature of island territories in relation to land acquired during the first phase of American expansion, see Bell, *Last Among Equals*, 12–21.

72. *Congressional Record*, 58th Cong., 3rd sess., 1905, 39, pt. 4: 3909–10.

73. Sheila M. Rothman describes a shift in the way Americans perceived tuberculosis during the late nineteenth century, arguing that it assumed more negative connotations when doctors traced its cause to a bacterium and established it as a contagious disease. At the same time, however, she notes that this development raised hopes that doctors could then diagnose the disease in its early stages and better effect a cure; see

Rothman, *Living in the Shadow of Death*, 194–210. These congressional debates suggest that these sanatoria were actually welcomed by communities who profited from the business generated by these institutions.

74. *Congressional Record*, 58th Cong., 3rd sess., 1905, 39, pt. 4: 3910.

75. Ibid., 3909. Representative Thetus Sims of Tennessee framed the pointed question, "Is it not a fact that these two Territories are practically a national sanitarium for all people in the United States affected with lung trouble, and would it not cease to be such a place and would not more people die by being deprived of that than you would save of lepers?"

76. Ibid. For example, Representative Joseph Sibley of Pennsylvania referred to this action as "absolutely destructive of States' rights," Representative John Dalzell of Pennsylvania asked if it was not "the worst kind of paternalism," while Delegate John Wilson of Arizona concurred that the idea of a national leprosarium should be defeated on the grounds that it represented "paternalism in the strongest sense, absolute paternalism."

77. Ibid., 3911. Explicitly expressed by Delegate Rodey, as well as by Representative Williams.

78. Ibid., 3910.

79. Ibid., 3911.

80. Ibid., 4001–2. In fact, the leprosy settlement only occupied part of the small, isolated Kalaupapa peninsula on the island. Mr. Kalaniana'ole, the delegate from Hawai'i, offered this correction the following day on the floor of the House, noting how Moloka'i supported farmers, fishermen, and plantation workers. He also took the opportunity to voice Hawaiians' objections to the importation of any mainland leprosy patients.

81. Ibid., 3911. The final vote measured 36 in favor and 180 opposed.

82. The issue did arise twice in the House during the intervening years, once in 1910 by Representative Wickersham, who suggested establishing a "detention hospital" in Alaska for the care of "Indians, Eskimos, and Creoles" with leprosy; and again in 1913. Both measures died in committee. *Congressional Record*, 61st Cong., 2nd sess., 1910, 45, pt. 8: 8448, regarding H.R. 26922; *Congressional Record*, 63rd Cong., 1st sess., 1913, 50, pt. 1: 87, regarding H.R. 1751.

83. Press coverage of Early's visit was cited by members of Congress in their debates over what should be done with Early and other Americans with leprosy; *Congressional Record*, 63rd Cong., 2nd sess., 1914, 51, pt. 14: 9823.

84. Early's history and campaign to gain improved conditions for leprosy patients are chronicled in Kalisch, "Strange Case of John Early," 291–305. His story is also explored in Gould, *Disease Apart*, 185–211.

85. "Leper J. Early Insane," *Washington Post*, 11 July 1913, 3. The former Lottie Early, known as Mrs. George Tauson after her remarriage, disputed accounts of her former husband's mental condition, contending that he had a long history of violence; she

claimed she had been desperate to escape from her marriage to protect herself and her children. See "Tells Story of Her Suffering as Wife of the Leper, John Early," *Washington Post*, 20 July 1913, 4.

86. Office of the Surgeon General, "Memorandum Relative to John Early," Central File 4712, Box 529, Record Group 90, National Archives and Records Administration.

87. *Congressional Record*, 63rd Cong., 2nd sess., 1914, 51, pt. 14: 9772–73, regarding H.R. 17011 and H.R. 17018; 9830, regarding H.R. 17040.

88. Ibid., 9822–23.

89. Ibid., pt. 15: 15190.

90. Ibid., 3rd sess., 1914, 52, pt. 1: 291, regarding H.R. 20040.

91. House Committee on Interstate and Foreign Commerce, *Prevention of Leprosy in the United States*, 1–2.

92. *Congressional Record*, 63rd Cong., 3rd sess., 1915, 52, pt. 5: 3814–15.

93. Ibid., 4546–47, and 4560, regarding H.R. 20040.

94. Congress considered a new slate of leprosy bills the following year. The House introduced two bills (H.R. 193 and H.R. 5777) in December 1915, while the Senate considered S. 4085 in January 1916. *Congressional Record*, 64th Cong., 1st sess., 1915, 53, pt. 1: 18, 294; *Congressional Record*, 64th Cong., 1st sess., 1916, 53, pt. 2: 1781.

95. Senate Committee on Public Health and National Quarantine, *Care and Treatment of Persons Afflicted with Leprosy*, 7. During the hearings themselves, Ransdell cited the precedent of federal Civil War pensions to assert that the government had a responsibility to care for those soldiers who acquired leprosy in the line of duty (121).

96. Ibid., 13, 38, 60.

97. Nancy Tomes discusses the nineteenth-century asylum as a site of both therapy and containment in *Generous Confidence*. Similar impulses led to the construction of homes for the mentally retarded in the twentieth-century U.S. South, as Steven Noll explores in *Feeble-Minded in Our Midst*.

98. Senate Committee on Public Health and National Quarantine, *Care and Treatment of Persons Afflicted with Leprosy*, 25, 39.

99. Ibid., 22. The fact that Louisiana law compelled patients diagnosed with leprosy to enter the home might have influenced their reported willingness to comply.

100. Ibid., 183.

101. John Early to Senator Ransdell, in Senate Committee on Public Health and National Quarantine, *Care and Treatment of Persons Afflicted with Leprosy*, 159.

102. Ibid., 146–47.

103. As quoted in Leavitt, *Typhoid Mary*, 180. In her examination of Mallon, Leavitt discusses the ways in which labels identifying people by the disease they carry dehumanize patients (126–61).

104. Senate Committee on Public Health and National Quarantine, *Care and Treatment of Persons Afflicted with Leprosy*, 25, 96.

105. Ibid., 125. The term "native" evoked notions of savagery, primitivism, and exoticism, enabling politicians and public health officials to position themselves as the

civilized counterpart to what they viewed as uncivilized peoples. For a discussion of the construction of the Hawaiian "native" in Euroamerican colonial discourse, see Wood, *Displacing Natives*. For discussions of the ways in which American and British literature represented Pacific Islanders as primitive, see Edmond, *Representing the South Pacific*. For a broader discussion of the ways in which American men such as Theodore Roosevelt drew on the discourse of civilization in support of U.S. imperialism and racial violence, see Bederman, *Manliness and Civilization*, 170–215.

106. Senate Committee on Public Health and National Quarantine, *Care and Treatment of Persons Afflicted with Leprosy*, 125.

107. Victor G. Heiser, "Leprosy—Its Treatment in the Philippine Islands by the Hypodermic Use of a Chaulmoogra Oil Mixture"; original examination record of Board of Health of Hawaii; and George W. McCoy, "Statistic Study of Leprosy in Hawaii," *Public Health Bulletin* 66 (1916), in Senate Committee on Public Health and National Quarantine, *Care and Treatment of Persons Afflicted with Leprosy*, 31–34, 123, 167–75.

108. Senate Committee on Public Health and National Quarantine, *Care and Treatment of Persons Afflicted with Leprosy*, 152–53.

109. Ibid., 197.

110. Ibid., 1–2.

111. *Congressional Record*, 64th Cong., 2nd sess., 1917, 54, pt. 2: 1807–8.

112. Senator Joseph Ransdell of Louisiana managed to convince the Senate to substitute the almost identical House bill instead. The House had passed H.R. 193 the previous session with little debate; *Congressional Record*, 64th Cong., 1st sess., 1916, 53, pt. 8: 7431. Ransdell presented his request on 25 January 1917, and President Woodrow Wilson signed the bill on 3 February 1917; *Congressional Record*, 64th Cong., 2nd sess., 1917, 54, pt. 2: 1965–66, 2776.

113. *Congressional Record*, 66th Cong., 3rd sess., 1921, 60, pt. 3: 2294.

Chapter 2

1. Traditional histories of late nineteenth century Hawai'i have portrayed the eventual annexation of the islands to the United States as the inevitable triumph of an "advanced" society over a "primitive" one. See, for example, Kuykendall, *Hawaiian Kingdom, Vol. 3*; Russ, *Hawaiian Revolution*; Daws, *Shoal of Time*; Stevens, *American Expansion in Hawaii*; and Fuchs, *Hawaii Pono*. Sahlins provides a richer examination of Hawaiian culture that challenges the idea of Pacific Islander inferiority, but still isolates Hawaiians within a static system. For an example of Sahlins's work, see *Islands of History*. For a critique of this work, see Obeyesekere, *Apotheosis of Captain Cook*. Obeyesekere has been criticized for silencing Hawaiian voices by interpreting their actions as the work of Western rationalists. See Sahlins, *How 'Natives' Think*. For an analysis of this debate, see Borovsky, "Cook, Lono, Obeyesekere, and Sahlins." More

recent scholarship has directly addressed the issue of U.S. imperialism in Hawai'i, focusing on Hawaiian resistance and the fragmented nature of colonial power to suggest that the Western overthrow of Hawaiian sovereignty was neither inevitable nor complete. See, for example, Trask, *From a Native Daughter*, 113–22. For an examination of how Hawaiians responded to, adapted, and were transformed by Anglo-American law, see Merry, *Colonizing Hawai'i*. Grounding her work in Hawaiian-language sources, Silva provides a path-breaking challenge to traditional accounts of Hawaiian passivity, demonstrating how Kanaka Maoli (Native Hawaiians) resisted political oppression and cultural assimilation. See Silva, *Aloha Betrayed*.

2. The 100th anniversary of the Spanish-American-Cuban-Filipino Wars has generated significant scholarly attention to events and issues surrounding American imperialism in 1898. Some of this scholarship has rightfully noted how the dominant strain of U.S. historiography has focused disproportionately on this year, treating the "rise of the U.S. empire" as an anomaly in U.S. history. See, for example, Campomanes, "1898 and the Nature of the New Empire." This emphasis on military conquest and political annexation particularly slights the history of U.S.-Hawaiian relations. The U.S. annexation of the Hawaiian Islands in 1898 emerged from a different set of historical processes than the wars that led to the acquisition of Puerto Rico, the Philippines, and Guam. The United States did not engage in an overt military struggle with another European colonial power to acquire Hawai'i. American business interests and missionaries played vital roles in the economic, legal, and cultural transformation of the islands, as well as the political changes that wrested control from native Hawaiians. The annexation of Hawai'i in 1898 is only one moment in a broader and longer history of U.S. imperialism in the islands. For a discussion of American colonial activity before 1898, see Silva, *Aloha Betrayed*. For American colonial activity during annexation and after, see Coffman, *Nation Within* and *Island Edge of America*. For an exploration of U.S. anti-imperialism, see Osborne, *"Empire Can Wait."*

3. For a discussion of this scholarship, see Porter, "Religion and Medicine," 1449–1468. Numbers and Amundsen emphasize the Judeo-Christian traditions embedded in the history of Western medicine in their edited collection, *Caring and Curing*. However, the essays in this volume reinforce the notion that religious understandings of sickness and health gave way to scientific views in the nineteenth century. Such an interpretation overlooks the ways in which religious beliefs continued to inform medical opinion and shape medical institutions.

4. Watts, *Epidemics and History*, 71–76.

5. Conservative estimates place the population of native Hawaiians at 250,000 in 1779; in the first year leprosy patients were sent to the Moloka'i settlement (1866), that number had dropped to 58,765. By 1890, the Hawaiian population stood at 40,622. See Nordyke, *Peopling of Hawai'i*, 174–78. Stannard uses archaeological and historical evidence to reevaluate previous demographic projections and argue that the Hawaiian population during the time of European contact was actually much higher, consisting of at least 800,000 people, in *Before the Horror*, 3–31.

6. Crosby, "Hawaiian Depopulation as a Model for the Amerindian Experience," 190–91. Crosby notes that while leprosy did not play a significant role in Hawaiian depopulation, it played into westerners' racist assumptions by primarily targeting the native-born residents. Crosby notes that in 1848–49 alone, epidemics of measles, whooping cough, and influenza took 10,000 lives.

7. As quoted in Mouritz, *Path of the Destroyer*, 29.

8. Ibid.

9. Maffly-Kipp has called attention to the need to recognize the role of the United States as an imperial power that has often used religion as a means of subjugation in "Eastward Ho!", 136.

10. "Report of Dr. G. L. Fitch, 1884," in *Appendix to the Report on Leprosy*, xxviii–xxix.

11. Silva, *Aloha Betrayed*, 35–39.

12. Land ownership shifted even more dramatically with the beginning of "The Great Mahele" in 1848, which provided individualized land holdings for native Hawaiians. Established by the monarchy with the intention of dissolving traditional relationships between chiefs and commoners, it made the practice of subsistence agriculture untenable for many Hawaiians who found themselves unable to pay the newly required land taxes on their holdings. Many therefore sold their land to westerners and often became laborers on the plantations that emerged. Buck discusses the disruption of Hawaiian culture brought on by these land reforms and the development of the sugar industry in *Paradise Remade*, 69–75. Campbell cautions against characterizing the Great Mahele as an "act of national betrayal," noting that the declining Hawaiian population left much of the land idle, threatening the economic viability of the new kingdom; see *History of the Pacific*, 86–88.

13. Watts, *Epidemics and History*, 65–66. Watts specifically challenges accounts suggesting that Chinese laborers were the sole source of the disease, pointing out that Norwegian immigrants were among those initially recruited to work the fields.

14. Mouritz, *Path of the Destroyer*, 33.

15. Hawaiians could not be said to have a "traditional" way of handling contagious disease, as there is no evidence to suggest that they had to deal with any before the late eighteenth century when Western contact brought such diseases. Hawaiians constructed their own ideas about leprosy from their evolving encounters with the series of illnesses that white settlers had brought to the islands' populations. They came to identify leprosy in part by the curious insistence among white settlers that this disease required unique treatment to arrest its spread, as reflected in one term for the disease, "maʻi hoʻokaʻawale"—the "separating sickness." For Hawaiians, care for the sick was a communal effort in which the healthy and ill intermingled and family and friends provided care for one another. Although Hawaiians (like westerners) could link sickness with wrongful behavior or punishment from (a) higher being(s), their rituals of healing required involvement of family and friends (unlike westerners), usually under the direction of a kahuna lapaʻau (healer or physician). See Bushnell, *Gifts of Civilization*, 64–67. Anyone seeking healing or forgiveness was to be accepted, and those who

refused risked generating their own misfortune. See, for example, Pukuai, Haertig, and Lee, *Nana I Ke Kumu*, 38, 64, 74–75.

16. Excerpt from the 1865 "Act to Prevent the Spread of Leprosy," as quoted in Mouritz, *Path of the Destroyer*, 63–65. The leprosy settlement was situated on what came to be known as the Kalaupapa (originally Makanalua) peninsula on Moloka'i. Those with leprosy initially settled on the eastern portion of the peninsula, in the region called Kalawao. The population gradually shifted to the west, settling within the land division known as Kalaupapa. The entire settlement would come to be identified by this name. The distance between the two regions of the peninsula is approximately 2.5 miles. For a further discussion of settlement, see Law, "Triumph of Spirit."

17. The other two patients were Chinese, see "Report of Arthur Mouritz—Resident Physician and Medical Superintendent at the Leper Settlement, Molokai," in *Appendix to the Report on Leprosy*, lxxxiii.

18. "Table Showing the Number of Lepers at the Settlement on Molokai, Mortality, and Number on the Books at the End of Each Year," in *Report of the Board of Health for the Biennial Period Ending Dec. 31, 1897* (Honolulu: Hawaiian Gazette, 1898), 166, hereafter *Report of the Board of Health*. The Hawaiian population for 1866 was 58,765, making the number of incarcerated Hawaiians with leprosy more than 2 people per 1,000.

19. Kuykendall, *Hawaiian Kingdom, Vol. 2*, 258–59.

20. Ibid.

21. *Report of the Board of Health, 1897*, 166.

22. Peter Kaeo maintained a correspondence with his cousin, Queen Emma, throughout his stay in the Moloka'i settlement, later published as *News from Molokai*.

23. Popular understandings of leprosy in Hawai'i have been dominated by the story of Father Damien, a narrative that portrays Damien as the white savior of powerless Hawaiians who improved conditions for unfortunate "lepers" and tragically died from the disease himself in the process. Moblo demonstrates how the story of Damien has served to justify Western efforts to both dominate Hawaiian political systems and develop harsh restrictions toward those with leprosy. See Moblo's "Defamation by Disease," and "Blessed Damien of Moloka'i," 691–726.

24. "Special Report from Rev. J. Damien, Catholic Priest at Kalawao, March 1886," in *Appendix to the Report on Leprosy*, cx–cxi.

25. Indeed, the interfaith alliance demonstrated the degree to which both Catholics and Protestants sought to make leprosy a platform for their worldwide missionary efforts. While Catholics would point to Damien as evidence of the Church's successful mission to the poor and suffering, Protestants viewed their monetary support of the priest's work as part of their broader commitment to the civilization and Christianization of the "natives." In this way, even the American Leprosy Missions, a Protestant organization, could refer to Father Damien as "A Christian Hero"; see Feeny, *Fight Against Leprosy*, 75–87.

26. For more recent biographies of Damien, see Daws, *Holy Man*, and Stewart, *Leper Priest of Moloka'i*.

27. "Report of Arthur Mouritz," in *Appendix to the Report on Leprosy*, lxxix–lxxx.

28. "Report by Dr. Edward Arning," in *Appendix to the Report on Leprosy*, liv.

29. This constitution, named for the violence that the Hawaiian League promised if the king refused to accept it, placed governing authority in the hands of the legislature; at the same time, it extended the franchise to a greater number of foreigners while imposing property qualifications that limited the number of Hawaiians who could vote for certain representatives. For a discussion of the rise of the Hawaiian League and their imposition of the new charter, see Andrade, *Unconquerable Rebel*, 44–52. For a discussion of the ways in which Kalākaua sought to retain a strong sense of Hawaiian identity within the islands even as he relinquished political authority, see Silva, *Aloha Betrayed*, 87–122.

30. Moblo examines the politicization of leprosy from the 1887 Bayonet Constitution to the 1893 overthrow of Lili'uokalani in "Leprosy, Politics, and the Rise of Hawaii's Reform Party," 75–89. While I agree with Moblo's contention that westerners used leprosy as a means of asserting their superiority over Hawaiians, I dispute her conclusion that only in Hawai'i did the disease carry "special status," that "leprosy was treated much like other diseases in most of the world." The politics of leprosy reverberated far beyond the boundaries of the Hawaiian Islands.

31. *Report of the Board of Health, 1890*, 2.

32. *Report of the Board of Health, 1902*, 13.

33. *Report of the Board of Health, 1890*, 4–5.

34. Ibid., 14.

35. For example, Dr. A. Lutz, commissioned by the board in 1890 to research leprosy, selected twenty patients "of intelligence and good will, whose affections promised well for treatment," to remain at Kalihi; *Report of the Board of Health, 1890*, 71. Chapter 4 further explores patient experimentation.

36. *Report of the Board of Health, 1890*, 9.

37. As described by Morrow, "Leprosy and Hawaiian Annexation," 586.

38. *Report of the Board of Health, 1890*, 63.

39. The Baldwin Home for boys was situated in the Kalawao region of the peninsula, while the Bishop Home for girls and women stood in Kalaupapa.

40. *Report of the Board of Health, 1890*, 46.

41. In 1853, Hawaiians represented 97 percent of the islands' population (71,000 of 73,000); by 1890, that number had dropped to less than 45 percent (40,000 of 90,000). Nordyke, *Peopling of Hawai'i*, 174–78.

42. *Report of the Board of Health, 1890*, 115. This number includes four Americans, four English, one Portuguese, one German, one Canadian, and one Russian. One Samoan and two Gilbert Islanders rounded off the list of residents identified by "nationality."

43. As reported by Resident Superintendent R. W. Meyer, many Hawaiians confined in the settlement refused to participate in planting efforts or other enforced labor, effectively undermining Board of Health plans, *Report of the Board of Health, 1890*, 47.

44. The weekly rations allocated each adult patient outside the homes in 1890 consisted of one bundle pa'i'ai (21 pounds) (used to make poi) or 12.5 pounds flour and 1 pound sugar, or 9 pounds rice plus 1 pound sugar, or 8.5 pounds bread with 1 pound sugar, or 50 cents cash; also, 7 pounds beef or mutton, if available, or 7 pounds fresh fish, or 3 pounds salt salmon. In addition, residents each month received 1 pound of soap, 5 pounds salt, and 4 packs of matches; each household received 1 quart of kerosene oil. *Report of Board of Health, 1890*, 125.

45. In 1890, this money amounted to $5,607.03. That the board maintained a method of examining all packages shipped into the settlement does reveal how it attempted to keep a close eye on the activities of the residents. *Report of the Board of Health, 1890*, 141.

46. *Report of the Board of Health, 1894*, 18.

47. In 1890, this represented approximately 950 out of 1,159 patients. The remaining patients lived under the supervision of religious workers in more institutional settings, such as the Bishop and Baldwin homes, *Report of the Board of Health, 1890*.

48. By the end of the 1892 fiscal period, the board owned 191 houses, while patients owned 236 houses. The Catholic Church owned an additional three houses occupied by patients. Accounting for a fluctuating patient population throughout the 1890–92 period, this meant that the average number of patients per house was little more than two. However, this does not account for the addition of kōkuas, nonpatient resident helpers. It is important to point out that the patients did not own the land on which these houses stood, only the structures. As patients constructed these houses themselves, with their own materials, the board considered them patient-owned and disavowed all responsibility for their maintenance. "Report of R. W. Meyer, Agent of the Board of Health," in *Report of the Board of Health, 1892*, 99–105.

49. Female kōkuas slightly outnumbered male kōkuas in 1890, 102 to 84. While many entered the settlement to assist their spouses, others came to help care for parents or friends. *Report of the Board of Health, 1890*, 116.

50. *Report of the Board of Health, 1890*, 139.

51. *Report of the Board of Health, 1892*, 88–89.

52. Report from David Dayton to Members of the Board of Health, 29 January 1891, Reports of Various Agents on Leprosy (1887–1893), DOH4–35, Department of Health Records, Hawai'i State Archives, hereafter HSA.

53. *Report of the Board of Health, 1890*, 138.

54. *Report of the Board of Health, 1892*, 117.

55. Ibid., 7, 118.

56. Morrow, "Leprosy and Hawaiian Annexation," 587.

57. "Report of Sidney B. Swift," in *Report of the Board of Health, 1892*, 85–87.

58. *Report of the Board of Health, 1890,* 43.

59. "Report of Sidney B. Swift," in *Report of the Board of Health, 1892,* 85–87.

60. *Report of the Board of Health, 1890,* 41–42.

61. "Report of R. W. Meyer," in *Report of the Board of Health, 1892,* 114–16.

62. Board president David Dayton termed the incident a "riot" but did not dwell on its implications. *Report of the Board of Health, 1892,* 8–9.

63. Health officials knew these enclaves existed, but found themselves unable to track down the people with leprosy who lived there. The board president reported in 1890, "Some very bad and unmistakable cases are in hiding in the fastnesses of the mountains or high up in the valleys, often being fed and secreted by their friends, while some mild cases change their places of residences so often as to baffle the efforts of the officers of the law for their arrest." *Report of the Board of Health, 1890,* 13.

64. Traditional U.S. accounts of this event tended to depict the coup d'etat as the inevitable triumph of white settlers over an ineffective Hawaiian government. For example, Russ explained that the "Royal Government under Kalakaua and Lili'uokalani was inefficient, corrupt, and undependable. That the powerful American minority disliked it is understandable, and that these same whites would wish to bring the islands under the control of the United States is equally understandable"; Russ, *Hawaiian Revolution,* 349. For a more critical view, see Dougherty, *To Steal a Kingdom.* For a discussion of Hawaiian resistance to both the coup and U.S. annexation efforts, see Silva, *Aloha Betrayed,* 123–63.

65. Board of Health Meeting, 17 May 1893, vol. 5, 45, Minutes of the Board of Health, HSA.

66. As Fuchs has noted, the majority of prominent government officials were related to missionaries; this held true for the Board of Health as well. Fuchs, *Hawaii Pono,* 33.

67. "Board of Health," *Daily Pacific Commercial Advertiser (DPCA),* 9 June 1893, 2.

68. Ibid.

69. Board of Health Meeting, 31 May 1893, vol. 5, 47; Board of Health Meeting, 16 June 1893, vol. 5, 52, Minutes of the Board of Health, HSA.

70. The incident is more fully described in an oral account by Pi'ilani, Ko'olau's wife, recorded by John G. M. Sheldon in 1906 and later translated into English by Frances N. Frazier as "The True Story of Kaluaiko'olau, or Ko'olau the Leper." Frazier's translation, along with a reprint of the original 1906 Hawaiian publication, has been republished as *True Story of Kaluaikoolau, as Told by His Wife, Piilani.* For contemporary press coverage, see "Shot by a Leper: The Shocking Fate of Deputy Sheriff Stolz of Waimea," *Daily Bulletin,* 29 June 1893, 3.

71. "Kauai Lepers: Preparations Being Made to Remove Them to Molokai," *DPCA,* 29 June 1893, 3.

72. "Dead or Alive: Lepers to Be Removed from Kalalau," *DPCA,* 30 June 1893, 3.

73. For a brief discussion of divided opinion in the wake of the overthrow of Lili'uokalani, see Bell, *Last Among Equals,* 27–28, and Fuchs, *Hawaii Pono,* 32–34. How-

ever, these works pay more attention to the response of the U.S. federal government than they do to competing interests within Hawai'i.

74. "Meddle and Muddle," *Daily Bulletin*, 29 June 1893, 2.

75. "Shame, Thou Royalist!" *DPCA*, 30 June 1893, 2.

76. "Shot by a Leper," *Daily Bulletin*, 29 June 1893, 3; "Squad Off for Kalalau," *Daily Bulletin*, 30 June 1893, 2; and [headline missing], *DCPA*, 30 June 1893, 4.

77. Board of Health Meeting, 1 July 1893, vol. 5, 57, Minutes of the Board of Health, HSA.

78. "At Bay: Koolau and His Backers Will Make a Stand," *DCPA*, 5 July 1893, 2.

79. Ibid., "Return from Kalalau: S.S. Waialeale Brings a Number of Surrendered Lepers," *Daily Bulletin*, 5 July 1893, 3.

80. "The Pele Arrives: The Situation Not Changed at Kalalau," *DPCA*, 8 July 1893, 3.

81. "Stronghold of the Lepers: An Impregnable Fastness where Koolau Will Die Before Yielding," *Daily Bulletin*, 8 July 1893, 3; "The Pele Arrives," *DPCA*, 8 July 1893, 3.

82. "Taste of Real War: Three Soldiers Killed in the Kalalau Expedition," *Daily Bulletin*, 10 July 1893, 3; "Killed by Koolau! Two Soldiers Shot by the Leper Bandit," *DPCA*, 10 July 1893, 5.

83. "Notes and Comments," *DPCA*, 10 July 1893, 3.

84. Anderson, "Excremental Colonialism."

85. "They All Came Back: The Troops Return from Kalalau without Koolau," *Daily Bulletin*, 13 July 1893, 2; "Koolau Provisioned," *Daily Bulletin*, 18 July 1893, 2.

86. "Flight of Koolau," *DPCA*, 14 July 1893, 5.

87. *Report of the Board of Health*, 1894, 60.

88. Kaluaikoolau, *True Story of Kaluaikoolau*, 36–46. For an examination of the multiple retellings of the story of Ko'olau's resistance and what they reveal about the contests among Euroamericans and Hawaiians over the management and mobility of people with leprosy, see Moran, "Telling Tales of Ko'olau." His story has inspired several fictional accounts, including the sensationalized short story by London, "Koolau the Leper," and Merwin's lyrical epic, *Folding Cliffs*.

89. Board of Health Meeting, 7 July 1893, vol. 5, 60, Minutes of the Board of Health, HSA.

90. "Rules and Regulations for Lepers and Kokuas Living at the Leper Settlement on Molokai, Promulgated in Accordance to Section 5b of Chapter XXXIII of the Laws of 1870, and Section 2 of Chapter LXI of the Laws of 1888," Rules and Regulations for Lepers and Kokuas at Leper Settlement, 1893, Box 35, DOH-4, Department of Health Records, HSA.

91. Board of Health Meeting, 3 May 1893, vol. 5, 37; 21 July 1893, vol. 5, 65, Minutes of the Board of Health, HSA.

92. *Report of the Board of Health*, 1894, 6.

93. Ibid., 1.

94. For an examination of the belief in the connection between clean houses and healthy living, see Tomes, *Gospel of Germs*, 135–54. For a discussion of the perceived

healthful effects of whitewashing and shifting notions of disease causation in the late nineteenth century, see Rosenberg, *Care of Strangers*, 124–41, and *Cholera Years*.

95. "Rules and Regulations for Lepers and Kokuas," 2–3, Department of Health Records, HSA.

96. Ibid., 4.

97. Board of Health Meeting, 2 January 1895, vol. 5, 214; 13 February 1895, vol. 5, 216, Minutes of the Board of Health, HSA.

98. In 1897, an equal number of male and female kōkuas lived in the Settlement (thirty-nine of each sex). Both men and women were expected to perform tasks for the general support of the settlement beyond the care of their loved ones. *Report of the Board of Health, 1897*, 58.

99. "Rules and Regulations for Lepers and Kokuas," 4–5, Department of Health Records, HSA.

100. *Report of the Board of Health, 1894*, 34.

101. Kalaupapa, Miscellaneous, 1896–1899, Box 36, DOH-4, Department of Health Records, HSA. I found lists for no other year than 1899 in the Board of Health of files. Most requests were handled on a case-by-case basis; that a board member attempted to tabulate the requests in 1899 apparently reflected a personal interest in the matter, as it was not the type of information regularly quantified and published in the board's annual reports.

102. Luki Mila to C. E. Cooper, 17 April 1899, Kalaupapa, Miscellaneous, 1896–1899, Box 36, DOH-4, Department of Health Records, HSA.

103. Letter from W. R. Castle to C. E. Cooper, 19 April 1899, Kalaupapa, Miscellaneous, 1896–1899, Box 36, DOH-4, Department of Health Records, HSA.

104. Mouritz, *Path of the Destroyer*, 58–59.

Chapter 3

1. "Bound for the Leper Land," *New Orleans Daily Picayune*, 17 April 1896, as quoted in Mulhane, *Leprosy and the Charity of the Church*, 147–53.

2. O'Connell discusses the intensive period of Catholic hospital building in the nineteenth and twentieth centuries to conclude that, ultimately, physical healing served only as a path to the more crucial goal of redeeming souls. This interpretation slights the degree to which religious workers embraced scientific medicine and to which religious beliefs continued to influence medical policies and institutions. See O'Connell, "Roman Catholic Tradition Since 1545." This view has been challenged by religious historians who have examined the religious dimensions of the public ministry of healing, whether on the battlefield, in immigrant neighborhoods, or in hospitals. See, for example, Stepsis and Liptak, *Pioneer Healers*, and Kauffman, *Ministry and Meaning*. While their work has offered a vital alternative to the religion-medicine dichotomy, there is a need to move beyond a focus on strictly sectarian institutions to demonstrate

how religious women health care workers helped shape public health policy and practice, bringing a tradition of discipline and order tempered with humanitarian concerns to a public institution under state and eventually federal authority.

3. In this regard I diverge sharply from Gussow, *Leprosy, Racism and Public Health*, 59–66.

4. The scholarship on Protestant women reformers' efforts to carve a public sphere for themselves grounded in their moral authority as women is vast. See, for example, Ginzberg, *Women and the Work of Benevolence*; Pescoe, *Relations of Rescue*; and Higginbotham, *Righteous Discontent*.

5. For a discussion of the distinctive role of Catholic women religious, see Coburn and Smith, *Spirited Lives*, 7–10.

6. Dyer, "Endemic Leprosy in Louisiana," 571.

7. "Leper Board Begins Its Work," *New Orleans Daily Picayune*, 2 December 1894, copy in Folder 11–5: History—John Smith Kendall, Box 11, MS-C-421 Public Hospital Historical Collection, National Library of Medicine.

8. Dyer, "History of the Louisiana Leper Home," 714–17.

9. For a discussion of the ways in which business leaders and elites attempted to downplay news of epidemics within the city under the belief that it would be bad for commerce, see Ellis, *Yellow Fever and Public Health*, 14–36.

10. *Report of the Louisiana State Board of Control of the Leper Home*, 1896, 4.

11. L. A. Wailes to Isadore Dyer, 5 January 1895, Folder 2, General Correspondence, Leper Home Board of Control, Leper Home Records (35–57), No. 2515, Louisiana State University Special Collections, hereafter LHBC.

12. L. A. Wailes to Board of Control, 30 June 1895, Folder 2, General Correspondence, LHBC.

13. Ibid.

14. L. A. Wailes to Board of Control, 13 August 1895, Folder 2, General Correspondence, LHBC.

15. Chaulmoogra oil emerged as a traditional treatment for leprosy in Southeastern Asia; Western medical practitioners came to use the treatment during the nineteenth century. See Parascondola, "Chaulmoogra Oil and the Treatment of Leprosy."

16. L. A. Wailes to Isadore Dyer, 5 January 1895, Folder 2, General Correspondence, LHBC.

17. L. A. Wailes to Board of Control, 30 November 1895, Folder 2, General Correspondence, LHBC.

18. *Report of the Louisiana State Board of Control of the Leper Home*, 1896, 5.

19. E. M. Cooper to the Board of Control, 1 May 1896, Folder 3, General Correspondence, LHBC.

20. For a discussion of the tradition of Catholic sisters and nursing in urban hospitals and their work during periods of epidemic disease, see Kauffman, *Ministry and Meaning*, 64–82, and Newhauser, "In Times of Epidemic," 69–85.

21. Sister Agnes Slavin to Mother Superior, 29 February 1896, Carville Correspondence, 1896–1899, Marillac West Province Archives, hereafter MWPA.

22. Ibid.

23. Transcript of contract between the State Board of Control of the Lepers' Home of Louisiana and the Order of the Sisters of Charity, signed by Isadore Dyer and Mother Marianna, 1 March 1896, Carville Correspondence, 1896–1899, MWPA.

24. Ibid.

25. Sister Beatrice to Sister Julianne, [May 1896], Carville Correspondence, 1896–1899, MWPA.

26. In addition to steam baths, the only other experimental therapy reported to the board at this time was red mangrove, either applied as a salve to patient skin ulcers or ingested. Like the baths, few patients actively participated in these informal medical trials. See Sister Beatrice to M. D. Lagan, 8 April and 22 April 1900, Folder 8, General Correspondence, LHBC.

27. For a discussion of the professionalization of nursing, see Melosh, *"Physician's Hand."* For a critique of how nursing scholarship has failed to acknowledge the role of religious orders in developing the profession, see Nelson, *Say Little, Do Much.*

28. Sister Beatrice to the Board of Control, 2 February 1901, Folder 9, General Correspondence, LHBC.

29. Sister Beatrice to Mother Superior, 6 July 1896, Carville Correspondence, 1896–1899, MWPA.

30. Sister Beatrice to M. D. Lagan, 9 June 1897, Folder 4, General Correspondence, LHBC.

31. Sister Beatrice to M. D. Lagan, 19 January 1897, Folder 4, General Correspondence, LHBC.

32. Ibid.

33. Sister Beatrice to M. D. Lagan, 27 May 1898, Folder 5, General Correspondence, LHBC.

34. Listings of all the donations to the Louisiana Leper Home accompanied each biannual and annual report of the Board of Control after the sisters assumed administrative responsibilities. See, for example, "Report of Sister Beatrice Acknowledging Donations, Etc.," in *Report of the Board of Control of the Leper Home*, 1898, 14–17.

35. Sister Beatrice to Sister Lucia, 18 May 1896, Carville Correspondence, 1896–1899, MWPA.

36. Sister Beatrice to Sister Josephine, 10 May 1896, Carville Correspondence, 1896–1899, MWPA.

37. Sister Beatrice to Sister Lucia, 18 May 1896, Carville Correspondence, 1896–1899, MWPA.

38. Sister Beatrice to Mother Superior, 4 August 1896, Carville Correspondence, 1896–1899, MWPA.

39. Sister Beatrice to Sister M. Felix, 24 January 1897, Carville Correspondence, 1896–1899, MWPA.

40. Sister Beatrice to Sister Lucia, 10 July 1896, Carville Correspondence, 1896–1899, MWPA.

41. Sister Beatrice to Sister M. Virginia, 18 May 1896, Carville Correspondence, 1896–1899, MWPA.

42. Sister Beatrice to Mother Superior, 15 August 1896, Carville Correspondence, 1896–1899, MWPA.

43. Sister Beatrice to Mother Superior, 8 March 1897, Carville Correspondence, 1896–1899, MWPA.

44. Sister Beatrice to M. D. Lagan, 31 October 1896, Folder 3, General Correspondence, LHBC.

45. Sister Beatrice to Mother Superior, 4 November 1897, Carville Correspondence, 1896–1899, MWPA.

46. Sister Beatrice to Mother Superior, 15 August 1896, Carville Correspondence, 1896–1899, MWPA.

47. Sister Beatrice to Sister Julianne, [May 1896], Carville Correspondence, 1896–1899, MWPA.

48. Sister Beatrice to Mother Superior, 6 July 1896; Sister Beatrice to Sister Josephine, 23 July 1896, Carville Correspondence, 1896–1899, MWPA.

49. Sister Beatrice to M. D. Lagan, 18 October 1897, Folder 4, General Correspondence, LHBC.

50. Sister Beatrice to Mother Superior, 15 October 1898, Carville Correspondence, 1896–1899, MWPA.

51. James Ware to Governor Murphy J. Foster, 21 June 1897, Folder 4, General Correspondence, LHBC.

52. L. H. Viallon to M. D. Lagan, 14 October 1896, Folder 3, General Correspondence, LHBC.

53. Sister Beatrice to M. D. Lagan, 7 May 1899, Folder 6, General Correspondence, LHBC.

54. Sister Beatrice to Albert Phelps, 2 February 1901, Folder 9, General Correspondence, LHBC.

55. J. F. Pollack to Sister Benedicta, 8 May 1907, Folder 14, General Correspondence, LHBC. Sister Benedicta Roache assumed the role of administrator in 1901, a position she held until 1917.

56. Sister Beatrice to M. D. Lagan, 20 February 1897, Folder 4, General Correspondence, LHBC.

57. Sister Beatrice to M. D. Lagan, 12 March 1897, Folder 4, General Correspondence, LHBC.

58. Sister Beatrice to M. D. Lagan, 13 June 1897, Folder 4, General Correspondence, LHBC. The letter did not include a list of the regulations, however, nor could I find such a list within the copious records of the Daughters of Charity or the Board of Control.

59. The organization of medical institutions in the late nineteenth and early twentieth centuries separated the sexes by alternating floors, wards, or wings for men and

women. See, for example, Tomes, *Generous Confidence*; and Rothman, *Living in the Shadow of Death*.

60. Sister Beatrice to Sister Lucia, 18 May 1896, Carville Correspondence, 1896–1899, MWPA.

61. Sister Beatrice to Mother Superior, 21 July 1896, Carville Correspondence, MWPA.

62. Sister Beatrice to M. D. Lagan, 7 February 1898, Folder 5, General Correspondence, LHBC.

63. Sister Beatrice to M. D. Lagan, 16 February 1898, Folder 5, General Correspondence, LHBC.

64. Ibid.

65. Sister Beatrice to M. D. Lagan, 1 March 1898, Folder 5, General Correspondence, LHBC.

66. Walter Abrams to Albert Phelps, 7 September 1902, Folder 9, General Correspondence, LHBC.

67. Sister Benedicta to Albert Phelps, 22 July 1903, Folder 10, General Correspondence, LHBC.

68. Sister Benedicta to Albert Phelps, 22 February 1904, Folder 10, General Correspondence, LHBC.

69. Sister Benedicta to J. F. Pollack, 5 July 1907, Folder 14, General Correspondence, LHBC.

70. A. Wilson, Henry Hayes, Henry Zimmerman, and John Drew to the Board of Control, 1 July 1907, Folder 14, General Correspondence, LHBC.

71. John Drew to Albert Phelps, 24 July 1907, Folder 14, General Correspondence, LHBC.

72. Ibid.

73. J. F. Pollack to Sister Mary Thomas, 6 August 1907, Folder 14, General Correspondence, LHBC.

74. This policy was not restricted to southern institutions. As Rosenberg makes clear, "locational segregation" remained a standard practice in northern hospitals that admitted both blacks and whites; see Rosenberg, *Care of Strangers*, 301.

75. Sister Beatrice to Albert Phelps, 15 June 1901, Folder 9, General Correspondence, LHBC.

76. Copy of draft report from the Sister Superior to the Board of Control, 30 April 1916, Carville Correspondence, 1916, MWPA.

77. Sister Benedicta to James Rainey, 25 May 1911, Folder 18, General Correspondence, LHBC.

78. President of the Board of Control to Sister Benedicta, 27 May 1911, Folder 18, General Correspondence, LHBC.

79. Sister Benedicta to P. E. Burke, 10 October 1912, Folder 20, General Correspondence, LHBC.

80. President of the Board of Control to Bourgois Robeaux, 11 October 1912, Folder 20, General Correspondence, LHBC.

81. Sister Benedicta to the Board of Control, 13 March 1905, Folder 11, General Correspondence, LHBC.

82. Sister Benedicta to J. F. Pollack, 7 January 1907, Folder 14, General Correspondence, LHBC.

83. Sister Benedicta to the Board of Control, 12 November 1907, Folder 14, General Correspondence, LHBC.

84. Ibid.

85. Sister Benedicta to Albert Phelps, 22 July 1903, Folder 10, General Correspondence, LHBC.

86. Harry Zimmerman to Albert Phelps, 20 August 1906, Folder 13, General Correspondence, LHBC.

87. Sister Benedicta to the Board of Control, 13 March 1905; Sister Benedicta to Albert Phelps, 3 July 1905, Folder 11, General Correspondence, LHBC.

88. Sister Benedicta to J. F. Pollack, 19 March 1906, Folder 12, General Correspondence, LHBC.

89. See, for example, the mention of patient "absconders" in letters from Sister Benedicta to Albert Phelps, 2 September and 30 December 1903 and 19 January 1904, Folder 10, General Correspondence; Albert Phelps to Sister Benedicta, 7 March 1906, Folder 12, General Correspondence, LHBC.

90. Sister Benedicta to J. F. Pollack, 26 March 1906, Folder 12, General Correspondence, LHBC.

91. Albert Phelps to the Board of Health, 30 March 1906, Folder 12, General Correspondence, LHBC.

92. J. F. Pollack to Harry Zimmerman, 9 November 1906, Folder 13, General Correspondence, LHBC.

93. Harry Zimmerman to Albert Phelps, 19 November 1906, Folder 13, General Correspondence, LHBC.

94. Citizens of Iberville [B. O. LeBlanc, Jules Carville, Louis Carville, Ralph Sumnaur, John Lapevoleu, R. R. Blauim, C. C. Cole, B. J. Engler, R. A. Richard, W. A. Wintz, J. A. Wintz, Jr., J. A. Wintz, Sr., and W. C. Templain] to the Board of Control, 16 November 1907, Folder 14, General Correspondence, LHBC.

95. J. F. Pollack to the Patients at the Leper Home, 18 November 1907, Folder 14, General Correspondence, LHBC.

96. Sister Benedicta to James Rainey, 10 July 1909, Folder 16, General Correspondence, LHBC.

97. Sister Benedicta to J. F. Pollack, 20 November 1907, Folder 14, General Correspondence, LHBC.

98. J. F. Pollack to Sister Benedicta, 26 November 1907, Folder 14, General Correspondence, LHBC.

99. Sister Benedicta to James Rainey, 13 June 1910, Folder 17, General Correspondence, LHBC.

100. Board of Control to Hon. Harold C. Newman, Commissioner of Public Safety, 5 November 1913, Folder 24, General Correspondence, LHBC.

101. Sister Benedicta to Robert Staigg, 27 July 1914, Folder 26, General Correspondence, LHBC.

102. S. W. Ray, Secretary of the Board of Control, to Sister Benedicta, 27 January 1914, Folder 27, General Correspondence, LHBC.

103. Board of Control to Sister Benedicta, 13 July 1914, Folder 27, General Correspondence, LHBC.

104. E. Olsen to Ralph Hopkins, 26 August 1914, Folder 27, General Correspondence, LHBC.

105. Sister Benedicta to R. J. Montagne, 2 December 1916, Folder 30, General Correspondence, LHBC.

106. The files of the Louisiana Leper Home contain many letters from creditors alternating between pleading and demanding that bills be paid. See especially Folders 27 through 31, LHBC.

107. Sister Benedicta to Governor R. G. Pleasant, 18 January 1917, Carville Correspondence, 1917, MWPA.

108. Sister Edith to Dr. Dowling, 26 May 1918, Carville Correspondence, January–May, 1918, MWPA. Sister Edith assumed the position of administrator in 1917.

109. See Chapter 1 and Kalisch, "Lepers, Anachronisms, and the Progressives," 519.

110. Sister Edith to Sister Visitatrix, 21 August 1920, Carville Leprosarium Letters, Folder II, MWPA.

111. Sister Catharine to Sister Visitatrix, 7 October 1920, Carville Leprosarium Letters, Folder II, MWPA.

112. The new institution would be identified by many names, including the National Home for Lepers and Marine Hospital No. 66. For the sake of clarity, it is generally referred to in this text as the U.S. National Leprosarium, a name that clearly identifies its function.

113. O. E. Denney to Sister Eugenia, 26 October 1920, Carville Leprosarium Letters, Folder II, MWPA.

114. Superintendent to the Most. Rev. John W. Shaw, 18 October 1920, Carville Correspondence, 1920, MWPA.

Chapter 4

1. The United States had initially annexed the islands in 1898.

2. *Report of the President of the Board of Health of the Territory of Hawai'i, 1902, 4,* hereafter *Report of the Board of Health.*

3. *Report of the Board of Health, 1902*, 13.

4. *Report of the Board of Health, 1901*, 3.

5. *Report of the Board of Health, 1902*, 270.

6. *Report of the Board of Health, 1901*, 3.

7. *Report of the Board of Health, 1902*, 289–91.

8. J. D. McVeigh, "Report of the Superintendent of the Leper Settlement," in *Report of the Board of Health, 1904*, 72.

9. Ibid., 74.

10. The Organic Act, a federal law that officially instituted Hawai'i as a U.S. territory, granted the right to vote in local elections to all male residents of age who were citizens of the Republic of Hawai'i in 1898. It did not extend the right to vote to Asian immigrants, though it did enfranchise native-born Hawaiians. Unlike the laws under the former Republic of Hawai'i, no property qualifications applied. While citizens could vote for territorial representatives and for the (nonvoting) delegate to Congress, the territorial governor was a federal appointment; see Daws, *Shoal of Time*, 293–96.

11. W. J. Feary to C. B. Reynolds, 9 November 1900, Superintendent's Correspondence—Leper Settlement, DOH4–36, Department of Health Records, HSA, hereafter DOH Records.

12. Assistant Superintendent W. J. Feary mentions several candidates speaking "from the deck of the sloop" on 29 September 1900, while closer to election day, Republican and Independent party candidates spoke on 3 and 4 November. W. J. Feary to C. B. Reynolds, 4 October 1900 and 9 November 1900, Superintendent's Correspondence—Leper Settlement, DOH4–36, DOH Records.

13. *Report of the Board of Health, 1904*, 14.

14. Ibid.

15. "Report of the Resident Physician," in *Report of the Board of Health, 1904*, 75.

16. *Report of the Board of Health, 1904*, 82.

17. Ibid., 75.

18. Ibid., 80.

19. S. Kapela to S. E. Pinkham, 12 October 1906, Kalaupapa Settlement, Correspondence, DOH4–49, DOH Records.

20. S. Kapela to S. E. Pinkham, 19 October 1906, Kalaupapa Settlement, Correspondence, DOH4–49, DOH Records.

21. S. E. Pinkham to S. Kapela, 22 October 1906, Kalaupapa Settlement, Correspondence, DOH4–49, DOH Records.

22. Clipping, *Evening Bulletin*, 9 August 1906, in Records Re: Mr. Lor Wallach, DOH4–36, Department of Health Records, HSA, hereafter Wallach Records.

23. Petition, 19 April 1907, Wallach Records.

24. Daws, *Shoal of Time*, 295. Daws identifies this effort by Home Rule legislators as an example of one of the "frivolous" measures of the party. Such an interpretation diminishes the importance Hawaiians placed in trying to reestablish social and cul-

tural practices in the islands, in this case by allowing Hawaiian kahunas to resume their place as healers within their communities.

25. *Report of the Board of Health, 1907*, 24–25.

26. S. E. Pinkham to President and members of the Senate of the Legislature of the Territory of Hawaii, 19 April 1907, Wallach Records.

27. Copy of House Resolution, 23 April 1907, Wallach Records.

28. Emma Makaweliweli et al. to S. E. Pinkham, 20 September 1907, Wallach Records.

29. Transcript of notes taken on Hearing in the Matter of the Petition of J. Lor Wallach to Treat Lepers at the Leper Settlement, 2 October 1907, Wallach Records.

30. Testimony of J. Lor Wallach, taken before S. E. Pinkham, 8 October 1907, Wallach Records.

31. For a discussion of how the AMA fought the patent medicine industry, see Starr, *Social Transformation of American Medicine*, 127–34. On unorthodox medical practice in the United States, see Young, *Medical Messiahs*.

32. As of 30 June 1907, 798 people with leprosy lived in the settlement. Of these, 556 lived outside the religiously administered facilities of the Bishop, Baldwin, and Bay View Homes, *Report of the Board of Health, 1907*, 133.

33. William Notely and Joseph K. Naukana to S. E. Pinkham, 10 October 1907, Wallach Records.

34. Hawaii Territorial Board of Health, *Molokai Settlement*, 5.

35. Charles Chillingworth, John Lane, Joseph Kalana, and John Pao to Board of Health, 10 October 1907, Wallach Records.

36. S. E. Pinkham to William Notely, 25 October 1907, Wallach Records.

37. Resolution, signed by William Notely et al., 11 November 1907, Wallach Records.

38. S. E. Pinkham to the Committee of Seven, 23 November 1907, Wallach Records.

39. Dr. J. T. Wayson, D. Kalauokalani, and Mark P. Robinson voted in favor of the petition, while Fred C. Smith, Dr. Baldwin, and Attorney General C. R. Hemenway voted against; S. E. Pinkham broke the tie vote. Clipping from the *Hawaiian Advertiser*, 21 November 1907, in "Newspaper Clippings re: Leprosy, 1907–1920," DOH4–37, DOH Records.

40. S. E. Pinkham to William Notely, 4 February 1908, Kalaupapa Settlement, DOH4–49, DOH Records.

41. William Notely to S. E. Pinkham, 7 February 1908, Kalaupapa Settlement, DOH4–49, DOH Records.

42. "Hedging Against Dr. J. Atcherley," *Hawaiian Gazette*, 5 May 1908, Newspaper Clippings re: Leprosy, 1907–1920, DOH4–37, DOH Records.

43. "Opinion Given on Segregation," *Evening Bulletin*, 21 December [1907], Newspaper Clippings re: Leprosy, 1907–1920, DOH4–37, DOH Records.

44. "Pinkham Scored in the Hawaiian Mass Meeting," *Hawaiian Advertiser*, [April 1908], Newspaper Clippings re: Leprosy, 1907–1920, DOH4–37, DOH Records.

45. *Report of the Board of Health, 1908*, 3.

46. "Board of Health Adopts Important Change in Policy," *Hawaiian Gazette*, 14 August 1908, Newspaper Clippings re: Leprosy, 1907–1920, DOH4–37, DOH Records.

47. In a letter to the U.S. surgeon general, board member W. O. Smith maintained that a new federal facility on Moloka'i would allow public health officials to tell territorial residents that they would provide "far better treatment than any which the Territory could afford" in Honolulu. W. O. Smith to Walter Wyman, 18 October 1906, Central File 4712, Box 526, Record Group 90, National Archives and Records Administration.

48. *Congressional Record*, 58th Cong., 3rd sess., 1905, 39, pt. 4: 3667. For a further discussion of this legislation, see Chapter 1.

49. Furman, *Profile of the United States Public Health Service*, 273.

50. J. D. McVeigh to J. K. Waiaimau, 21 June 1906, Letterbooks of the Superintendent of the Leper Settlement (1901–1911), HSA.

51. Furman, *Profile of the United States Public Health Service*, 274.

52. Bushnell, "United States Leprosy Investigation Station," 84.

53. Gibson, *Under the Cliffs of Molokai*, 15–16.

54. Ibid., 44.

55. Ibid., 21.

56. On the emergence of mainland concerns regarding interracial relationships between black men and white women in the post–Civil War era, see Hodes, "Sexualization of Reconstruction Politics." For a discussion of Ida B. Wells's challenge to the black rapist myth, see Bederman, *Manliness and Civilization*, 45–76. For an analysis of the intersections between race, sex, and imperialism, see Stoler, *Race and the Education of Desire*. On colonial preoccupation with miscegenation, see Young, *Colonial Desire*, 90–117.

57. Gibson, *Under the Cliffs of Molokai*, 2.

58. Ibid., 19, 71. Emma Gibson went so far as to refuse to meet with the sisters who served as nurses at the Bishop Home, claiming that she feared they might bring contagion into the home (53).

59. Bushnell, "United States Leprosy Investigation Station," 87. Currie had replaced Brinckerhoff as the director of the facility in April 1909.

60. Gibson, *Under the Cliffs of Molokai*, 88.

61. Ibid., 104–5.

62. "Report of the Resident Physician," in *Report of the Board of Health, 1910*, 139.

63. Michael, "Public Health Service Leprosy Investigation Station on Molokai," 203–9.

64. Ibid., 209.

65. *Congressional Record*, 67th Cong., 2nd sess., 1922, 62, pt. 9: 8989.

66. Ibid., pt. 12: 12677.

67. *Congressional Record*, 67th Cong., 1st sess., 1921, 61, pt. 7: 7261.

68. *Congressional Record*, 67th Cong., 4th sess., 1923, 64, pt. 4: 3583–84.

69. A. W. Mellon to the Chairman, Committee on Appropriations, 13 June 1922, in *Congressional Record*, 67th Cong., 4th sess., 1923, 64, pt. 4: 3583.

70. Ibid., 3584.

71. The president signed S. 3721, the act "providing for the erection of additional suitable and necessary buildings for the National Leper Home," on 20 February 1923; *Congressional Record*, 67th Cong., 4th sess., 1923, 64, pt. 5: 4357.

72. Sister Edith to Lawrence Fabacher, 8 February 1921, Carville Correspondence, Marillac West Province Archives.

73. Stein, *Alone No Longer*, 100–101.

74. "Regulations for the Apprehension, Detention, Treatment, and Release of Lepers," 3152–53. Specifically, such bans were outlined in regulation 6: "Retention and discipline of patients afflicted with leprosy.—(a) No patient shall, under any circumstances, proceed beyond the limits of the reservation set aside for the detention of patients suffering from leprosy. (b) Patients shall, on no account, visit the quarters allotted to, or hold communication with, patients of the opposite sex, unless authorized to do so by special permission of the medical officer in charge. Visitation between patients of the opposite sex shall be permitted in the appointed visiting place only and at such hours as may be set aside for that purpose."

75. "Regulations," 3152–54.

76. See Chapter 5.

77. "Regulations," 3152.

78. Denney, "Leprosy Problem in the United States," 926.

79. Ibid.

80. Ibid., 928–29.

81. Lavinder, "Only National Leprosarium in the Continental United States," 413.

82. Denney, "Leprosy Problem," 927–28.

83. No further explanation of the practice was offered. Sister Martha and Sister Catherine, "National Leper Home," 795.

84. Ibid., 797–800.

85. Ibid., 799.

86. Denney, "Leprosy Problem," 929.

87. "Recovered Lepers Discharged from National Leprosarium," 563.

88. "Science Wins Again," *New York Illustrated News*, 16 March 1925, Newspaper Clippings File, Gillis W. Long Hansen's Disease Center Library, Carville, La.

89. Denney, "National Leper Home, 1926," 2595.

90. Denney, "Social Aspects of Leprosy and Leper Treatment," 22. The text beneath the title of the article spoke of the work at Carville in more dramatic terms, proclaiming, "Once the Cause of Benumbing Terror, Leprosy Is No Longer a Hopeless Disease, As Modern Therapeutic Measures Are Increasing Cured and Non-Dangerous Cases."

91. Denney, "Leprosy Problem," 929.

92. Denney, "National Leper Home, 1927," 814–15.

93. de Souza-Araujo, *Leprosy: Survey Made in Forty Countries*, 34.

94. Denney, "National Leper Home, 1927," 812.

95. In this regard, the National Leprosarium more closely resembled the modern hospital than did the settlement at Kalaupapa, as many hospitals during the 1920s and 1930s added research units where doctors could conduct clinical studies of patients. The perceived successes of scientific medicine made the public more accepting of medical experimentation involving human subjects; many came to view such practices as a necessary step toward medical progress. See, for example, Lederer, *Subjected to Science*, 126–38. On the limitations of the hospital for clinical research, see Marks, *Progress of Experiment*, 50–53.

96. Denney, "National Leper Home, 1929," 3169.

97. *Report of the Board of Health*, 1929, 9.

Chapter 5

1. Few scholarly accounts of leprosy in the mainland United States pay more than scant attention to the patient perspective. Gussow, a sociologist, focuses on the stigma surrounding the disease and its influence on medical policy in *Leprosy, Racism, and Public Health*; see also Gussow and Tracy, "Stigma and the Leprosy Phenomenon." For an exception to this trend, see Parascondola, "An Exile in My Own Country," which incorporates the viewpoints of patients Stanley Stein and Betty Martin in a discussion of federal leprosy policy at Carville. The stories of Stein and Martin are also explored in Gould, *Disease Apart*, 237–71. See also Fairchild, "Community and Confinement."

2. Judd, *Lawrence M. Judd & Hawai'i*, 140–42.

3. H. A. Kluegel, "Kalaupapa, Molokai. Special Investigation, Bureau of the Budget, Honolulu, Territory of Hawaii," 30 June 1930, n.p., Board of Hospitals and Settlement, Hawaiiana Collection, Hamilton Library, University of Hawai'i.

4. Bell explores the issue of Hawaiian statehood in the 1930s in *Last Among Equals*, 57–70. See also Fuchs, *Hawaii Pono*.

5. In 1930, the total population of Hawai'i was 368,336; the largest group of residents were Japanese (139,631), followed by Caucasians (80,373), Filipinos (63,052), Hawaiians (50,860), Chinese (27,179), Koreans (6,461), Blacks (563), and "Other" (217). Of those identified as Caucasians, 27,588 were Portuguese, 6,671 were Puerto Rican, and 1,219 were Spanish. See Nordyke, *Peopling of Hawai'i*, 178–79, table 3-1.

6. For a discussion of labor conditions in Hawai'i, including worker resistance and the rise of labor unions, see Beechert, *Working in Hawai'i*. For a discussion of the link between labor unrest and anti-Japanese sentiment, see Okihiro, *Cane Fires*.

7. The prosecution presented a tenuous case against the five men; post-trial analyses have indicated that none of the accused could have committed the crime. Daws analyzes the racial dimensions of the Massie trial and surrounding events in *Shoal of Time*, 317–27. Wright, a reporter at the trial, provides a comprehensive narrative of the events in *Rape in Paradise*. Stannard uses the two trials surrounding the Massie case as

a means of illustrating the resistance of an interethnic local community to a white oligarchy in *Honor Killing*.

8. Kluegel was referring to the U.S. National Leprosarium in Carville and the Culion leprosy settlement in the Philippines; Kluegel, "Special Investigation."

9. Ibid.

10. Ibid.

11. "Report of the Governor's Advisory Committee on Leprosy in Hawaii," October 1930, 9, HI 290, Leprosy in Hawaii, Hawaii Medical Library. The committee's report was released to the public two months later and published in one of the prominent English-language dailies, with the most startling proposal publicized in a front-page banner headline: "Kalaupapa Abandonment Urged," *Honolulu Star-Bulletin*, 20 December 1930, 1.

12. "Report of the Governor's Advisory Committee," 8.

13. Ibid.

14. Ibid., 9–10.

15. Consider, for example, patient protests mobilized on behalf of obtaining Indian herbalist J. Lor Wallach and to close down the U.S. Public Health Service extension service within the settlement, as discussed in Chapter 4.

16. *Annual Report of the Superintendent, Board of Hospitals and Settlement of the Territory of Hawaii for the Fiscal Year Ending June 30, 1932*, 1, 23. Hereafter *Report of the Superintendent*.

17. Walter Scratch, "New Day Ahead for Kalaupapa Colony People," *Honolulu Star-Bulletin*, 6 July 1931, 1.

18. H. A. Kluegel to the Board of Leper Hospitals and Settlement, 30 June 1932, frontispiece to *Report of the Superintendent, 1932*.

19. *Report of the Superintendent, 1932*, 8.

20. Ibid. Ironically, leprosy was also endemic among the Scandinavian-American population.

21. Ibid., 3–4.

22. Ibid., 73.

23. R. L. Cooke, "Report of the Resident Superintendent, Leprosarium Kalaupapa," in *Report of the Superintendent, 1932*, 7.

24. Ibid., 4.

25. L. F. Luckie, "Report of the Resident Physician, Leprosarium Kalaupapa," in *Report of the Superintendent, 1932*, 1.

26. Ibid., 2.

27. Greene, *Exile in Paradise*, 384–422.

28. The imperialistic international dimensions of leprosy eradication efforts have been under-explored, in large part because of what Anderson has criticized as the creation of a "disciplinary enclave of implicitly nationalist historians of medicine," in "Where Is the Postcolonial History of Medicine," 523. For works that have discussed various international leprosy conferences (the first of which took place in Berlin in

1897) within a national framework, see Silla, *People Are Not the Same*, and Gussow, *Leprosy, Racism, and Public Health*. Vaughan briefly mentions the international charitable appeal of leprosy in *Curing Their Ills*, 92–94.

29. *Report of the Superintendent, 1932*, 1.

30. Ibid., 81.

31. V. S. K. Houston to Governor Lawrence Judd, 27 February 1931, Leprosy, Epidemiological Survey, Territorial Departments—Board of Health, Governor's Files—Judd, HSA.

32. *Congressional Record*, 72nd Cong., 1st. sess., 1931, 75, pt. 1: 95.

33. Lawrence Judd to Hugh Cumming, 7 December 1931, and Cumming to Judd, 22 December 1931, in *Congressional Record*, 72nd Cong., 1st sess., 1932, 75, pt. 8: 8969–70.

34. House Committee on Territories, *Federal Aid—Hawaii*, 34.

35. *Congressional Record*, 72nd Cong., 1st sess., 1932, 75, pt. 7: 7829.

36. *Congressional Record*, 72nd Cong., 1st sess., 1932, 75, pt 8: 8972.

37. Ibid., 8971.

38. President Hoover signed H.J. Res. 361 into law on 15 July 1932; see *Congressional Record*, 72nd Cong., 1st sess., 1932, 75, pt. 14: 15747.

39. House Committee on Territories, *Federal Aid—Hawaii*, 20.

40. Ibid., 21–22.

41. *Report of the Superintendent, 1932*, 12.

42. Ibid.

43. For discussion of the historical development of eugenicist arguments in the United States, see Kevles, *In the Name of Eugenics*; Haller, *Eugenics*; and Ludmerer, *Genetics and American Society*. For a discussion of the emergence of sterilization as an approved eugenics tool, see Reilly, *Surgical Solution*. For a discussion of eugenicist arguments among birth control advocates, see Gordon, *Woman's Body, Woman's Right*, 118–32. For a discussion of the ethnic and class components of state-administered eugenics programs, see Kline, *Building a Better Race*, and Stern, *Eugenic Nation*.

44. By the 1930s, the annual number of sterilizations in state institutions exceeded 2,500, spurred by the Supreme Court approval of the procedure in its 1927 *Buck v. Bell* ruling; see Larson, *Sex, Race, and Science*, 119.

45. The advisory committee members themselves referred to children of patients as "worse than orphans," noting that they had to deal not only with the loss of their parents but also with the stigma of being associated with leprosy; see Hawaii Territorial Legislature, Senate Committee on Public Health, *Standing Committee Report No. 296 of the Senate of the Legislature of the Territory of Hawaii on Governor's Message No. 27, Relative to the Report of the Governor's Advisory Committee on Leprosy* (Honolulu, 1931), 5.

46. Minutes of the Board of Hospitals and Settlement, 24 October 1934, vol. 2, 29–30, HSA.

47. Some eugenicists argued that birth control would not effectively pose a solution

to rising births among the poor because they were incapable of using it properly; see Gordon, *Woman's Body, Woman's Right*, 304.

48. Gugelyk and Bloombaum, *Separating Sickness*, 38–41.

49. Minutes of the Board of Health, 5 June 1929, vol. 26, 54–58, HSA.

50. *Report of the Superintendent, 1932*, 12.

51. Senate Committee on Public Health, *Standing Committee Report No. 296*, 5.

52. Eric Fennel to Dr. Cooke, 11 August 1933, Eric Fennel Papers, HI 292, Leprosy in Hawaii, Hawaii Medical Library.

53. Scholars have produced an extensive body of work on the development of social welfare programs in the United States. For a discussion of the maternalist roots of the welfare state, see Koven and Michel, *Mothers of a New World*; Ladd-Taylor, *Mother-Work*; and Muncy, *Creating a Female Dominion*. For a discussion of the ways in which Civil War and mothers' pensions marked the origins of social welfare programs, see Skocpol, *Protecting Soldiers and Mothers*. Gordon examines the gendered roots of U.S. welfare programs and unpacks the way in which welfare recipients have come to be stigmatized in *Pitied but Not Entitled*.

54. E. V. Paris to the Superintendent of Hospitals and Settlement, regarding "Request of Alexander Stone for Admission of Wife to Kalaupapa as a Kokua to Board," 22 November 1933, Eric Fennel Papers, HI 292, Leprosy in Hawaii, Hawaii Medical Library.

55. This policy of regular visitation was established in the 1930 reorganization of the Board of Hospitals and Settlement; see Report of the Governor's Advisory Committee on Leprosy in Hawaii, October 1930, HI 290, Leprosy in Hawaii, Hawaii Medical Library; for reports of the social workers' visits, see the Minutes of the Board of Hospitals and Settlement throughout the 1930s.

56. "Application for Transfer of William Kupele, a Minor, Residing at the Kalihi Hospital, by Mr. and Mrs. David Kupele, to the Board of Hospital and Settlements, Territory of Hawaii," 24 October 1934, 1, Eric Fennel Papers, HI 295, Leprosy in Hawaii, Hawaii Medical Library.

57. Lederer has revealed that some physicians defended the use of "minimal risk" experimentation on orphans in part through the belief that such children's participation in scientific experiments enabled them to "repay their debt to society." For a discussion of children used in medical experiments before World War II, see Lederer, *Subjected to Science*, 15–16, 106–9.

58. "Application for Transfer of William Kupele," 1.

59. F. J. Pinkerton, Acting Chairman of the Board of Hospitals and Settlement, to Attorney General W. B. Pitman, 1 November 1934, Eric Fennel Papers, HI 295, Leprosy in Hawaii, Hawaii Medical Library.

60. Attorney General W. B. Pitman to F. J. Pinkerton, Acting Chairman of the Board of Hospitals and Settlement, 9 November 1934, Eric Fennel Papers, HI 295, Leprosy in Hawaii, Hawaii Medical Library.

61. Ernie Pyle, column, *Honolulu Advertiser*, 8 January 1937, reprinted in mimeographed collection, "Kalaupapa," by Eric Fennel, HI 294, Leprosy in Hawaii, Hawaii Medical Library.

62. Ibid.

63. Stein, *Alone No Longer*, 118–21. While Stein revealed his given name as Sidney Maurice Levyson, I will use the name he assumed as a patient a Carville, an identity he continued to embrace for the duration of his life.

64. Starr, *Social Transformation of American Medicine*, 348. For AMA opposition to veterans' hospitals, see Stevens, *In Sickness and in Wealth*, 128–29.

65. Watson B. Miller, American Legion, to O. E. Denney, Medical Officer in Charge, 19 November 1931; General Subject Files 1924–1935, Carville; PHS General Records, Record Group 90 (RG 90); National Archives Records Administration, hereafter NARA.

66. R. P. Sanddidge, Senior Surgeon, U.S. Treasurer Department, Public Health Service, U.S. Marine Hospital Inspection Report, August 1939; General Classified Records, 1936–1939; Group IV—Marine Hospitals, Carville; PHS General Records, RG 90; NARA.

67. Stein initiated the publication of the first Carville newspaper, *The Sixty-six Star*, in 1931. However, that paper ceased publication in 1933 after its readership objected to an editorial critical of the Catholic Church's role in keeping "the stigma of leprosy alive in the public mind." See Stein, *Alone No Longer*, 69, 160–61.

68. Stanley Stein to H. E. Hasseltine, n.d.; General Classified Records, 1940–1944; Group IV—Marine Hospitals, Carville; PHS General Records, RG 90; NARA.

69. H. E. Hasseltine to S. L. Christian, 29 February 1940; General Classified Records, 1940–1944; Group IV—Marine Hospitals, Carville; PHS General Records, RG 90; NARA.

70. However, higher officials in the PHS, particularly the Public Information Officer, shared Hasseltine's concerns and chafed at their inability to regulate what was printed in the paper.

71. Martin, *Miracle at Carville*, 8.

72. Ibid., 68–70.

73. H. E. Hasseltine to S. L. Christian, 29 February 1940; General Classified Records, 1940–1944; Group IV—Marine Hospitals, Carville; PHS General Records, RG 90; NARA.

74. Patients explained the meaning of the name in the first issue of *The Star*, September 1941.

75. As proclaimed in the newspaper's mission statement, printed in every issue.

76. In 1946, for example, 312 patients signed a petition in support of a fifteen-point plan for improvements recommended by patient activists; see Stein, *Alone No Longer*, 235.

77. Recent examples of scholarship emphasizing the repressive aspects of medical authority include Kraut, *Silent Travelers*; and Markel, *Quarantine*.

78. See, for example, Leavitt, *Typhoid Mary*; Rothman, *Living in the Shadow of Death*; and Noll, "Sterilization of Willie Mallory."

79. "After Two Score and Seven," *The Star*, November 1941, 3–4.

80. G. H. Faget, "Courage," *The Star*, December 1941, 3–4.

81. D. J. Soviero, "Nationalization of a Disease: A Paradigm?," 403. For a discussion of the development of sulfone treatment at Carville, see Parascondola, "Miracle at Carville," 59–66.

82. "After Two Score and Seven," *The Star*, November 1941, 3–4.

83. G. H. Faget, "Annual Report, Fiscal Year ending June 30, 1944, United States Marine Hospital, Carville, Louisiana"; General Classified Records, 1940–1944; Group IV—Marine Hospitals, Carville; PHS General Records, RG 90; NARA.

84. "Latest Report on Promin," *The Star*, November–December 1944, 17.

85. This list first appeared in the December 1942 issue of *The Star*.

86. National Field Service, The American Legion, Report of Visit of Claude A. Brown, 5 August 1944; General Classified Records, 1940–1944; Group IV—Marine Hospitals, Carville; PHS General Records, RG 90; NARA.

87. "And Thousands Mourn," *The Star*, February 1942, 3. For examples of international connections, see note from Panama in the July 1943 issue. The world outreach effort drew more responses after World War II.

88. See, for example, the "Global Glimpses" column, including a news report from a patient in Chacachacare, Trinidad, highlighting the number of new quarters for married couples under construction there, in *The Star*, November 1945, 16.

89. "William's Chin Waggin," *The Star*, September 1944, 9.

90. "Ann Page's The Ladies," *The Star*, September 1944, 10.

91. "Regulations for the Apprehension, Detention, Treatment, and Release of Lepers," 3152–3154.

92. G. H. Faget, "What the Patient Should Know About Hansen's Disease, Article 9, Rules and Regulations," *The Star*, April 1943, 2–3.

93. "Revise and Revoke," *The Star*, May 1943, 6; Martin, *Miracle at Carville*.

94. Stein, *Alone No Longer*, 167–70.

95. "Revise and Revoke," *The Star*, May 1943, 5.

96. "Carville Bill of Wrongs," *The Star*, February 1944, 5–7.

97. Martin, *Miracle at Carville*, 146.

98. "Carville Bill of Wrongs," *The Star*, February 1944, 6.

99. "Tragedy of Misinformation," *The Star*, April 1942, 3–4.

100. These figures are based on the patient statistics for 1944: 125 of 384 patients were foreign-born, with the largest contingents from Mexico (64) and China (17); 8 patients came from the British West Indies; 33 patients came from the U.S. possessions of Hawai'i, the Philippines, Puerto Rico, and the Virgin Islands. Annual Report, Fiscal Year ending 30 June 1944, United States Marine Hospital, Carville, Louisiana; Folder 1850–15 (1940–1944), Box 319; Group IV—Marine Hospitals, Carville; PHS General Records, RG 90; NARA.

101. The federal annual reports from the 1940s categorized patients by nationality rather than race, so precise figures regarding the number of African American patients are not available. However, the records of the Daughters of Charity provide evidence of separate cottages for African American, as well as Asian, patients during this time period; see Carville Annals, 1940–1949, Book 2, Marillac West Province Archives.

102. *The Star*, January 1942–August 1945, *passim*.

103. Betty Martin, "Why Am I Not Free," *The Star*, July 1945, 1–2.

104. Cover, *The Star*, July 1945.

105. Martin, "Why Am I Not Free," 1–2.

106. For a discussion of African American civil rights activism during the 1940s, see Blum, *V Was for Victory*, 215–19, and Perry, "It's Time to Force a Change."

107. Stein, *Alone No Longer*, 232–33.

108. Martin, *Miracle at Carville*, 249.

109. Hornbostel recounted her story to Kathleen Dean, "Shameful Stigma of Leprosy," in Senate Subcommittee on Health of the Committee on Labor and Public Welfare, *National Leprosy Act*, 83.

110. Martin, *Miracle at Carville*, 250.

111. Stein, *Alone No Longer*, 248–49.

112. Martin, *Miracle at Carville*, 251.

113. *The Star*, September 1946, cover.

114. Gertrude Hornbostel, "Rebuttal," *The Star*, October 1946, 12.

115. Ralph Coghlan, "Truth about Leprosy Now Gaining in Struggle Against Stigma Put on Victims by Misunderstanding," *St. Louis Post-Dispatch*, 17 March 1947, in Senate Subcommittee on Health, *National Leprosy Act*, 86–89; Stein, *Alone No Longer*, 250; and Martin, *Miracle at Carville*, 257.

116. Martin, *Miracle at Carville*, 258.

117. "Truth about Leprosy," *St. Louis Post-Dispatch*, 29 January 1947, in Senate Subcommittee, *National Leprosy Act*, 85–86.

118. The complete list of demands is as follows:

1. Abolish compulsory segregation, in the light of modern scientific knowledge, and make institutionalization voluntary. 2. Establish out-clinics for early diagnosis and treatment in other parts of the country in an effort to reach the thousand or more cases not at Carville. 3. Revoke the common-carrier ban. 4. Set up a small hospital or clinic outside the endemic focus to test the effect of climate on response to treatment. 5. Expand research facilities and invite the Leonard Wood Memorial to conduct some of their work at Carville. 6. Engage a plastic surgeon, resident or part-time, for Carville. 7. Make provision for financial aid to the families of bread-winners segregated at Carville. 8. Inaugurate a program of coordinated occupational therapy. 9. Grant more liberal vacations. 10. Provide quarters for married couples. 11. Provide quarters and meal service for visitors. 12. Launch a program to educate the public about the true nature of the disease. 13. Recognize 'Hansen's dis-

ease' as an official term for so-called leprosy. 14. Abolish from hospital regulations such terms as 'parole,' 'abscond,' and others with similar criminal connotation. 15. Continue the Advisory Committee as a permanent group.

The list is recorded in Stein, *Alone No Longer*, 232–35.

119. R. C. Williams, "Summary of the Recommendations of the Advisory Committee on Leprosy in the United States," *The Star*, January 1947, 9.

120. For an excellent discussion of issues of citizenship and racial tensions in Hawai'i during World War II, see Bailey and Farber, *First Strange Place*.

121. Minutes of the Board of Hospitals and Settlement, 13 January 1942, vol. 3, 99, HSA.

122. Greene, *Exile in Paradise*, 524.

123. Ibid., 525.

124. Kluegel, "Board of Hospitals and Settlement War Emergency Activities, 1941–1944," reprint from the *Hawaii Medical Journal* (March–April 1945), Hawaiiana Collection, University of Hawai'i Library.

125. Greene, *Exile in Paradise*, 528.

126. Kluegel, "Board of Hospitals and Settlement," 1.

Chapter 6

1. G. H. Faget, "Hope is Reborn Here," *The Star*, September 1946, 1.

2. Lerner, *Contagion and Confinement*, 56, 116–38. Lerner's study focuses on the forced confinement of a "subset of extremely unreliable, uncooperative Skid Road patients" (8), showing how officials insisted that quarantine remained a useful means of maintaining order within tuberculosis institutions.

3. *The Star*, September 1946, 10–11.

4. Gertrude Hornbostel, "Rebuttal," *The Star*, October 1946, 12; Faget, "Hope is Reborn," 1.

5. Stein, *Alone No Longer*, 233–34.

6. Key Pitt, "Under Your Hat," *The Star*, November 1946, 14–15.

7. Stein, *Alone No Longer*, 234.

8. Ibid., 235. The signatures were from all patients, excepting those who were incapacitated or on leave from the facility.

9. Ibid., 232–33.

10. The National Advisory Committee consisted of Dr. G. W. McCoy and Dr. David E. Brown, both of New Orleans; Dr. James E. Perkins and Dr. E. R. Kellersberger, both of New York; Dr. J. A. Doull and Dr. L. F. Badger, both of the U.S. Public Health Service; Sister Catherine Sullivan, Daughter of Charity of St. Vincent de Paul and former Carville nurse; Claude A. Brown of the American Mission to Leprosy; Louis L. McCormick; and Perry Burgess. See R. C. Williams, "Summary of the Recommenda-

tions of the Advisory Committee on Leprosy in the United States," *The Star*, January 1947, 9–10.

11. Editor's comment, *The Star*, January 1947, 13.

12. G. H. Rarey, "Opportunities for Service to Mankind," *The Star*, July 1946, 11–18.

13. G. H. Rarey, "Comments on Recommendations," *The Star*, February 1947, 11.

14. Stein, *Alone No Longer*, 244.

15. Medical scholars tend to view patient activism as a more recent phenomenon, pointing to significant numbers of relatively affluent and well-educated patients and supporters who have mobilized to fight for research funding for such diseases as AIDS and breast cancer; see, for example, Padgug and Oppenheimer, "Riding the Tiger," 245–78; Patton, *Inventing AIDS*; and Lerner, *Breast Cancer Wars*.

16. Senate Subcommittee on Health of the Committee on Labor and Public Welfare, *National Leprosy Act*, 49, 1–9. The remaining points were as follows: Second, the Public Health Service would be authorized and directed to establish a system of treatment centers that made care more accessible to patients. Third, a permanent National Advisory Council with bi-annual meetings would be established. Fourth, the act would create a rehabilitation and reemployment program that would provide educational and vocational training to patients and ensure hiring preferences for discharged patients. Fifth, a Patients' Welfare Fund would be created to provide financial assistance to severely disabled patients and their dependents. Sixth, physically disabled patients would receive monetary compensation upon their discharge from the hospital. Seventh, research into the disease would be expanded, with the Public Health Service stimulating interest in such research at other public and private institutions with monetary and structural support.

17. Hartman L. Lichtwardt, "Hansen's Disease—A New Name for an Old Condition," *Journal of the Michigan State Medical Society* 45 (September 1946): 1221–25, in Senate Subcommittee on Health, *National Leprosy Act*, 51.

18. Senate Subcommittee on Health, *National Leprosy Act*, 9–13.

19. "Statement of Hon. Claude Pepper, United States Senator from the State of Florida," Senate Subcommittee on Health, *National Leprosy Act*, 15–17. *The Star* noted the New York policy on its back page, "Further Facts," along with the parenthetical aside, "1 down, 47 to go"; see, for example, *The Star*, February 1945.

20. "Statement of Paul Strachan, president, American Federation of Physically Handicapped, Washington, D.C.," Senate Subcommittee on Health, *National Leprosy Act*, 56.

21. "Pancho Case—an Example," *The Star*, in Senate Subcommittee on Health, *National Leprosy Act*, 73.

22. The story of how Gertrude Hornbostel and her husband came to Carville is discussed in Chapter 5.

23. "Statement of Ignace LeBlanc, president, Patients' Federation; Stanley Stein, editor of *The Star*; Tom Quarnstrom, Commander, American Legion Post 188; and

Gertrude C. Hornbostel, President, American Federation of the Physically Handicapped, Lodge 86," Senate Subcommittee on Health, *National Leprosy Act*, 54.

24. Senate Subcommittee on Health, *National Leprosy Act*, 108. The creation of these research institutes represented a significant expansion of federal involvement in medical research. The National Cancer Institute (1937) and the National Heart Institute (1948) became two of the earliest branches of the National Institute (later Institutes) of Health, which had expanded from the Hygienic Laboratory in 1930; see Starr, *Social Transformation of American Medicine*, 340–44. Strickland demonstrates that increased funding did not necessarily result in developing cures in *Politics, Science, and Dread Disease*.

25. For a discussion of how material conditions associated with the Western world such as sanitation and nutrition altered patterns of disease, see Brandt, "Behavior, Disease, and Health," 53–77.

26. Stein, *Alone No Longer*, 404.

27. Although patients at Carville campaigned for the use of "Hansen's disease," the term leprosy continued to have widespread usage among medical practitioners and public health officials in Hawai'i until a Kalaupapa patient campaign convinced the state legislature to end the use of "leprosy" in favor of Hansen's disease. I agree with the patient argument that the term "leprosy" evokes a stigmatized and foreign contagion. I nevertheless continue to use this name in the context of postwar Hawai'i to reflect its use by territorial officials during these years.

28. "Post-War Suggestions, Medical Department and Staff, Kalaupapa Settlement," unpublished ms. submitted [April 1945] to Harry A. Kluegel, Kalaupapa Misc. Reports and Evaluation, Lawrence McCully Judd Collection (M–420), HSA, hereafter Judd Collection.

29. "Post-War Suggestions," Judd Collection.

30. Norman R. Sloan, Resident Physician, "Kalaupapa Hospital Annual Report, July 1, 1945 to June 30, 1946," Kalaupapa Hospital Annual Reports, Judd Collection.

31. Kalaupapa Hospital Monthly Report, June 1947, Kalaupapa Monthly Hospital Reports, Judd Collection.

32. Norman R. Sloan, Resident Physician, "Kalaupapa Hospital Annual Report, July 1, 1946 to June 30, 1947," Kalaupapa Hospital Annual Reports, Judd Collection. Emphasis in the original.

33. "Post-War Suggestions," Judd Collection.

34. "Report on Mainland Trip by Dr. Norman R. Sloan, Delegate from Hawaii, to the International Leprosy Congress held at Havana, Cuba," Correspondence, Dr. Norman Sloan, Judd Collection.

35. Kalaupapa Hospital Monthly Report, November 1948, Kalaupapa Monthly Hospital Reports, Judd Collection.

36. "Report on Mainland Trip by Dr. Norman R. Sloan," Judd Collection. Whereas the average Kalaupapa patient arrived at the settlement less than a year after originally

displaying symptoms of the disease, the average length of time from first symptom to commitment at Carville was three to four years.

37. Sloan, "Kalaupapa Hospital Annual Report, July 1, 1946 to June 30, 1947," Judd Collection.

38. Ibid.

39. Kalaupapa Hospital Monthly Report, January 1948, Kalaupapa Monthly Hospital Reports, Judd Collection.

40. Kalaupapa Hospital Monthly Report, September 1948, Kalaupapa Monthly Hospital Reports, Judd Collection.

41. Copy of patient petition, 4 June 1948, Correspondence, Dr. Norman Sloan, Judd Collection.

42. For popular press accounts of Sloan's drug trials, see, for instance, "New Hope for Leprosy Patients Seen in Use of Three New Drugs," *Honolulu Star-Bulletin*, 9 October 1947, 24, and "Leprosy Parley Reveals Success of New Drugs," *Honolulu Advertiser*, 16 June 1948, 2.

43. Minutes of the Board of Hospitals and Settlement, 27 July 1948, vol. 4, 50, HSA.

44. For an example of the sense of community felt by Kalaupapa residents, see "My Big Kalaupapa Family," in Gugelyk and Bloombaum, *Separating Sickness*, 62–64. This oral history describes the sense of dislocation experienced by one patient after being declared "negative" and discharged from the settlement.

45. Walter D. Ackerman, Attorney General, to Charles L. Wilbar, 11 September 1950, Kalaupapa Release of Patients, Judd Collection.

46. Charles L. Wilbar to the Director of the Board of Hospitals and Settlement, 22 November 1950, Kalaupapa Release of Patients, Judd Collection.

47. Lawrence M. Judd to the president of the Board of Health, 29 November 1950, Kalaupapa Release of Patients, Judd Collection.

48. Dr. C. V. Caver, medical director of Kalaupapa Settlement, to Lawrence M. Judd, 28 November 1950, Kalaupapa Release of Patients, Judd Collection. Caver had replaced Sloan, who voluntarily left his position.

49. Greene, *Exile in Paradise*, 548–49.

50. Minutes of the Board of Hospitals and Settlement, 25 March 1947, vol. 4, 4, HSA; Harry Kluegel to Harold W. Boss, Director of Personnel and Classification, 16 April 1947, Kalaupapa Employment, L. Judd, Judd Collection.

51. Judd, *Lawrence M. Judd & Hawai'i*, 245–48.

52. Ibid., 248–52.

53. Lawrence M. Judd to Harry Kluegel, 1 July 1947, Kalaupapa Recreation, Judd Collection; Thomas H. Rickman to Lawrence M. Judd, 31 December 1948, Kalaupapa Voc. Rehabilitation and Employment, Judd Collection.

54. Resident Superintendent's Report for June 1947, Kalaupapa Res. Supt. Reports, Judd Collection.

55. Resident Superintendent's Report for December 1948, Kalaupapa Res. Supt. Reports, Judd Collection.

56. E. K. Chung-Hoon, Chief of Medical Services, to Senator Eugene S. Capellas, 7 January 1950, Kalaupapa Medical Treatment, Judd Collection.

57. Resident Superintendent's Reports for July 1947 and August 1947, Kalaupapa Res. Supt. Reports, Judd Collection.

58. Transcript of talk by Lawrence M. Judd, Resident Superintendent, Kalaupapa Settlement, to Charter Day Meeting of the Kalaupapa Lion's Club, 24 April 1948, Kalaupapa Lion's Club, Judd Collection.

59. Timothy L. Wiaamau, president of the Kalaupapa Entertainment Club, to Lawrence M. Judd, 3 May 1948, Kalaupapa Recreation, Judd Collection.

60. Erlene McGuire, Secretary of the Molokai Girl Scouts, to Lawrence M. Judd, 13 October 1948, Kalaupapa Recreation, Judd Collection.

61. Resident Superintendent's Report for June 1947 from Lawrence M. Judd to Harry Kluegel, 30 June 1947, Kalaupapa Res. Supt. Reports; Report from Lawrence M. Judd to Charles L. Wilbar, 18 December 1950, Kalaupapa Misc. Reports and Evaluation, Judd Collection.

62. Richard K. C. Lee to Lawrence M. Judd, 17 May 1949, Kalaupapa Release of Patients, Judd Collection.

63. Lawrence M. Judd to Harry Kluegel, 6 December 1948, Kalaupapa Air Service, Judd Collection.

64. Charles L. Wilbar to the County Health Officer (Hawaii), Acting County Health Officer (Maui), and Acting County Health Officer (Kauai), 26 March 1949, Kalaupapa Air Service, Judd Collection.

65. Memo from Lawrence M. Judd to Harry Kluegel, 8 April 1949, Kalaupapa Air Service, Judd Collection.

66. Lawrence M. Judd to Harry Kluegel, 1 November 1948, Kalaupapa Budget, Judd Collection.

67. Lawrence M. Judd to Jack T. Waterhouse, 27 December 1948; Jack T. Waterhouse to Lawrence M. Judd, 6 January 1949, Kalaupapa Budget, Judd Collection.

68. It was at this point that individuals involved with the care of the disease in Hawai'i began regularly substituting the term Hansen's disease for leprosy, and I have mirrored this shift in my discussion of this period.

69. Lawrence M. Judd to Charles L. Wilbar, 16 June 1949, Kalaupapa Administration, General, Judd Collection.

70. Charles L. Wilbar to Lawrence M. Judd, 28 June 1949 and 9 December 1949, Kalaupapa Administration, General, Judd Collection.

71. E. Bell to Hon. Ingram M. Stainback, 2 June 1949, Kalaupapa Patients Personal, Judd Collection.

72. Ibid.

73. Lawrence M. Judd to Charles L. Wilbar, 6 June 1949, Hale Mohalu, Misc., Judd Collection.

74. *Halemohalu News*, 31 August 1950, Hale Mohalu Newsletter, Judd Collection.

75. Band program, 26 August 1951; Memo from Hecules S. Mendonca, institution

administrator at Hale Mohalu, to Lawrence M. Judd, 28 August 1951, Hale Mohalu Band, Judd Collection.

76. E. K. Chung-Hoon, Chief of Medical Services, to Lawrence M. Judd, 11 October 1951, Hale Mohalu Band, Judd Collection.

77. Lawrence M. Judd to E. K. Chung-Hoon, 12 October 1951, Hale Mohalu Band, Judd Collection.

78. Charles L. Wilbar to Lawrence M. Judd, 17 October 1951, Hale Mohalu Band, Judd Collection.

79. Lawrence M. Judd to Charles L. Wilbar, 13 September 1951, Kalaupapa Employment, L. Judd; Statement of Resignation, 22 October 1951, Hale Mohalu Band, Judd Collection.

80. Stephen Dawson to Lawrence M. Judd, 4 September 1947, Correspondence, Dawson, Judd Collection.

81. Stanley Stein to Lawrence M. Judd, 13 January 1949, Kalaupapa Rules and Regulations, Judd Collection.

82. "Move to Relax Segregation Laws on Leprosy Backed by Patients," *Honolulu Star-Bulletin*, 28 March 1949, 9.

83. Public Health Regulations, Board of Health, Territory of Hawaii, Chapter 27: Hansen's Disease, HI 289, Leprosy in Hawaii, Hawaii Medical Library.

84. "Copy of Resolution from the Board of Health of the Territory of Hawaii to the Delegate to Congress from Hawaii, Requesting the Delegate to Exert His Efforts to Have the Congress of the United States Arrange for Appropriation of Funds for Personnel in the United States Public Health Service to be Assigned to the Hansen's Disease Program in Hawaii or for Grant-in-Aid Funds for This Portion," Director of the Board of Health Correspondence, HSA.

85. House Subcommittee on Territories and Insular Possessions, *Treatment of Hansen's Disease in the Territory of Hawaii*, 5–6.

86. See Chapter 4 for a discussion of the 1930s effort to solicit funds from the federal government.

87. Charles L. Wilbar, "Resolution from the Board of Health of the Territory of Hawaii to the Delegate to Congress from Hawaii," in House Subcommittee on Territories and Insular Possessions, *Treatment of Hansen's Disease*, 11–12.

88. Ibid., 12–15.

89. House Subcommittee on Territories and Insular Possessions, *Treatment of Hansen's Disease*, 24.

90. *Congressional Record*, 82nd Cong., 2nd sess., 1952, 98, pt. 6: 7369, 7450, 8172.

91. "Hansen's Disease Set-Up Praised by U.S. Official," *Honolulu Star-Bulletin*, 30 March 1951, 2.

92. "Annual Report for the Period Ending December 31, 1950, from the Medical Director of Kalaupapa Settlement to the Director of the Division of Hospitals and Settlement," 7 February 1951, Director of the Board of Health Correspondence, HSA.

93. "Inspection of Kalaupapa Settlement by the Committee on Health on March 6, 1951," 21 March 1951, Director of the Board of Health Correspondence, HSA.

94. Lief Erikson to Lawrence M. Judd, 24 June 1952, Kalaupapa Voc. Rehabilitation and Employment, Judd Collection.

95. Kaneo Kishimoto, Representative of Maui County, to Charles L. Wilbar, 22 September 1952, Director of the Board of Health Correspondence, HSA.

96. Routing slip to the Director of Hansen's disease from Charles L. Wilbar, 23 September 1952, Director of the Board of Health Correspondence, HSA.

97. Stanley Stein to Lawrence M. Judd, Kalaupapa Rules and Regulations, Judd Collection.

98. R. T. Hollinger to Dr. Hunt, Assoc. Chief Bureau of Medical Services, 22 October 1952, Patient Cottages Correspondence, Public Health Service Hospitals Historic Collection, National Library of Medicine, hereafter PHSHHC.

99. Copy of Supplemental Appropriations Bill, Hearings Before the Subcommittees of the Committee on Appropriations, 84th Cong., 2nd sess., 6 June 1956, Patient Cottages Correspondence, PHSHHC.

100. "Demolition of Patient Cottages at Carville is Scheduled Soon," *Baton Rouge Morning Advocate*, 16 August 1956.

101. Stein, *Alone No Longer*, 307–14.

102. Memo to the Surgeon General from James F. Kelly, Acting Director of Administration re: Future Status of Payments to Hawaii for Care of Persons Afflicted with Leprosy, 18 August 1959, Hawaii Correspondence, PHSHHC.

Epilogue

1. Stoler with Bond, "Refractions Off Empire," 101.

2. Gugelyk and Bloombaum, *Separating Sickness*, 12.

3. With improved air transportation to the settlement in 1965, this became a viable job opportunity for patients. In that year, approximately 3,000 tourists visited Kalaupapa; see *Annual Report, Department of Health, State of Hawaii, 1966*, 12.

4. Strange, "Symbiotic Commemoration," 91–92.

5. Ibid., 88–89.

6. The NPS Kalaupapa website, for example, prominently features images of Damien on its main page and begins its description of the site with a discussion of his arrival at Kalawao; see "Kalaupapa National Historical Park, Hawaii," National Park Service, <http://www.nps.gov/kala>.

7. See, for example, Levin, *Kalaupapa: A Portrait*, and Cahill, *Yesterday at Kalaupapa*.

8. The armadillo was the first animal other than humans known to contract Hansen's disease.

9. The registered prevalence of disease at the beginning of 2006 was 219,826

cases. The WHO identified a 27 percent decrease in the number of cases from the previous year; see "Leprosy Today," World Health Organization, <http://www.who.int/lep/en>.

10. "Carville Centennial Celebration, 1894–1994," *The Star*, July–August 1994, 6–7.

11. "History of the National Hansen's Disease Programs," National Hansen's Disease Programs, <http://bphc.hrsa.gov/nhdp/HISTORY__MAIN__PAGE.htm>.

12. Markel, *When Germs Travel*, 211.

Archival Collections

Bishop Museum Archives, Honolulu, Hawai'i
    Photographs Collection
Daughters of Charity of St. Vincent DePaul West Central Province Archives, St.
        Louis, Missouri
    Carville Annals, 1921–1959
    Carville Correspondence, 1896–1922
Gillis W. Long Hansen's Disease Center Library, Carville, Louisiana
    Newspaper Clippings File
Hawaii Medical Library, Honolulu, Hawai'i
    Hawaiiana Collection
        Eric Fennel Papers
        Leprosy in Hawaii
Hawai'i State Archives, Honolulu, Hawai'i
    Series 259, Minutes of the Board of Health, 1893–1959
    Series 326, Director's Internal Correspondence
    Series 330, Minutes of the Board of Hospitals and Settlement, 1931–1949
    DOH-4, Department of Health Records
        Hansen's Disease Records and Correspondence, 1883–1913
        Letterbooks of the Superintendent of the Leper Settlement, 1901–1916
    GOV7, Governor's Records, Lawrence Judd
    M-420, Lawrence McCully Judd Collection
Louisiana State University Archives, Baton Rouge, Louisiana
    Leper Home Records, 1893–1921
National Archives and Records Administration, College Park, Maryland
    Paramount Pictures, Inc., Collection
    Record Group 90, Public Health Service
        Marine Hospital Records
National Library of Medicine, Bethesda, Maryland
    Public Health Service Hospitals Historical Collection
        Series 3: National Hansen's Disease Center, Carville, Louisiana

University of Hawai'i Hamilton Library
 Hawaiiana Collection

Newspapers, Annals, and Periodicals

Congressional Record
Daily Bulletin, Honolulu
Daily Pacific Commercial Advertiser, Honolulu
Honolulu Advertiser
Honolulu Star-Bulletin
New York Times
Public Health Reports
Reports of the Board of Control for the Louisiana Leper Home
Reports of the Board of Health, Territory and State of Hawai'i
Reports of the Superintendent, Board of Hospitals and Settlement, Territory of Hawai'i
The Star, Carville, Louisiana
Washington Post

Government Documents

Hawaii Territorial Legislature, Senate Committee on Public Health. *Standing Committee Report No. 296 of the Senate of the Legislature of the Territory of Hawaii on Governor's Message No. 27, Relative to the Report of the Governor's Advisory Committee on Leprosy*. Honolulu, 1931.

U.S. House Committee on Interior and Insular Affairs. *Treatment of Hansen's Disease in the Territory of Hawaii*. Hearings, before the Subcommittee on Territories and Insular Possessions of the Committee on Interior and Insular Affairs, on H.R. 1739. 82nd Cong., 1st sess., 24 April 1951.

U.S. House Committee on Interstate and Foreign Commerce. *Care and Treatment of Lepers in Hawaii*. H. Rept. 4624. 58th Cong., 3rd sess., 16 February 1905.

U.S. House Committee on Interstate and Foreign Commerce. *Leprosarium for the Segregation of Lepers, Etc*. H. Rept. 4599. 58th Cong., 3rd sess., 13 February 1905.

U.S. House Committee on Interstate and Foreign Commerce. *Prevention of Leprosy in the United States*. H. Rept. 1286. 63rd Cong., 3rd sess., 15 January 1915.

U.S. House Committee on Territories. *Federal Aid—Hawaii*. Hearings, before the Committee on Territories, on H.R. 306. 72nd Cong., 1st sess., 9 and 15 February 1932.

U.S. Senate Committee on Labor and Public Welfare. *National Leprosy Act*. Hearing, before the Subcommittee on Health of the Committee on Labor and Public Welfare, on S. 704. 81st Cong., 1st sess., 9 May 1949.

U.S. Senate Committee on Public Health and National Quarantine. *Leprosarium for the Segregation of Lepers, Etc.* S. Rept. 3874. 58th Cong., 3rd sess., 13 February 1905.

U.S. Senate Committee on Public Health and National Quarantine. *Letter from the Surgeon-General of the Marine-Hospital Service Presenting a Report Relating to the Origin and Prevalence of Leprosy in the United States.* S. Doc. No. 269. 57th Cong., 1st. sess., 24 March 1902.

U.S. Senate Committee on Public Health and National Quarantine. *Care and Treatment of Persons Afflicted with Leprosy.* S. Rept. 306. 64th Cong., 1st sess., 25 March 1916.

Published Sources

Anderson, Warwick. *The Cultivation of Whiteness: Science, Health and Racial Destiny in Australia.* New York: Basic Books, 2003.

——. "Disease, Race, and Empire." *Bulletin of the History of Medicine* 70, no. 1 (1996): 62–67.

——. "Excremental Colonialism: Public Health and the Poetics of Pollution." *Critical Inquiry* 21 (Spring 1995): 640–69.

——. "Immunities of Empire: Race, Disease, and the New Tropical Medicine, 1900–1920." *Bulletin of the History of Medicine* 70, no. 1 (1996): 94–118.

——. "Leprosy and Citizenship." *Positions* 6, no. 3 (1998): 707–30.

——. "Where Is the Postcolonial History of Medicine?" *Bulletin of the History of Medicine* 72, no. 3 (1998): 522–30.

Andrade, Ernest Jr. *Unconquerable Rebel: Robert W. Wilcox and Hawaiian Politics, 1880–1903.* Niwot, Colo.: University Press of Colorado, 1996.

Appendix to the Report on Leprosy of the President of the Board of Health to the Legislative Assembly of 1886. Honolulu: Pacific Commercial Advertiser, 1886.

Arnold, David. *Colonizing the Body: State Medicine and Epidemic Disease in Nineteenth-Century India.* Berkeley: University of California Press, 1993.

Bailey, Beth, and David Farber. *The First Strange Place: Race and Sex in World War II Hawaii.* Baltimore: Johns Hopkins University Press, 1994.

Bailey, Thomas A. "The Lepers of Asia." *Missionary Review of the World* 29 (November 1906): 818–24.

Bailey, Wellesley C. "Mission Work Among the Lepers." *Missionary Review of the World* 23 (June 1900): 449–55.

Ballantyne, Tony, and Antoinette Burton, eds. *Bodies in Contact: Rethinking Colonial Encounters in World History.* Durham, N.C.: Duke University Press, 2005.

Bates, Barbara. *Bargaining for Life: A Social History of Tuberculosis, 1876–1938.* Philadelphia: University of Pennsylvania Press, 1992.

Bederman, Gail. *Manliness and Civilization: A Cultural History of Gender and Race in the United States, 1880–1917.* Chicago: University of Chicago Press, 1995.

Beechert, Edward D. *Working in Hawai'i: A Labor History*. Honolulu: University of Hawai'i Press, 1985.

Bell, Roger. *Last Among Equals: Hawaiian Statehood and American Politics*. Honolulu: University of Hawai'i Press, 1984.

Bernabeu-Mestre, Josep, and Teresa Ballester-Artigues. "Disease as a Metaphorical Resource: The Fontilles Philanthropic Initiative in the Fight Against Leprosy, 1901–1932." *Social History of Medicine* 17, no. 3 (2004): 409–21.

Big Jim McClain. Produced by Robert Fellow and John Wayne. Directed by Edward Ludwig. 90 min. Warner Home Video, 1985 [orig. 1952]. VHS.

Bix, Amy Sue. "Diseases Chasing Money and Power: Breast Cancer and Aids [*sic*] Activism Challenging Authority." In *Health Care Policy in Contemporary America*, edited by Alan Marcus and Hamilton Cravens. University Park: Pennsylvania State University Press, 1997.

Blum, John Morton. *V Was for Victory: Politics and American Culture During World War II*. San Diego: Harcourt Brace Jovanovich, 1976.

Booty, John E. "The Anglican Tradition." In *Caring and Curing: Health and Medicine in the Western Religious Traditions*, edited by Ronald L. Numbers and Darrel W. Amundsen. New York: Macmillan, 1986.

Borovsky, Robert. "Cook, Lono, Obeyesekere, and Sahlins." *Current Anthropology* 38 (1997): 255–82.

Boston Women's Health Book Collective. *Our Bodies, Ourselves*. New York: Simon and Schuster, 1973.

Brandt, Allan M. "Behavior, Disease, and Health in the Twentieth Century United States." In *Morality and Health*, edited by Allan M. Brandt and Paul Rozin, 53–77. New York: Routledge, 1997.

——. *No Magic Bullet: A Social History of Venereal Disease in the United States since 1880*. Exp. ed. New York: Oxford University Press, 1987.

Briggs, Laura. *Reproducing Empire: Race, Sex, Science, and U.S. Imperialism in Puerto Rico*. Berkeley: University of California Press, 2002.

Brody, Saul Nathaniel. *The Disease of the Soul: Leprosy in Medieval Literature*. Ithaca, N.Y.: Cornell University Press, 1974.

Brumberg, Joan Jacobs. *Fasting Girls: The History of Anorexia Nervosa*. New York: Plume Books, 1989.

Bryder, Linda. *Below the Magic Mountain: A Social History of Tuberculosis in Twentieth Century Britain*. Oxford: Clarendon Press, 1988.

Buck, Elizabeth. *Paradise Remade: The Politics of Culture and History in Hawai'i*. Philadelphia: Temple University Press, 1993.

Burton, Antoinette, ed. *After the Imperial Turn: Thinking with and through the Nation*. Durham, N.C.: Duke University Press, 2003.

——. *Burdens of History: British Feminists, Indian Women, and Imperial Culture, 1865–1915*. Chapel Hill: University of North Carolina Press, 1994.

Bushnell, A. O. *The Gifts of Civilization: Germs and Genocide in Hawai'i*. Honolulu: University of Hawai'i Press, 1993.

——. "The United States Leprosy Investigation Station at Kalawao." *Hawaiian Journal of History* 2 (1968): 76–94.

Cahill, Emmett. *Yesterday at Kalaupapa: A Saga of Pain and Joy*. Honolulu: Mutual Publishing, 1990.

Campbell, I. C. *A History of the Pacific Islands*. Queensland: University of Queensland Press, 1990.

Campomanes, Oscar V. "1898 and the Nature of the New Empire." *Radical History Review* 73, nos. 1–3 (1999): 130–46.

Coburn, Carol K., and Martha Smith. *Spirited Lives: How Nuns Shaped Catholic Culture and American Life, 1836–1920*. Chapel Hill: University of North Carolina Press, 1999.

Coffman, Tom. *The Island Edge of America: A Political History of Hawai'i*. Honolulu: University of Hawai'i Press, 2003.

——. *Nation Within: The Story of America's Annexation of the Nation of Hawai'i*. Kane'ohe, Hawai'i: Tom Coffman/EPICenter, 1998.

Cohn, Bernard S. *Colonialism and Its Forms of Knowledge: The British in India*. Princeton, N.J.: Princeton University Press, 1996.

Cooper, Frederick, and Ann Laura Stoler, eds. *Tensions of Empire: Colonial Cultures in a Bourgeois World*. Berkeley: University of California Press, 1997.

Coordinating Centers for Infectious Diseases, Division of Mycotic and Bacterial Diseases. "Hansen's Disease (Leprosy)." <http://www.cdc.gov/ncidod/dbmd/diseaseinfo/hansens_t.htm>. 18 October 2006.

Craddock, Susan. *City of Plagues: Disease, Poverty, and Deviance in San Francisco*. Minneapolis: University of Minnesota Press, 2000.

Crosby, A. W. "Hawaiian Depopulation as a Model for the Amerindian Experience." In *Epidemics and Ideas: Essays on the Historical Perception of Pestilence*, edited by Terence Ranger and Paul Slack. New York: Cambridge University Press, 1994.

Davis, Rebecca Harding. "Leprosy in America." *Littel's Living Age* (17 May 1890): 448.

Daws, Gavan. *Holy Man: Father Damien of Molokai*. Honolulu: University of Hawai'i Press, 1984.

——. *Shoal of Time: A History of the Hawaiian Islands*. Honolulu: University of Hawai'i Press, 1968.

de Souza-Araujo, H. C. *Leprosy: Survey Made in Forty Countries, 1924–1927*. Rio de Janeiro: Oswaldo Cruz Institute, 1929.

de Veuster, Pamphile. *Life and Letters of Father Damien, the Apostle of the Lepers*. London: Catholic Truth Society, 1889.

Debroey, Steven. *Father Damien: The Priest of the Lepers*. London: Burns & Oates, 1996.

Demaitre, Luke E. "The Relevance of Futility, Jordonu de Ture on the Treatment of Leprosy." *Bulletin of the History of Medicine* 70, no. 1 (1996): 25–61.

Denney, O. E. "The Leprosy Problem in the United States." *Public Health Reports* 41, no. 20 (1926): 923–29.

——. "The National Leper Home (Marine Hospital No. 66), Review of the More Important Activities During the Fiscal Year Ended June 30, 1926." *Public Health Reports* 41, no. 46 (1926): 2593–97.

——. "The National Leper Home (United States Marine Hospital), Carville, La., Review of the More Important Activities During the Fiscal Year Ended June 30, 1927." *Public Health Reports* 43, no. 14 (1928): 810–17.

——. "The National Leper Home (United States Marine Hospital), Carville, La., Review of the More Important Activities During the Fiscal Year Ended June 30, 1929." *Public Health Reports* 44, no. 52 (1929): 3169–76.

——. "Social Aspects of Leprosy and Leper Treatment." *Nation's Health* 9, no. 5 (1927): 21–23+.

Dougherty, Michael. *To Steal a Kingdom*. Waimanalo, Hawaiʻi: Island Press, 1992.

Douglas, Mary. "Witchcraft and Leprosy: Two Strategies of Exclusion." *Man*, n.s., 26, no. 4 (1991): 723–36.

Duffy, John. *The Sanitarians: A History of American Public Health*. Urbana: University of Illinois Press, 1990.

——, ed. *The Rudolph Matas History of Medicine in Louisiana*. Vol. 1. Baton Rouge: Louisiana State University Press, 1958.

Dutton, Charles Judson. *The Samaritans of Molokai*. New York: Dodd, Mead & Co., 1932.

Dwyer, Ellen. *Homes for the Mad: Life Inside Two Nineteenth-Century Asylums*. New Brunswick, N.J.: Rutgers University Press, 1987.

Dyer, Isadore. "Endemic Leprosy in Louisiana: With a Logical Argument for the Contagiousness of This Disease." *Philadelphia Medical Journal* 2, no. 12 (1898).

——. "The History of the Louisiana Leper Home." *New Orleans Medical and Surgical Journal* 54 (May 1902): 714–17.

Edmond, Rod. *Representing the South Pacific: Colonial Discourse from Cook to Gauguin*. New York: Cambridge University Press, 1997.

Ellis, John H. *Yellow Fever and Public Health in the New South*. Lexington: University Press of Kentucky, 1992.

Eperjesi, John R. *The Imperialist Imaginary: Visions of Asia and the Pacific in American Culture*. Hanover, N.H.: Dartmouth College Press, 2005.

Epstein, Stephen. *Impure Science: AIDS, Activism, and the Politics of Knowledge*. Berkeley: University of California Press, 1996.

Fairchild, Amy L. "Community and Confinement: The Evolving Experience of Isolation for Leprosy in Carville, Louisiana." *Public Health Reports* 119, no. 3 (2004): 362–70.

Farrow, John. *Damien the Leper*. New York: Sheed & Ward, 1951.

Feeny, Patrick. *The Fight Against Leprosy*. New York: American Leprosy Missions, 1964.

Fett, Sharla M. *Working Cures: Healing, Health, and Power on Southern Slave Plantations*. Chapel Hill: University of North Carolina Press, 2002.

Foster, Burnside. "Leprosy and the Hawaiian Annexation." *North American Review* 167 (September 1898): 300–305.

Foucault, Michel. *Madness and Civilization: A History of Insanity in the Age of Reason.* Translated by Richard Howard. New York: Vintage Books, 1988.

Fox, Daniel M., and Christopher Lawrence. *Photographing Medicine: Images and Power in Britain and America since 1840.* New York: Greenwood Press, 1988.

Fuchs, Lawrence H. *Hawaii Pono: An Ethnic and Political History.* Honolulu: Bess Press, 1961.

Furman, Bess. *A Profile of the United States Public Health Service, 1798–1948.* Washington, D.C.: Government Printing Office, 1960.

Gaudet, Marcia. *Carville: Remembering Leprosy in America.* Jackson, Miss.: University Press of Mississippi, 2004.

Gibson, Emma Warren. *Under the Cliffs of Molokai.* Fresno, Calif.: Academy Library Guild, 1957.

Ginzberg, Lori D. *Women and the Work of Benevolence: Morality, Politics, and Class in the Nineteenth-Century United States.* New Haven, Conn.: Yale University Press, 1990.

Gordon, Linda. *Pitied but Not Entitled: Single Mothers and the History of Welfare, 1890–1935.* New York: Free Press, 1994.

——. *Woman's Body, Woman's Right: Birth Control in America.* Rev. ed. New York: Penguin Books, 1990.

Gould, Tony. *A Disease Apart: Leprosy in the Modern World.* New York: St. Martin's Press, 2005.

Greene, Linda W. *Exile in Paradise: The Isolation of Hawai'i's Leprosy Victims and Development of Kalaupapa Settlement, 1865 to the Present.* Historic Resource Study. Denver, Colo.: National Park Service, Pacific Northwest Planning Branch, 1985.

Gugelyk, Ted, and Milton Bloombaum, eds. *The Separating Sickness—Ma'i Ho'oka'awale: Interviews with Exiled Leprosy Patients at Kalaupapa, Hawaii.* Honolulu: The Separating Sickness Foundation, 1979.

Gussow, Zachary. *Leprosy, Racism and Public Health: Social Policy in Chronic Disease Control.* Boulder, Colo.: Westview Press, 1989.

Gussow, Zachary, and George S. Tracy. "The Phenomenon of Leprosy Stigma in the Continental United States." *Leprosy Review* 43, no. 2 (1972): 85–93.

——. "Stigma and the Leprosy Phenomenon: The Social History of a Disease in the Nineteenth and Twentieth Centuries." *Bulletin of the History of Medicine* 44 (1970): 425–49.

Hall, Melvin F. *Poor People's Social Movement Organizations: The Goal Is to Win.* Westport, Conn.: Praeger, 1995.

Haller, Mark H. *Eugenics: Hereditarian Attitudes in American Thought.* New Brunswick, N.J.: Rutgers University Press, 1963.

Hawaii Territorial Board of Health. *The Molokai Settlement (Illustrated), Territory of Hawaii, Villages Kalaupapa and Kalawao.* Honolulu: Hawaiian Gazette, 1907.

Higginbotham, Evelyn Brooks. *Righteous Discontent: The Women's Movement in the Black Baptist Church, 1880–1920*. Cambridge, Mass.: Harvard University Press, 1993.

History of the National Hansen's Disease Programs. National Hansen's Disease Programs, May 2002. http://bphc.hrsa.gov/nhdp/HISTORY_MAIN_PAGE.htm. 9 May 2002.

Hodes, Martha. "The Sexualization of Reconstruction Politics: White Women and Black Men in the South after the Civil War." *Journal of the History of Sexuality* 3 (1992): 402–17.

Hoganson, Kristin. "Cosmopolitan Domesticity: Importing the American Dream." *American Historical Review* 107, no. 1 (2002): 55–83.

Hudson, Robert P. *Disease and Its Control: The Shaping of Modern Thought*. Westport, Conn.: Greenwood Press, 1983.

Hudson, Tim, and Jim Genesse. "Hansen's Disease in the United States." *Social Science and Medicine* 16, no. 9 (1982): 999–1001.

Hunt, Nancy Rose. *A Colonial Lexicon of Birth Ritual, Medicalization, and Mobility in the Congo*. Durham, N.C.: Duke University Press, 1999.

Inglis, Kerri A. "'A Land Set Apart': Disease, Displacement, and Death at Makanalua, Moloka'i." Ph.D. diss., University of Hawai'i, 2004.

Jacobson, Matthew Frye. *Barbarian Virtues: The United States Encounters Foreign Peoples at Home and Abroad, 1876–1917*. New York: Hill and Wang, 2000.

Joseph, D. George. "'Essentially Christian, Eminently Philanthropic': The Mission to Lepers in British India." *História Ciências Saúde: Manguinhos* 10, supp. 1 (2003): 247–75.

Joseph, Gilbert M., Catherine C. LeGrand, and Ricardo D. Salvatore, eds. *Close Encounters of Empire: Writing the Cultural History of U.S.-Latin American Relations*. Durham, N.C.: Duke University Press, 1998.

Judd, Lawrence M., as told to Hugh W. Lytle. *Lawrence M. Judd & Hawai'i: An Autobiography*. Rutland, Vt.: Charles E. Tuttle Company, 1971.

Kaeo, Peter. *News from Molokai, Letters between Peter Kaeo & Queen Emma, 1873–1876*. Edited by Alfons L. Korn. Honolulu: University of Hawai'i Press, 1976.

Kalisch, Philip A. "Lepers, Anachronisms, and the Progressives: A Study in Stigma, 1889–1920." *Louisiana Studies* 12, no. 3 (1973): 489–531.

———. "The Strange Case of John Early: A Study of the Stigma of Leprosy." *International Journal of Leprosy* 40, no. 3 (1972): 291–305.

Kaluaikoolau, Piilani. *The True Story of Kaluaikoolau, as Told By His Wife, Piilani*. Translated by Frances N. Frazier. Lihue, Hawai'i: Kauai Historical Society, 2001.

Kaplan, Amy. *The Anarchy of Empire in the Making of U.S. Culture*. Cambridge, Mass.: Harvard University Press, 2002.

———. "'Left Alone with America': The Absence of Empire in the Study of American Culture." In *Cultures of United States Imperialism*, edited by Amy Kaplan and Donald E. Pease. Durham, N.C.: Duke University Press, 1993.

Kauffman, Christopher J. *Ministry and Meaning: A Religious History of Catholic Health Care in the United States*. New York: Crossroad, 1994.

Kevles, Daniel J. *In the Name of Eugenics: Genetics and the Uses of Human Heredity*. New York: Knopf, 1985.

Kline, Wendy. *Building a Better Race: Gender, Sexuality, and Eugenics from the Turn of the Century to the Baby Boom*. Berkeley: University of California Press, 2001.

Korn, Alfons L., ed. *News from Molokai: Letters between Peter Kaeo and Queen Emma, 1873–1876*. Honolulu: University of Hawai'i Press, 1976.

Koven, Seth, and Sonya Michel, eds. *Mothers of a New World: Maternalist Politics and the Origins of Welfare States*. New York: Routledge, 1993.

Kraut, Alan M. *Silent Travelers: Germs, Genes, and the 'Immigrant Menace.'* New York: Basic Books, 1994.

Kunzel, Regina G. *Fallen Women, Problem Girls: Unmarried Mothers and the Professionalization of Social Work, 1890–1945*. New Haven, Conn.: Yale University Press, 1993.

Kuykendall, Ralph S. *The Hawaiian Kingdom, Vol. 2: 1854–1874, Twenty Critical Years*. Honolulu: University of Hawai'i Press, 1953.

———. *The Hawaiian Kingdom, Vol. 3: 1874–1893, The Kalakaua Dynasty*. Honolulu: University of Hawai'i Press, 1967.

Ladd-Taylor, Molly. *Mother-Work: Women, Child Welfare, and the State, 1890–1930*. Urbana: University of Illinois Press, 1994.

Larson, Edward John. *Sex, Race, and Science: Eugenics in the Deep South*. Baltimore: Johns Hopkins University Press, 1995.

Latour, Bruno, and Steve Woolgar. *Laboratory Life: The Social Construction of Scientific Facts*. Vol. 80. Sage Library of Social Research. Beverly Hills, Calif.: Sage Publications, 1979.

Lavinder, C. H. "The Only National Leprosarium in the Continental United States." *Modern Hospital* 19, no. 5 (1922): 412–15.

Law, Anwei Skinsnes. "A Triumph of Spirit." Introduction to *Kalaupapa: A Portrait*. Photographs by Wayne Levin. Honolulu: Bishop Museum Press, for the Arizona Memorial Museum Association, 1989.

Leavitt, Judith Walzer. *Brought to Bed: Child-Bearing in America, 1750–1950*. New York: Oxford University Press, 1986.

———. *Typhoid Mary: Captive to the Public's Health*. Boston: Beacon Press, 1996.

Lederer, Susan. *Subjected to Science: Human Experimentation in America before the Second World War*. Baltimore: Johns Hopkins University Press, 1995.

Leigh, Robert D. *Federal Health Administration in the United States*. New York: Harper & Brothers, 1927.

Leprosy Elimination Group. *Leprosy, the Disease*. World Health Organization, 23 April 2002. http://www.who.int/lep/disease/disease.htm. 30 April 2002.

Lerner, Barron. *The Breast Cancer Wars: Hope, Fear, and the Pursuit of a Cure in Twentieth Century America*. New York: Oxford University Press, 2001.

——. *Contagion and Confinement: Controlling Tuberculosis along the Skid Road*. Baltimore: Johns Hopkins University Press, 1998.

Levin, Wayne. *Kalaupapa: A Portrait*. Photographs by Wayne Levin, introduction by Anwei Skinsnes Law. Honolulu: Bishop Museum Press, for the Arizona Memorial Museum Association, 1989.

Levine, Philippa. *Prostitution, Race, and Politics: Policing Venereal Disease in the British Empire*. New York: Routledge, 2003.

London, Jack. "Koolau the Leper." In *Stories of Hawaii*. Edited by A. Grove Day. Honolulu: Mutual Publishing, 1994.

Ludmerer, Kenneth M. *Genetics and American Society: A Historical Appraisal*. Baltimore: Johns Hopkins University Press, 1972.

Lunbeck, Elizabeth. *The Psychiatric Persuasion: Knowledge, Gender, and Power in Modern America*. Princeton, N.J.: Princeton University Press, 1994.

Lupton, Deborah. *Medicine as Culture: Illness, Disease, and the Body in Western Societies*. London: Sage Publications, 1994.

Lyons, Maryinez. *The Colonial Disease: A Social History of Sleeping Sickness in Northern Zaire, 1900–1940*. New York: Cambridge University Press, 1992.

Maffly-Kipp, Laurie F. "Eastward Ho! American Religion from the Perspective of the Pacific Rim." In *Retelling U.S. Religious History*, edited by Thomas A. Tweed. Berkeley: University of California Press, 1997.

Markel, Howard. *Quarantine! East European Jewish Immigrants and the New York City Epidemics of 1892*. Baltimore: Johns Hopkins University Press, 1997.

——. *When Germs Travel: Six Major Epidemics That Have Invaded America Since 1900 and the Fears They Have Unleashed*. New York: Pantheon Books, 2004.

Marks, Harry M. *The Progress of Experiment: Science and Therapeutic Reform in the United States, 1900–1990*. Baltimore: Johns Hopkins University Press, 1997.

Martin, Betty. *Miracle at Carville*. Garden City, N.Y.: Doubleday & Company, 1950.

Melosh, Barbara. *"The Physician's Hand": Work Culture and Conflict in American Nursing*. Philadelphia: Temple University Press, 1982.

Merry, Sally Engle. *Colonizing Hawai'i: The Cultural Power of Law*. Princeton, N.J.: Princeton University Press, 2000.

Merwin, W. S. *The Folding Cliffs: A Narrative*. New York: Alfred A. Knopf, 1998.

Michael, Jerrold M. "The Public Health Service Leprosy Investigation Station on Molokai, Hawai'i, 1909–13—An Opportunity Lost." *Public Health Reports* 95, no. 3 (1980): 203–9.

Moblo, Pennie. "Blessed Damien of Moloka'i: The Critical Analysis of Contemporary Myth." *Ethnohistory* 44, no. 4 (1997): 691–726.

——. "Defamation by Disease: Leprosy, Myth and Ideology in Nineteenth Century Hawai'i." Ph.D. diss., University of Hawai'i, 1996.

——. "Leprosy, Politics, and the Rise of Hawaii's Reform Party." *Journal of Pacific History* 34, no. 1 (1999): 75–89.

Mohr, James C. *Plague and Fire: Battling Black Death and the 1900 Burning of Honolulu's Chinatown*. New York: Oxford University Press, 2005.

Montgomery, Douglass W. "Leprosy in San Francisco." *Journal of the American Medical Association* 23 (28 July 1894): 137.

Moran, Michelle T. "Colonizing Leprosy: Imperialism, Patients, and the Politics of Public Health in Hawai'i and Louisiana." Ph.D. diss., University of Illinois, Urbana-Champaign, 2002.

——. "Telling Tales of Ko'olau: Containing and Mobilizing Disease in Colonial Hawai'i." In *Moving Subjects: Mobility, Intimacy, and Gender in a Global Age of Empire*, edited by Tony Ballantyne and Antoinette Burton. Urbana: University of Illinois Press, forthcoming.

Morris, Aldon D., and Carol McClurg Meuller, eds. *Frontiers in Social Movement Theory*. New Haven, Conn.: Yale University Press, 1992.

Morrow, Prince A. "Leprosy and Hawaiian Annexation." *North American Review* 165 (November 1897): 582–90.

Mouritz, Arthur A. St. M. *The Path of the Destroyer: A History of Leprosy in the Hawaiian Islands and Thirty Years Research into the Means by Which It Has Been Spread*. Honolulu: Honolulu Star-Bulletin, 1916.

Mulhane, L. W. *Leprosy and the Charity of the Church*. Chicago: D. H. McBride and Company, 1896.

Mullan, Fitzhugh. *Plagues and Politics: The Story of the United States Public Health Service*. New York: Basic Books, 1989.

Muncy, Robyn. *Creating a Female Dominion in American Reform, 1890–1935*. New York: Oxford University Press, 1991.

National Hansen's Disease Programs. "History of the National Hansen's Disease Programs." <http://bphc.hrsa.gov/nhdp/HISTORY_MAIN_PAGE.htm>. 18 October 2006.

National Park Service, U.S. Department of the Interior. "Kalaupapa National Historical Park, Hawaii." <http://www.nps.gov/kala>. 18 October 2006.

Nelson, Sioban. *Say Little, Do Much: Nurses, Nuns, and Hospitals in the Nineteenth Century*. Philadelphia: University of Pennsylvania Press, 2001.

Newhauser, Duncan. "In Times of Epidemic." In *Pioneer Healers: The History of Women Religious in American Health Care*, edited by Ursula Stepsis and Dolores Liptak, 69–85. New York: Crossroad, 1989.

Noll, Steven. *Feeble-Minded in Our Midst: Institutions for the Mentally Retarded in the South, 1900–1940*. Chapel Hill: University of North Carolina Press, 1995.

——. "The Sterilization of Willie Mallory." In *'Bad Mothers': The Politics of Blame in Twentieth-Century America*, edited by Molly Ladd-Taylor and Lauri Umansky, 41–57. New York: New York University Press, 1998.

Nordyke, Eleanor C. *The Peopling of Hawai'i*. 2nd ed. Honolulu: University of Hawai'i Press, 1989.

Numbers, Ronald L., and Darrel W. Amundsen, eds. *Caring and Curing: Health and Medicine in the Western Religious Traditions*. New York: Macmillan, 1986.

O'Connell, Marvin. "The Roman Catholic Tradition Since 1545." In *Caring and Curing: Health and Medicine in the Western Religious Traditions*, edited by Ronald L. Numbers and Darrel W. Amundsen, 108–45. New York: Macmillan, 1986.

Obeyesekere, Gananath. *The Apotheosis of Captain Cook: European Mythmaking in the Pacific*. Princeton, N.J.: Princeton University Press, 1992.

Okihiro, Gary Y. *Cane Fires: The Anti-Japanese Movement in Hawai'i, 1865–1945*. Philadelphia: Temple University Press, 1991.

Osborne, Thomas J. *"Empire Can Wait": American Opposition to Hawaiian Annexation, 1893–1898*. Kent, Ohio: Kent State University Press, 1981.

Padgug, Robert A., and Gerald M. Oppenheimer. "Riding the Tiger: AIDS and the Gay Community." In *AIDS: The Making of a Chronic Disease*, edited by Elizabeth Fee and Daniel M. Fox, 245–78. Berkeley: University of California Press, 1992.

Parascondola, John. "Chaulmoogra Oil and the Treatment of Leprosy." *Pharmacy in History* 45, no. 2 (2003): 47–57.

———. "An Exile in My Own Country: The Confinement of Leprosy Patients at the United States National Leprosarium." *Medicina nei Secoli* 10, no. 1 (1998): 111–25.

———. "Miracle at Carville: The Introduction of the Sulfones for the Treatment of Leprosy." *Pharmacy in History* 40, nos. 2–3 (1998): 59–66.

Patterson, James T. *The Dread Disease: Cancer and Modern American Culture*. Cambridge, Mass.: Harvard University Press, 1987.

Patton, Adell Jr. *Physicians, Colonial Racism, and Diaspora in West Africa*. Gainesville: University Press of Florida, 1996.

Patton, Cindy. *Inventing AIDS*. New York: Routledge, 1990.

Peard, Julyan G. *Race, Place, and Medicine: The Idea of the Tropics in Nineteenth-Century Brazilian Medicine*. Durham, N.C.: Duke University Press, 1999.

Perry, Earnest L. Jr. "It's Time to Force a Change: The African-American Press's Campaign for a True Democracy during World War II." *Journalism History* 28, no. 2 (2002): 85–95.

Pescoe, Peggy. *Relations of Rescue: The Search for Female Moral Authority in the American West, 1874–1939*. New York: Oxford University Press, 1990.

Pi'ilani. "The True Story of Kaluaiko'olau, or Ko'olau the Leper." Recorded by John G. M. Sheldon in 1906. Translated by Frances N. Frazier. *The Hawaiian Journal of History* 21 (1987): 1–41.

Porter, Roy. "Religion and Medicine." In *Companion Encyclopedia of the History of Medicine*, edited by W. F. Bynum and R. Porter, 1449–68. Vol. 2. London: Routledge, 1993.

Pukuai, Mary Kawena, E. W. Haertig, and Catherine A. Lee. *Nana I Ke Kumu. Look to the Source*. Vol. 1. Honolulu: Hui Hanai, 1972.

Reagan, Leslie J. "Engendering the Dread Disease: Women, Men, and Cancer." *American Journal of Public Health* 87, no. 11 (1997): 1779–87.

——. *When Abortion Was a Crime: Women, Medicine, and Law in the United States, 1867–1973*. Berkeley: University of California Press, 1997.

"Recovered Lepers Discharged from National Leprosarium." *New Orleans Medical and Surgical Journal* 77 (1924–25): 563.

"Regulations for the Apprehension, Detention, Treatment, and Release of Lepers." *Public Health Reports* 37 (22 December 1922): 3152–53.

Reilly, Philip R. *The Surgical Solution: A History of Involuntary Sterilization in the United States*. Baltimore: Johns Hopkins University Press, 1991.

Renda, Mary A. *Taking Haiti: Military Occupation and the Culture of U.S. Imperialism, 1915–1940*. Chapel Hill: University of North Carolina Press, 2001.

Richards, Peter. *The Medieval Leper and His Northern Heirs*. Cambridge: D. S. Brewer Ltd., 1977.

Risse, Guenter. " 'A Long Pull, A Strong Pull, and All Together': San Francisco and Bubonic Plague, 1907–1908." *Bulletin of the History of Medicine* 66, no. 2 (1992): 260–86.

Rogers, Naomi. *Dirt and Disease: Polio Before FDR*. New Brunswick, N.J.: Rutgers University Press, 1992.

Rosenberg, Charles E. *The Care of Strangers: The Rise of America's Hospital System*. New York: Basic Books, 1987. Reprint, Baltimore: Johns Hopkins University Press, 1995.

——. *The Cholera Years: The United States in 1832, 1849, and 1866*. 1962. Reprint, with a new afterword, Chicago: University of Chicago Press, 1987.

——. "Framing Disease: Illness, Society, and History." In *Framing Disease: Studies in Cultural History*, edited by Charles E. Rosenberg and Janet Golden. New Brunswick, N.J.: Rutgers University Press, 1992.

Rothman, David J. *The Discovery of the Asylum: Social Order and Disorder in the New Republic*. Boston: Little, Brown, 1971.

Rothman, Sheila M. *Living in the Shadow of Death: Tuberculosis and the Social Experience of Illness in American History*. New York: Basic Books, 1994.

Russ, William Adam. *The Hawaiian Revolution, 1893–94*. Selinsgrove, Pa.: Susquehanna University Press, 1959.

Ryer, Washington M. *The Conflict of the Races*. San Francisco: P. J. Thomas, 1886.

Sahlins, Marshal. *How 'Natives' Think, About Captain Cook, for Example*. Chicago: University of Chicago Press, 1995.

——. *Islands of History*. Chicago: University of Chicago Press, 1985.

Said, Edward. *Orientalism*. New York: Vintage Books, 1978.

St. George, Robert Blair. "Introduction." In *Possible Pasts: Becoming Colonial in Early America*, edited by Robert Blair St. George, 1–29. Ithaca, N.Y.: Cornell University Press, 2000.

Santiago-Valles, Kelvin. "On the Historical Links Between Coloniality, the Violent Production of the 'Native' Body and the Manufacture of Pathology." *Centro* 7, no. 1 (1995): 108–18.

Schoen, Johanna. *Choice and Coercion: Birth Control, Sterilization, and Abortion in Public Health and Welfare*. Chapel Hill: University of North Carolina Press, 2005.

Shah, Nyan. *Contagious Divides: Epidemics and Race in San Francisco's Chinatown*. Berkeley: University of California Press, 2001.

Shilts, Randy. *And the Band Played On: Politics, People, and the AIDS Epidemic*. New York: St. Martin's Press, 1987.

Silla, Eric. *People Are Not the Same: Leprosy and Identity in Twentieth-Century Mali*. Portsmouth, N.H.: Heinemann, 1998.

Silva, Noenoe K. *Aloha Betrayed: Native Hawaiian Resistance to American Colonialism*. Durham: Duke University Press, 2004.

Sister Martha [no last name] and Sister Catherine [no last name]. "The National Leper Home." *The American Journal of Nursing* 24, no. 10 (1924): 795–800.

Skocpol, Theda. *Protecting Soldiers and Mothers: The Political Origins of Social Policy in the United States*. Cambridge, Mass.: Harvard University Press, Belknap Press, 1992.

Smith, Susan L. *Japanese American Midwives: Culture, Community, and Health Politics, 1880–1950*. Urbana: University of Illinois Press, 2005.

———. "Medicine, Midwifery, and the State: Japanese Americans and Health Care in Hawai'i, 1885–1945." *Journal of Asian American Studies* 4, no. 1 (2001): 57–75.

———. *Sick and Tired of Being Sick and Tired: Black Women's Health Activism in America, 1890–1950*. Philadelphia: University of Pennsylvania Press, 1995.

Sontag, Susan. *Illness as Metaphor* and *AIDS and Its Metaphors*. 1977, 1988. Reprint, 2 vols. in 1, New York: Doubleday, 1990.

Soviero, D. J. "The Nationalization of a Disease: A Paradigm?" *Public Health Reports* 101 (July–August 1986): 399–404.

Stannard, David E. *Before the Horror: The Population of Hawai'i on the Eve of Western Contact*. Honolulu: Social Science Research Institute, 1989.

———. *Honor Killing: How the Infamous "Massie Affair" Transformed Hawai'i*. New York: Viking. 2005.

Starr, Paul. *The Social Transformation of American Medicine*. New York: Basic Books, 1982.

Stein, Stanley, with Lawrence G. Blochman. *Alone No Longer: The Story of a Man Who Refused to Be One of the Living Dead!* New York: Funk & Wagnalls, 1963. Reprint, with additional text, Carville, La.: The Star, 1974.

Stepsis, M. Ursula, and Dolores Liptak, eds. *Pioneer Healers: The History of Women Religious in American Health Care*. New York: Crossroad, 1989.

Stern, Alexandra Minna. *Eugenic Nation: Faults and Frontiers of Better Breeding in Modern America*. Berkeley: University of California Press, 2005.

Stevens, Rosemary. *In Sickness and in Wealth: American Hospitals in the Twentieth Century*. Baltimore: Johns Hopkins University Press, 1989.

Stevens, Sylvester K. *American Expansion in Hawaii, 1842–1898*. 1945. Reprint, New York: Russell & Russell, 1968.

Stevenson, Robert Louis. "Father Damien, an Open Letter to the Reverend Doctor Hyde of Honolulu." 1890. Reprinted in *Dr. Hyde and Mr. Stevenson*. Tokyo: Tuttle, 1973.

Stewart, Richard. *Leper Priest of Moloka'i: The Father Damien Story*. Honolulu: University of Hawai'i Press, 2000.

Stoddard, Charles Warren. *Father Damien: The Martyr of Molokai*. San Francisco: Catholic Truth Society, 1901.

Stoler, Ann Laura. *Carnal Knowledge and Imperial Power: Race and the Intimate in Colonial Rule*. Berkeley: University of California Press, 2002.

——. *Race and the Education of Desire: Foucault's* History of Sexuality *and the Colonial Order of Things*. Durham: Duke University Press, 1995.

——. "Tense and Tender Ties: The Politics of Comparison in North American History and (Post) Colonial Studies." *Journal of American History* 88, no. 3 (2001): 829–65.

Stoler, Ann Laura, with David Bond. "Refractions Off Empire: Untimely Comparisons in Harsh Times." *Radical History Review* 95 (2006): 93–107.

Strange, Carolyn. "Symbiotic Commemoration: The Stories of Kalaupapa." *History & Memory* 16, no. 1 (2004): 86–117.

Strickland, Stephen. *Politics, Science, and Dread Disease: A Short History of United States Medical Research Policy*. Cambridge, Mass.: Harvard University Press, 1972.

Takaki, Ronald. *Strangers from a Different Shore: A History of Asian Americans*. New York: Penguin Books, 1989.

Tayman, John. *The Colony: The Harrowing True Story of the Exiles of Molokai*. New York: Scribner, 2006.

Thorne, Susan. " 'The Conversion of Englishmen and the Conversion of the World Inseparable': Missionary Imperialism and the Language of Class in Early Industrial Britain." In *Tensions of Empire: Colonial Cultures in a Bourgeois World*, edited by Frederick Cooper and Ann Laura Stoler. Berkeley: University of California Press, 1997.

Tomes, Nancy. *A Generous Confidence: Thomas Story Kirkbride and the Art of Asylum-Keeping, 1840–1883*. New York: Cambridge University Press, 1984.

——. *The Gospel of Germs: Men, Women, and the Microbe in American Life*. Cambridge: Harvard University Press, 1998.

Transactions of the Congress of American Physicians and Surgeons, Third Triennial Session. New Haven, Conn.: Published by the Congress, 1894.

Transactions of the Second Annual Conference of State and Territorial Health Officers. Washington, D.C.: Government Printing Office, 1904.

Transactions of the Third Annual Conference of State and Territorial Health Officers with the United States Public Health and Marine-Hospital Service, May 15, 1905. Washington, D.C.: Government Printing Office, 1906.

Trask, Haunani-Kay. *From a Native Daughter: Colonialism and Sovereignty in Hawai'i*. Rev. ed. Honolulu: University of Hawai'i Press, 1999.

Trautman, John R. "Epidemiological Aspects of Hansen's Disease (HD)." *Bulletin of the New York Academy of Medicine*, 2nd ser., 60, no. 7 (1984): 722–31. Revised and reprinted in *The Star*, 49, no. 2 (1989).

Treichler, Paula. "AIDS, HIV, and the Cultural Construction of Reality." In *The Time of AIDS: Social Analysis, Theory, and Method*, edited by Gilbert Herdt and Shirley Lindenbaum. Newbury Park, Calif.: Sage Publications, 1992.

——. *How to Have Theory in an Epidemic: Cultural Chronicles of AIDS*. Durham, N.C.: Duke University Press, 1999.

Vaughan, Megan. *Curing Their Ills: Colonial Power and African Illness*. Stanford, Calif.: Stanford University Press, 1991.

Wailoo, Keith. *Dying in the City of the Blues: Sickle Cell Anemia and the Politics of Race and Health*. Chapel Hill: University of North Carolina Press, 2001.

Washburn, Walter L. "Leprosy Among Scandinavian Settlers in the Upper Mississippi Valley, 1864–1932." *Bulletin of the History of Medicine* 24 (March–April 1950): 123–48.

Watts, Sheldon. *Epidemics and History: Disease, Power, and Imperialism*. New Haven, Conn.: Yale University Press, 1997.

Waxler, Nancy E. "Learning to Be a Leper: A Case Study in the Social Construction of Illness." In *Social Contexts of Health, Illness, and Patient Care*, edited by Elliot G. Mishler, 169–74. New York: Cambridge University Press, 1981.

Weber, Timothy P. "The Baptist Tradition." In *Caring and Curing: Health and Medicine in the Western Religious Traditions*, edited by Ronald L. Numbers and Darrel W. Amundsen. New York: Macmillan, 1986.

Wexler, Laura. *Tender Violence: Domestic Visions in an Age of U.S. Imperialism*. Chapel Hill: University of North Carolina Press, 2000.

WHO/Leprosy Today. "Leprosy Elimination." <http://www.who.int/lep/en/>. 18 October 2006.

Williams, William Appleman. *Empire as a Way of Life*. New York: Oxford University Press, 1980.

Wilson, Rob. *Reimagining the American Pacific: From South Pacific to Bamboo Ridge and Beyond*. Durham, N.C.: Duke University Press, 2000.

Wood, Houston. *Displacing Natives: The Rhetorical Production of Hawai'i*. Lanham, Md.: Rowman & Littlefield, 1999.

Worboys, Michael. "Tropical Disease." In *The Companion Encyclopedia of the History of Medicine*, edited by W. F. Bynum and Roy Porter. Vol. 1. London: Routledge, 1993.

Wright, Theon. *Rape in Paradise*. Honolulu: Mutual Publishing, 1966.

Young, James Harvey. *The Medical Messiahs: A Social History of Health Quackery in Twentieth-Century America*. Rev. ed. Princeton, N.J.: Princeton University Press, 1992.

Young, Robert J. C. *Colonial Desire: Hybridity in Theory, Culture and Race*. New York: Routledge, 1995.

186–90; as acting director of Division of Hospitals and Settlement, 190–93; resignation of, 193, 199

Kaeo, Peter, 53
Kahahawai, Joseph, 137. *See also* Massie case
Kahunas, 60, 109, 110
Kalākaua (king of Hawai'i), 54
Kalalau Valley (Kaua'i, Hawai'i), 13, 62–67
Kalaupapa, leprosy settlement on: confinement of people with leprosy at, 1, 3, 13, 25, 126; and children, 2, 12, 60–61, 70–71, 148–52, 168, 205; and Father Damien, 8, 53–54, 60; and patient activism, 9, 10, 12, 14, 111–14, 116–18, 134, 150–51, 193–95, 198–99, 209; and Western medicine, 9, 14, 104–5, 108–11, 118–23, 139, 143–44; and patient community, 10, 12, 14, 15, 16, 58–61, 73, 168–69, 170, 173, 181, 185–86, 187–88, 191–92, 202–3, 205–7; and World War II, 15, 164, 167–69; creation of, 51; escapes from, 54, 59–60, 68; religious workers at, 57–58, 60–61, 75, 138; marriage and families at, 59, 69–71, 147–52, 160, 205; relationship with neighbors, 59–60, 187–88; and traditional medicine, 60, 108–9; regulation of, 68–72, 106–7; visits to, 71–72, 105–6; patient activities at, 84–85, 187–88; and voting, 107–8, 115; and Lor Wallach case, 111–18; and U.S. Leprosy Investigation Station, 118–23; compared to Carville, 130–31, 160, 174, 182–83, 193–94, 199, 200–201; 1930s reforms at, 136, 138–44; and sterilization, 147–48; and sulfone drug treatments, 181–82, 183, 184–86; and relaxing regulations, 188–90, 193–95; and patient concerns about Hale Mohalu, 190–92, 197–98; end of incarceration at, 206; as tourist site, 206–7
Kalaupapa National Historical Park, 206
Kalawao, 59, 60–61, 119–23, 187. *See also* Kalaupapa, leprosy settlement on

Kalihi Boys' Home (Honolulu, Hawai'i), 148
Kalihi Hospital and Detention Center. *See* Kalihi Receiving Station
Kalihi Receiving Station (Honolulu, Hawai'i), 104, 144; and containment of people with leprosy, 13, 48, 54, 72, 119, 126, 131; creation of, 51; and medical examinations, 55, 57; and Lor Wallach, 111–12, 115, 116; and U.S. Leprosy Investigation Station, 121, 122, 181, 186, 190, 195; and expansion plans, 139, 141; and patient transfers, 150, 168; closure of, 190–91
Kamehameha III (king of Hawai'i), 50
Kamehameha IV (king of Hawai'i), 50
Kamehameha V (king of Hawai'i), 51
Kapiolani Girls' Home (Honolulu, Hawai'i), 148
Kimball, J. H., 55
Kingsley, J. Donald, 178
Kishimoto, Kaneo, 198–99
Kluegel, Harry A., 135, 136, 138–39, 141, 189
Kōkuas, 59, 68, 69–70, 149, 185
Ko'olau, 63–68, 72
Kupele family, 150–51

Lanham, Fritz, 124–25
Lee, Richard K. C., 188
"Leper," as stigmatized term, 2, 5, 7, 8, 12, 36, 42, 43, 48, 154, 155, 156, 162, 211 (n. 4). *See also* Leprosy: and stigma
Leprosy: biblical representations of, 2, 4–5, 7, 19, 20–21, 40, 155, 209; and stigma, 2, 4–5, 7–8, 12, 20, 38, 40, 41–42, 43, 51, 74–75, 77, 102, 111, 115, 124, 141–42, 152, 154–55, 156, 157, 162, 165, 174, 177, 181, 185, 187, 188, 190–91, 198, 202, 204–5, 206; and imperialism, 2–3, 5–8, 12, 13–16, 19, 28, 35, 40–41, 48, 76, 133–34, 138, 204, 208–9; contemporary medical understandings of, 4; as foreign threat, 4, 7, 11, 16, 18, 26, 27, 35–36, 43, 48, 154–55, 209; and Christianity, 5, 8, 13, 20–21, 42, 48–49, 49–50, 53, 55, 57, 60–61, 63, 69, 72–73, 74–76, 79–

New Orleans, La., 19, 74, 75, 76, 77, 85, 98
Notely, Charles, 113, 114

O'Connor, James, 123
Organic Act, 107

Page, Ann, 158–59
Paris, E. V., 149
Parran, Thomas, 164
Parsons, Claude, 145–46
Paschoal, M. G., 198
Patient activism, 3, 12, 15–16, 192, 205–6, 209
—at Carville, 152–61; and veterans' groups, 152–54; and public health campaign, 155–56, 157–59; and sexuality, 158–59; during World War II, 161–64; and Hornbostel publicity, 164–67; and protests against segregation, 175–80; and National Leprosy Act of 1949, 177–78; and Cottage Grove controversy, 200
—and citizenship, 107, 134, 161–64, 166, 170
—and drug therapies, 172–73, 201
—at Kalaupapa, 8, 111–18, 194, 199; and resistance to family regulation, 149–52; and challenge to physicians, 184–85; and resistance to medical examination, 185–86; and demands for government support, 197–98
—at Louisiana Leper Home: and sexual segregation, 88–92; and resistance to medical regulations, 94–98
—and medical knowledge, 9–10, 155–56
—and racial issues, 160–61, 167, 170–71
—and renaming of leprosy as Hansen's disease, 155–56
Patients. See People with leprosy
Patients' Committee for Social Improvement and Rehabilitation, 164
People with leprosy, 24, 38, 42, 123, 132, 145; and stigma, 5, 49, 54, 124, 181; and imperialism, 7, 19, 23, 47–48, 72, 139, 141–42, 204; and enforced segregation in medical

institutions, 14, 18, 37, 40, 53, 55, 74, 76–77, 86, 119; as patients, 20, 33, 41, 59, 91, 94–95; medical surveillance of, 57, 126, 190, 194–95, 199–200; and resistance to government authority, 62–67, 102; and families, 70–71, 105, 151; and experimental treatments, 111–16, 121, 130, 156–57; sexual regulation of, 146–48, 159–60
Pepper, Claude, 179, 180
Perkins, George, 25
Phelps, Albert, 90, 91, 96
Philippines, 1, 2, 3, 41, 46, 101, 127, 164, 167; as U.S. possession, 5–6, 34, 37, 44, 177
Pinkerton, F. J., 151
Pinkham, S. E., 110, 112, 113, 114, 115, 116, 117
Pitman, W. B., 150–51
Platt, Orville, 23
Pollack, J. F., 94
Promin, 156–57, 172, 175, 181, 182. *See also* Sulfone drugs
Promizole, 172, 175. *See also* Sulfone drugs
Public health policy: and imperialism, 3, 6, 9, 11, 27–28, 32, 45–46, 62, 71, 73, 104–5, 122, 131, 133, 136, 141, 170, 204–5; and germ theory, 5; and patient activism, 7, 107, 112, 150–51, 156–57, 159, 165–66, 175, 178, 193–94; at state and local levels, 12, 18–19, 74, 77; at national level, 17–18, 20, 21–23, 32, 44–45, 164; and medical segregation, 22, 27, 42, 118, 142, 148, 169, 174, 181; and images of leprosy, 29; and religious workers, 74–75, 82, 87, 101, 102. *See also* U.S. Public Health Service
Public Health Service. *See* U.S. Public Health Service
Pyle, Ernie, 151–52

Ransdell, Joseph, 41
Rarey, G. H., 177, 178, 180
Reynolds, C. B., 66, 67
Roache, Benedicta. *See* Sister Benedicta Roache
Robeaux, Bourgois, 93